Consumer
Socialization

Other Titles of Interest from Lexington Books:

The Role of Affect in Consumer Behavior
Emerging Theories and Applications
Robert A. Peterson, Wayne D. Hoyer, University of Texas at Austin, and
William R. Wilson, Rice University, editors
ISBN 0-669-12874-0   208 pages

Children as Consumers
Insights and Implications
James U. McNeal, Texas A&M University
ISBN 0-669-13087-7   240 pages

The Future of Consumerism
Paul N. Bloom, University of North Carolina at Chapel Hill, and Ruth Belk
Smith, University of Maryland, editors
ISBN 0-669-09428-5   240 pages

Personal Values and Consumer Psychology
Robert E. Pitts, Jr., DePaul University, and Arch G. Woodside, University
of South Carolina, editors
ISBN 0-669-06937-X   336 pages

Advertising and Consumer Psychology
Larry Percy, HBM/CREAMER, Inc., and Arch G. Woodside, University of
South Carolina Business Partnership Foundation, editors
ISBN 0-669-05766-5   432 pages

The Bibliography of Marketing Research Methods
Second Edition
John R. Dickinson, University of Windsor
The Marketing Science Institute Series
ISBN 0-669-12373-0   832 pages

Meta-Analysis in Marketing
Generalization of Response Models
John U. Farley and Donald R. Lehmann, Columbia University
The Marketing Science Institute Series
ISBN 0-669-14039-2   144 pages

The Baby Boom
A Selective Annotated Bibliography
Greg Byerly, Kent State University, and Richard E. Rubin, Akron-Summit
County Public Library
ISBN 0-669-08903-6   240 pages

Consumer Socialization

A Life-Cycle Perspective

George P. Moschis
Georgia State University

Lexington Books
D.C. Heath and Company/Lexington, Massachusetts/Toronto

Library of Congress Cataloging-in-Publication Data

Moschis, George P., 1944–
    Consumer socialization.

    Bibliography: p.
    Includes index.
    1. Consumers. 2. Marketing research. I. Title.
HF5415.3.M66   1987   658.8'342   85-45165
ISBN 0-669-11244-5 (alk. paper)

Published simultaneously in Canada
Printed in the United States of America
Casebound International Standard Book Number: 0-669-11244-5
Library of Congress Catalog Card Number: 85-45165

The paper used in this publication meets the minimum requirements of American National Standard for Information Sciences—Permanence of Paper for Printed Library Materials, ANSI Z39.48-1984.

∞™

87 88 89 90 8 7 6 5 4 3 2 1

To my parents,
Parthenios and Anastasia

Contents

Figures and Tables

Preface

The marketplace is characterized by continuous changes in market composition, business practices, and structure. Shifts in customer age composition over the life cycle, the emerging minority markets, the increasing affluence among consumers, and women's participation in the labor force are examples of changes affecting the demand for goods and services. Parallel to these demographic changes are technological developments and innovations that provide new ways of delivering products and services, as well as new methods of communicating with consumers in the marketplace. These latter developments create new environments for buyer-seller interaction and business transactions.

To assume that consumer behavior does not change as a result of these developments would deny us the opportunity to increase our understanding of consumer behavior in the context of these dynamic changes. The assumption would be unwise for marketers, who must adapt to the changing environment for survival and profits; for public policymakers, who are interested in consumer well-being and in making the marketplace more efficient; for consumer educators, who must understand how to prepare consumers better for efficient and effective interaction with the marketplace; and for students of consumer behavior and social scientists, who wish to understand human behavior in general better.

The purpose of this book is to help the reader develop an understanding of the nature of the changes in consumer behavior that are likely to occur, how they occur, and why. It seeks to provide information about the processes likely to bring about these changes, with the hope that such an understanding will help those interested in consumer behavior better serve the needs of the consumer and society as a whole.

We have witnessed a plethora of studies attempting to explain consumer behavior. In spite of the progress made, research often suggests that it is particularly difficult to generalize findings across situations, consumers, and time. Because of the many factors that can affect consumer behavior, researchers often must confine their efforts to certain nonrandom phenomena in the marketplace that lend themselves to scientific investigation, such as brand and store loyalty and product preferences. It would seem far more desirable to attempt to understand such patterns of behavior and the processes related to them rather than to try to understand other aspects of consumer choice for which little or no empirical regularity can be observed.

The main objective of this book is to help the reader develop an understanding of the formation, persistence, change, and extinction of the consumption-related patterns of thoughts and actions that comprise consumer behavior. The book is similar to other books written on the topic in that it, too, synthesizes research, seeking to understand consumer behavior. It differs, however, in its approach. Unlike previous approaches, which tend to use a specific theory and research findings in isolation from other theories, the approach used here attempts to integrate several theories and much of the research on the topic into a unified framework, reflecting current trends in approaches used in other disciplines to understand and study human behavior. Another unique feature is the emphasis placed on the interpretation of empirical findings reported in previous studies in the context of specific theories that are viewed as part of the general approach used to study consumer behavior.

Briefly, the approach presented consists of the adaption of the general socialization framework used in other disciplines to construct a model of consumer socialization, which serves as a framework for integrating specific theories and research findings. The model is based on the notion that consumer behavior is dynamic; it constantly undergoes development and change over a person's life cycle.

To support the main theories, the information presented is organized in a way useful to marketers, consumer educators, and policymakers who must analyze consumer behavior and formulate policy. It focuses on consumer behaviors that characterize segments of consumers—children, adolescents, adults, the elderly, and various subcultures and ethnic groups. The consumer behaviors of individuals in these segments are described, and explanations are offered as to why certain behavior patterns occur. The approach integrates several perspectives into a unified framework of socialization, reflecting current thinking in the fields of sociology, psychology, cultural anthropology, gerontology, and communications. The empirical findings are organized around key linkages in the consumer socialization model and are interpreted in the context of socialization theories. Many influences on consumer behavior come into this discussion, including family, peer, mass media, maturational, socioeconomic, racial, gender-related, and ethnic influences.

This project represents the contribution of a large number of individuals. My current thinking reflects the thoughts of several colleagues, former students, and teachers with whom I have interacted and from whom I have benefited a great deal. I owe a word of appreciation to them. My early interaction with Steve Chaffee, Jack McLeod, and Gil Churchill at the University of Wisconsin helped me develop the bases and the general conceptualization of the approach presented in this book. My long-term association with Roy Moore at Wisconsin and later as a colleague at Georgia State University has helped me enormously. Many of the ideas and research efforts reported here are the result of collaboration with him. Also, Ruth B. Smith, now at the University of Maryland, has provided the opportunity for me to gain deeper insights into the subject matter.

I also thank several graduate students, especially Preecha Srisakhirun, Turgut Guvenli, Suprano Antijanto, and Linda Mitchell, who provided research assistance. I thank Barbara Jatkola for her excellent copyediting. Barbara Anne Hines and Aquila Sermons bore the burden of typing, and I thank them for their patience, cooperation, promptness, and good humor. The Georgia State University College of Business Administration through the Research Professorship Program provided research support for this effort.

Finally, I owe a large debt to my wife, Nancy. Evening and weekend writing took precious time from her. I thank her for her understanding and support.

1
Introduction

The study of consumer behavior has enjoyed increasing popularity among several groups of people, including marketing practitioners, public policymakers, consumer educators, and students of human behavior in general. With a changing orientation from a product-oriented to a customer-oriented society in the post–World War II years, marketers have focused their attention on the consumer. Thus, the need to take consumer needs and wants into account before producing and selling products and services has spurred the increasing need for understanding consumer behavior.

The marketers' need to understand consumers better recently has intensified and spread to other groups, particularly public policymakers, as a result of charges made by various consumer groups regarding the effects of various business activities on public welfare. Policymakers have become interested in research that will shed light on the issues surrounding the effects of marketing activities on people, while marketers concurrently have become interested in generating information that will protect and justify their practices, thus helping them avoid government interference in their operations.

The formation of numerous consumer groups has suggested to public policymakers the need to protect consumers from unfair business practices and has triggered the need for consumer research. Such research has revealed information that is useful in understanding consumer capabilities in dealing with the marketplace and has suggested additional ways of protecting and educating the consumer. Thus, the focus and scope of consumer research and the subsequent interest in the field have been expanded to include consumer educators who wish to know more about consumers as a means of preparing them for effective interaction with the marketplace.

The need for information on consumer behavior among marketers, public policymakers, and consumer educators has had a subsequent effect on commercial, private, and government institutions capable of generating the needed information. Therefore, researchers from various disciplines have become increasingly interested in the study of consumer behavior.

Explanations of Consumer Behavior

Researchers traditionally have borrowed various theoretical perspectives from a wide range of disciplines in their efforts to understand and predict consumer behavior. Such disciplines include psychology, sociology, anthropology, and economics. Even within a given discipline, different theoretical perspectives have been used, sometimes as competitive and sometimes as complementary explanations of consumer behavior. For example, within psychology one finds research based on different psychological themes such as theories of social, child, and developmental psychology. These efforts have been more useful in revealing the perplexity of consumer behavior rather than providing explanations for it. They have been particularly useful in identifying a large number of potential explanations for consumer behavior.

Explanations for consumer behavior vary according to the location of the causal force as being in the social organization, within the person, or in the relationship between people. People occupying a given position in the social organization are said to face a similar set of social stimuli and produce rather uniform behavior as a result (McLeod and O'Keefe 1972, 126). For example, research findings suggest that the consumer behavior of individuals in various social classes is rather different (Engel et al. 1978). In many cases, variables in social organizations fail to indicate functional explanations of consumer behavior beyond locating consumer behavior patterns within the particular social structure. While one probably could predict the homogeneity of behavior within a social grouping, there is usually little indication of the particular form of behavior expected in the specific social grouping (McLeod and O'Keefe 1972).

Approaches using intrapersonal characteristics have emphasized the individual's internal (usually psychological) characteristic(s) as the main explanation of consumer behavior. Common perspectives applied from this category include personality, motivation, and attitude theories. Several consumer researchers, for example, have investigated the relationship between consumer personality variables and a variety of consumer behaviors such as product choice, brand, and store loyalty (Engel et al. 1978). Similarly, attitudinal theories have been used extensively to explain several aspects of consumer behavior such as brand choice and store patronage (see, for example, Wilkie and Pessemier 1973).

Intrapersonal personality variables have not been very successful predictors of consumer behavior (Kassarjian 1971), perhaps because of their definition as transitional properties of the individual (McLeod and O'Keefe 1972). Personal values (lifestyles) recently have been used with some success, particularly in studies of product and service use (Wells 1975). The fact that life-styles often are defined as consumer behaviors presents the danger of tautologically mistaking description for actual explanation. For example, a person defined as a "sports enthusiast" is expected to be a heavier consumer of sports magazines than a person not possessing this characteristic. Thus sports magazine readership might be a domain of this personality construct—that is, it defines the concept rather than predicts a certain type of behavior.

Finally, informal social relations between people are the focus of several interpersonal theories, stemming from sociological rather than psychological perspectives. For example, theories of reference group influence have been used to explain brand choice (Engel et al. 1978). Sociological theories have been rather useful in providing explanations of various aspects of consumer behavior. The concern seems to lie primarily in conceptualizing and measuring the influence processes of social relations (see, for example, Robertson and Ward 1973, 29).

While no single theory is capable of explaining consumer behavior better than others, it is believed that some theoretical formulations offer better explanations than others under certain conditions. Thus, a single theory might adequately explain consumer behavior in certain circumstances, making the contextual factors of consumer behavior important conditional variables. This has given rise to a more explicit treatment of contextual variables such as situational variables, high and low involvement of consumer behavior, product innovations, and the like.

Figure 1–1 graphically summarizes previous efforts to explain consumer behavior. The figure shows the four major sets of factors that have been offered as explanations or approaches to the study of consumer behavior. The solid lines and arrows show how efforts have been explicitly directed at the examination of consumer behavior primarily by marketing and consumer researchers. The dotted lines show relationships reported by researchers in the consumer field as well as by researchers in other disciplines. These relationships show an indirect influence on consumer behavior through an intervening variable—that is, they show how one factor affects another variable, which in turn might directly or indirectly affect consumer behavior. For example, relationships between intrapersonal factors (for example, motives) and interpersonal processes have been the focus of much communications research (see, for example, Katz et al. 1974). Similarly, investigation of the relationship between sociocultural factors and specific interpersonal variables has been the subject of a great deal of sociological research (see, for example, Hess 1970). Explanations for the relationships between the sets of factors are sought in psychological, sociological, and social-system theories.

Because of the perplexity and variety of causal factors offered as potential explanations of consumer behavior, several formal comprehensive models of consumer behavior attempt to integrate the various types of causal factors derived from many theoretical areas (see, for example, Nicosia 1966; Howard and Sheth 1969; Engel et al. 1978). Comprehensive models appear to be useful in providing a framework for integrating several theories, as there appears to be no single unified theory of consumer behavior. Such models often have been criticized for their lack of explicit treatment of the interrelationships among variables and difficulties in defining and measuring variables (Robertson and Ward 1973). Unfortunately, comprehensive models deal only with selected, often limited, aspects of consumer behavior such as brand choice, which usually is conceived to be the outcome of evaluative processes preceding purchase. Recent research, however, suggests that consumer behavior researchers often are interested in several other dimensions of consumer

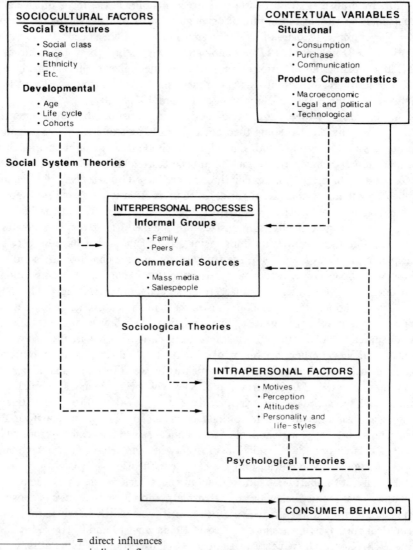

= direct influences
= indirect influences

Figure 1-1. A Conceptual Model of Consumer Behavior

behavior (Olshavsky and Granbois 1979); in addition, little prepurchase evaluation seems to take place among adult consumers, with much of consumer behavior
occurring as a result of a person's learning experiences acquired earlier in life
(Olshavsky and Granbois 1979).

Several observations on the approaches traditionally used to study consumer
behavior follow:

1. Since no single theory appears to explain consumer behavior adequately, there seems to be a need for multitheoretical models that integrate existing theories.

2. Most theories and research on consumer behavior have focused on adults, ignoring increasingly specialized segments of the market (children, adolescents, the elderly, and ethnic groups).

3. Theories and models should be appropriate in helping us explain a wide spectrum of consumer behavior aside from brand choice.

4. There seems to be a need for theories that would help researchers and practitioners understand differences in the consumer behavior of social groupings, including subcultures such as blacks and Hispanics.

One approach to the study of consumer behavior that appears to hold particular promise from a theoretical perspective and from the point of view encompassing existing research is the general conceptual framework of socialization. The socialization approach uses multitheoretical perspectives rather than one particular theory or approach, and the assumption is that behavior is continuously subject to formation and change over a person's life. The socialization model unifies intrapersonal, interpersonal, and social-system theories into a more cohesive, and perhaps more powerful, model, making the use of such an approach fairly attractive, as it helps us understand individual as well as group differences. Finally, the socialization approach provides opportunities for studying a wide spectrum of consumer behaviors over a person's life cycle.

Origins of Consumer Socialization

Similar to so many other approaches to the study of consumer behavior, consumer socialization has its origins in the social sciences. In this section, I will describe the emergence of socialization in general, followed by the emergence of consumer socialization in particular.

Socialization

The term *socialization* was around long before social scientists began to study it as a concept. One source notes its presence in *The Oxford Dictionary of the English Language* in 1828 (Clausen 1968a). Early usage of the term was confined to "making one fit for living in society," while more recent uses of the concept include the development of values, attitudes, and behaviors, both socially functional and dysfunctional (Clausen 1968a).

Socialization has been the concern of several writers in various areas of the social sciences. In sociology, the concept was first addressed around the turn of the century. Cooley (1902) was among the first to express an interest in the development of self through the process of social interaction, recognizing the importance of primary reference groups in the development of personality. Similarly, Thomas saw the emergence of the person as a product of both social demands and internal individual (mostly biological) processes (Thomas and Znaniecki 1918–1920). Other early writers contributing to the development of socialization include Park and Burgess (1921), who were among the first to address socialization processes contributing to the development of a person in the society, and Dewey (1922), whose work had a profound influence not only on sociologists but also on social psychologists, anthropologists, and students of child development (see also Clausen 1968a).

George H. Mead (1934) was the first to address the socialization process directly by focusing on the development of self through the process of modeling. He is credited with the development of the symbolic interaction approach. More recent contributors to the field of socialization include Dollard (1935 and 1939), who set forth criteria for studying socialization.

Psychologists developed an interest in socialization at a later time. Their work was influenced greatly by that of early sociologists (see also Clausen 1968a). Perhaps the greatest contribution comes from students of child psychology (see, for example, Piaget 1926 and 1932; Anderson 1936) and several social psychologists, including Allport, Lewin, Hull, Hoveland, and Sears. Psychologists' contributions to socialization include the reinforcement mechanism of learning and the integration of the sociological and psychological approaches responsible for the development of the social learning point of view and specific learning processes (see Maccoby 1968). This early work has led to the development of three major approaches that are now popular in socialization research: stimulus-response analysis of the neo-Hullians; functional analysis, which is closely related to Skinner's position; and the social learning theories (see, for example, Zigler and Child 1969).

Anthropologists also have contributed to the field of socialization in their study of how culture is transmitted from one generation to the next. Margaret Mead is credited with most of the work in this area, although several other researchers have contributed as well. For example, major contributions were made by Kluchon and his students, who distinguished between socialization and culturation and between individual development and culture changes.

Finally, communications researchers have contributed to the study of socialization, borrowing from several other disciplines. Early studies dealing with public opinion formation and influence (see, for example, Katz and Lazarsfeld 1955) focused mostly on the effects of significant others on the individual's changes in cognitions and behaviors. The effects of other communication processes (such as the mass media) were assumed to have little significance (Klapper 1960). While these studies did not directly address socialization, more recent research places greater emphasis on interpersonal and mass media influences on consumer socialization. For example, studies have found socialization to be influenced by family interaction patterns (see, for example, Miller and Swanson 1958; McLeod and Chaffee 1972) and mass media uses and gratifications (Katz et al. 1974). These later approaches are more elaborate in specifying the communication processes and the type of learning taking place.

Consumer Socialization

The field of consumer socialization as an area of scientific inquiry is relatively new. Early contributions came from researchers outside the field of marketing who wished to understand human behavior better. For example, Guest's (1942, 1944, 1955) early attempts to understand the development of brand preferences were among the first descriptive psychological studies. Similarly, Parsons and others (1953), as well as Riesman and others (1956) and Riesman and Roseborough (1955), were among the first sociologists to speculate on consumer socialization processes and outcomes.

The major contribution to the emergence of consumer socialization comes from communications research. During the late 1960s, Steven H. Chaffee and Jack M. McLeod, codirectors of the Mass Communication Center in the School of Journalism at the University of Wisconsin, developed a family interaction process typology (Chaffee et al. 1966) and were engaged in a significant amount of research in political socialization. Among their students were Scott Ward, Chuck Atkin, and Danny Wackman, all of whom went on to do a great deal of work in consumer socialization. Scott Ward is credited with the introduction of consumer socialization to the study of consumer behavior. In a monograph, Ward (1974b) observed that political socialization and consumer socialization had several things in common, making both areas amenable to a similar research approach. His early thinking and research influenced some of his colleages at the Harvard University School of Business, former professors at Wisconsin, and students (such as Roy Moore, Ron Faber, and myself) studying under Chaffee and McLeod.

Interest in the area of consumer socialization by communications researchers was developed in part because of the issues raised by consumer advocate groups in the late 1960s and the Federal Trade Commission's (FTC) efforts to respond to these groups during the 1970s. For this reason, early efforts to use the socialization approach to the study of the consumer behavior of young people were limited to the effects of advertising. Later attempts more systematically examined variables derived from the socialization model (see, for example, Moore and Stephens 1975; Moschis and Churchill 1978), while more recently the socialization approach has been suggested as a means for understanding consumer behavior over an individual's life cycle (Moschis 1981b; Smith and Moschis 1985a).

The Concept of Socialization Today

Parallel to the development of consumer socialization, the definition of the concept has been changing. Several definitions have been applied to the concept. Some of the more recent ones deserve particular attention. According to one source, for example:

> Socialization is a broad term for the whole process by which an individual develops, through interaction with other people, his specific patterns of socially relevant behavior and experience. (Zigler and Child 1969, 474)

Brim refines this view by referring specifically to the content of learning, defining socialization as:

> The process by which individuals acquire the knowledge, skills and dispositions that enable them to participate as more or less effective members of groups and the society. (Brim 1966, 3)

The socialization perspective focuses on the development of learning properties (cognitions and behaviors) necessary for performing a given role. For example, researchers have investigated socialization to roles such as spouse, employee, and prisoner (Hill and Alders 1969; Tannenbaum and McLeod 1967; Brim 1966; Wheeler 1969).

Furthermore, the study of socialization is no longer restricted to the learning that occurs during childhood but applies to the study of learning over the life span (Albrecht and Gift 1975; Brim 1966; Brim 1968; Clausen 1967; Riley et al. 1969; Rosow 1974). Individuals proceeding through the middle and later years must continually learn to play new or altered roles and to relinquish old ones. Moreover, with the trend toward increased longevity, more mature people are expected to be called upon to play a variety of roles in society (Riley et al. 1969). Thus, there is a continuous need for socialization in adulthood. Learning to respond to new demands does not stop at the end of childhood (Albrecht and Gift 1975).

In viewing socialization from a life-span perspective, Inkeles (1969) writes:

> In adulthood the main *issue* is the degree to which the individual accepts, and the quality of his performance in, the whole panoply of roles which accompany the statuses of adulthood such as husband, father, earner of a living, member of a religious community . . .
>
> In older age there is an analogue to the main *issue* of infancy and early childhood, in that adjustment to physical changes comes again to oblige us to acquire new skills and change established habits . . . A main part of the older individual's *task* is to learn to renounce or abandon previously held positions . . . The learning of entirely, or largely, new roles may also be required, such as dealing with total leisure. (pp. 628–629)

To view transition into old age in terms of socialization is not unusual, given its traditionally close association with other widely known developmental stages such as childhood and adulthood (Piaget 1952; Kohlberg 1969; Long et al. 1980). As people grow older, there seems to exist a developmental tie with learning.

In terms of the use of the concept for aging individuals, Dowd and others note that aging is not an automatic process whereby the older person is "fashioned from the whole cloth of the middle-aged recruit" (Dowd et al. 1981, 359). Rather, the transition to a new life span is more appropriately conceptualized as a series of interactions between an individual and others in his or her environment, and recognition is given to the idea that older people, like their younger counterparts, can be socialized.

Rosow (1974) also has described the transition to old age in terms of socialization, as have Riley et al. (1969) and Baltes and his associates in life-span developmental psychology (Baltes 1978; Baltes et al. 1977). Within a communication context, the concept of the socialization of the elderly has been applied by some researchers (for example, Dimmick et al. 1979) interested in the mass media as a socialization agent. Finally, in the field of consumer affairs, Stampfl (1978) viewed consumer education needs from a life-cycle perspective and suggested the need for socializing the same person into new and changing consumer roles over the entire life cycle.

Consumer Socialization

The adaptation of the socialization approach to consumer research was only recently proposed as a vehicle to the study of consumer behavior (Ward 1974a). The area of consumer socialization has received considerable interest and attention mainly as a result of various contemporary issues related to public and corporate policy formulation (Ward 1974a).

The concept of consumer socialization has been applied to the development of consumption-related cognitions, attitudes, and behavior in children and in adolescents. In fact, Ward defines consumer socialization as the "process by which *young people* [emphasis added] acquire skills, knowledge, and attitudes relevant to their effective functioning as consumers in the marketplace" (p. 2).

Socialization researchers and students of consumer behavior, however, recently have viewed the area as a fruitful approach to the study of consumer behavior throughout a person's life cycle. For example, researchers in various disciplines increasingly have applied socialization perspectives to help them understand and explain select aspects of human behavior over a person's life cycle (see, for example, Baltes et al. 1980; Denhardt and Jeffress 1971; Brim 1968; Baltes and Schaie 1973; Riesman et al. 1950; Riesman and Roseborough 1955; Goslin 1969). Similarly, there is an increasing tendency among researchers of consumer behavior to suggest the use of the socialization approach (see, for example, Olshavsky and Granbois 1979; Davis 1976; Ferber and Birnbaum 1977; Moschis 1981b; Smith and Moschis 1985a).

Specific research efforts utilizing the socialization approach to the study of consumer behavior include research by Stampfl, Moschis, and Lawton (1978), who used consumer socialization perspectives to study preschoolers' consumer learning; work by Moschis and Moore (1979b), who used socialization perspectives to study the development of consumer decision-making patterns among adolescents; Bellenger's and Moschis's (1981) presentation of the socialization approach to explain consumer store patronage behavior; and later efforts to use the socialization approach to study the consumer behavior of the elderly (Smith et al. 1981, 1982, 1985, 1986; Smith and Moschis 1984a, 1984b, 1985a, 1985b, 1987).

In summary, it has been recognized that psychological and social factors affect the consumer socialization of children and adolescents (Ward 1974a; Ward et al. 1977). Some evidence in consumer socialization research also suggests what general socialization researchers are acknowledging: that socialization occurs throughout the life span and affects the cognitions, attitudes, and behaviors of older adults (Ahammer 1973; Dowd et al. 1981; Riley et al. 1969; Rosow 1974).

The tendency to view consumer socialization as a lifelong process is not unreasonable given the increasing number of empirical studies and theoretical perspectives in support of the approach. For example, although it often is assumed that adult brand preferences and brand loyalty are outcomes of evaluative processes preceding purchase (see, for example, Engel et al. 1978), recent research suggests that these orientations are likely to be acquired early in life as part of the general socialization process (Olshavsky and Granbois 1979). Similarly, a recent brand loyalty study by Yankelovich, Skelly, and White concluded that: "Significant decision making does occur during the teen years, and once the decision making process is accomplished, these teenagers will hold on to the brand for a significant period of time" (Madison Avenue 1980, 91).

Thus, although previous studies of brand preference and brand loyalty have focused on adult consumers, it appears that the study of the development of preferences and loyalties for brands during the preadult years might be of at least equal interest, as such orientations are likely to be maintained and translated into purchases later in life. This observation appears to be consistent with the more general belief that attitudes and behavior patterns established during late adolescence can be carried over into adulthood and become a way of life (see, for example, Sofranko and Nolan 1972; Hurlock 1968). As Ward (1974b) put it: "At least some patterns of adult consumer behavior are influenced by childhood and adolescent experiences, and the study of these experiences should help us to understand not only consumer behavior among young people, but the development of adult patterns of behavior as well" (p. 49).

Additional evidence in support of the socialization perspective over the life cycle comes from a vast amount of research presented in this book. For example, a recent study examined the formation of desires for products and brands during adolescence. The findings indicate that the development of such desires might occur throughout a person's life cycle, with preferences for products and brands likely to be formed and changed at various stages. The authors suggest that the learning of such orientations is better understood as a life-span developmental phenomenon rather than a cognitive developmental process restricted to the preadult years (Moschis and Moore 1981a).

Riesman and his colleagues (1956) in their book *The Lonely Crowd* were among the first sociologists to present the study of consumer behavior among adults from a socialization perspective. Gradually, consumer behavior researchers have recognized that the consumer behavior of adults undergoes formation and change throughout the later years in a person's life cycle. Similarly, it has long been recognized by marketers that certain behavior patterns change over the life cycle (Engel et al. 1978; Wells and Gubar 1966). Even in L.H. Clark's (1955) earlier work *The Life Cycle and Consumer Behavior*, it was noted that older housewives might be both more difficult to educate through advertising and more brand loyal than younger housewives (Miller 1955).

Finally, the evidence suggests that the consumer behavior of older adults differs from the consumer behavior of younger persons. For example, table 1–1, which shows expenditure by age, indicates that elderly families spend a greater proportion of their income than younger families on the following: food eaten at home, housing (except furnishings), health care, personal care, and vacation and pleasure trips. Recent data also point out that people over fifty are among the largest spenders in the country for items such as stocks, bonds, furs, jewelry, and expensive clothing (Bartos 1980).

Research during the past twenty years has found particularly that the consumer behavior of the aged is different from the consumer behavior of younger people and that there are significant differences in consumer behavior among the aged. Unfortunately, the research has been descriptive, fragmented, and void of analysis based on sound theoretical perspectives (Meadow et al. 1981).

Retirement and old age are characterized by the relinquishment of certain consumption categories (such as consumer durables and children's education expenses) and the assumption of others (such as health care, securities and investments, and travel), within the context of the role shift. To keep pace with these changes in behavior patterns, the consumer must continuously learn, forming new attitudes and skills and changing old ones (Mauldin 1976). Therefore, in much the same way socialization applies to young adult consumers' learning in a general context, it also should apply to the development and change of adult and elderly consumers' cognitions, attitudes, and behaviors toward marketing stimuli. For example, as people grow older, they tend to interact differently with various sources of consumer information, particularly in their increased exposure to the mass media (Real et al. 1980). The criteria for media use preference also seem to change with age (Bernhardt and Kinnear 1976; Hendricks and Hendricks 1977; Phillips and Sternthal 1977). A recent review of the literature in the field of consumer behavior provided support for the socialization approach in studying the consumer behavior of the elderly (Moschis 1981b).

To summarize, the purpose of this book is to suggest that the adaptation of the socialization approach to the study of consumer behavior over the life cycle not only is in line with theoretical notions advanced in other disciplines but also is supported by empirical research. It will be argued that the socialization perspective used to study human behavior in other disciplines provides a conceptual framework that accommodates diverse theoretical perspectives and might provide a fruitful approach to the study of changes in consumer behavior over the life cycle.

Table 1-1
Annual Consumer Expenditures by Age of Family Head

	Under 25	25-34	35-44	45-54	55-64	65 and Over
Total expenditures	$11,617	$19,271	$24,296	$24,718	$19,497	$12,346
Food	1,835	2,949	4,046	4,166	3,328	2,288
At home	965	1,806	2,612	2,728	2,194	1,660
Away from home	870	1,143	1,434	1,438	1,134	628
Alcoholic beverages	343	356	322	307	260	133
Housing	3,410	6,409	7,494	6,870	5,374	4,123
Shelter	2,151	3,915	4,411	3,658	2,697	2,073
Owned	325	2,059	3,087	2,449	1,792	1,134
Rented	1,681	1,637	937	761	538	699
Other	145	219	386	448	367	240
Fuel, utilities, public services	688	1,305	1,789	1,969	1,701	1,342
Household operations	115	359	327	226	208	267
House furnishings and equipment	475	831	968	1,016	767	440
Apparel and apparel services	782	1,071	1,428	1,366	933	515
Transportation	2,623	4,052	4,758	4,991	3,656	1,972
Vehicles	1,046	1,703	1,934	1,809	1,148	606
Gasoline and motor oil	745	1,073	1,308	1,493	1,145	603
Other vehicle expenses	706	1,047	1,263	1,421	1,082	575
Public transportation	126	229	253	267	281	189
Health care	307	547	753	936	1,056	1,228
Entertainment	581	977	1,294	1,075	799	390
Personal care	92	148	203	223	213	166
Reading	74	121	154	153	140	106
Education	489	180	343	590	197	45
Tobacco	139	196	249	290	244	116
Miscellaneous	119	244	347	356	329	198
Cash contributions	100	297	695	925	754	665
Personal insurance, pensions, and Social Security	772	1,724	2,209	2,469	2,155	401
Life insurance and other personal insurance	64	205	353	434	324	154
Retirement, pensions, and Social Security	659	1,519	1,855	2,035	1,830	247

Source: Bureau of Labor Statistics, "Consumer Expenditure Survey Results from 1982–83" (interview survey) (Washington: Bureau of Labor Statistics, 1985), tables 3 and 11.

Rationale

The adaptation of the socialization perspective to consumer behavior explanations appears to be logical for several reasons. Consumer behavior does not seem to be amenable to any particular theory; rather, each of the several theories used might offer meaningful insights into the understanding of consumer behavior. The socialization model seems to provide such a multitheoretical perspective (Moschis and Churchill 1978; Robertson and Feldman 1976; Smith and Moschis 1985a; Ward 1978). In addition, the socialization model suggests a framework for integrating existing theories by providing an approach that unifies several theories previously used in isolation to explain consumer behavior. For example, learning theories might be useful in understanding how people acquire consumer orientations from the mass media; consumer motives, which are subject to change over a person's life cycle, might explain the individual's interaction with socialization agents (such as media use) and age-related demands for decision making (Morrison 1979); reference group influence might be viewed in isolation (see, for example, Churchill and Moschis 1979) as well as in relation to other socialization agents in the form of a two-step flow model (see, for example, Chaffee et al. 1970); and cognitive developmental theories might apply to nearly every stage in a person's life cycle (see, for example, Long 1980). In addition, specific theories might help explain changes in behavior at specific stages. For example, several theories have been advanced regarding the later stages of life-span development, including disengagement, subculture, personality, and social breakdown theory (see, for example, Young 1979).

Furthermore, because socialization involves continual adjustment between the individual and the situation (role), it is likely to result in changes in an individual's orientation toward his or her environment. In such cases, the individual is expected to relearn specific patterns of behavior. This process is commonly known as resocialization, with antecedent variables and socialization processes again playing an important role (Riesman and Roseborough 1955).

Socialization perspectives also might be more useful in improving our understanding of several aspects of adult consumer behavior, as opposed to, for example, information-processing research. Olshavsky's and Granbois's (1979) findings, for example, show that little prepurchase decision making takes place, with much of the behavior occurring as a result of a person's experiences earlier in life.

While other approaches to consumer research examine learning, they usually are limited to learning occurring from a single instance or, at best, from experiences within a limited time. The socialization perspective appears to be more powerful than these approaches because it not only focuses on how learning might take place within a specific (limited) time frame, but it also provides opportunities for studying how learning is affected by progression through the life cycle.

The socialization approach can help us better understand specific approaches used to study consumer behavior. For example, it has been argued that information-processing skills can best be understood in the context of a life-span perspective (Baltes et al. 1980). Since it is possible to adopt a life-span perspective without studying individuals of all ages, researchers examining adult consumer behavior can benefit a great deal by applying theoretical notions within the broader conceptual framework of socialization over the life span. Such an approach might suggest the inclusion or control of antecedent variables and provide a better understanding of the effects of previous experiences.

Using life-span developmental perspectives to study human behavior has become a rather popular approach in recent years among psychologists (see, for example, Baltes et al. 1980; Baltes and Schaie 1973), sociologists (see, for example, Brim 1966 and 1968), and more recently communications researchers (see, for instance, McLeod and O'Keefe 1972; Dimmick et al. 1979). Even advocates of cognitive developmental theories, which presumably are most applicable to children and adolescents, have viewed these theories from a life-span developmental perspective (see, for example, Kohlberg 1973; Baltes et al. 1980; Long et al. 1980). Thus, the socialization perspective provides opportunities for studying consumer behavior over a person's life cycle. It is not limited to preadult years. Because consumer behavior appears to change over a person's life cycle (see, for example, Wells and Gubar 1966), socialization theory might help us explain what changes take place, as well as how and why these changes occur. Thus, consumer behavior might be viewed from a life-span developmental perspective.

Several practical marketing problems and issues are better understood and addressed by socialization theory. For example, the individual's response to marketing communications is likely to vary on the basis of the level of cognitive development (see, for example, Adler et al. 1980). By understanding how cognitive development relates to the way the individual responds to marketing communications, marketers can design more effective messages directed at groups in different developmental stages.

If consumer socialization is indeed a lifelong process, marketers must identify the stage(s) at which desires for various products and brands are likely to start developing or changing and then attempt to influence the development of these orientations. The latter task requires a better understanding of the processes leading to the development of consumer behavior.

Consumer educators have become interested in the area mainly as a result of the consumerism movement and the subsequent need for preparing present and future consumers for effective interaction with the marketplace. In recent years, consumer education not only has been targeted at preadults in schools, but it also has focused on adults, especially minorities. Some individuals have argued for life-span education because the process of learning consumer skills appears to take place throughout a person's life cycle (see, for example, Stampfl 1978; Birren and Woodruff 1973; Ryles 1980). For example, consumer educators are interested in developing programs to aid the acquisition and use of consumption skills by the elderly. Evidence of this interest is found in the growing number of special programs for the elderly consumer (Baltes et al. 1977; Burton and Hennon 1980).

Consumer socialization is of interest to public policymakers who wish to understand consumer behavior, especially that of the young and the elderly, in an effort to address public concerns better and pass legislation. For example, in addition to the obvious need to protect the elderly consumer from deceptive or misleading advertising, high-pressure sales tactics, and outright fraud (Baltes 1978), policymakers realize that the elderly are an increasingly powerful political force (Bureau of Labor Statistics 1972–1973). Groups such as the Gray Panthers are becoming more vocal in demanding their rights, and they are getting results.

Finally, social scientists and students of consumer behavior have shown a concern for the socialization of select groups. For example, with respect to the behavior of elderly consumers, economists are interested in the macroeconomic effects of population aging on consumption (Amann et al. 1980; Atchley 1972), as well as the microeconomic effects of aging (Atkin 1976b), while gerontologists have shown an interest in the elderly's sources and uses of information (Bearden et al. 1979). Research in the individual's development of consumer knowledge, attitudes, and skills also should be of interest to students of consumer behavior. Consumer socialization not only addresses questions concerning the consumer behavior of adults, but it also deals with the consumer behavior of various subcultures, focusing on the formation and acquisition of values, attitudes, and behaviors over the life cycle.

2
A Conceptual Model of
Consumer Socialization

Socialization explanations of consumer behaviors are quite different from the single theoretical explanations discussed briefly in chapter 1. They are more elaborate and demand more data to validate them. These requirements are reflected in a key assumption of the socialization approach: *"to understand human behavior, we must specify its social origins and the processes by which it is learned and maintained"* (McLeod and O'Keefe 1972, 127–28).

While most alternative explanations of consumer behavior often are limited to one type of variable (for instance, personality or attitudes), the socialization perspective is more demanding because it includes five types of variables (McLeod and O'Keefe 1972):

1. age or life-cycle position of the influencee
2. social structural constraints affecting learning
3. agent or source of the influence
4. learning processes involved in socialization
5. content or criterion behavior

This chapter discusses these variables and incorporates them in a conceptual model of consumer socialization. To illustrate the relevance and applicability of the model, an example is given of how one specific aspect of consumer behavior (store patronage) might be viewed from a socialization perspective.

The Model

Age or Life-Cycle Position

Age or life-cycle position refers to a specific time in a person's life when socialization occurs. Although the study of socialization was once restricted to learning that takes place during childhood, it has been extended in recent years to include the study of learning that occurs throughout a person's lifetime (Brim 1966). Because people learn continuously and because they learn different things at different times in their lives from different sources, the emphasis is on changes in cognitions and behaviors as an individual moves through the life cycle, specifically in the postadolescent period when the person gets married, takes a job, and so forth. The term *life cycle* is preferred over *age* as a more relevant variable in adult socialization because life-styles associated with particular cycles become more crucial in terms of the reorganization of various cognitions and behaviors (McLeod and O'Keefe 1972). Theory and research also suggest that people at different ages or life-cycle stages might be influenced differently by environmental factors (Kagan and Moss 1962; Baldwin 1969; Ward et al. 1977; Crandall et al. 1958) and might respond differently to stimuli in general and to commercial stimuli in particular (Wells and Gubar 1966; Phillips and Sternthal 1977). Thus, all generalizations are dependent on a particular phase in the developmental process or life cycle, and a different cluster of variables tends to dominate each stage.

For example, perhaps the consumer socialization of children and adolescents prior to the era of television occurred in a different fashion than it does today. The same can be said about the consumer socialization of the elderly. For example, Kubey (1980) has hypothesized that since adult socialization is thought to occur more readily when it builds on previously established experiences, television (and presumably other mass media) might have a more profound impact on future cohorts of the aged, who will have a more extensive history of exposure to mass communications. Similarly, technology is likely to introduce changes in an individual's environment, and this might result in changes in the person's orientation toward consumption as well as changes in the individual's relationships with the various sources of consumer learning.

Because people continuously learn different things at different times from different soruces, it is necessary to consider some index of the passage of time relative to the individual. The aging process involves biological, psychological, and social aspects occurring in different environments. The use of only one index, that of chronological age, would be an incomplete indicator. Therefore, it is useful to separate age effects (biological, psychological, and social aging) from period effects (environmental changes such as the availability of television) and cohort effects (historical differences in socialization, genetic change, and cohort composition) (Reynolds and Rentz 1981).

Social Structural Constraints

Social structural constraints refer to the social environment within which a person's learning takes place. Variables such as social class, sex, and race locate a person in a social grouping whose members' behaviors tend to be relatively homogeneous. As a result, they can directly, as well as indirectly, affect consumer socialization and often are useful control variables in socialization research. Social structural variables can be conceived as subcultural factors, locating the individual within specific subcultures that are likely to exhibit different patterns of consumer behaviors. Subcultural variables, unfortunately, are not well defined in consumer research. For example, while it is often easier to assume subcultures within social classes, it is more difficult to assign a person to a specific ethnic subculture on the basis of the person's ethnic background, which can be mixed. Similarly, the extent to which a variable can be used to define subcultures often is an empirical question. For example, using variables such as religion and life-styles to categorize individuals into religious and life-style subcultures could present problems because often very little is revealed regarding the extent to which a person possesses the specific attribute or the extent to which subcultural categories are mutually exclusive.

Socialization Agents

A socialization agent can be a person or an organization directly involved in socialization because of frequency of contract with the individual, primacy to the individual, and control over rewards and punishments given to the individual (Brim 1966). These agents are of high salience to the learner and continue to influence the development of the individual's character, even as new agents are added and older ones are displaced. The result of these interactions is the development of a series of self-other systems in which the individual is oriented toward the evaluations of significant others and their role prescriptions. Such conceptual notions can be traced to Cooley's (1902 discussion of the "looking-glass self" and Mead's (1934) "generalized other."

The main implication of including specific agents in the socialization model is that the unit of analysis becomes the agent-learner relationship (McLeod and O'Keefe 1972). Talmon (1963) put these agent-learner relationships into four categories on the basis of the formality of the type of agent and role of the learner:

1. formal organization (agent), role of learner specified (for example, school)
2. formal organization, role of learner not specified (for instance, mass media)
3. informal organization, role of learner specified (for example, family)
4. informal organization, role of learner not specified (for instance, peers)

Previous research suggests that the mass media, family, peers, and school are important agents of consumer socialization among children and adolescents (see, for example, Moschis 1981b; Adler et al. 1977). Previous research also suggests that mass media and personal sources are important agents of socialization in general (see, for example, Schramm 1969; Riley et al. 1969 and of consumer socialization in particular in later stages of the life cycle (see, for example, Kubey 1980; Smith, Moschis, and Moore 1981 and 1982; Riesman and Roseborough 1955). As Hess (1972) notes, however, in the socialization of the older person, who must confront drastic role changes, no socializers are vastly superior in age. Older persons must rely on age mates, such as a spouse, friends, or siblings, or on younger people, such as young or adult offspring.

There appears to be ample opportunity for parents to learn from their off-spring. Studies also have found relatives to be important sources of consumer information for the elderly (Klippel and Sweeney 1974; Schiffman 1971). While most older people prefer to live in their own households, about 90 percent of older people in the United States live within one hour's commuting distance from at least one child, and about 28 percent live with one of their children (U.S. Bureau of the Census 1979). The majority of older Americans have at least two children (Cowgill 1979). Neugarten, Moore, and Lowe (1968) also found a preference for maintaining a separate household near children or relatives and a tendency to see family members frequently. Even when the generations are separated geographically, they are not sociologically isolated; both generations prefer to be close and to see family members regularly (Cowgill 1979).

Learning Processes

Learning processes refer to the ways in which the learner acquires specific values and behaviors from socialization agents while interacting with them. Learning processes fall into three categories: modeling, reinforcement, and social interaction. *Modeling* explanations involve imitation either through a conscious attempt to emulate the socialization agent or because the agent's behavior is the most salient alternative open to the person. For example, a child does the same things his parents do in an effort to be like them. This type of learning process has been referred to as observational or imitation learning.

Observational learning refers to any learning proceeding from a vicarious experience—that is, from observation of the behavior of some model, either live or symbolic. It can include process variables such as imitation, role-playing, and identification. A wide variety of behavior has been shown to derive from the observation of models. Such learning is a function of attentional, retentional, motoric, and motivational processes, all of which might be affected by various factors in the modeling stimuli, the observation and performance context, and individual capacities (Bandura 1969).

Common operational definitions of modeling processes are correlations between the agent's and learner's behavior. Bandura (1969) points out several problems inherent in using agent-learner similarity measures to tap modeling processes. For example, many behavior similarities result from direct tuition, selective exposure to settings and activities, and the influence of common reinforcement contingencies in specific cultural subgroups. Behaviorial similarities cannot always be attributed to modeling processes, and the identification of the sources of emulated behavior also becomes problematic. Children in particular are continuously exposed to multiple models, including teachers, peers, other adults, and models on television.

Bandura cites examples to support the notion that people show no greater similarity to their actual parents than to randomly selected parental figures and that measures of identification might indeed assess generally conditioned patterns of behavior basic to all members of a given subculture. Furthermore, lack of a significant correlation does not mean that there is no relationship between the two variables but only that the linear relationship has not been demonstrated for the range of variables studied. Although matching behavior is a usual measure of observational learning, a distinction between acquisition and performance is necessary (Bandura 1973). While matching behavior indicates that learning has occurred, failure to perform matching behavior need not mean that acquisition has not occurred. Individuals who originally fail to imitate behavior they observe might display this behavior later when sufficient incentives are provided. For example, children might observationally acquire behaviors associated with adult roles that can be performed only when the child reaches adulthood.

Reinforcement explanations of learning involve either reward (positive reinforcement) or punishment (negative reinforcement) mechanisms. The person learns to duplicate past behaviors that have been rewarded by the socializing agent and to avoid repeating those behaviors for which she has been punished (McLeod and O'Keefe 1972). Among the more common examples of operational definitions of positive and negative reinforcement are affection and psychological punishment by the parent, respectively.

The *social interaction* mechanism is less specific concerning the exact type of learning involved. It might involve a combination of modeling and reinforcement (McLeod and O'Keefe 1972). This explanation maintains that the characteristic social norms involved in the person's interactions with other significant persons shape the individual's attitudes, values, and behaviors. Thus, what is learned is a series of interpersonal relationships relating to a given social role (Brim 1960 and 1966; Thorton and Nardi 1975).

The *social interaction* process can have content and structure. Content often refers to expectations (norms) held by agents as to what the prescribed role should be; these can be attitudinal, behavioral, or cognitive (Thorton and Nardi 1975). Specific examples in consumer socialization would include parental norms regarding saving and spending (Ward et al. 1977) and skills in selecting and using products rationally, which normally are taught in school (Gavian and Nanassy 1955). Alternatively, the structure of the social interaction mechanism usually refers to agent-learner relations concerning power and communication. For example, with respect to parent-child relations, one finds power structures such as "controlling-permissive" and "traditional-modern" types of families, while parent-child communication relations include "socio-oriented" and "concept-oriented" communication structures (Chaffee et al. 1971), with specific examples of consumer socialization such as "lectures" (one-way talks by the parent to the child regarding consumer activities) and two-way communication between parent and child regarding consumption (Ward and Robertson 1970).

There are several methods of operationalizing social interaction. For example, in a model of educational and occupational achievement, best friends' plans and parental encouragement are viewed as modeling and social interaction processes, respectively, depicting the influence of significant others (Haller and Portes 1973). Frequency of social interaction often is used to measure social influence processes. The theoretical justification for using frequency of interaction to capture this complex process is found in various social learning theories (see, for example, Gewirtz 1969). For instance, learning resulting from the repetitive nature of television advertising—that is, frequency of interaction with the television—and associating attractive outcomes with advertised products (or unattractive outcomes with failure to use advertised products) might be linked to theories of classical and instrumental conditioning (Bandura 1971a and 1971b).

In the classic situation of childhood socialization, children are helped by parents (as socializing agents) to learn certain values, norms, and definitions to guide their behavior. Through processes of modeling, reinforcement, and social interaction, children learn how to behave. In a model of later life socialization, however, major modifications of the familiar early learning model must be made. Although it has received little attention, one aspect of socialization that is unquestionably important in later life roles derives from the reciprocal relationship between parent and offspring. This reciprocal relationship might play a part in socializing the parent during the middle years (Riley et al. 1969). Riesman and Roseborough (1955) called this retroactive socialization. Retroactive socialization processes have been documented in the field of consumer socialization (see, for example, Bowen 1977), and they have emerged across cultural settings (see, for example, Alexander 1964).

Recent overviews suggest that the social learning of adult roles occurs through modeling, imitation, and identification (social interaction) (Parke 1972). Such learning can be by trial and error or can occur in a no-trial situation where correct behavior responses are acquired through observation (Bandura 1965). For example, one of the ways in which the aging individual might learn appropriate behavior for the later years is through observation of the mass media (Young 1969). Learning also can take place through personal interaction. For example, Schiffman (1972a) found that the level of social interaction of the elderly consumer affects the amount of perceived risk in a new product trial, while more recent studies found social interaction with significant others to be associated with the development of a variety of consumption-related cognitions (Smith et al. 1981, 1982 and 1985). Further, it has been suggested that social interaction might be a more important process later in life than in youth, when modeling and reinforcement are more likely the important processes (Ahammer 1973).

Content or Criterion Behavior

Content or criterion behavior refers to the *learning properties* (cognitions and behaviors) necessary for the performance of a given social role. Relevant learning properties often are a function of the particular role under consideration. Often these include specific behavioral acts as well as cognitive components such as values, attitudes, and beliefs. For example, among the attributes often considered to be related to a person's political role are political interest, political activity, and political knowledge; political party and candidate differences; party identification; and usage of mass media for political news (Jennings and Niemi 1968). Learning properties can be divided into (a) those properties that help a person function in any given social system and (b) those properties that are related to the person's individual behavior, regardless of the standards set by any larger system (McLeod and O'Keefe 1972).

The criteria relevant to the functioning of a given social system are prescribed by society; they are based on normative theories of human behavior and, in a sense, are efforts on the part of some of society's members to regulate the behavior of other members so that certain desirable consequences follow (Brim 1966). Alternatively, the criteria relevant to individual behavior include cognitions and behaviors that enable a person to perform a given social role, regardless of whether the behaviors are functional or dysfunctional to any larger system. While one cannot entirely ignore gratuitous assumptions about human behavior (assumptions such as "the world would be better off if people conformed to socially prescribed behaviors"), it seems particularly useful in socialization research to sort out those behaviors that are defined in terms of their relevance to performing some function for society and those cognitions and behaviors defined in terms of their relevance only to the individual (McLeod and O'Keefe 1972).

Consumer Role. Criterion variables defining a person's consumption role might represent a fairly wide spectrum of consumption-related variables in regard to occupation (Riesman and Roseborough 1955; Ferber 1976), acquisition of strategic items (Gredal 1966; Arndt 1976), purchasing and consuming (Nicosia and Mayer 1976; Arndt 1976), and sex roles in family decision making (Herbst 1952; Davis 1976). Among these, however, only purchasing and consuming can be viewed as useful in defining a person's consumer role from a societal perspective, as society appears to have some prescribed norms of behavior regarding purchase and use of products (for example, comparative shopping and energy conservation) (Churchill and Moschis 1979, 24), but imposes few norms on occupational choice, purchase of products, and sex roles in family decisions.

From a social perspective, an individual can be said to be socialized when he or she has learned to think and feel according to society's expectations. Deviance from society's norms and expectations is explained as the consequence of poor socialization; it might be a consequence of deviant socialization experiences—that is, socialization to deviant norms—or of an incomplete or inadequate communication of norms, or it might result from the individual's emotional or rational rejection of norms (Clausen 1968b).

Consumer Behavior. One surprising discovery students of consumer behavior often make is that definitions of consumer behavior vary widely, with boundaries often extended to include noneconomic decisions, such as consumption of time, fertility, and deviant consumer behaviors such as shoplifting (see, for example, Moschis et al. 1987; Powell and Moschis 1986). Most researchers, however, seem to limit consumer behaviors to cognitive and overt acts preceding, determining, and following the act of purchase (see, for example, Engel et al. 1978). Such acts can be categorized into several clusters, each relating to stages in the decision-making process, as well as to broad types of consumer decisions such as spending versus saving decisions, assortment decisions, product decisions, brand or store decisions, and consumption decisions (Nicosia and Mayer 1976; Arndt 1976).

Figure 2–1 presents a conceptual framework for classifying various types of consumer behaviors, thus defining the individual's learning properties. The highest order of consumer decisions is whether to spend or save. The next level of purchase decisions involves assortment decisions, or general budget allocation decisions—that is, decisions concerning the allocation of one's income to various assortments of goods or expense items such as transportation and recreation

STAGE	1	2 Search for Information		3	4	5 Postdecisional/ Consumption Activities
DECISION	Consumption Needs	Internal	External	Alternative Evaluation	Decision/ Purchase	
Saving vs. Spending						
General Budget Allocation Decision						
Acquisition of Strategic Items						
Generic Product or Service Decision						
Variant Selection						

Source: A modification of Arndt's (1975) conceptual framework.

Figure 2–1. Elements of Consumer Behavior: Classification by Type of Decision and Stage in Decision-making Process

(Alderson 1957; Runyon 1977; Solow 1968). Lower order consumer decisions can be broken down further into various types of product decisions, which in turn are broken down into strategic and generic product or service decisions (Chaffee and McLeod 1973; Arndt 1976; Solow 1968). Finally, variant selection includes more specific decisions, such as those related to store patronage and brand decisions (Engel et al. 1978; Runyon 1977).

At any given level of this consumer decision hierarchy, concepts examined most often relate to some type of cognitive, effective, and behavioral aspect of consumer behavior. Examples of cognitive orientations include consumer knowledge, consumer skills, and information-processing patterns; affective orientations often are expressed in terms of preferences, attitudes, and dispositions; and behavioral concepts often are defined in terms of either single or repeat choices. These can be classified in terms of the traditional stages in the consumer decision-making process (figure 2–1).

Another type of classification of socialization outcomes is by relevance to the consumer decision process and level of cognitive complexity (Moschis 1976a, 1978a, 1981b). Some skills, attitudes, and knowledge are *directly* relevant to consumption behavior and the transaction itself. Examples include evaluation of alternatives and brand preferences. Skills and attitudes that motivate consumption, such as materialistic values, are *indirectly* useful in the purchasing decision or transaction itself. Consumption-related orientations also can be classified into *simple* and *complex* categories. The former category might include simple definitional statements (such as brand identification), while the latter includes relational statements (such as brand X is better than brand Y).

These two dimensions (consumption relevance and cognitive complexity) provide a fourfold typology of consumer behaviors: direct-simple, direct-complex, indirect-simple, and indirect-complex skills. Previous socialization research has used typologies for classifying socialization outcomes in line with this typology (see, for example, Ward 1974a; Wackman et al. 1972; Moore and Stephens 1975; Moschis 1976a and 1981a).

Socialization explanations of consumer behavior are concerned with the examination of how consumers learn to develop patterns of behaviors and cognitions. In presenting evidence supporting the socialization model in this book, we have adopted a minimal definition of relevant literature as any study that describes a person's consumer behavior specific to the person's age or life cycle. Although this definition does not specify the nature of the dependent variables, it does suggest that criterion variables might be different over the person's life cycle. Stampfl (1978), for example, has elaborated on this issue and has suggested variables specific to the person's stage in the life cycle. Although such a framework would seem to focus consumer socialization research on rather specific dependent variables, it also might be misleading, as many learning properties relevant to a specific stage in a person's life cycle might be acquired prior to reaching that stage. Riesman and Roseborough (1955) and Merton (1957) have called this type of learning anticipatory socialization.

Anticipatory Consumer Socialization. Hess and Torney (1967) describe three types of anticipatory socialization: the acquisition of attitudes and values about adult roles that have limited relevance for the child but serve as a basis for subsequent learning; the acquisition of specific information not directly applied until later in life; and the acquisition of skills that can be practiced immediately and called into play when appropriate. In the study of consumer behavior, Riesman and Roseborough (1955) used the term to refer to prospective housekeeper roles young people assume prior to reaching the age of role enactment. They suggest that anticipatory socialization specifically might entail development of expectations regarding career, product ownership, and adaptive patterns of consumer behavior.

Research on consumer socialization proliferated during the 1970s, focusing almost exclusively on the development of consumer orientations and norms among children and adolescents that can be enacted immediately. Many cognitions, however, might have little practical application at the time they are learned, as direct spending by children and adolescents is rather limited (Ward 1974a). For example, a child might see adults, either directly or in the mass media, consuming various material goods, but the child is too young to participate in such consumption. Such learning might consist of "implicit often unconscious learning for roles which will be assumed sometime in the future" (Ward 1974a, 2). Although a good deal of childhood and adolescent socialization is learning in advance of adult roles in preparation for the future, a great deal of adult socialization during the middle years is learning roles for later life (Riley et al. 1969).

A limited number of consumer socialization studies have investigated learning skills that can be considered anticipatory. Our earlier research (Moschis and Moore 1978) examined adolescents' cognitions and perceptions of the consumer role, including the functions, obligations, position, and rights associated with the purchasing and consumption processes. These include skills such as budgeting one's money and conserving energy, which can be practiced immediately or called into play throughout life. Another study (Moschis and Moore 1979b) that examined adolescent conceptions of husband and wife involvement in a variety of household decisions found that most adolescents already had acquired such conceptions, although this type of information normally is not directly applied until later in life. One study (Moschis and Churchill 1978) also investigated adolescents' ability to price specific items in atypical family budget and consumer affairs knowledge likely to be useful only in the later stages of socialization described by Hess and Torney (1967). A more recent study investigated the development of anticipatory consumption-related skills (Moschis and Moore 1984). We found that early acquisition of consumer (anticipatory) skills does occur among adolescents.

Thus, consumer skills acquired early might affect the learning of skills, attitudes, and behaviors later in life, or they might affect the development of other cognitions in a given period of time. It should be noted, however, that just because a person has acquired certain skills, that person will not necessarily use them. A study by Rudd and Dunsing (1972) found that although family members had closely related attitudes and knowledge about savings, they did not translate those cognitions into action.

Although questions dealing with the effects of early learning on later learning remain relatively unexplored among children and adolescents, our small-scale experimental study suggested that the sequence in which preschoolers were taught various consumer concepts affected their ability to learn (Moschis, Lawton, and Stampfl 1980). Similarly, analysis of our longitudinal data over more than a one-year time interval revealed that an adolescent's level of acquisition of a specific consumption orientation at an earlier time is likely to affect future learning from advertising (Moschis and Moore 1982). Finally, there is ample evidence to suggest the linkage between earlier acquired skills (such as, attitudes) on later learning (such as, behaviors) (Engel et al. 1978; Assael 1984) with respect to adult consumer socialization; less evidence is available to suggest relationships between earlier acquired skills and consumer behaviors of the elderly.

To summarize, the socialization perspective suggests that consumer behavior is acquired through interaction between the person and various agents in specific social settings. The emphasis is on changes in the content or criterion behavior at different ages or stages in the life cycle. All generalizations apply only to a given phase in a person's life cycle because a different set of variables might be dominant at each stage of the person's development or life cycle. A given factor varies in influence according to the person's age or life-cycle stage and the environment.

Figure 2–2 outlines a general conceptual model of consumer socialization, which incorporates the types of variables as well as linkages between them (Moschis 1978a; Moschis and Churchill 1978). The main elements of the models are classified into antecedent variables, socialization processes, and outcomes. The socialization process incorporates both the socialization agent and the type of learning process actually operating. Socialization processes directly affect content or criterion variables, which are viewed as outcomes of socialization. Social structural variables and age or life-cycle position are antecedent variables. They might affect the acquisition of consumer learning properties (outcome) directly and indirectly through their impact on the socialization processes.

An antecedent variable is said to have a direct effect on socialization when it produces a statistically significant effect that is the result of a functional relationship between the antecedent factor and a specific learning property. An indirect effect is the outcome of the variable's functional relationship with a specific socialization process, which in turn directly (or again indirectly via another socialization process) affects a specific aspect of consumer behavior. Learning resulting from interaction or contact with socialization agents can be the result of one or more socialization processes. For this reason, in the review of the literature we chose to distinguish content of learning (consumer behavior)—that is, what is learned—from specific effects of socialization or learning processes—that is, how consumer behavior is learned. Finally, when the effects of a socialization agent are contingent

Antecedents   **Socialization Processes**   **Outcomes**

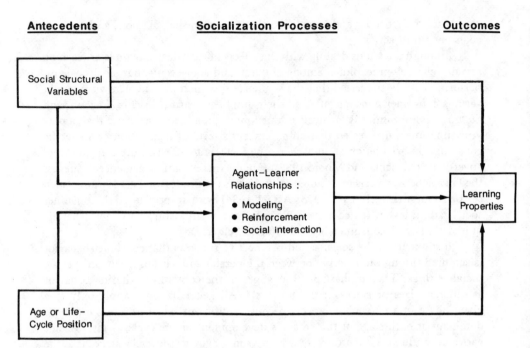

Source: George P. Moschis and Gilbert A. Churchill, "Consumer Socialization: A Theoretical and Empirical Analysis." Reprinted from *The Journal of Marketing Research* 15 (November 1978), published by the American Marketing Association.

Figure 2–2. A Conceptual Model of Consumer Socialization

upon the learner's interaction with another socialization agent, the former agent's influence is said to be mediated by the latter agent.

A Socialization Model of Retail Patronage: An Example

To illustrate the applicability of the model in a specific context of consumer behavior, let us consider retail patronage in the context of socialization (figure 2–3). This particular aspect of consumer behavior appears to be broad enough to accommodate the various types of socialization, including the socialization of young people into specific aspects of the consumer role (shopping and purchasing), the socialization of adults into new roles defined by environmental changes (opportunities for at-home shopping by phone or home computer), and resocialization into new shopping communities as a result of changes in residence. The outcomes of interest include two interrelated sets—behavioral outcomes and cognitive (mental) outcomes.

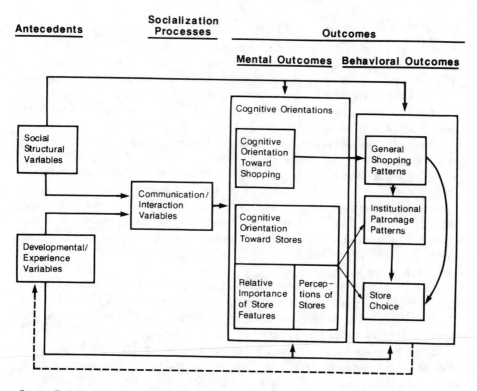

Source: Bellenger and Moschis (1981, 375).

Figure 2–3. A Socialization Model of Retail Patronage

Behavioral outcomes include the consumer's general store patronage patterns (behaviors such as store loyal versus non-store loyal), institutional patronage patterns (behaviors such as frequent use of discount stores versus department stores), and patterns of store choice (the selection of store A versus store B). The behaviors are believed to be the manifestation of various mental outcomes (earlier acquired learning), which can be called cognitive orientations. In terms of retail patronage, two types of cognitive orientations are applicable—cognitive orientations toward shopping and cognitive orientations toward stores (both specific and general types of stores). Shopping orientations are mental states that might affect various general shopping patterns. For example, a housewife with a strong desire for convenience might exhibit a pattern of shopping at stores close to her home. This pattern can, in turn, affect the institutional shopping patterns and individual store choice decision. Cognitive orientations toward stores have a more direct impact on institutional shopping patterns and store choice. These store-related mental states include the relative importance of specific store attributes and images. The socialization perspective assumes that the cognitive orientations toward both shopping and stores undergo formation and change.

Effects of Early Learning

Several studies on adult consumers have established linkages between earlier acquired cognitive orientations toward marketing stimuli and subsequent behaviors. The assumption of relationships between attitudes and subsequent behaviors is basic to attitude research. Examples of these relationships can be found in research on store selection. Doyle and Fenwick (1974–1975), for instance, examined how store image affects the selection of a grocery store.

Research also has supported the linkage between a shopper's cognitive orientation toward stores and the behavioral outcome of institutional shopping patterns. For example, Schiffman, Dash, and Dillon (1977) showed a relationship between the relative importance of various store features and shopping at different types of retail institutions for the same merchandise. Their findings indicated that the expertise of the retail salespeople and the assortment of brands and models were critical to patrons of audio equipment specialty stores, while department store customers were concerned primarily with convenience of store location and guarantee or warranty policies.

A relationship between supermarket attribute preference and consumer shopping orientations was found in a study of supermarket shoppers by Darden and Ashton (1974–1975). Specifically, a significant percentage of those shoppers who prefer supermarkets offering stamps gave a high score on the "special shopper" shopping orientation scale, suggesting a relationship between the general shopping pattern of selecting supermarkets that offer stamps and a favorable cognitive orientation toward shopping for specials. Looking at the effect of another type of general shopping pattern, Goldman (1977–1978) examined the relationship between store loyalty and the consumer's shopping style (cognitive orientation toward shopping). In general, he concluded that store loyalty appears to be part of a low search, a low knowledge, and a low utilization level shopping style.

Effects of Socialization Processes

The findings of several studies support the relationship between socialization processes and patronage outcomes, although in many cases this is not the major focus of the work. One study (Moschis 1976c) does center on information use and shopping orientations. The study related various shopping orientations (store-loyal shopper, special shopper, problem-solving shopper, and the like) to selected communication variables (such as sources of information used for new products and source credibility) for cosmetics shoppers. The findings showed that shoppers possessing different orientations exhibited different communication behaviors; they had different information needs and preferences for sources of communication. A rather clear link was established between communication patterns and cognitive orientations toward shopping.

Kelly 1967) also examined the role of information in the patronage decision. The manner in which both formal and informal information flows among prospective customer groups was found to have a profound influence on the patronage decision process associated with new retail outlets. This exploratory research suggested that there is a hierarchy of influence in the determination of patronage decision outcomes: The effect of in-store experiences was found to be most influential, followed by personal influences, while newspaper advertising had less impact than might have been expected. Again, these relationships point to the significance of sources of consumer information (socialization agents) in developing preferences for new retail outlets.

Bearden, Teel, and Durand (1978) reported a study of the differences in demographics, psychographics, and media usage of patrons versus nonpatrons of four different types of retail institutions (convenience stores, department stores, discount stores, and fast-food outlets). Several significant differences in media usage patterns were found between patrons and nonpatrons of the four different types of retail institutions. Similarly, a study by Darden, Lennon, and Darden (1978) showed that out-shoppers (that is, those shopping outside their local trading areas) have different media behavior than in-shoppers (that is, those shopping locally). Different types of out-shoppers also used significantly different information sources, pointing to a relationship between general shopping patterns and communication or interaction variables. A number of other studies have found that advertising and other sources of consumer information can have a powerful impact on consumers' perceptions of a store as well as on their patronage behavior (see, for example, Engel et al. 1978; Assael 1984).

Research by Hisrich, Dornoff, and Kernan (1972) suggested that the relationship between information seeking and store selection is moderated by perceived risk. As the perceived risk increases, the extent of information seeking about alternative stores increases up to a point, suggesting the role of situational variables in the socialization process. In general, research supports a linkage between socialization processes as measured by communication and interaction variables and those measured by retail patronage outcomes. A significant linkage with both mental and behavioral outcomes has been found in both cases. It should be noted that many variables in both sets have not been addressed adequately from a theoretical standpoint, but findings to date, albeit exploratory, tend to support this linkage in the socialization model.

Effects of Developmental or Experience Variables

Developmental variables indexing an individual's previous amount of interaction with his or her environment—that is, experience—are likely to have some direct and indirect effect on selected aspects of consumer patronage behavior. First, with respect to the direct effect of such variables, previous research suggests that experience is an important factor in store selection. For example, a study by Bellenger, Hirschman, and Robertson (1976–1977) found age to be significantly related with store selection among female shoppers. Similarly, Steilen (1972) found that the retail selection process of new residents tended to be experimental and might affect institutional store patronage.

Age and life cycle also have been found to have an effect on cognitive orientations toward shopping (Lazer and Wyckham 1969). In another study, age was found to be positively related to store loyalty (Reynolds et al. 1974). These findings suggest that maturation or experience might affect the development of loyalty to stores.

Developmental variables are likely to influence store patronage behavior indirectly by affecting the socialization process—that is, the person's frequency of interaction with various socialization agents. For example, toward the later stages of the life cycle, people tend to interact more frequently with the mass media and less frequently with peers (Bernhardt and Kinnear 1976; Phillips and Sternthal 1977). These agents, in turn, are likely to have a differential impact on a person's cognitions and behaviors regarding store patronage.

Effects of Social Structural Variables

Social structural variables also might have direct and indirect effects on the cognitive and behavioral outcomes that comprise store patronage. First, with respect to the direct effects, a number of studies have found certain socioeconomic variables to be associated with store selection. Tate (1961) reports an inverse relationship between education and loyalty to grocery stores. Enis and Paul (1970) also found education to be inversely related to customer loyalty to grocery stores. In a study of female shoppers, Bellenger, Hirschman, and Robertson (1976–1977) found education to be strongly related to store choice regarding the purchase of specific categories of merchandise. In another study of the image of the store-loyal customer, education was again inversely related to store loyalty (Reynolds et al. 1974).

Income and Occupation also appear to be strong predictors of store choice. They have been found to be associated mainly with grocery store patronage (Enis and Paul 1970; Tate 1961). Family income, in particular, was found to be negatively related to store loyalty (Reynolds et al. 1974). Income was also found to be related to cognitive orientations toward shopping (Cort and Dominguez 1977–1978). Working status per se also is likely to affect a person's shopping behavior (McCall 1977).

Myers and Mount (1973) suggest that income is superior to social class in the consumer store choice for a wide variety of home furnishings, appliances, and ready-to-wear product categories, as well as some services. Hisrich and Peters (1974) also found income superior to social class in explaining store choice behavior. Thus, the relative importance of income and social class as a predictor variable seems to vary depending on the type of store patronage under investigation.

Sex also might be an important antecedent of store patronage, but its effects have not been fully examined. There is some evidence to indicate that loyalty to banks might be higher among males than females (Fry et al. 1973). Ethnicity is another factor that is likely to relate to cognitive and behavioral orientations toward stores. For example, several studies found significant differences among Mexican-

Americans and Anglo-Americans with respect to selected shopping orientations (see, for example, Bellenger and Valencia 1982; Boone et al. 1974; Valencia 1982). Similarly, Feldman and Star (1968) found racial differences in the behavior of Chicago shoppers.

Similar social structural variables have been found to be related to vendor or institutional loyalty. For example, consumers who are loyal to department stores have the following characteristics: they are white-collar workers, have higher incomes, and have more education (Rich and Jain 1968). Similarly, shoppers who tend to patronize discount stores normally are blue-collar workers, are younger, and have children living at home (Cox 1971).

Finally, social structural variables are likely to affect the respondent's general shopping patterns. For example, the extent to which a person is loyal to stores in general is affected by educational background, income level, occupation, and number of children living at home (Peters and Ford 1972). In addition to their relationship to behavioral outcomes, social structural variables have been found to relate to cognitive outcomes such as shopping orientation. Bellenger, Robertson, and Greenberg (1977), for example, found that various demographic variables such as income and occupation relate to women's shopping orientations with respect to shopping centers.

Social structural variables also are likely to have an indirect effect on outcomes by affecting specific socialization processes. For example, socioeconomic characteristics are likely to affect a person's frequency of interaction with the various socialization agents, which might in turn have a differential impact on patronage behavior. Specifically, studies of media use have found that television is consumed heavily by individuals who tend to be of lower socioeconomic status, have less education, and tend to be from a minority background. Alternatively, newspaper reading is most likely to take place among upper-class and more educated consumers (Schramm et al. 1961; Moschis 1981b). Similarly, a study of female shoppers found significant differences among working and nonworking women with respect to their frequency of interaction with various socialization agents, including personal and commercial sources of information (McCall 1977). Several other antecedent variables are likely to be associated with different socialization processes. For example, marital status, education, urbanity (that is, extent of shopping opportunities), income, and ethnicity are likely to be related to different preferences for the mass media and other sources of consumer information (Allen and Clarke 1980; Engel et al. 1978; Urban 1980).

Summary and Discussion

This chapter has presented a model of consumer socialization based on the notion that consumer behavior is acquired and is likely to change at specific points in a person's life cycle. Research findings concerning store patronage were presented to illustrate the applicability of the model. It was suggested that much of the research in consumer behavior can be viewed from a socialization perspective. Research in retail patronage was presented as an example of how patronage can be viewed in the context provided by such a model. Although the purpose here was to show how data fit the model, later in this book the same data are interpreted in the context of theory, supporting the value of socialization as a general framework for studying retail patronage behavior.

Certain requirements must be met before the socialization perspective can become a viable approach to research in consumer behavior. First, the key variables related to socialization in a consumer behavior context must be clearly established. Second, the measurement of these variables is necessary to achieve uniformity in future research. Third, linkages between variables must be established to provide adequate justification for the model as an approach to the study of consumer behavior. Fourth, the theoretical justification for linkages between variables must be spelled out. The importance of variables at different stages of the consumer's life cycle should be explored. Fifth, relevant criterion variables for different segments of the population (subcultures such as ethnic groups, teens, and the elderly) should be identified.

Chapter 3 addresses measurement issues and methods related to the consumer socialization model, while chapter 4 presents theoretical foundations for the socialization approach and translates these theories into the specific context of consumer socialization. Chapters 5 through 13 present empirical findings organized around the key linkages of the consumer socialization model and interpret these findings in the light of socialization theories. Finally, chapter 14 summarizes the key points of this book regarding the socialization perspective as an approach to consumer behavior. It also presents general directions for future research and states views on how the consumer socialization approach can be expanded to explain various dimensions of consumer behavior.

3
Measurement Models

A conceptual framework is useful in the study of consumer socialization because it not only specifies relevant types of variables and relationships between them, but it also suggests the theories and types of data required to validate specific relationships. Specific variables, however, must be operationalized and measured before one attempts to conduct a study of consumer socialization or interpret results. Thus, as in any other area of scientific inquiry, measurement becomes an important aspect of the study of consumer socialization for at least three main reasons:

1. It helps the researcher translate abstract concepts into operational variables whose relationships with other variables can be statistically tested.

2. It helps researchers accumulate findings by using measures that are fairly similar across studies.

3. It provides opportunities for increasing reliability and validity in the findings by developing valid and reliable measures over time.

Thus, understanding what to measure and how to measure variables in the model helps focus research on relevant factors and accumulate research findings.

This chapter deals with the measurement of the conceptual model of consumer socialization discussed in chapter 2. Specifically, it discusses how various elements of the model are measured or should be measured. Each type of variable in the model is described briefly and is conceptually defined; operational definitions and measures are then presented. While this chapter does not intend to present every possible measure for every possible variable that could be included in the model, a rather broad sample of the types of variables and their measures are presented when several options are available. Measures of age and life cycle, along with several social structural variables, are discussed first, followed by measurement models pertaining to agent-learner relationships. The discussion focuses on the three main elements of the models: antecedent variables, socialization processes, and outcomes.

Antecedent Variables

Antecedent variables have been classified into social structural variables and developmental or maturational factors. Among the commonly used social structural variables researched in the context of consumer socialization are social class, race, ethnicity, sex, and urbanity. Developmental variables include age (both biological and cognitive) and life cycle.

Most antecedent variables have been measured as continuous, and they have been used either as continuous or as categorical variables. Thus, it has been a very common approach in socialization research to measure an antecedent variable on an interval scale and then change the scale to a categorical scale for analysis purposes (for instance, comparison between groups of respondents belonging to a social structure or age group.)

Social Structures

Social Class. Social stratification of consumers is a difficult task because of the many variables that can be used to define social class and also because of the lack of accurate information on the relative importance of these variables at a given point in time. Variables such as occupation, education, income, and dwelling area often are used as single indexes of a person's socioeconomic status. Among the more frequently used measures of socioeconomic status are Duncan's (1961) index of occupation, which reports the prestige of 425 occupations on a percentile basis. Measures of other indexes of social class (income, education, dwelling area) tend to be more arbitrary in the construction and specification of categories such as number of income brackets, intervals and treatment of the quality of characteristics such as education (for example, trade school versus college), and location of house within an area.

To overcome deficiencies in single measures of social class, researchers often use multiple indexes of socioeconomic status, which combine several factors believed to measure social class. Some popular composite measures of social class are Warner's Index of Status Characteristics (ISC), which combines occupation, source of income, house type, and dwelling area; the U.S. Bureau of Census Socioeconomic Status (SES) Score, which combines occupation, family income, and education; the Two-Factor Index of Social Position, which combines occupation and education; the Index of Urban Status; and the Index of Cultural Classes (see, for example, Schiffman and Kanuk 1983).

Although measures of social class and socioeconomic status often are used as continuous variables in socialization research, reseachers often must form categories of SES for comparison purposes. Unfortunately, few criteria are available in forming such categories other than population percentage estimates falling into each specific class, which can vary considerably depending on the typology used. For example, using Warner's (1972) classification, one can include as much as 55 percent of the population in the lower classes, while more recent typologies suggest that only 16 percent fall into those classes (Coleman 1983).

Unfortunately, popular measures of social class are out of date, as most of them were developed in the 1940s and 1950s. It is very likely that the perception of various characteristics that define and measure social class (such as type of occupation) and their importance have changed in the past thirty to forty years. Coleman (1983) discusses these and other limitations of existing instruments and suggests revised measures.

Ethnic Background. The term *ethnic* refers to large groups of people with the same national, regional, or racial origin, according to common cultural traits and customs. Individuals in these groups are expected to share the same culture—that is, the values, norms, traits, and customs that characterize a particular culture.

Ethnic background usually is identified by self-report of the respondent's descent or background. For example, the U.S. Bureau of Census method for identifying ethnic background consists of asking the respondent to select the category (black, Anglo, Mexican-American, Chicano, Cuban, Puerto Rican) that best describes his or her ethnic affiliation. This method is easy to use, has face validity, and can be compared to census data. Its major drawback is that it forces the person to report one ethnic background and provides very little information on the degree to which the person identifies with one or more cultures or subcultures. To overcome these shortcomings, it is advisable to use culture or ethnic identification scales in which respondents can indicate the extent to which they identify with one or more culture (ethnic background) on a number of dimensions that define ethnicity, such as language, religion, customs, and cultural traits, making possible both valid and reliable measures. Examples of efforts to measure one's ethnic background as a continuum include the work by Hirschman (1981) and more recently Valencia's (1985) attempt to measure "Hispanicness."

Age and Life Cycle

While both age and life cycle are used as indexes of a person's developmental/maturational process, the appropriateness of each and their importance in socialization research vary on the basis of the specific age span under investigation. Age is a crucial variable in the socialization of young people, children in particular, because significant changes in a person's cognitive structure are believed to be taking place within short age intervals. Similarly, age becomes an important variable at late stages in a person's life, when significant physical and biological changes occur. While such changes do not necessarily have a strong (direct) impact on a person's cognitive abilities, they often are important because they alter the person's patterns of interacting with socialization agents, thereby indirectly affecting the person's consumer learning.

Life cycle appears to be a much more appropriate variable than age in the study of consumer socialization during middle life. Although cognitive changes do occur throughout a person's life (see, for example, Long et al. 1980), such changes are not as important in consumer socialization as those occurring as a result of a person's changes in life cycle. The latter have a stronger influence on the person's communication relationship with existing as well as new or different socialization agents (such as co-workers, spouse, and children), who can significantly influence the person's cognitions and behaviors (Thorton and Nardi 1975).

Age can be measured in several ways. First, chronologically, age can be defined as the number of years lived or as the distance from birth. Age also can be defined nonchronologically. Nonchronological age variables include biological age, social age, and social-psychological age. Biological age refers to an individual's present position in relation to his or her potential life span. Social age is defined in terms of the social roles and habits the person assumes while passing through the life cycle. Finally, social-psychological age can refer to subjective age, personal age, and other-perceived age (Barak and Schiffman 1981). Subjective age refers to the individual's self-perception in terms of reference age groups. Personal age is a construct of four types of self-perceptions: feel-like, look-like, do-like, and interest-like age measured in terms of units of years. Other-perceived age refers to subjective evaluation of the person's age by others. More recently, Barak and Gould (1985) assessed additional alternative age-related measures among adults. The results of their study suggest the usefulness of using nonchronological measures of age.

The extent to which one measure is more appropriate than another depends on the research question at hand. For example, in studying the consumer socialization of children, chronological age becomes an important measure of age because changes in the cognitive structures of the child are believed to be associated with advancing age-related stages (narrow age brackets). On the contrary, in the study of the consumer socialization of the elderly, cognitive or personal age becomes more important than chronological age because changes in cognitive structures are related to long age-span intervals and because studies suggest that cognitive age might be a more powerful predictor of elderly socialization than chronological age (see, for example, Smith and Moschis 1984b).

Chronological age has been measured in a variety of ways in socialization studies. The most common approach involves asking respondents to specify their chronological age either by checking age-response categories or specifying number of years (such as grade in school for younger people). While accurate chronological age frequently is obtained by asking individuals to report their birthday, this variable is used often as a nominal rather than an interval scale. It should be noted that appropriate age ranges for classifying individuals into age brackets are open to debate, especially in later life when researchers arbitrarily tend to use sixty-five as the cutoff point for old age as well as several age brackets to show transition into old age (see, for example, Roedder-John and Cole 1986; Smith and Moschis 1985a).

The rationale for using nominal scales consisting of several age groups, rather than using age as a continuous variable, is based on cognitive development theories. According to these theories, one expects little variation in cognitive structures and behaviors of individuals of different ages within an age bracket.

A similar rationale exists for using stages in a person's life cycle. Unfortunately, little research in consumer socialization has been conducted with adults using the life-cycle variable. The life-cycle variable appears to have two drawbacks: First, the number of stages varies depending on the specific operational definition used; second, the stages must be treated as discrete variables rather than continuous. Furthermore, in revised versions of life-cycle concepts (see, for example, Murphy and Staples 1979), the latter problem is magnified because such modern measures of life cycle contain several stages (categories), with a relatively small number of individuals in the sample belonging to a specific stage.

Although researchers recently proposed alternative definitions of family life cycle to accommodate the increasing variety of family types, thus increasing the number of stages, empirical testing of alternative formulations suggests that increasing the number of stages might not improve the predictive validity of life-cycle models (Wagner and Hanna 1983).

Researchers similarly have questioned the value of age as an independent variable in the socialization literature. For example, Wohlwill (1970) argued that the greatest usefulness of age is as a temporal dimension along which change is mapped. Danowski (1975) presented data that supported his contention that "informational age" is more important in the life cycle than chronological age. Danowski's view assumes that individuals age along psychological and social dimensions.

Socialization Processes

Socialization agents transmit norms, attitudes, and values to the learner by communicating certain expectations and behavioral patterns. Thus, the study of the effects of socialization agents requires an examination of the communication processes and consequences of such communications—that is, agent-learner communication relationships.

While there is a tendency to look within the individual for explanations of human behavior, the study of communication requires an interpersonal rather than an intrapersonal perspective. At least two persons must be involved in it (source and receiver or audience), and an object of communication must be present. As a result, communication research can be conceptualized in line with Newcomb's (1953) A-B-X paradigm.

The Newcomb model assumes that two persons, A and B, are attracted to one another positively or negatively and are co-oriented to an object of communication, X. Newcomb's co-orientation model has been particularly useful in the study of interpersonal communications because it is applicable to groups and to the actual interpersonal relations among people and their cognitions and perceptions. In addition, the model provides a useful framework for conceptualizing the differences in orientation between two general approaches to social communciation research.

Social communication theorists can be divided roughly between those who are concerned with the interactants' cognitive orientations to events and issues in the world outside their immediate context (A-X and B-X relationships) and those who stress elements of interpersonal relationships (A-B relationships). The first group of theorists typically is interested in several aspects of public opinion (see, for example, Chaffee and McLeod 1968; McLeod and Chaffee 1972), but the approach also is amenable to the study of institutionalized relationships such as parent-child and husband-wife (O'Keefe 1973; Pasdirtz 1969). The second group of theorists typically is interested in person perception research, psychiatrist-patient interaction, marital discord, and the communication of relationship information (see also Chaffee and Tims 1976).

In the context of mass media communications, the A-B-X model is only one among many consistency or balance theories that have generated a vast amount of attitude change research during the past thirty years. The mass media can create an imbalance structure that the consumer must restore by changing his or her beliefs about the source or the object of communication.

A socialization agent (the source) might communicate certain information (object of communication) to the learner (receiver) through various mechanisms. First, by performing certain acts, an agent might consciously or unconsciously communicate certain norms and expectations. The communication in this case is likely to take place at a cognitive level, and consumer learning is likely to be the result of observation or imitation of these behaviors. For example, a child might make a conscious effort to emulate the behavior of a television character because the model's behavior is the most salient alternative open to the child—that is, the child does the same thing the model does in an effort to be like the model. Common operational definitions of such modeling processes include source-learner similarity of behaviors and attitudes (McLeod and O'Keefe 1972). It should be noted, however, that while a high level of similarity might be a necessary condition for such cognitive communication effects, it is hardly a sufficient one, as the learner might develop similar orientations through other processes, such as overt communication. Furthermore, the learner's interpretation of the source's behavior or intent might differ, as could the source's actual or usual behavior outside the communication context. Awareness of the source's behavior also is necessary for such communication to take place. For example, in one of the few consumer socialization studies measuring modeling processes, adolescents' awareness of parental consumer behaviors was related to the extent to which the adolescents performed similar types of behaviors (Moschis, Moore, and Smith 1984).

Second, a socialization agent might influence the consumer behavior of others by using various reinforcement mechanisms, both positive and negative. In attempting to communicate certain desires to others, for example, a person might reward certain behaviors that are consistent with such desires and punish others that are inconsistent. For example, in interpersonal settings, reinforcement might involve overt communication, such as praise for (positive) and complaining about (negative) using a product; it also might involve cognitive communication in which a person might dictate his or her desires to others by, for example, showing affection (positive reinforcement) or psychologically punishing them (negative reinforcement). In fact, affection and psychological punishment are common examples of operational definitions of positive and negative reinforcement, respectively (McLeod and O'Keefe 1972). Similar reinforcement mechanisms might operate with respect to mass communication (Bandura 1971b).

Finally, socialization agents can affect the consumer behavior of the learner through overt communication processes. This often is referred to as the social interaction mechanism. The social interaction mechanism is less specific, and it might involve a combination of modeling and reinforcement (McLeod and O'Keefe 1972). During the course of a person's interaction with socialization agents, he or she might acquire certain attitudes, values, and behaviors, which often are communicated explicitly.

Social interaction processes can have content and structure. Content includes expectations (norms) held by the communicator as to what the desirable or prescribed behaviors should be, or it can be information about consumption. Structure has different connotations. When it refers to interpersonal processes, structure can be interpreted in the context of power and communication relations. For example, with respect to parent-child relations, one finds power structures such as controlling-permissive and traditional-modern types of families. In a consumer behavior context, such power relations are applied only to adult family member relations (such as husband dominant or wife dominant); they are not relevant to parent-child relations, perhaps because of the relatively low power children exert on parents. Parent-child communication relations include socio-oriented and concept-oriented family communication structures (Chaffee et al. 1971) and parental encouragement (Haller and Portes 1973). In the study of consumer behavior, for example, consumer learning has been associated with family communication patterns and structures (see, for example, Moore and Moschis 1981b; Moschis and Moore 1979c and 1979d). These communication processes account for significant differences in consumer socialization *beyond* differences already accounted for by other types of family communication processes (Moschis, Moore, and Smith 1984).

With respect to the mass media, structure refers to how information is presented. One finds methods such as one-sided and two-sided messages, climax and anticlimax, order of presentation, and various types of appeals, such as humorous, fearful, and novelty appeals.

Interpersonal Processes

Measurement of communication processes often focuses on overt agent-learner interaction, with an emphasis on the frequency, content, and structure of communication.

Most studies of consumer socialization, for example, have used measures of overt parent-child interaction about consumption (see, for example, Moschis 1981b). Considerably less attention has been paid to measuring the content of family communication, which usually is inferred from correlational data. Thus, for example, if one finds a relationship between parent-child interaction about consumption and the child's ability to price products accurately, the assumption is made that such communication focuses on prices. The child's ability to price products accurately, however, does not necessarily develop as a result of family communication but might be due to a third variable (such as development of product desires), which can result both in greater awareness of product attributes and in child-initiated communication with family members. Finally, the structure of interaction has been investigated in relatively few studies, such as in those examining the effects of family communication patterns (see, for example, Moore and Moschis 1980 and 1981b; Moschis and Moore 1979c and 1979d).

Following Newcomb's model, McLeod and Chaffee (1972) developed a typology of parent-child communication structures and patterns. While parent-child relations usually are described as a unidimensional portrayal of the power situation within the family, such as autocratic-democratic, controlling-permissive, and traditional-modern, studies of parent-child communication processes consistently have found two relatively uncorrelated dimensions of communications structure (McLeod and Chaffee 1972). The first (which is analogous to the types of social power) is called *socio-oriented,* the type of communication designed to produce deference and foster harmonious and pleasant social relationships at home. In terms of Newcomb's (1953) paradigm, this type of communication stresses A-B relationships. Children in homes characterized by such a communication structure might be taught to avoid controversy and repress their feelings on extrapersonal topics, for example, by not arguing with adults and giving in on arguments rather than risk offending others.

The second type of communication structure is called *concept-oriented,* a pattern that focuses on positive constraints that help a child to develop his or her own views about the world, stressing A-X relationships. The parents might, for example, encourage the child to weigh all alternatives before making a decision or expose the child to controversy—either by differing openly on an issue or by discussing it with guests at home (McLeod and Chaffee 1972). The two general dimensions of parent-child communication produce a fourfold typology of family communication patterns expressed in co-oriented terms using Newcomb's A-B-X paradigm: laissez-faire, protective, pluralistic, and consensual (McLeod and Chaffee 1972).

Laissez-faire families (low concept-oriented, low socio-oriented) lack emphasis on both kinds of communication; there is little parent-child communication in these families. *Protective* families (low concept-oriented, high socio-oriented) stress obedience and social harmony in their communication; there is little concern over conceptual matters. *Pluralistic* families (high concept-oriented, low socio-oriented) encourage open communication and discussion of ideas without insisting on obedience to authority; the child is encouraged to explore new ideas and to express them without fear of retaliation. The emphasis in this communication structure appears to be mutuality of respect and interests. *Consensual* families (high concept-oriented, high socio-oriented) stress both types of communication; the child is encouraged to take an interest in the world of ideas but to do so without disturbing the family's hierarchy of opinion and internal harmony.

Extensive evidence has lead researchers to assume that family communication patterns help guide the individual in coping with various situations encountered outside the immediate family context—for instance, situations in relation to public affairs issues and mass media use (see, for example, Chaffee et al. 1971; Chaffee et al. 1966; McLeod and Chaffee 1972). In addition, the evidence suggests that "the influence of family communication, as generalized to other situations, persists well into adulthood; it appears to become part of the developing individual's personality that he carries outside the home" (Chaffee et al. 1971, 331).

Researchers have made limited efforts to develop patterns and structures of communication in other interpersonal settings such as between spouses, peers, and siblings. One notable exception is the work of Chaffee and Tims (1976), who developed peer communication patterns using revised measures of family communication structures.

It should be noted that because the family communication typology grew out of social-psychological theory, it is itself no theory. Rather, it might reflect certain value and belief systems that exist in various subcultures (Tims and Masland 1985). In addition, these measures might not provide an accurate description of the family as a social unit but rather a description of the parenting communication behavior of the subject's mother or father (Ritchie 1985).

Mass Communication Processes

Because researchers interested in examining the role of mass communication on consumer socialization come from different disciplines, their measures of mass media communication processes vary across two dimensions: level of aggregation of mass communication exposure/use and the basis on which measures were constructed (that is, the approach).

Level of Aggregation of Mass Media Exposure/Use. Studies of mass media effects vary considerably with respect to the level of aggregation of mass media use measures. First, there are studies assessing media effects at a very aggregate level, with mass media exposure/use measures defined in terms of the individual's use of (or exposure to) the mass media. Such measures usually combine specific measures of exposure/use into one total index of overall exposure or frequency of using several types of media. Furthermore, they fail to account for audience orientations toward the medium (attention or content preference, for example), other activities taking place while the person interacts with the medium, and the relative importance of various media.

Second, there are studies assessing the aggregate effects of exposure/use of specific media. While mass media measures for specific media enable the researcher to decompose aggregate mass media measures, they are still problematic because they do not tap audience orientations toward stimuli in the medium or level of attention.

Third, there are studies tapping more direct interactions of the audience with the medium content (such as advertising, programming, and editorial). Specific measures such as exposure to televised news and entertainment allow for selective exposure to, or use of, mass media content.

Approaches to Measurement. Measures of mass media interaction and influence have been constructed from the point of view of the influencee, the medium, and the researcher. When such measures are approached from the influencee's standpoint, the focus is on asking respondents to assess their response to the mass media content, such as awareness of products in ads and advertising influence on their consumer decisions. Quite often measures of such responses are constructed by asking individuals in the influencee's immediate environment to report such responses. For example, parents are asked to report a child's requests for advertised products. Measures of mass media interaction also have been approached from the influencee's standpoint by focusing on the respondent's gratifications sought or received from the mass media. While self-reported measures of mass media influence might help researchers isolate media effects from other third variables likely to produce similar responses, they rely on the respondent's ability to assess the medium's influence.

Measures focusing on the media emphasize the message content and structure found in the medium. The measures often are constructed by means of content analysis, while the medium's influence is inferred from its content. While measures of media content can improve the accuracy of the individual's exposure to selected stimuli, especially if supplemented with frequency of exposure measures (see, for example, Robertson et al. 1979), they tend to be used as surrogate measures of mass media effects. In addition, content analysis is subject to rater judgments requiring interrater reliability coefficients, which seldom are reported.

Finally, researchers have used measures of mass media interaction based on the respondent's assessment of media use and analysis of media content, inferring media influence from a statistically significant relationship between media use/exposure and consumer orientations. The researcher's goal is to falsify the existence of a relationship rather than to confirm it. When a significant relationship is found, the inference is that variation in consumer orientation is due to media content. Lack of a significant relationship suggests that the media might not influence consumer orientations or that the influence might not be linear.

Outcomes of Socialization

Measures of the effects of socialization agents and antecedent variables present a rather different picture in that both relative and absolute measures can be used. Measures of the relative effects of socialization agents are assessed in terms of the communicator's intent, attitudes, and cognitions by pitting the source's (agent's) orientations against the audience's (or learner's) orientations toward the object of communication. Thus, the emphasis shifts from the individual's orientation (absolute measures) to co-orientation (relational measures) and from sampling individuals as units of analysis to sampling dyads, groups, or collectivities. Absolute measures often consist of cognitive, affective, and behavioral outcomes measured in relation to some norm or expected direction. For example, learning about products (awareness) and developing skills in budgeting (behaviors) are used as unidirectional measures of the effects of advertising and parent-child communication about consumption, respectively. When such measures are used, the assumption often is made that the agent's intention is to change the level of cognitions and behaviors to the desired direction.

Relative Measures

Co-orientation Models. The term *co-orientation* refers to the simultaneous orientation of two persons to one another as well as to some external object (Newcomb 1953). Currently there are three co-orientation models, which were developed independently and simultaneously. The first model is the General Co-Orientation Model, which was developed by Chaffee and McLeod in the study of communications (see, for example, Chaffee and McLeod 1968; McLeod and Chaffee 1972 and 1973). The second model was developed by Laing and his associates in the field of clinical psychology and is called the Model of Reciprocal Perspectives (Laing et al. 1966). The third model, the Model of Group Consensus, was developed by Scheff, a sociologist (Scheff 1967).

Although these models were developed independently, they have at least two things in common. First, the unit of analysis is not the individual but the social system of which the individual is a part. The social system can range from a small dyadic relationship such as parent-child to large collectivities such as consumers. Second, the main variables under study are not individual traits but relationships between the cognitions of two or more persons. The justification for using interpersonal units of analysis to study various aspects of human behavior (including communication) rests on the assumption that a social system is not composed of many persons (atoms) but of many interpersonal relationships (molecules) (Chaffee 1973, 466).

General Co-orientation Model. This model consists of a system of beliefs and cross-perceptions between two persons. The model assumes that each person has two sets of cognitions: his own beliefs about objects in his environment and his estimate or perception of the other person's orientations toward the same objects. An object is broadly defined as anything that exists psychologically for any person; it can be substantive, synthetic, or quite abstract. The empirical test is whether the person recognizes the object and can discuss it (Carter 1965). The main variables in the model are not individual cognitions but relationships among them.

There are three types of relationships between persons in the general co-orientation model. These relationships are called overlap, congruency, and accuracy. *Overlap* consists of the degree of similarity of cognitions (what one thinks) between the two persons in the co-orientational situation. When there is overlap in terms of values (that is, whether something is good or bad), there is agreement; when there is overlap of cognitions in nonevaluative cases (what the facts are), there is understanding.

Congruency refers to the extent to which each person thinks that the other person's cognitions resemble his; it is a comparison of what one thinks about an object with his perception of the other person's cognitions about the same object of orientation. Finally, *accuracy* refers to the relationship between one person's estimate of the other person's cognitions and the other person's actual cognitions; the extent to which these cognitions overlap indicates the degree of accuracy. Accuracy closely resembles the concept of empathy. It is considered to be the single best criterion for assessing communication effectiveness.

This model was first used to study interpersonal communication. Shortly after its introduction, researchers began to apply it to a variety of situations involving not only dyads but also larger social entities. Thus, the term *person* has been expanded to groups and collectivities such as reporters and communities (see, for example, Chaffee 1973).

Model of Reciprocal Perspectives. Laing, Phillipson, and Lee (1966) have developed a model that operates under the assumption that paired individuals sharing experiences over time come to develop what they call a spiral of reciprocal perspectives. In such a spiral, they classify reciprocal perspectives as direct perspective, metaperspective, and meta-metaperspective. A direct perspective is what the person thinks about the object of orientation. A metaperspective is what one person thinks about how the other evaluates an object. A meta-metaperspective is what person A thinks person B thinks about person A's evaluation.

The interpersonal variables are co-orientational indexes of agreement, understanding, the feeling of being understood, and realization. *Agreement* (or disagreement) refers to the degree of similarity (or dissimilarity) between both persons' direct perspectives; it is measured by comparing these perspectives. *Understanding,* for Laing and his associates, is similar to Chaffee's and McLeod's *accuracy*; it is the extent to which one person's metaperspective resembles the other's direct perspective. The *feeling of being understood* and misunderstood is similar to Chaffee's and McLeod's *congruency*; it is obtained by comparing a person's meta-metaperspective with his or her own direct perspective. *Realization* (or failure to realize that one is understood) is the extent to which one person's meta-metaperspective resembles the other person's metaperspective on the same object.

Model of Group Consensus. Scheff (1967) developed a model somewhat similar to that of Laing and others to conceptualize degree of consensus within groups. Scheff generalizes across additional levels of reciprocal cognitions and labels several levels of consensus. The first level, called *zero-order* consensus, is agreement, but only in the sense that both individual members concerned positively agree on the object of orientation. The second level, *first-degree* concensus, is similar to Laing's metaperspective. The third level is *second-degree* consensus, which is similar to the meta-metaperspective. Scheff suggested that complete consensus depends on a series of reciprocal understandings among the members of the group regarding the object of orientation. He also regarded the type and extent of coordination as a behavioral component of consensus or co-orientation variables.

Assumptions. Co-orientation models make the following basic assumptions (McLeod and Chaffee 1973, 494):

1. Person A is simultaneously oriented to Person B and to the object of orientation (X).

2. The elements of X perceived by A are identical to those in B's orientation to X.

3. A is oriented toward the B-X orientation that he perceives.

4. A sees the B-X orientation as relevant to his A-B and A-X orientations.

5. The A-X and B-X orientations are communicable to B and to A, respectively.

Assumption 5 will not be fully satisfied when co-orientation is applied to groups or collectivities. The extension of the co-orientation concept to larger groups rests on the assumption that a person is oriented to a group or collectivity as a unified entity; this kind of orientation is called reification. In consumer research, it is common to reify individual entities and speak of them as if they were units. For example, researchers often use terms such as *consumers* and *public*. In the case of reification, a person's estimate of the group's or collectivity's cognitions has been referred to as mass empathy (Van Zelst 1952).

These models have been used extensively in studies of human communication, especially in co-orientational measurements in family studies. Pasdirtz (1969), for example, reported relationships between communication and co-orientation variables using a sample of fifty-one husband-wife pairs; he also compared the family communication patterns (FCP) typology with co-orientation variables. Co-orientational measures in family studies, however, most often are applied in studies examining parent-child communications (see, for example, McLeod and Chaffee 1972). Some applications of select co-orientational concepts are found in studies of consumer behavior. For example, co-orientational variables were used to explain consumer use of information and susceptibility to reference group influence (Moschis 1976b and 1980).

Co-orientational assumptions must be checked before applying the model. At times, interpersonal communication effects on consumer learning assessed using co-orientational variables are difficult to evaluate in terms of exactly the same elements of X (object of communication). Although both A and B rarely would perceive exactly the same elements of X, some similarity of orientation to the object of communication is necessary to apply the model sensibly at the co-orientational level. At times, the availability of symbols of X (often referred to as codability) might hamper communication, as would connotation, a term that describes variance between A and B in their respective usage of words to denote Xs (McLeod and Chaffee 1973).

Absolute Measures

Communication effects on consumer learning can be not only in terms of overlaps, in line with the co-orientation model, but also in terms of changes in or developments of cognitive and behavioral patterns. For example, much consumer socialization literature suggests that parent-child communication about consumption is related to the child's development of several cognitive and behavioral orientations about consumption (Moschis 1981b). In addition, other messages or cues can be communicated, often unintentionally, from one person to another during the course of interaction. Thus, it is often the effect rather than the perceived intent of the communication that should be measured. Because of the several ways in which family members can influence one another, several types of indexes of communication effectiveness often are recommended in assessing interpersonal communication and influence. For purposes of measurement, it is necessary to assess a set of attributes of the role-incumbent group that are particularly relevant to that role and to obtain corresponding measures of the same attributes on the role-aspirant group. The particular set of attributes to be assessed is a function of the particular role under consideration. Such attributes include values, beliefs, attitudes, and specific behaviors.

To assess the degree of socialization, indexes of communality between the role-aspirant and role-incumbent groups are required. The degree of communality between the two groups can be indexed by a number of measures. For example, Tannenbaum and McLeod (1967) suggested several indexes, including similarity of factor structure, relative factor salience, difference in concept judgments using the D statistic, differentiation between concepts, degree of role identification, homogeneity of judgments, and meaningfulness. In the study of consumer socialization, Rossiter and Robertson (1979) used confirmatory factor analysis to assess the similarity of factor structures between mothers and their children.

One of the difficulties encountered in trying to demonstrate the effectiveness of socialization agents in teaching behaviors is that learning involves at least two stages: acquisition and performance (see, for example, Comstock et al. 1978). Failure to perform a behavior previously observed does not mean that acquisition has not taken place (Bandura 1973). Unfortunately, it often is impossible to determine whether a behavior has been acquired unless it is performed. A behavior previously acquired might not be performed immediately, however, but will be performed later if or when the appropriate eliciting conditions occur. Developmentalists have referred to this phenomenon as a sleeper effect, while sociologists have referred to it as anticipatory socialization.

Because acculturation—that is, the process by which one is socialized into a culture other than that into which one is born—is considered to be part of socialization (see, for example, Clausen 1968a; O'Guinn and Faber 1985; O'Guinn, Lee, and Faber 1986), some researchers are interested in assessing the process by which ethnic groups are assimilated into a given culture. Given the significant trends in ethnic populations, it is expected that acculturation will become increasingly important within the context of consumer socialization.

Several sociologists and psychologists have developed measures of acculturation (see, for example, Campisi 1947; Chance 1965; Graves, 1967; Olmedo and Padilla 1978; and Olmedo et al. 1981). In the study of consumer behavior, few attempts have been made to develop measures of consumer acculturation. Hair and Anderson (1972) were the first to use the Campisi scale in the context of consumer behavior. More recently, Schiffman, Dillon, and Ngumah (1982) developed their own consumer acculturation scale in their study of personality factors in consumer behavior.

Reliability and Validity

Reliability and validity are necessary conditions for sound consumer socialization research if knowledge about the area is to be systematically accumulated over time. Issues of reliability and validity are magnified when the researcher works with groups of people at extreme stages in the life cycle (that is, children and the elderly). This is because these people exhibit relatively greater difficulty in responding to questions or questionnaires. Thus, an instrument could be shown to be reliable and valid when adult subjects are used but unreliable or invalid when applied to children or the elderly.

Consumer socialization involves continuous adjustment to one's environment, along with learning new attitudes, values, and norms or modifying existing ones. Because not all orientations develop or change simultaneously, interrelationships among items expected to measure a particular construct frequently are low. Correlations of the same measure over time (test-retest reliability) are low as well because socialization involves the formation and change of orientations regarding a specific role. Thus, it is more likely to achieve a higher reliability of constructs when working with subjects who are expected to have developed certain attitudes, values, and behaviors than with subjects who are in the process of developing or modifying such orientations.

Another related problem that applies to both reliability and validity stems from the fact that responses to an instrument are likely to be significantly affected by the person's background characteristics. Factors such as race, age, social class, and sex are likely to affect both reliability and validity. For example, while Rossiter's (1977) objective test for measuring children's attitudes toward television commercials was found to be highly reliable, analysis of the instrument by income level suggested significant differences in responses. Similarly, Allen and Chaffee (1977) found that the two-dimensional model of communication structures did not fit the black subculture as well as it does the white subculture from which it was derived.

Differences in responses to the instrument across social groupings could be due to a number of reasons. First, socialization might not occur at the same rate within groups of a social structure. Second, different norms, values, and beliefs might be emphasized in different subcultures. Third, subcultural variables might affect the respondents' communication skills and even the quality and meaningfulness of responses. Finally, third variables (such as I.Q.) might be related both to a specific subculture and to items making up the instrument (for instance, in measuring attitudes toward advertising).

Several problems related to reliability and validity can be mitigated if specific steps are taken. It appears that specification of the attitudes, values, and behaviors that define the consumer role, or consumer behavior in general, has a lot to do with how persons from different backgrounds respond to measures of these variables. If the constructs and domains related to the focal variables are of nearly equal relevance to respondents, regardless of their background characteristics, reliability and validity should be improved.

Researchers also should be cognizant of the dangers associated with borrowing measures from other disciplines. Such measures must be revised to reflect consumption behavior, and the revised instrument should be validated using the original measures. This task involves obtaining responses on both original and revised items and validating them, for example, by factor analyzing both sets simultaneously to ensure validation before the revised items are used in consumer socialization studies.

Researchers also can test measures for validity and reliability within specific social groupings. To the extent that the scales are reliable and valid for specific groupings, reliability and validity for the aggregate sample should be high as well. Cronback's coefficient alpha is the recommended statistic for reliability purposes. Alternative reliability tests, such as split halves, are inferior to coefficient alpha because the former can vary depending on the way items are split. Test-retest reliabilities also are inappropriate for consumer socialization studies because cognitive and behavioral orientations toward consumption are presumed to be developing and changing throughout a person's life cycle.

Coefficient alpha could be tested across social groupings to ascertain a satisfactory level and correspondence. As a rule of thumb, Nunnally (1967) has suggested that for basic research, reliabilities of .50 to .60 suffice and increasing reliabilities beyond .80 are a waste of time and funds. The researcher always should strive, however, for reliabilities in excess of .70 (Nunnally 1978). Coefficient alpha can be increased by deleting a number of the original items used to measure a variable. This suggests the desirability of using several items to measure a construct and its domains. In conjunction with the heuristic search for higher alphas, it is useful to analyze the item-to-total correlations, which indicate the degree of agreement between an item and the rest of the items in the scale. A low item-to-total correlation coefficient can single out group-specific problems that could be eliminated. The items that drop out in this analysis could be idiocyncratic to a particular group or be poorly understood by respondents in that group. Idiosyncratic items might be valuable information because they could represent a portion of the construct's domain that is not directly comparable between social groups. If the item is poorly understood, however, it should be eliminated from the analysis.

Finally, measures should be validated across social groupings of respondents. Construct validity can be evaluated by factor analysis of the same set of items designed to measure a variable (construct) for each social group. The factor structure solutions can then be compared across groups. This analysis is designed to confirm the presence of the same constructs and their respective items, which purportedly measure them. Valid transgroup items would be those that load significantly on the same construct in each group, with high loadings (approximately .30 or greater) on the hypothesized factor and low loadings (less than .30) on the other factors. The coefficient of factor congruency can be used as an index of the degree of agreement between the separate factor solutions. The coefficient of factor congruency, which is analogous to a correlation coefficient, measures the extent to which the agreement between two factor structures is similar (see, for example, Cattell 1978).

4
Theoretical Perspectives

T he model presented in chapter 2 suggests the types of variables and linkages between them that are to be supported by theory and research data to satisfy the socialization perspective. Unfortunately, the existing theories and supportive research are far from ideal in satisfying these conditions. Quite often more than one theory might provide a rationale for the linkage between two variables. Available research findings also are far from ideal in supporting all linkages of the model. The task of organizing research data becomes more complex, partly because of the richness of the study of consumer behavior in terms of dependent variables. According to the hierarchy of consumer decisions discussed in chapter 2, each decision conceivably can involve predecisional stages such as information seeking and alternative evaluation stages (see, for example, Chaffee and McLeod 1973; Arndt 1976). Decision making at each stage might in turn involve the operation of different types of skills, knowledge, motives, attitudes, and behaviors (Moschis and Churchill 1978).

This chapter presents major theoretical perspectives on socialization and discusses their applicability to consumer socialization.

Theories

Generally, three types of theories have been used to explain consumer socialization over a person's life cycle. For discussion purposes, these can be classified into developmental, social learning, and social-system theories.

Developmental Theories

Within the developmental category, we include maturational theories as well, although the distinction and relationship between the two is worth noting. Developmental changes involve sociopsychological changes, many of which can be caused by biological changes, while maturational changes merely reflect biological changes and organic growth. Examples of developmental theories include theories of cognitive development and life-span developmental theories.

When socializtion is viewed from a cognitive developmental perspective, the emphasis is placed on a person's maturation (often indexed by age). With maturation, content of learning (criterion variables) is expected to undergo formation and change as psychological adjustment to the environment occurs. Because the cognitive developmental approach recently has been extended into later adolescence and adulthood, and socialization research in general has been extended to learning throughout a person's lifetime, life cycle rather than age has been suggested as a proxy variable of the person's developmental process (see, for example, Baltes and Schaie 1973). The developmental approach has been used to understand changes not only in the individual's decision-making processes but also in family consumer decisions (Hill 1965). The latter area has been a topic of sociological research pioneered by Hill and his associates (1957).

Views of life-span development often are referred to as stage theories. Stage theories, like those proposed by Piaget and Erikson, emphasize qualitative changes and differences believed to appear in a relatively fixed sequence. The developmental perspective views development over the life cycle similar to the biological concepts of growth and maturation. A change is classified as developmental if it is universal qualitative, sequential, irreversible, and endstate-oriented (see also Baltes et al. 1980).

Life-span development not only involves unidirectional and cumulative change functions extending from birth to death but also multilinear and discontinuous developmental processes. For example, cognitive and social behaviors acquired in childhood can be maintained, transformed, or extincted in later life when the acquisition of new behaviors is likely to occur (Baltes et al. 1980). One rather comprehensive model of life-span development has been presented by Kimmel (1974), who attempted to chart the dimensions along which people develop from infancy to old age. He noted that the human organism develops along four dimensions: (a) the inner-biological, (b) the individual-psychological, (c) the cultural-sociological, and (d) the outer-physical. Specifically, a person's progression through life could be independently examined in terms of cell structure growth and death (biological), the development of attitudes and learning abilities (psychological), the development of communicative and interpersonal relationships (sociological), and outward appearance and size (physical). Although these progressions should be examined independently, it is very unlikely that any one would present a complete and accurate picture of life-span development in an individual.

Riegel (1975) suggests that these four domains should be viewed as planes of progression along which people and society change. Because very little is known in adult development concerning the inner-biological, Riegel (1975) believes that it is appropriate to treat inner (a) and outer (d) together as a biophysical plane. Combining the remaining two dimensions (b and c) in Kimmel's typology, Riegel presents biophysical and psychosocial events and changes that have implications for socialization (table 4–1).

Planes of progression through life can be seen as three-dimensional spirals that are analogous to life-span position, cohort, and period (Dimmick et al. 1979).

Table 4-1
Positions and Events in the Life Cycle

Life-Span Position	Psychosocial	Biophysical
Level I (1-7 years): Childhood—egocentric	Cognitive development Nonsymbolic Communication skills Family dependence Beginning of sex-role identification	Cognitive development Neural patterning Motor coordination (crawling, walking, talking)
Level II (7-12 years): Middle childhood— concrete operational	Importance of peer relationships Exploration of hobbies and interests Conforming behavior Development of multiple roles (daughter/son, student friend, sister/brother)	Eye–hand coordination Growth spurts Complex memory system
Level III (12-18 years): Adolescence—formal operational	Attraction to others Attempts at independence Testing of physical capabilities Rebellion Career plans Egocentric behavior	Physical maturation Sexual maturation Conceptual/abstract ability
Level IV (18-25 years): Pre-adulthood	College/first job Marriage First child	First child (F)[a]
Level V (25-30 years) Early adulthood	Second job/loss of job (F) Other children Children in preschool First home	Other children (F)
Level VI (30-35 years): Early-middle adulthood	Move Promotion Children in school	
Level VII (35-50 years): Middle adulthood	Second home Promotion/second career (F) Departure of children	Loss of stamina
Level VIII (50-65 years): Older adulthood	Unemployment/retirement Isolation Grandparenting Death of parents Death of friends Head of kin	Menopause (F) Illness
Level IX (65+ years): Elderly	Loss of partner Deprivation	Sensory-motor deficiencies

Source: Adapted from Riegel (1975). J. Dimmick, T. McCain, and W.T. Bolton, "Media Use and the Life Cycle Span," *American Behavioral Scientist*, Vol. 23, No. 1 (September/October 1979), 17. Copyright © 1979 by Sage Publications, Inc. Reprinted by permission of Sage Publications, Inc.
[a](F) = female only or predominantly female.

Socialization in the life cycle is a function of these three factors working on a spiral of progression—the biophysical and the psychosocial spiral. For example, the life-span position marks the individual's progression in the psychosocial spiral, since society expects certain types of behavior at various ages, while the time a person is both (birth cohort) determines to a large extent his or her interpretation of the environment.

Most of the research in consumer socialization has used age as an explanatory variable, with less emphasis on other concepts related to time or life span. For this reason, information on consumer behavior differences is presented in this book as they might relate to age for broad age groupings (children, adolescents, adults, and older adults).

Life-span theories are in the early stages of development, but they generally address changes in priorities and one's view of oneself and the world. These changes are likely to be caused by changes in one's physical, psychological, and social well-being. For example, in later years physical changes include deterioration of the ability to sense and perceive, such as the deterioration of visual and hearing abilities, changes that affect the individual's information-processing skills. Psychosocial changes include changes in personality traits (such as self-concept), internal locus of control, job-related and family responsibilities and future expectations. They also include the emotional changes associated with mid-life crisis (see also Lepisto 1985).

Social Learning Theories

The social learning model views socialization as an outcome of environmental forces on the person rather than internal biopsychological processes, focusing almost exclusively on socialization agents. When socialization is viewed as a social process, the emphasis is on socialization agents transmitting norms, attitudes, motivations, and behaviors to the learner; socialization is assumed to take place during the course of the person's interaction with these agents in various social settings.

Social learning theories can be divided into formal connectionist learning theories and interaction theories. The first kind are represented by the stimulus-response contiguity theories of Watson and Guthrie and by the reinforcement theories of Skinner, Miller, and others. For example, social learning theory, based on Skinner's operant conditioning principles and the classical conditioning paradigms, describes behavior changes as a function of stimuli provided by the social environment. The key assumption of social learning theory is that all behavior potentially is learned and can be changed.

> Behavior change occurs when discriminative conditions and response contingencies change. These are expected to change when even an individual interacts with people he has not interacted with before or whenever he comes into a new environmental setting. Since people are assumed to interact with new people throughout the life span (such as children, spouse, friends, colleagues, neighbors, etc.),

and/or come into new environmental settings (such as different jobs, countries, neighborhoods, dwellings, etc.) they are expected to show behavior change throughout the entire life span. (Ahammer 1973, 257)

In general, connectionist theories view the process as being externally controlled, regardless of the person's state (active or passive). For example, classical conditioning stimulus-response theories view learning as the outcome of externally imposed reward contingency schedules, with an external agent having complete control over the process. Similarly, instrumental conditioning theories focus on learning that occurs as a result of rewards and punishments rendered by the external agent because of the learner's active behavior.

In contrast to the connectionist learning theories, interaction theories stress an active view of the individual in the socialization process. Within this school of thought, symbolic interaction theorists attempt to explain the individual's behavior in relation to his or her environment, which is symbolic as well as physical in nature. The individual is viewed as an active participant in the learning process, and the development of values, attitudes, and behaviors results from interaction with others and the cues received from them about those behaviors and attitudes. Cooley's (1902) notion of looking-glass self is the cornerstone of this theory.

Several theorists in their effort to explain imitation have offered detailed analyses of modeling phenomena in terms of associative and classical conditioning mechanisms, reinforcement theories of instrumental conditioning, or instinctual propensities (see also Bandura 1969). Bandura argues that such approaches do not specify how new response patterns are acquired observationally, specifically the variables regulating observational response acquisition, the factors influencing long-term retention of previously learned matching responses, and the conditions affecting degree of behavioral reproduction of modeling stimuli.

Bandura (1969) has proposed a social learning theory of identification that is more explicit than previous theoretical formulations. According to this theory:

> Matching behavior is acquired on the basis of contiguity of modeling stimulus sequences and symbolic verbal coding of observational inputs. These representational symbolic events, in conjunction with appropriate environmental cues, later guide overt enactment of appropriate matching responses. Performance of observationally learned identificatory responses, on the other hand, is primarily governed by reinforcing events that may be externally applied, self-administered, or vicariously experienced. Moreover, emphasis is given to the differential consequences of emulating the behavior of models possessing distinctive characteristics. (Bandura 1969, 255)

Bandura contends that virtually all learning phenomena that result from direct experiences can occur on a vicarious basis through observation of other people's behavior rather than from experimental reinforcement. The individual, according to Bandura, can imitate the behavior of competent models exhibiting proper modes of response and avoid dangerous mistakes that can result from tedious trial and error practice. Behavioral inhibitions can be induced as well by observing punishment of others for their actions. Bandura proposes that most behaviors are learned deliberately or inadvertently. Dangerous mistakes can be avoided by observing competent models who demonstrate the proper mode of response.

Bandura's approach differs from contemporary analyses. He proposes four sub-processes that govern modeling: attention, retentional processes, motoric reproduction processes, and reinforcement and motivational processes. The initial process is *attention*. Here the observer is exposed to the modeling stimuli, selectively attends to, recognizes, and differentiates specific aspects of the model's behavior. *Retentional processes* involve coding of images and verbal symbols of observed phenomena. *Motoric reproduction processes* require certain skills on the part of the observer to execute the behavioral response. Finally, *reinforcement* and *motivational processes* determine whether the acquired behavior will be expressed as overt behavior. The translation of neutral acquisition to behavioral performance is facilitated by positive incentives, especially observed reinforcement contingencies (see also Atkin 1976a). As Bandura puts it:

> When observed outcomes are judged personally attainable, they create incentive motivation. Seeing others' success can function as a motivation by arousing in observers expectations that they can gain similar rewards for analogous performances. In addition, evaluation of people and activities can be significantly altered on the basis of observed consequences. Ordinarily, observed punishment tends to devaluate the models and their behavior, whereas the same models become a source of emulation when their actions are admired. (Bandura 1978, 22).

Early social learning and operant conditioning theories of modeling required overt performance of a response matching modeled stimulus cases. Positive reinforcement of the imitative behavior followed. Bandura's view differs from these formulations in that he distinguishes between acquisition (learning) and actual performance of the behavior. Learning occurs when stimuli elicit mental representation of the behavior, while performance is determined on the basis of reinforcement experienced by the model and the learner.

Overt performance of identificatory behavior is influenced not only by response consequence to a model but also by certain status-conferring symbols and model attributes. A vast amount of research in social psychology has demonstrated that models who display discriminative characteristics (such as prestige, power, competence, socioeconomic status, and expertise) are imitated to a greater extent by both children and adults than models who lack these qualities. Under certain conditions, modeling also can be significantly influenced by a real or perceived similarity between the observer and the model. According to Stotland's theoretical interpretation of identification, individuals have a strong need to achieve cognitive consistency in their self-concept. When they perceive themselves as having some characteristics in common with a model, they will interject other attributes of the model into their self-image to maintain cognitive or perceptual consistency (Bandura 1969). Thus, there is considerable evidence (Bandura 1969) to suggest that observation of rewarding or punishing consequences to a model affects the extent to which observers willingly engage in identification behavior.

Finally, role theorists view the individual both as a passive and an active participant in the socialization process. Some early theorists subscribed to the view that roles are externally constructed without the individual's input, while others saw roles as socially structured but stress the individual's active participation in learning, performing, and modifying roles in the process of socialization (see, for example, Thorton and Nardi 1975). Symbolic interaction and role theory are valuable tools for studying socialization throughout an individual's life cycle because both theories recognize that the individual changes group affiliations and confronts new environments in the course of a lifetime.

One recent approach to role acquisition (Thorton and Nardi 1975) posits a series of four stages. Each stage involves interaction between individuals and external expectations (the content of which might be behavioral, attitudinal, or cognitive), and a role is not fully acquired until each stage has progressed.

> The first stage of role acquisition is the period prior to incumbency in a social position during which . . . those aspiring to membership in groups begin to adopt group values, thus becoming prepared for future transitions into groups. (p. 874)

At this stage, several agents can play an important role in helping the person acquire role conceptions, with the mass media considered to be the most important (Thorton and Nardi 1975).

> In the second phase of role acquisition the individual, now in a social position, experiences the role as an incumbent and shifts from viewing it from an outside perspective to viewing it from inside. (p. 876)

The expectations at this stage arise from those enacting the same roles, those enacting strictly reciprocal roles, and the incumbent himself, who tends to form role conceptions in response to the expectations others have of him.

The third, or informal, stage involves encounters with unofficial or informal role expectations. Primary sources of these expectations include peers, work groups, cliques, and other people encountered in daily activities.

> Like anticipatory and formal expectations, informal ones may be either explicit or implicit and may refer to behavior, attitudes, knowledge and skills; but they tend to be implicit and to refer to the attitudinal and cognitive features of role performance. (p. 879)

Learning about norms associated with the new role at this stage is expected to take place by trying to enact the role.

The final step in role acquisition involves individuals imposing their own expectations and conceptions on roles and modifying role expectations. This stage focuses on the individual's personality, past experience, skills, values, and beliefs and these factors' effect on and subsequent modification of his role.

Thus, according to this model, role acquisition and role enactment consist of a gradual process, with the person being passive at first and becoming increasingly more active in the process. The media play an important role in forming initial (anticipatory) expectations. Next, significant others (members of the group) develop expectations about the person's behavior and exert pressure for compliance. The third stage involves active interaction of the learner with the role itself, and much learning is expected to be acquired through trial and error experiences. In the final stage, the person is expected to contribute to the refinement and modification of role expectations. It appears that part of the person's function in the last stage is to resocialize others to modified role expectations.

Social System Theories

Social system theories contend that the source of influence is within an organization or group of which the learner is part. The individual is expected to acquire the norms and behaviors that are specific to a particular segment of society, often referred to as a culture or subculture. Because socialization involves the learning of one's culture, the learning process often is known as enculturation (Clausen 1968a, 47). Different cultures show different norms, behaviors, and value orientations, so the content of learning outcomes is expected to differ across cultures and subcultures. Anthropological perspectives are particularly useful in explaining the consumer socialization and behavior of different cultures and subcultures (see, for example, Heskel and Semenik 1983; Hirschman 1985a). It should be noted that these differences might be due not only to the accepted norms but also to different socialization processes that might operate differently in each specific social structure.

In using social-system models, it becomes necessary to separate the direct effects from the indirect effects of the social organization with which a person is identified. Learning, which can be a function of developmental as well as sociological perspectives, might be a function of the individual's active interaction with a specific environment (direct learning); it also might be due to differences in learning processes unique to a specific culture or subculture. Unfortunately, social-system theories are far from being explicit in specifying the learning processes and their functional relationships to criterion variables.

Theoretical Perspectives over the Life Span

Childhood and Adolescence

Developmental Perspectives. For children and adolescents, cognitive developmental perspectives appear to be most applicable to explanations of consumer socialization and behavior. Two major theories of cognitive development are Piaget's theory of intellectual development and Ausubel's learning theory. Piaget's theory suggests that learning occurs through interaction between the child and the environment (Piaget 1970). Learning is viewed as an active process involving manipulative and exploratory interaction with concrete objects and events. Intellectual development is expected to occur as a series of stages characterized by specific cognitive operations, and the course of development is an invariant sequence.

Studies utilizing the cognitive developmental approach attempt to explain socialization as a function of qualitative changes (stages) in cognitive organization occurring between infancy and adulthood. Stages are defined in terms of environment at different stages. Piaget describes four stages during which the child's cognitive development is expected to occur:

1. sensimotor operations (from birth to 1½ years)
2. preoperational stages (ages 2 to 7)
3. concrete operations (ages 7 to 10)
4. formal operations (ages 11 to 14)

As children move from one stage to another, they are assumed to be developing and integrating various intellectual skills, which have taxonomical relationship to each other. Thus, age is used as a proxy variable for cognitive development. It is worth noting that children at the preoperational stage are expected to have difficulty in forming stable concepts and constructing valid propositions.

Ausubel describes cognitive structure in terms of concepts and propositions arranged in hierarchical structures (see, for example, Ausubel 1960; Ausubel and Robinson 1969). It is expected that meaningful learning will occur when the individual can relate new knowledge nonarbitrarily to established ideas previously learned. This type of learning is expected to reduce rote learning and enhance long-term memory. Ausubel proposes that meaningful learning can best be promoted by the use of general ideas that, once learned, are expected to provide a potentially meaningful set of anchoring ideas under which subsequently presented subordinate knowledge can be subsumed. Ausubel places a major emphasis on sequential transfer. Ideas must be first identified and taught in order of abstractiveness or generalizability, with the more abstract ideas taught first, followed by the teaching of more specific concepts. Thus, contrary to Piaget, Ausubel posits that better learning cannot occur simply by means of interaction with one's environment but also requires improving the level and kind of interaction.

In the context of consumer socialization, Piaget's theory of early childhood education would lead one to conclude that it would be very difficult to teach consumer socialization to preschool children because they are expected to be at a preoperational level of development. Alternatively, Ausubel's theory suggests that preschool children can be taught these abstract concepts through utilization of a sequence going from general ideas to more specific concepts and facts.

The proposition that even young children can learn consumer skills has received some empirical support in a recent study. Moschis, Lawton, and Stampfl (1980) exposed two- to six-year-olds who were enrolled in a preschool program to two different educational programs. One was based on Piagetian cognitive development theory, the other on Ausubel's learning theory. Children taught concepts in line with the Ausubelian program developed better consumption skills than children in the Piagetian program.

Although cognitive developmental models (such as Piaget's) suggesting that all socialization occurs by the age of fifteen have been widely accepted, some researchers have presented findings suggesting that some kinds of socialization—particularly political—take place after fifteen years of age. Therefore, it is no surprise to find evidence, albeit cross-sectional, that consumer learning (and hence, consumer socialization) occurs through high school (Jennings and Niemi 1968).

Piaget's (1972) recent position on the attainment of the formal operations level of cognitive development indicates that the time span from ages 15 to 20 reflects a period of diversification of aptitudes and a degree of generality of cognitive structures acquired between 12 and 15. Piaget further argues that all normal subjects attain the formal operations or structuring stage, if not between 11–12 and 14–15 years, at least between 15 and 20 years. "However, they reach this stage in different areas according to their aptitudes and their professional specializations" (p. 10). According to this view, speed of development might vary from one environment to another, placing greater significance on the environmental influences.

Flavell (1970), who has made important suggestions for extending Piaget's theory of cognition, suggests that the meaning of *developmental* should not be seen as restricted to biological changes. Instead, he points to experience as a "far more promising source of cognitive changes than are biological events" (p. 250). This notion suggests that a person's increasing experience with the marketplace, which is associated with an increasing variety of needs for products and services, is likely to result in the formation of and change in his or her cognitive structure.

Social Learning Theories. Social learning models of consumer socialization differ from developmental models with respect to the emphasis and importance of environmental forces—that is, socialization agents. While cognitive developmental theories view the individual as playing an active role in the socialization process, with socialization agents being rather passive, social learning perspectives view the individual as playing a rather passive role, with the socializers being more instrumental in shaping attitudes and behaviors. Theories of social learning often are inexplicable, with the effects of learning from socialization agents often inferred from the socializee's interaction with the various agents. In the study of consumer socialization, for example, learning from television ads (as a result of a person's frequency of advertising viewing) has been attributed to instrumental conditioning, modeling, and cognitive learning (Adler et al. 1977). Similarly, learning from parents might be attributed to modeling processes (Ward et al. 1977), positive and

negative reinforcement (Moschis et al. 1984), and cognitive learning involving purposive consumer training (Ward et al. 1977). One of the difficulties in using social
learning theories stems from reciprocal relationships and influences—that is, the
indirect effects of socialization agents (see, for example, Moschis 1985; Moschis
and Moore 1982).

Socioeconomic Effects. Socioeconomic effects on consumer socialization can
be interpreted in the context of social-system perspectives. The direct effects of
social class can be viewed from a life-space perspective (Lewin 1951). With increasing
socioeconomic status comes an expanded life space for the individual, resulting
in increased availability of products and brands that fall into one's environment
and are more likely to be consumed and preferred. Speculations by Riesman and
his associates (1956), as well as those by Ward (1974a), appear to be in line with
the life-space notion; they suggest that youths from more affluent families are likely
to have more experience with money and might be more aware of the range of consumer goods available than youths from less-affluent families. Similary, Hess (1970)
states that: "The relative isolation of the lower-class person from the paths of experience of the dominant middle class is one antecedent of his relatively low skill
and experience in obtaining and evaluating information about events and resources
that affect or might affect his life" (p. 408).

Adulthood and Late Adulthood

Differences in adult behavior can be viewed from a life-span perspective. According to this view, "a developmental orientation is needed whenever the behavior
identified involves a change process and is better understood if placed in the context of chains and patterns of antecedent and subsequent events" (Baltes et al. 1980,
66). Figure 4–1 summarizes three representative life-span theories that have been
used to explain differences and changes in adult behavior. Unfortunately, little
research into adult consumer behavior has been conducted using the socialization
framework. Data on differences in adult consumer behavior, however, can be interpreted from a socialization perspective (see, for example, Moschis 1981b).

Most explanations of differences in the behavior of older individuals are closely
tied to theories of alterations in sociopsychological and biophysical stages of life-
span development. Sociopsychological perspectives include both sociological and
psychological theories. Examples of the first type are the disengagement, activity,
social breakdown, and subculturation theories, whereas psychological approaches
include mostly personality theories. Biophysical theories derive from developmental
perspectives. These theories, arising from different disciplines, are neither com-
patible nor mutually exclusive. For example, several researchers have suggested that
activity theory, also called engagement theory, and disengagement theory are com-
patible; rather, they are explanations of different levels of activity or types of adaptation to aging (see, for example, Maddox 1964).

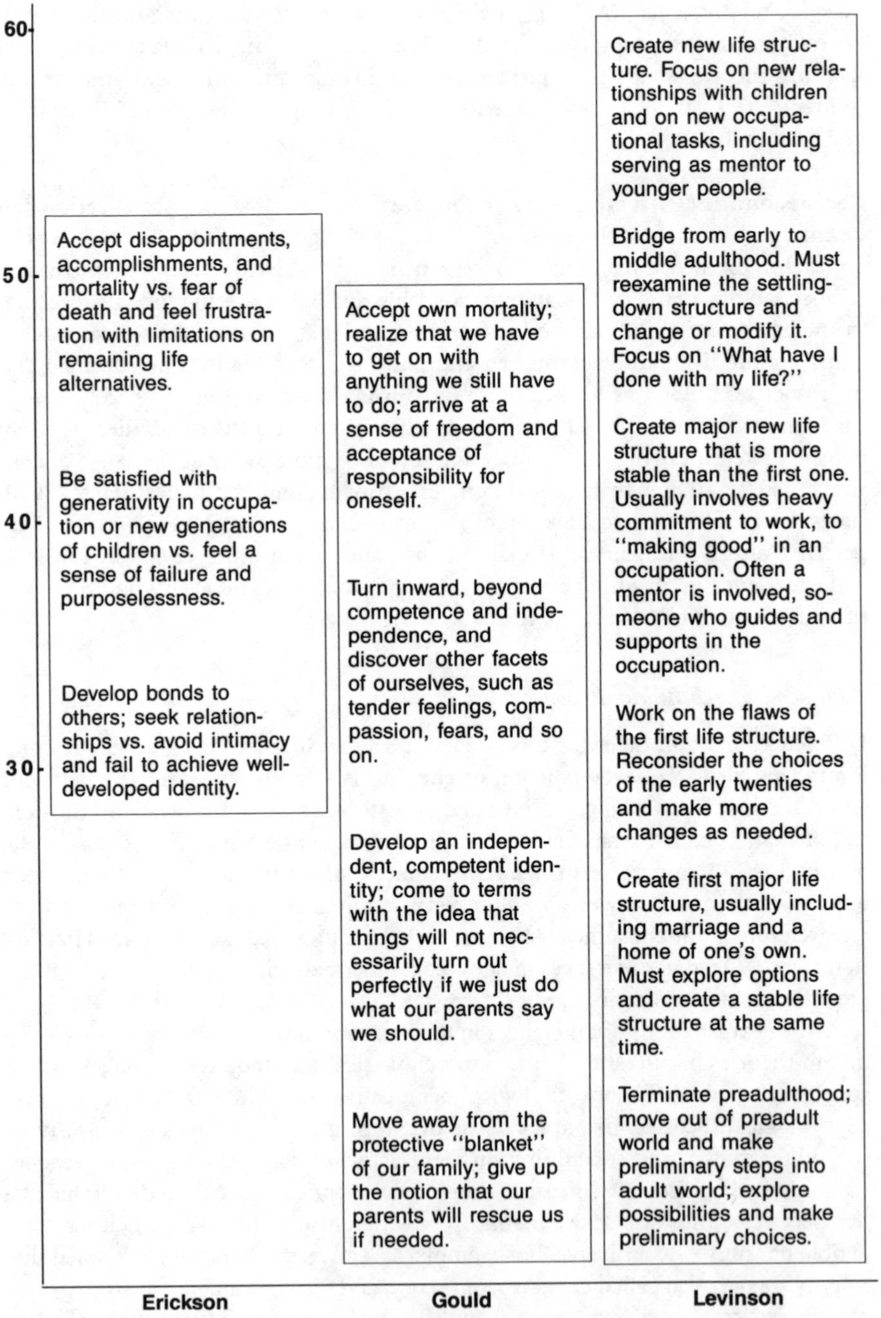

60—

50—

40—

30—

Erickson column:

Accept disappointments, accomplishments, and mortality vs. fear of death and feel frustration with limitations on remaining life alternatives.

Be satisfied with generativity in occupation or new generations of children vs. feel a sense of failure and purposelessness.

Develop bonds to others; seek relationships vs. avoid intimacy and fail to achieve well-developed identity.

Gould column:

Accept own mortality; realize that we have to get on with anything we still have to do; arrive at a sense of freedom and acceptance of responsibility for oneself.

Turn inward, beyond competence and independence, and discover other facets of ourselves, such as tender feelings, compassion, fears, and so on.

Develop an independent, competent identity; come to terms with the idea that things will not necessarily turn out perfectly if we just do what our parents say we should.

Move away from the protective "blanket" of our family; give up the notion that our parents will rescue us if needed.

Levinson column:

Create new life structure. Focus on new relationships with children and on new occupational tasks, including serving as mentor to younger people.

Bridge from early to middle adulthood. Must reexamine the settling-down structure and change or modify it. Focus on "What have I done with my life?"

Create major new life structure that is more stable than the first one. Usually involves heavy commitment to work, to "making good" in an occupation. Often a mentor is involved, someone who guides and supports in the occupation.

Work on the flaws of the first life structure. Reconsider the choices of the early twenties and make more changes as needed.

Create first major life structure, usually including marriage and a home of one's own. Must explore options and create a stable life structure at the same time.

Terminate preadulthood; move out of preadult world and make preliminary steps into adult world; explore possibilities and make preliminary choices.

| Erickson | Gould | Levinson |

Source: Adapted from Lepisto (1985), who summarized Bee and Mitchell (1980).

Figure 4-1. Three Representative Life-Span Developmental Theories

Disengagement Theory. This theory maintains that as a natural consequence of aging, the elderly and our social systems are mutually withdrawn from each other. According to this theory, aging is associated with a voluntary severing of social ties and a retreat into isolation. After this inevitable process gradually shifts the relationship between self and society, a new equilibrium emerges that is mutually gratifying to both self and society. It is characterized by the constriction of previous interpersonal contracts and the increased interiority of the individual (Cumming and Henry 1961). Schramm (1969) was among the first to suggest that the elderly use the mass media to help combat disengagement. More recently, Smith and her colleagues (1982 and 1985) applied disengagement theory to consumer behavior.

Engagement Theory. This theory, also called activity theory, claims that there is a contraction of the aged individual's life space, which is an involuntary exile imposed by society on the elderly. The aged individual, given a choice, will seek out other activities to substitute for previous role behaviors. If successful substitution is made, the individual's psychological well-being is enhanced (Lemmon et al. 1972). Activity theory was espoused by early gerontologists and more recently has been applied to other fields (see, for example, Amann et al. 1980). For example, a media perspective known as activity substitution has emerged from activity theory in the study of mass communication (Graney and Graney 1974). Recent efforts of consumer researchers to apply this perspective to socialization include the work of Smith and her colleagues (1981, 1982, 1985, 1986) and Weeks (1986).

Social Breakdown Theory. Social breakdown theory suggests that aging individuals approaching retirement are faced with a "roleless role" and are likely to assume the role that they perceive is expected of them (Young 1979). Older people are surrounded by unfamiliar circumstances resulting from role loss without adequate preparation, and they reach out for some cues to advise them how to behave. Because perceptions of the elderly among younger age groups generally are negative (Young 1975), older persons gradually, almost inadvertently, adopt some of the negative characteristics ascribed to them (Kuypers and Bengston 1973). Riley et al. (1969) were among the first to suggest that the process of aging and retirement can be viewed as socialization into a new role. More recently researchers have found that other role-related aspects of behavior are related to advancing age (see, for example, Fulgraff 1978). Neugarten, Moore, and Lowe (1968) found that "as the individual ages, he becomes increasingly aware of age discriminations in adult behavior and of the system of social sanctions that operate with regard to age appropriateness" (pp. 27–28). Because the consumer role changes significantly for the aging individual (Mauldin 1976) and it might be affected by negative prescriptions, older consumers might perceive their role as declining, as opposed to the developing of the consumer role in childhood and adolescence (Smith 1982).

Subculturation. This perspective views the elderly as a unique and identifiable subculture. Because of common role changes, common generational experiences in a rapidly changing society, and physical limitations, the elderly exhibit a positive affinity for one another (Rose 1965) and constitute a subsociety, much like the adolescent subsociety (Philibert 1965). As a result, the aged interact more often with their peers, identifying with informal reference groups (Streib 1968) and making an effort to attain status within such groups by means of good mental and physical health and maintenance of social activity (Rose 1965). No direct effort has been made to apply this perspective to the study of consumer behavior and socialization, although some descriptive data can be interpreted in the context of subculturation (McMillan and Moschis 1985).

Personality Theory. This theory attempts to explain behavior by identifying personality characteristics of the aging individual that predict behavior, as the consensus among social gerontologists and personality theorists is that personalities do not change dramatically with age (see, for example, Havighurst 1968; Neugarten 1972; Neugarten, Havighurst, and Tobin 1968). Reichard, Livson, and Peterson (1962), for example, identified five types of personalities indicative of successful and unsuccessful aging: mature, rocking chair, and armored (successful); angry and self-hating (unsuccessful). One application of personality theory to the study of elderly consumer behavior was by LaForge, French, and Crask (1981), who tested Reichard et al.'s (1962) personality typology of the elderly for its utility in market segmentation.

Developmental Perspective. In contrast to the theories that attempt to explain sociopsychological changes in aging, the developmental perspective focuses on alterations in behavior due to biological and physiological changes. For example, cognitive problems in the decision process are thought to be age-related (Baltes and Labouvie 1973). Similarly, other aspects of behavior development and change are thought to be due to biophysical changes.

Hormonal change is one biological change that occurs during aging. The male's production of testosterone and the female's production of estrogen (both primary sex hormones) diminish gradually in the male (climacterium) and more abruptly in the female (menopause) (Finch and Hayflick 1977). The result is that the small amount of estrogen normally found in males and the small amount of androgens normally found in females have noticeable effects on the aging man or woman (Finch and Hayflick 1977), who as a result become biologically and psychosocially alike (Birren 1964).

Several other biophysical changes might help us understand differences in the behavior of older persons. Biophysical changes include: visual, auditory, and other sensory declines; changes in mental capacity; and a decline in manual dexterity and mobility.

Visual Declines. Several aspects of the human visual system deteriorate with age, including acuity, smooth pursuit, light-level attention, and contrast sensitivity. Acuity refers to how clearly a person sees detail. Acuity begins to decline at about age fifty and sharply deteriorates after age seventy. This decline is believed to occur because of changes in the general focusing ability, which is affected by the ciliary bodies and their muscular losses, and because of loss in near vision (near presbyopia), which is caused by hardening of the lenses (Carter 1982). It is believed that 15 to 25 percent of the elderly population has vision of 20/50 or worse, with a large percentage of this attributable to senile muscular degeneration, cataracts, and other causes (Marmor 1977; Pitts 1982). Although some acuity problems can be corrected (by wearing glasses, for example), many are difficult to correct (Christman 1979). Furthermore, older people tend to seek no correction because of factors such as cost and immobility, and they tend to accept the decline as part of the self-perception of their aging role (Heatherton and Fouts 1985).

Smooth pursuit is used when a person tracks an object across the visual field. With increasing age, the eye movement mechanism that controls pursuit is likely to deteriorate, resulting in loss of the ability to follow an object that moves quickly across the visual field.

Light-level attention changes with increasing age because there is a reduction of light at the retina resulting from the yellowing of the lens and cornea and a shrinking pupil, which causes a similar visual field and the scattering of light as it passes through the vitreous body (Sekuler et al. 1982). Lower light level suggests that older people might have to adjust their television to a higher intensity. It is believed that the major light attention often occurs for green and blue wavelengths, for which the light can be decreased by a factor of 8 to 9 (Ordy et al. 1982). Changes in light attention, which for a sixty-year old is one-third the light that reaches a twenty-year-old's retina, have been cited as reasons for increasing preferences for blue colors (Davis and Edwards 1975).

Also with increasing age comes a reduction in *contrast sensitivity*, which makes it difficult for older people to detect images with low contrast. Contrast is possible when there are variations between the highest and the lowest luminances within the image.

Auditory Declines. These include hearing loss, slower central speech processing, and distractibility. *Hearing loss* begins after the age of fifty and becomes a disability by the age of sixty (Botwinick 1978). It is estimated that approximately 28 percent of people sixty-five and over report hearing impairments (U.S. Department of Health and Human Services 1979). This figure understates the percentage of older people with hearing impairments because many do not know they have a hearing loss. Others know they have a hearing loss but do not attempt to correct it because of financial or personal reasons. Still others believe that this is just part of growing old (Colavita 1978).

Increasing age also brings changes in *central speech processing*. Older people have difficulty comprehending messages presented at a fast rate of speed (Schow et al. 1978). This has been attributed to a longer persistence of auditory trace of one sound or word interfering with the processing of the next sound or word (Botwinick 1978).

Distractibility deals with the way new information affects learning. Although the introduction of relevant information does not necessarily affect an older person's ability to learn (see, for example, Birren 1974), aging does affect an older person's ability to learn when irrelevant information or distracting stimuli are present. According to Phillips and Sternthal (1977), this is attributable to the aging person's inability to ignore the distracting information.

Lower Mental Capacity. Age also causes changes in information-processing patterns, abilities, and skills. One characteristic associated with aging is the decline in the individual's ability to process new information. This is due partly to memory loss, which is believed to be associated with the aging process. Aging individuals are more likely to experience short-term memory loss, such as the type used to remember a phone number before dialing, than to experience long-term memory loss, such as the type used in dealing with brand preferences (Roedder-John and Cole 1986). An older person also needs more time to process new information because of the loss of fluid intelligence—that is, the ability to see and use abstract relationships and patterns—the decreasing ability to screen out irrelevant information, and the physical aging of the nervous system. Alternatively, crystalized intelligence—that is, the individual's ability to recall information accumulated over a lifetime—continues to rise as long as the person remains healthy.

Loss of Manual Dexterity and Mobility. With advancing age, individuals experience a loss in grip strength, known as manual dexterity. Their ability to perform work in terms of magnitude and duration is significantly altered. The optimum grip strength of females is significantly less than that of males, something that applies not only to aged individuals but to people at any age. In general, aging individuals experience loss of tactile strength, muscle control, and physical strength in general.

Individuals also are likely to become less mobile with increasing age. Decreasing mobility is a function of several changes, including a decrease in arm span and the presence of crippling arthritis. Among individuals sixty-five and older, 44 percent are likely to have arthritis (U.S. Department of Health and Human Services 1979).

Reasons for Changes. Some developmental psychologists and social gerontologists believe that certain aspects of the aging individual's behavior can be explained by biological and physiological factors (see, for example, Long et al. 1980; Clark and Anderson 1967). For example, data have supported a reverse horizontal decalage hypothesis—that is, that cognitive skills acquired most recently disappear first (compare Long, McCrary, and Ackerman 1980). Similarly, Clark and Anderson (1967) posit a development theory of aging involving five adaptive tasks, including redefinition of physical and social life space, substitution of alternative sources of need satisfaction, and reassessment of criteria for evaluation of self. The theory further posits that environmental constraints on life space (such as illness or loss of companions) might limit available sources of gratification and force substitution of alternative sources. Environmental forces, motivations, and other developmental factors interact with and contribute to the individual's need structure, which is likely to affect behavior (see, for example, Pressey and Kuhlen 1957; Yarrow 1963). The developmental perspective has been used quite successfully in the study of consumer socialization (see, for example, Smith 1982; Smith et al. 1982).

Researchers in several disciplines, including psychology, sociology, education, and political science, are concerned with integrating existing gerontological research into theoretical frameworks that would illuminate variables of critical importance and their linkages. Most of the researchers (see, for example, Harris and Bodden 1978) who have tested activity theory versus disengagement theory seem to support activity theory. The results of a limited number of studies in consumer socialization also support activity theory (see, for example, Smith et al. 1985; Smith 1982). Others are beginning to explore the developmental perspective (Papalia 1972; Baltes and Labouvie 1973) and personality theory (LaForge et al. 1981). In the study of consumer socialization, developmental perspectives seem to account for several differences in the consumer behavior of older adults (see chapter 9).

Effects of Early Learning

One question that remains relatively unexplored deals with the effects of early learning on later learning. Theory and research in consumer socialization suggest that early consumer learning might affect later learning. Our small-scale experimental study suggested that the sequence in which preschoolers were taught various consumer concepts affected their ability to learn, in line with Ausubel's theory of learning and cognitive development (Moschis et al. 1980). Similarly, preliminary analysis of our longitudinal data over more than a one-year time interval revealed that an adolescent's level of acquisition of a specific consumption orientation at an earlier time is likely to affect future learning from advertising (Moschis and Moore 1982). Also, frequency of participation in leisure activities as a youth was found to be positively related to higher levels of participation in such activities among adults (Sofranko and Nolan 1972).

Riesman and Roseborough (1955) speculated that different occupational expectations might affect a person's expectations regarding the purchase of products and brands, suggesting that occupational learning might precede consumer learning. Similarly, Straus (1962a) suggested that people with high occupational aspirations might delay entry into the labor force in order to secure higher education, resulting in the deferment of one's economic needs. Ward (1974a), drawing on empirical findings, speculated that achievement motives might be demonstrated through consumption practices. Research by Dorvan and Adelson (1966) also showed that a teenager's perception of the future might determine his or her adjustment in later life, suggesting that the learning of such perceptions might have implications for consumer learning.

At a later stage in the life cycle, certain orientations toward self might affect an individual's behavior in general and consumer behavior in particular. As the social roles of aging individuals change or are lost, there might be detrimental effects on the self-perception of the elderly. Loether (1975) has noted the importance of the self-concept in a study of aging. In many instances, chronological age and biological changes are less important indexes of an individual's behavior than is self-concept (Loether 1975). Self-perception among the elderly has been found to relate to several aspects of consumer behavior (Smith et al. 1982).

The way elderly persons report themselves to look, feel, and act also has been found to have an impact on their level of social interaction. If an older individual feels, looks, and acts younger than his or her chronological age, the level of activity tends to be greater than for one who feels, looks, and acts old. Blau (1956) for instance, found that those elderly who thought of themselves as younger than their age engaged in more activity. In a more recent study, informal and formal levels of social interaction on consumption matters were negatively related to cognitive age (Smith 1982).

Thus, consumer skills acquired earlier might affect the learning of other skills, attitudes, and behaviors later in life, or they might affect the development of other cognitions in a given period of time. Several examples in the consumer behavior field provide theoretical support for consumer learning properties affecting others. For example, cognitive theories of attitude formation suggest that behavior follows the development or change of attitudes, while hierarchy of effects models view the learning of consumer properties relating to new products, with earlier acquired properties affecting the development of later acquired properties (Lavidge and Steiner 1965).

Trends and Prospects in Socialization Theory

Consumer socialization theory and research rely a great deal on socialization developments in other areas. Thus, changes in socialization perspectives and research approaches are likely to affect research in consumer socialization. It would, therefore, be useful to review developments in socialization research in other areas because such developments are likely to set the stage for consumer socialization research in the years to come.

Perhaps the most significant development is the tendency to use socialization perspectives to understand human behavior (see, for example, Baltes and Labouvie 1973). This trend is not surprising, given that no single theory can adequately explain human behavior. The socialization approach can incorporate several theories, providing a more realistic perspective on the explanation of human behavior.

Another trend closely related to the first is the use of socialization perspectives to explain behavior over the life cycle. While early work on socialization focused on children, researchers gradually have applied socialization explanations to other age groups. For example, Brim (1968) has viewed the development of values, attitudes, and skills related to the enactment of various roles during adulthood, while other researchers (see, for example, Riley et al. 1969; Kuypers and Bengston 1973) have used socialization approaches to understand behavior at later stages in the life cycle.

More recent developments include revisions of socialization theories and integration of theories. An example of the first type include Piaget's theory of intellectual development, which has been extended by Flavell (1970), as well as the, cognitive developmental perspective, which has been extended to adulthood and late adulthood (see, for example, Kohlberg 1973; Long et al. 1980). Not only have social scientists been modifying existing socialization theories, but they also have integrated them into broader socialization perspectives. The two main lines of research and theory—psychology and sociology—have been converging in the past 25 years into a new social science perspective for the study of aging over the life course. Baltes, Reese, and Lipsitt (1980) have summarized these developments:

> The convergence of these and other trends makes the current scene friendly to a life-space developmental approach . . . a large supportive context is provided by parallel developments in other disciplines, particularly sociology . . . largely because of demographic and other changes, the design and delivery of health and economic services are based increasingly on life-span conceptions. (p. 69)

Finally, there have been developments in the methodologies used to study socialization and test socialization theories. While early studies used cross-sectional (stage-related designs), more recent approaches have used longitudinal and causal designs. Causal designs that order variables in line with the expected (hypothesized) flow of influence have been a logical outgrowth of the integration of several theories.

Several research avenues are open to those interested in consumer socialization. These directions are suggested in part from developments in socialization theory and research in other disciplines. One opportunity exists in applying socialization perspectives to the study of consumer behavior over the life cycle. While most of the research has focused on the study of young people, more recent research has addressed later stages (see, for example, Smith and Moschis 1985a). The application of socialization perspectives to several stages would be a logical extension of socialization theory and research in other disciplines.

Adult stages in the life cycle will be asociated not only with learning different consumption-related variables but also with changes in existing patterns of behavior. The latter type of learning has been referred to as resocialization (Riesman and Roseborough 1955). In this category, one could include the learning of new roles related to consumption, such as shopping at home through the assistance of a home computer (Moschis et al. 1985), and learning new consumption-related skills and behaviors because of relocation.

Socialization perspectives also provide opportunities for understanding differences among subcultures. Students of consumer behavior find few theoretical bases for explaining demographic and socioeconomic differences in consumer behavior. The socialization approach provides opportunities for understanding such differences because subcultural differences are tied into socialization theories of subcultures (such as age groups, social classes, races, and ethnic groups). It also provides bases for understanding consumer acculturation processes (see, for example, O'Guinn and Faber 1985; O'Guinn, Lee, and Faber 1986).

Research in consumer socialization could be enhanced through the use of multitheoretical perspectives. Because the development and change of consumer behavior are influenced by several factors, no single theory of socialization is likely to describe the entire picture accurately. Developmental perspectives should be integrated into other theoretical perspectives, including learning theories and social-system theories. This approach would not necessarily involve devising new models but rather incorporating existing theories into a broader model. Such a model would have to include a larger number and variety of variables, which would be derived from socialization theories.

5
Family Influences

lthough informal interpersonal communication processes occur in several types of social settings (for example, with peers or siblings), the family context of interpersonal communication is believed to have the greatest influence on consumer socialization. This chapter presents theory and research concerning the effects of family on consumer socialization. Based on these theoretical and research perspectives, a set of propositions is developed. Finally, existing knowledge in the area is summarized, and directions for future research are suggested.

Types of Family Influence

With respect to family communication effects on consumer learning, research suggests that family influences as a result of such communication and dyadic relations might be of four types:

1. parental influence on child
2. child's influence on parent
3. spouse's influence on spouse
4. siblings' influence on sibling

Parental Influence

The effects of parental-initiated communication on a child's consumer learning have been the focus of several studies. For example, Ward and his colleagues (1977) examined methods mothers use to teach children consumer skills, such as giving lectures on consumption matters. Similarly, in more recent consumer socialization studies, Moschis and his associates examined the effects of family communication patterns regarding consumption on consumer skill acquisition (Moschis and Moore 1979c and 1979d; Moschis, Moore, and Smith 1984).

Select sections of this chapter have been adapted from Moschis (1985) with permission of the *Journal of Consumer Research*.

With respect to parent-child communication in a dyadic setting, communication and influence relationships can be of four dyadic types: mother-daughter, mother-son, father-daughter, and father-son. The majority of studies have examined parent-child interactions in a broad context, without addressing specific parent-child dyadic relations. Although some studies have addressed more specific units of analysis, they were not addressed in the context of family communication processes. For example, Saunders and her colleagues (1973) investigated the degree of agreement or disagreement between mother and daughter in selecting the daughter's school clothing. They found a higher percentage of consensus of mother-daughter opinion for expressive items (such as coats) than for nonexpressive items, and they found less conflict when the money used for purchases was provided by the parent than when the money was earned by the daughter. Another study of high school students found greater parental influence on the clothing behavior of boys than on that of girls (Hamilton and Warden 1966).

Child's Influence

While the effects of parental-initiated communication have been studied in the context of the consumer socialization of young people, the effects of children on parental consumer learning have been studied in a variety of situations over a person's life cycle. For example, Ward and Wackman (1972) studied the effects of a child's product requests on the mother's consumer behavior (yielding). Similarly, Atkin (1978a) studied child-initiated communication on the mother's purchasing behavior for cereal products. Such yielding to children's requests might have a long-term effect on behavior modification of the parent. This observation is in line with Riesman and Roseborough's (1955) notion of retroactive socialization, in which the child serves as an agent of change in parental consumer behaviors.

Spouse's Influence

While reciprocal influence between child and parent have been investigated in the context of communication, a spouse's influence on consumer learning traditionally has been examined in the context of household decision making. The focus is on power relations (for instance, syncratic or husband-dominant) rather than on communication processes, with communication assumed to be a given (see, for example, Engel et al. 1978). Research on the effects of communication between spouses on their consumer socialization is sparse.

Siblings' Influence

Siblings are likely to discuss consumption among themselves, and the outcome of such communication is likely to affect consumer learning. The effects of such communication, however, have not been investigated adequately. One study of adolescent consumer socialization, for example, assessed the influence of siblings (Moore et al. 1976). Others examined the influence of older siblings on clothing behavior (Vener 1957; Vener and Hoffer 1959). In studies of the adult consumer, the effects of siblings are subsumed under "relatives" as sources of information and influence on consumer decisions (see, for example, Engel et al. 1978). In this chapter the term *family* is confined to parent-child relations. It excludes sibling relations, which are addressed in chapter 8.

Communication with family members, both overt and cognitive, plays an important role in shaping consumer learning. The effects of this communication can be direct or indirect, and they can mediate the effects of other nonfamily sources of consumer information. *Direct* influences of family communication on a person's consumer behavior involve the acquisition of consumption-related information and the subsequent formation of patterns of beliefs, norms, and behaviors from other members. *Indirect* influences involve the learning of patterns of interaction with other sources of consumer information, which in turn might affect consumer learning. Finally, family communication might affect consumer learning by *mediating* the effects of other sources of consumer learning outside the family, such as the mass media and peers.

Childhood and Adolescence

Direct Influences

For discussion purposes, the direct effects of family are grouped into three categories:

1. consumer behavior—those aspects of consumer behavior young people learn from their parents without reference to specific communication processes, cognitive or overt
2. the effects of various types of family communication processes—that is, how the family influences consumer learning
3. effects of specific structures and patterns of overt family communication processes

Consumer Behavior. Riesman and Roseborough (1955) and others (Parsons et al. 1953) have speculated that the family is instrumental in teaching young people basic rational aspects of consumption, including basic consumer needs. Support for this speculation is provided by several studies. Ward and Wackman (1973) found that parents' general consumer goals for their children included learning price-quality relationships. In addition, Ward, Wackman, and Wartella (1977) found that such goals included experiences with use of money and learning to shop for quality products. Similarly, parent-adolescent communication about consumption predicted fairly well the child's knowledge of prices of selected products (Moore and Stephens 1975) and rational consumer behaviors such as managing money and comparative shopping (Moschis 1976a). In another study, the frequency of parent-child communication about consumption was positively associated with the adolescent's tendency to use price reduction (sales) as a criterion for choosing among brands (Moschis and Moore 1980).

In an earlier study of expenditure patterns and money management practices among approximately fifty-two thousand teenage girls, Hurt (1961) found that 47 percent of the seventh-graders reported parental assistance in deciding how to spend their money. This proportion declined with age, with only 27 percent of the twelfth-graders reporting parents' help. Similar findings were reported by Remmers and Radler (1957) in a study of teenagers (ninth- through twelfth-graders) over a fifteen-year period.

Parental influence on offspring consumer learning appears to extend beyond the rational elements of consumer decision making. Data reported in one study (Moore and Moschis 1978b) suggest that parents might encourage their children to work to save money for anticipatory consumption, especially for large ticket items. Another study found parental influence on both economic and social motivations for consumption (Churchill and Moschis 1979).

A study by Moschis and Moore (1984) revealed a significant relationship between family communication about consumption matters and the adolescent's career decision, suggesting that intrafamily interactions might provide opportunities for occupational socialization, a finding consistent with data reported by Levine (1976) and Kahl (1953). In addition, such interaction was associated with the adolescent's development of role perceptions regarding effective consumer behavior. These findings suggest that parents might be instrumental in teaching general as well as specific rational orientations regarding consumption, and they might emphasize normative consumer skills while interacting with their children.

Finally, parental influence might be an important factor in the development of several other dimensions of consumer behavior. For example, the study of Moschis and Moore (1984) found overt parent-child interactions to be associated with the development of desires for major types of products teenagers do not normally buy (such as a house). Similarly, two other studies suggested that the family might affect the development of materialistic orientations (Moore and Moschis 1978b and 1981b). Furthermore, a longitudinal study investigating the effects of family on adolescent consumer learning, both in the short run and in the long run, found parent-child interaction about consumption to have some long-run influence on the development of brand preferences as well as on the adolescent's ability to distinguish facts from exaggerations in advertising messages (Moschis 1984). Parental influence on adolescent brand preferences also is reported by Fauman (1966), Arndt 1971), and Yankelovich, Skelly, and White (Madison Avenue 1980), although the latter study inferred influence from mother-daughter similarity in brand preferences. Unfortunately, it is not clear from these studies how family communications affect brand preference development and whether such influence is the result of purposive parental training or is simply due to the availability of brands at home—that is, convenience. For example, a study of brand preferences among 1,346 college students indicated considerable influence of parents on bank patronage, with 93 percent of the freshmen patronizing the same bank their parents did. Such loyalty, however, might not be due to the child's preference but to the father's preference for convenience (Fry et al. 1973).

To summarize, there appears to be reasonably good supportive evidence that the family is instrumental in teaching young people basic rational aspects of consumption. It influences the development of rational consumption orientations related to a hierarchy of consumer decisions delineated by previous writers (see, for example, Arndt 1976; Olshavsky and Granbois 1979): spending and saving, expenditure allocation, and product decision, including some evaluative criteria. Considerably less is known about how parents influence their children's development of decision patterns regarding variant decisions such as brand and store preferences, as well as motives and information-processing skills.

Proposition 5.1: Parents are likely to influence the development of their offspring's selective preferences in the marketplace and processes leading to such preferences. They are likely to influence the development of:

    (a) preferences for brands
    (b) preferences for stores
    (c) motivations for consumption
    (d) skills relating to evaluation of information in advertising

The effects of family communication on the development of decision-making patterns appear to vary across stages of the decision-making process and type of product. For example, a cross-sectional study of the development of adolescents' decision-making process, with a greater likelihood of influence at the information-seeking stage than at the product-evaluation stage (Moschis and Moore 1979b). In a longitudinal analysis, family communication effects were found to be stronger on the development of information-seeking patterns than product-evaluation criteria (Moschis and Moore 1983).

Proposition 5.2: Parental influence on the consumer learning of their offspring is present, although not similar, across the main stages of the decision-making process. It is likely to affect the:

    (a) need-recognition stage
    (b) information-seeking stage
    (c) product-evaluation stage
    (d) purchase stage
    (e) postpurchase stage

Findings of a study of 608 adolescents also suggested that the effects of the family on adolescent consumer behavior might vary by type of product (Moschis et al. 1977). The data indicated that purchasing role structures vary significantly across selected items that are likely to be consumed by adolescents. Specifically, the data suggested that adolescent shopping goods (clothing) tend to be purchased jointly by the adolescent consumer and family members, whereas purchases of adolescent specialty goods (records or tapes, sporting equipment, and movie tickets) tend to be purchased in the absence of family members. Within the shopping goods category, the extent of adolescent–family member involvement in purchasing appears to be related to the social visibility and price of the product. These findings suggest that the degree of adolescent–family member involvement in purchasing might be a function of the socioeconomic risk present in a purchasing situation.

Another study of the development of decision-making patterns found that the extent to which adolescents take parental preferences or suggestions into account in choosing among brands might be a function of the perceived risk associated with the specific decision, with higher parental influence more likely to be present in purchases of high-risk products (Moschis and Moore 1979b). Other studies also have shown that family influence in the adolescent decision-making process is a function of product type. For example, research on child and adolescent decision making by Hamilton and Warden (1966), Vener (1957), Saunders et al. (1973), Mehrotra and Torges (1977), Belch et al. (1985), and Ward and Wackman (1972) suggested variation in parental influence by type of product.

Proposition 5.3: Parental influence on the consumer learning of their offspring varies by product characteristic.

(a) It is greater for decisions concerning shopping goods than for convenience or specialty goods.

(b) It is greater for decisions concerning products of high perceived risk.

Finally, family influence on the development of the youth's consumer decision-making patterns appears to be based on certain parent and child characteristics such as age, social class, and sex. Generally, youths attain greater family independence in decision making with age (see, for example, Moschis and Moore 1979b; Moschis et al. 1977; Vener 1957; Vener and Hoffer 1959), although the degree of independence varies by product type. The extent to which young people attain family independence in decision making might be conditioned by specific characteristics such as social class and sex. For example, middle-class adolescents appear to attain less independence in purchasing as they grow older than do adolescent consumers in lower and upper social classes. This finding has been attributed to middle-class families' greater consciousness of the normative standards of their class and their subsequent greater desire to supervise their children's activities closely in an effort to socialize them into the class norms (Moschis et al. 1977; Psathas 1957).

Alternatively, it can be attributed to the youth's ability to attain independence from the family as a result of contributions to the family. Parental power and control over the offspring's activities outside the home, including purchasing, appear to be influenced by the economic resources available to the child (Saunders et al. 1973). Once children begin to earn money outside the family, they are less subject to parental control by manipulation of resources. Studies show that adolescents from working classes are more likely to be needed for help in the home and as a result might attain greater independence from their parents. For the middle-class child who has long-range plans (such as college attendance), parents are better able to continue exercising influence through control of resources (Clausen 1968b).

Thus, socioeconomic influences might apply to stages in the decision-making process (need-recognition, information-seeking, product-evaluation, purchase, and postpurchase stages). In fact, in a more recent study, socioeconomic status was positively related with the adolescent's propensity to mention the need for a variety of products to parents but negatively related ($r = -.21$, $p < .01$) to the child's propensity to purchase these products (Moschis and Mitchell 1986).

Parental influence on the development of consumer behavior also appears to be affected by the sex of the child. For example, the greater need for conformity to group norms found among female adolescents (see, for example, Cannon et al. 1952; Saunders et al. 1973; Vener 1957) was reflected in their purchasing patterns through greater family independence (thus less influence) in purchasing products relevant to physical appearance, such as health care products and clothing (shirts and jeans) (Moschis et al. 1977).

Finally, parental influence on the consumer socialization of their children is likely to be affected by family characteristics. Aldous (1974), for example, speculated that children of working mothers might be socialized better or faster because they often are expected to take on more consumer responsibilities than children of non-working mothers. In fact, some studies have found that teenage girls of working mothers are brand conscious and tend to shop for specific brands (Quick Frozen Foods 1979). Similarly, advertisements for *Seventeen* magazine claim that 62.5 percent of teenage girls do food shopping for the family and spend 40 percent of the family's food budget (Advertising Age 1984), suggesting that parents might award their teenage girls greater independence in making family decisions or encourage greater involvement in family decisions. In fact, one study found female teenagers to be more likely than their male counterparts to have major influences on all stages of family decisions (Moschis and Mitchell 1986). Such interactions might affect consumer learning.

Proposition 5.4: Parental influence on the consumer learning of their offspring is affected by the child's sociodemographic characteristics.

(a) Parental influence on consumer decision declines with age to a significantly greater extent among lower- and upper-class youths than among middle-class youths.

(b) Parental influence on stages in the consumer decision process is greater among middle-class than among lower- and upper-class youths.

(c) For products of high social risk, parental influence on decision-making patterns of their offspring is stronger on boys than on girls.

(d) Parental influence on consumer learning is greater among girls than among boys.

Socialization Processes. While the family is believed to be an important source of consumer information, the ways in which it influences the child's consumer learning are not clearly known. Engel and his colleagues (1978), for example, after reviewing related literature, concluded that "the family plays an important role in interpersonal communication in the socialization of children," but the specific ways it might influence consumer learning were not clear (p. 280). Similarly, Ward (1974b) summarized much of the consumer socialization literature and concluded:

> The studies show that there is a great deal of parental activity, both purposive and non-purposive, which is related to children's experience with money, attitudes toward consumption, purchase influence attempts and the success of those attempts, and so forth. These studies were far from explicit, however, concerning how family members influence children in ways which affect their present, if limited, behavior as consumers or the patterns of consumer behavior they will adopt in the future. (pp. 31–32)

Ward and his colleagues (1977) identified five methods mothers use to teach children consumer skills:

1. prohibiting certain acts
2. giving lectures on consumer activities
3. holding discussions with the child about consumer decisions
4. acting as an example
5. allowing the child to learn form his or her own experiences

Their research further showed that most mothers use relatively few teaching methods and that there is considerable variation among mothers in how they teach their child consumer skills.

Most consumer socialization research examining family influences has focused on overt interaction processes, in particular, communication about consumption (see, for example, Moschis 1985; Ward and Wackman 1971). These studies have investigated how such interactions affect consumption-related properties. Overt interaction processes could be classified as social interaction mechanisms, according to McLeod and O'Keefe (1972), lacking a specific structure or pattern, although a few studies (see, for example, Moore and Moschis 1981b; Moschis and Moore 1978) recently have examined family communication structures and patterns in line with McLeod and Chaffee's (1972) typology. Consumer learning has been found to be related not only to frequency but also to the patterns or quality of communication that takes place within the home (Moschis 1985). This is in line with family communication patterns (FCP) research in political socialization, where patterns were found to have a more important influence than frequency or amount of parent-child interaction (McLeod and Chaffee 1972).

Although the family plays an important role in the consumer socialization of the young, parental influence often is incidental, far from purposive consumer training. In fact, the study by Ward and his associates (1977) suggests that parents often expect their children to learn through observation. Parent-child discussions about consumption are most likely to be initiated as a result of the child's request for a product he or she sees advertised.

Moschis, Moore, and Smith (1984) examined the effects of several communication processes simultaneously. The results suggest that different processes might be used in the transmission of consumer cognitions and behaviors from parent to child. Parents, in general, make limited attempts to teach their children consumer skills. Such limited efforts seems to focus on the desirability of performing certain acts (behaviors) but provide little education or understanding (cognitions). Cognitions appear to be acquired from parents (especially consumer behavior norms) through observation, suggesting that parents might try to act as role models to their children and then expect them to learn such roles through observation.

In an earlier study, Marshall and Magruder (1960) found that children are more knowledgeable of the use of money when they are given wide experience and opportunity in saving and spending and when their parents handle the family income wisely. Knowledge of the use of money was not increased by giving an allowance or providing an opportunity to earn money at home. Fairly similar findings were reported by Phelan and Schvaneveldt (1969). These findings suggest that money management skills might develop as a result of purposive consumer training, positive reinforcement, or observation of parental consumer behaviors.

Studies examining reinforcement mechanisms are almost nonexistent. A recent study of adolescent consumer socialization suggests that positive reinforcement might encourage the development of effective consumer behaviors, whereas negative reinforcement might constrain the development of consumer knowledge (Moschis, Moore, and Smith 1984).

These findings suggest that two types of communication processes might be of primary importance in transmitting cognitive and behavioral orientations from parent to child. Overt communication processes might be important in teaching behavioral dimensions, while modeling influences might be important in transmitting cognitive and effective norms.

Proposition 5.5: Different communication processes, both overt and cognitive, operate in the transmission of consumer behaviors from parent to child.

    (a) Parental purposive consumer training of their offspring focuses on performing socially desirable consumer behaviors.

    (b) Observation of parental behavior by the offspring is likely to lead to the development of socially desirable consumer values and norms.

    (c) Positive reinforcement encourages the development of socially desirable consumer behaviors.

    (d) Negative reinforcement constrains the development of consumer knowledge.

Furthermore, theory and research suggest that socialization processes vary by sociodemographic characteristics, including age, sex, social class, and race. Specifically, adolescents' frequency of interaction with the family regarding consumption matters has been shown to decline with age (see, for example, Moschis and Churchill 1978; Moschis, Moore, and Smith 1984), but this does not necessarily imply that the family's influence over the youth's consumer behavior declines. For example, the study reported by Moore and Moschis (1983) found that although overt communication about consumption declines with age, the adolescent's tendency to observe parental behaviors is not related to age. This observational measure was a strong predictor of some aspects of the adolescent's consumer behaviors, especially consumer role perceptions. Reinforcement mechanisms (such as giving the child an allowance) are likely to be frequent during early childhood (Ward et al. 1977). With increasing age, children might find other sources of income, thus reducing their economic dependence on parents. This, in turn, might diminish the importance of the reinforcement mechanism and, consequently, parent-child interaction about consumption.

Another study examined the effects of sex and other characteristics on various family communication processes, including overt parent-child communication about consumption, modeling processes, reinforcement (positive and negative), and family communication patterns (Moschis, Moore, and Smith 1984). Males were found to be less likely than females to communicate overtly with their parents about consumption and less likely to receive positive reinforcement; they were more likely to receive negative reinforcement. These findings suggest that parents might treat their offspring differently (on the basis of their sex) while interacting with them about consumption matters. The results of another study (Moschis and Moore 1979a) seem to support this line of reasoning. Specifically, the study investigated relationships between several adolescent-parent interactions and selected dependent variables by sex. Frequency of adolescents' communication with their parents was correlated with their ability to retain information in advertisements and level of knowledge about consumer matters only among females, suggesting that purposive consumer training might focus on teaching the female child more than the male child.

The extent to which parents influence a child's consumer socialization does not appear to depend only on the youth's sex but also on the sex of siblings and birth order position among siblings. In further analyzing data used in the Moschis and Moore (1979b) study, we assessed the influence of various socialization processes, including various measures of family communication processes, on the development of several consumer orientations among males with older male siblings versus females with older female siblings. Significant differences in the effectiveness of socialization processes emerged between the two groups. For example, negative reinforcement provided by parents was more significant in producing negative effects among later-born girls with older sisters than among later-born boys with older brothers; positive reinforcement was more effective among adolescents in the latter group. Family interaction about consumption was positively associated with only one criterion variable among girls (desirable consumer behaviors), suggesting that the presence of older siblings might diminish the influence (effectiveness) of parents in the consumer socialization processes—that is, parents might not talk to later-born children as frequently as they talk to firstborns about consumption matters.

Furthermore, previous theory and research suggest that communication processes vary by social class and race of the child. For example, socialization theory suggests that socialization practices tend to vary among families of different socioeconomic characteristics (Hess 1970). This also appears to be the case in the specific area of consumer socialization. Previous research has suggested that purposive parental training of youths is more likely to occur among upper social class families than among families from lower socioeconomic backgrounds (Ward and Wackman 1973). Similarly, another study of adolescents examined relationships between measures of adolescent-parent interactions and several dependent variables among lower-, middle-, and upper-class adolescents (Moschis and Moore 1979a). The data showed that parent-child communication about consumption is associated with the youth's consumer role perceptions only among children from upper social classes, suggesting that purposive consumer training might occur only in upper social strata. Discussions about consumer matters with parents among middle-class adolescents appear to focus on product attributes (such as price), while in lower classes they focus on product brand names.

In the study by Moschis, Moore, and Smith (1984), the effects of adolescent observation of parental behaviors also were assessed by socioeconomic and racial factors. Observation of parental behaviors was associated with increasing brand preferences among lower-class and black adolescents but with decreasing preferences for brands and increasing consumer knowledge among middle-class adolescents. These findings suggest that such learning might be due to the middle-class family's inclination to "shop around"—thus consider a larger number of alternatives (e.g., Engel et al. 1978)—a behavior which can be imitated by the youngster and expressed in terms of weak brand loyalties. Lower-class and black youths, on the other hand, might develop preferences for brands as a means of avoiding mistakes in decision making (Bauer et al. 1965). In another study, observation of parental behaviors was found to be more frequent among white than among black adolescents (Moschis and Moore 1985). This appeared to be the case even after controlling for socioeconomic status.

Proposition 5.6: Parental communication processes and their effects on children's consumer learning vary by socioeconomic characteristics.

(a) Overt parent-child communication about consumption declines with age.

(b) Overt parent-child communication is more frequent between parents and their male children than between parents and their female children.

(c) Purposive consumer training is more likely to be directed at the female child than the male child.

(d) Purposive consumer training is more likely to be present in upper-class than lower-class families.

(e) Purposive consumer training is more likely to be directed at firstborn than later-born children.

(f) Negative reinforcement is more likely to constrain development of desirable consumer behaviors among females with older sisters than among males with older brothers.

(g) White youths are more likely than their black counterparts to learn consumer behavior through observation.

Structures and Patterns of Communication. Socialization studies also have examined the effects of family communication structures on consumer learning. Ward (1974b) speculated that families stressing conformity to others might implicitly encourage children to "learn to purchase and to derive satisfaction from their purchases, on the basis of the perceived effects on others" (p. 40). Thus, it can be speculated that a socio-oriented communication structure, which encourages the child to develop respect for others and other social orientations, might lead to the development of materialistic orientations and the learning of expressive aspects of consumption.

The data presented in two studies support this line of reasoning. The correlations between a socio-oriented family communication structure and materialism were statistically significant, while the relationship between a concept-oriented communication structure and materialism was insignificant (Moore and Moschis 1978b and 1981b). The findings further suggested that parents who emphasize the importance of pleasant social relationships in the family (a socio-oriented structure) in their communication with their children might implicity encourage their children to evaluate their actions (including consumption behaviors) on the basis of their perceived effects on others. This might result in the development of materialistic orientations in the children's consumer behavior.

With respect to the adolescent's preference for kinds of information, previous research had speculated that the socio-oriented person would be sensitive to social kinds of information, while the concept-oriented person would be sensitive to information regarding functional aspects of the situation (McLeod and Chaffee 1972). The data presented in one study appear to support this line of reasoning. Emphasis on socio-oriented communication at home correlated positively with the adolescent's preferences for social kinds of information and negatively with preferences for functional or rational types of information (Moore and Moschis 1978b).

The importance of socio-orientation also was illustrated in a study by Stone and Chaffee (1970). Subjects were presented with a list of twenty topics and asked to indicate for each whether "who says it" or "what is said" is more important. It was found that high socio-oriented subjects (protective and consensual) were more source-oriented ("who says it"), while the low socio-oriented subjects (pluralistic and laissez-faire) were more message-oriented. When the subjects were given messages in which the expertise of the source was manipulated, the high socio-oriented subjects showed higher overall levels of attitude change.

The effects of parent-child communication structures also were evaluated at the group (family) level by asking the adolescent's mother to indicate the extent to which the child mentions the need for products, discusses purchases, decides what or where to buy, and actually buys products for the child's and the family's use (Moschis and Mitchell 1986). The data revealed that a socio-oriented communication structure was negatively related with the adolescent's likelihood to make consumer decisions for himself or his family. Although the correlations between concept orientation and the adolescent's role at the same stages of the decision process were not statistically significant, the findings suggest that such communication processes might have a stronger impact at the individual than at the group level.

If family communication structures influence consumer learning, one would expect youths from homes stressing the socio-oriented family communication dimension (A-B relationships in line with Newcomb's [1953] A-B-X model) to behave according to a nonrational or social influence model, while those from concept-oriented families stressing A-X and B-X relationships would behave according to a rational or economic model (see also Bauer 1964 and 1967).

Other aspects of consumer behavior likely to be affected by a socio-oriented communication structure include social attribution processes and gift-giving behavior. A person's desire to conform to the perceived expectations of others—a definition of normative social influence (Deutsch and Gerard 1955)—is likely to prevail among individuals characterized by a socio-oriented family communication structure. Judging others as persons on the basis of their consumption habits most likely would be a tendency among individuals from a socio-oriented family communication background. Similarly, gift-giving often is viewed as an expected obligation and is found within the nuclear family and among close kin (James, Lehman, and James 1985). Again, such normative expectation is most likely to be of greatest importance to those who value interpersonal (A-B) relationships—that is, those who come from a socio-oriented communication background. Consumer behavior differences by family communication structure at home can be summarized in the following propositions:

Proposition 5.7: A socio-oriented family communication structure fosters the development of consumer needs and behaviors geared to evaluating others and conforming to generally accepted norms.

    (a) It contributes to the youth's development of desires for products of social significance.

    (b) It contributes to the develpment of gift-giving behavior.

Proposition 5.8: A concept-oriented family communication structure fosters the development of consumer needs and behaviors geared to evaluating alternatives according to their objective (nonsocial) attributes.

    (a) It contributes to the youth's development of economic motivations for consumption.

    (b) It contributes to the development of rational (nonimpulse) oriented consumer behaviors.

With respect to the influence of the specific family communication patterns on consumer learning, the results of recent research are fairly similar to those found in the study of political socialization. Specifically, children from families characterized by insistence on conceptual matters and absence of social constraints on their communications (pluralistics) were found to have more knowledge about consumer-related matters; they were better able to filter puffery in advertising and to manage a typical family budget; they had more information about products and their characteristics; and they were more likely to perform socially desirable consumer behaviors (Moore and Moschis 1978b; Moschis and Moore 1979c and 1979d). In addition, pluralistic children had significantly greater preferences for functional kinds of information than did children from the other three groups. Thus, it would seem that preferences for functional types of information might develop when the family communication structure is characterized by a positive impetus for self-expression and lacks social constraints.

The study by Moore and Moschis (1978b) also examined the extent to which adolescent preferences for type of information sources vary by family communication pattern. Previous research suggested that laissez-faire children, in the absence of any parent-child communication at home, might tend to rely less on parents and more on external sources of consumer information, such as peer groups (McLeod and Chaffee 1972). Pluralistic children, who seem to show a relatively higher regard for their parents' opinions, were expected to prefer this source of consumer information more than their counterparts in the other groups. Since they are trained to evaluate several alternatives prior to decision making, they would show relatively higher preferences for sources of consumer information containing a large number of alternative solutions, such as *Consumer Reports* (Chaffee et al. 1966; McLeod and Chaffee 1971). Protective children were expected to be more susceptible to (therefore, have greater preferences for) consumer information from both peer groups and persuasive messages in the mass media (Eswara 1968; Stone and Chaffee 1970).

It was found that laissez-faire children, as expected, tended to rely relatively less on their parents as a source of consumer information. They did not, however, necessarily tend to rely more on peers; rather, they were less likely to rely on peer groups. Pluralistic children tended to prefer parental advice to a greater extent than did children from the other three groups, and they showed relatively greater preferences for information contained in *Consumer Reports*, as posited. Children from pluralistic homes also were more likely to pay attention to consumer news in the mass media than were their counterparts, and they tended to prefer information from a variety of communication sources, in line with the researchers' expectations. The data also seem to support the reasoning that children from protective homes are highly receptive to (thus susceptible to) consumer information from external sources such as peers and to a lesser extent television advertisements. This susceptibility to outside influences has been attributed to parental efforts to protect children from controversy within the home (McLeod and Chaffee 1972).

The influence of family communication patterns as they affect similar consumer learning properties also was investigated among 734 adolescents in rural and urban Georgia (Moore and Moschis 1980 and 1981b). As expected, adolescents from pluralistic homes were found to know more about consumer matters, and they were more likely to perform consumer activities portrayed as socially desirable. In addition, these children tended to score lower on materialism than their counterparts. Additional analysis of these data found pluralistics to be more likely than their counterparts in other FCP groups to have preferences for brands, negative attitudes toward the marketplace, greater purchasing independence, and egalitarian sex role perceptions. Consensuals were more likely to have positive attitudes toward the marketplace and be dissatisfied with the products they bought or used (Moschis et al. 1986).

In another study of the development of consumer skills among children, it was found that children learned consumer skills when they were given opportunities to participate in consumer decision making and share family responsibilities (Turner and Brandt 1978). Although the study did not directly examine the effects of family communication patterns, those practices found to foster the development of consumer skills were more likely to be present among pluralistic families than any other type of family (Moschis 1985). The Moschis et al. (1986) study clearly shows that youths in pluralistic homes have greater opportunities to participate in family decisions.

When adolescents were asked to report how disagreements among family members regarding purchases usually were resolved, pluralistics were more likely to report joint participation (voting) by family members and were less likely to report that the father dominated the conflict resolution process. Father dominance in the conflict resolution process was greater among protectives than among adolescents in any other FCP group. This is not surprising, given that parental authority is better recognized in a traditional sex role setting (husband dominant, wife dominant), and this is likely to result in fewer requests from children (Davis 1976).

> Proposition 5.9: The family communication patterns to which a young person is exposed early in life directly influence the development of his or her consumer behavior.
>
> (a) A pluralistic FCP pattern fosters the development of consumer competencies.
>
> (b) A pluralistic FCP pattern fosters the development of egalitarian sex role attitudes.
>
> (c) A protective FCP pattern contributes to a person's susceptibility to influences outside the home, both commercial and noncommercial.

Indirect Influences

In addition to direct effects family communication processes appear to have on consumer learning, such processes might affect consumer behavior indirectly. Indirect influence can take place when family communication processes influence the offspring's interaction with other sources of consumer information, which, in turn, directly (or again indirectly) affect the development of consumer behaviors. The findings of several studies have established the presence of relationships between family communication processes, including family coimmunication patterns, and an individual's interaction with other socialization agents (see, for example, Lull 1980b; McLeod, Fitzpatrick, Glynn, and Fallis 1982), which subsequently affect behavior. This indirect pattern of family influence also has been found in studies of consumer socialization. In fact, path analysis suggests that different communication processes that take place within the home might lead to differential exposure to and use of the mass media (newspapers and television), which, in turn, could lead to the development of various consumer orientations (Moore and Moschis 1981b). Thus, indirectly, family communication might influence a child's interaction with other socialization agents, which then might influence consumer learning.

Previous researchers have reported that purposive consumer training is a rare occurrence at home (Ward 1974a; Ward et al. 1977), suggesting that the effect of family communication on consumer and political skill acquisition is strongly related to the child's frequency of reading and viewing consumer or political news, which is influenced by the family communication structures at home (Chaffee et al. 1971). Similarly, the results of a longitudinal study (Moschis and Moore 1982) suggest that learning from television might be a second-order consequence of interpersonal processes, including family communication. These results appear to be consistent with longitudinal findings in political socialization (Atkin and Gantz 1978), and they are in line with speculations about learning from television based on cross-sectional data (Moschis and Churchill 1978).

Learning from the mass media might be a direct consequence of the family communication environment that prevails at home. If the environment imposes strain, the person is likely to be motivated to "get away from it all" by becoming immersed in fantasy (Maccoby 1954). Television in particular is rich in fantasy-oriented programming. Findings reported by Schramm and his colleagues (1961) show that adolescents who report conflict with their parents tend to watch more television than those who experience less parental friction. Similarly, McLeod and Chaffee (1972) attributed the greater inclination among consensuals to view fantasy-oriented programs to conflict that is likely to be created by the two rather diverse family communication structures.

With respect to other types of influence of specific parent-child communication processes on mass media use, one study examined whether motivations for television viewing could be the result of the family communication structure at home (Moore and Moschis 1981b). It was speculated that a socio-oriented communication structure might implicitly encourage the child to pay attention to the mass media as a means of learning how to behave in various social settings. The results were in line with this expectation, suggesting that families characterized by a socio-oriented communication structure might be encouraging their children to turn to the media to learn social orientations or consumption behaviors appropriate to certain roles. This might then lead to the learning of materialistic orientations, as people are believed to learn expressive aspects of consumption from the mass media (see, for example, Moschis and Moore 1982; Parsons et al. 1953). Similar findings are reported by Lull (1980b), whose research has shown that socio-oriented individuals use television for social purposes.

Additional support for these speculations comes from previous research (Moschis 1976a; Ward and Wackman 1971), which also found that materialistic attitudes are related to social motivations for watching television commercials and programs (for example, watching commercials and programs to learn what products to buy to make good impressions on others) and that such motivations are the result of the family communication structure at home (Moore and Moschis 1981b; Moschis and Moore 1979b).

Moreover, these studies show that a concept-oriented family communication structure is positively associated with exposure to public affairs information in the mass media (see, for example, Chaffee et al. 1971), which in turn might have a positive impact on consumer knowledge and other consumer competencies (Moschis and Moore 1979c and 1979d; Moschis, Moore, and Smith 1984). For example, the results of a path analysis of 301 Wisconsin adolescents (Moschis and Moore 1979c and 1979d) suggest that a concept-oriented family communication structure leads to exposure to public affairs information in the mass media, which subsequently might lead to the learning of consumer skills. The influence does not appear to be direct or to be totally explained by the antecedent variables. Specifically, age and a concept-oriented family communication structure were the best predictors of an adolescent's frequency of interacting with the media regarding public affairs content (frequency of reading advertisements and news about the economy and government, and frequency of viewing national and local news on television). Similar findings emerged from data collected in Georgia (Moore and Moschis 1981b).

Additionally, family influences might operate indirectly by affecting the child's social relations with peer groups. Social comparison theory (Festinger 1954) suggests that adolescents need to evaluate some of their perceived knowledge about consumption acquired from their parents by comparing it with the knowledge of other persons who are likely to have similar value perspectives about consumption. Such persons are likely to be peers (Sebald 1968), and empirical findings are in line with this type of reasoning. For example, a study of adolescent females by Brittain (1963) showed that in areas such as taste in clothes, in which girls perceived their ideas to be like those of their peers, the girls tended to favor peer-suggested alternatives. Similarly, several other studies suggest that the typical teenager is responsive to peer opinions on topics about which they have similar interests, opinions, and attitudes, such as clothes choice and hairstyle (Moschis and Moore 1979b; Remmers and Radler 1957; Saunders et al. 1973; Vener 1957). Another study demonstrated a positive relationship between frequency of communication about consumption with peers and frequency of communication about consumption with parents (Moore and Moschis 1978a). While these findings do not show explicitly how family communication processes affect peer relations, they do suggest that the youths are likely to discuss topics discussed at home with peers.

It also is possible that peer communications initiated outside the home are likely to be discussed with parents. One study that attempted to determine the flow of influence of interpersonal communication was not successful in isolating the effects of family communication about consumption on peer communication about consumption and vice versa. The data show, however, that family communication about consumption might lead to communication with peers about such matters, a finding that can be interpreted in line with Festinger's theory of social comparison (Churchill and Moschis 1979). Thus, a child's need to evaluate some consumption-related cognitions learned at home might cause that child to seek out others who are similar and to initiate discussions with them. This need also is likely to be magnified by the straining of parent-child relationships, a consequence of several psychosocial and biological processes.

> The adolescent's search for identity, rapid intellectual development, preoccupation with the projection of a positive physical image, evolving sexual drive, and an almost overwhelming need for peer acceptance all contribute to another unique characteristic of this stage in the life cycle, the straining of parent-child relationships. Conflicts between parents and teenagers often result from the adolescent's

repeated attempts at achieving independence and defending emerging personal values which are not yet in harmony with an adult world. Adolescents desire freedom from parental restrictions involving courtship, selection of friends, use of leisure time, hairstyles and dress, academic performance, selection of career goals, and domestic responsibilities, among others. Thus, early and mid-adolescence might be described as a period of attempted escape from parental influence, and frequent disassociation from other members of the family unit. (Avery 1979, 55)

Other researchers view the influence of parent-child interaction on other socialization agents as a by-product of family or family member characteristics. For example, poor adjustment among family members is likely to result in a greater orientation of children toward peer groups rather than toward family members (Bowerman and Kinch 1959). Similarly, Donohue (1975b) showed that emotionally disturbed teenagers who have trouble identifying with their parents and have difficulty exhibiting appropriate behaviors are more likely to imitate the behavior of their favorite television character.

One rather unexplored area concerns the effect of specific family communication patterns on other parent-child communication processes. Analysis of our Georgia data used in the Moschis and Moore (1981a) study suggested that family communication patterns might relate to the effectiveness of other parent-child interaction processes. Specifically, the parent-child similarity of attitudes and behaviors (which often is used as a measure of modeling processes; see chapter 4) varied in family communication patterns. The strength of the relationship (similarity) between attitudes toward the marketplace and consumer discontent was significant only for laissez-faire families; attitudes toward money were most similar among protective families; and positive (effective) consumer behaviors were most similar for consensual families. These findings suggest that family communication patterns might affect other family communication processes.

In sum, the findings suggest that family communication processes lead to rather different interaction patterns with other agents of consumer socialization, which in turn affect consumer learning. Considerably less is known about the specific family communication processes leading to specific interactions and how these subsequently affect consumer learning. The preceding discussion can be summarized as:

Proposition 5.10: Family communication about consumption, including frequency and structure of family communication that takes place within the home, indirectly affects consumer learning by affecting interaction with other socialization agents.

    (a) A concept-oriented family communication structure leads to higher use of public affairs information in the mass media.

    (b) A socio-oriented family communication structure leads to higher use of the mass media for social purposes.

(c) The frequency of a youth's interaction with parents about consumption leads to communication with peers about such matters.

(d) Family communication patterns affect other types of parent-child communication processes.

Mediating Effects

There is considerable evidence to suggest that family communication processes modify the effects of other socialization agents, particularly television (Comstock et al. 1978; McLeod, Fitzpatrick, Glynn, and Fallis 1982). The mediating role of family communication also has been investigated in the context of consumer socialization. After reviewing studies on the effects of television advertising, Robertson (1979) concluded that parents mediate such affects. Additional studies (Churchill and Moschis 1979; Moschis and Moore 1982) found that the effects of television advertising on consumer learning were contingent on the adolescent's frequency of communication with parents about consumption matters, with television advertising effects having a stronger impact among families where discussions about consumption were less frequent.

Parental mediation often is the result of a child's requests for advertised products. For example, Atkin (1982) found that parents and children often discuss and argue over consumer purchase decisions that are stimulated by television advertising. Such discussions and opportunities for mediation can be attributed to high adult-child coviewing behavior, which has been estimated to be as high as 70 percent of prime-time programming (Nielsen 1975).

While the family's mediating role is well documented, the nature and consequences of parental mediation are not very clear. Reviews outside the field of consumer behavior suggest that parental mediation of television effects are either strengthened or weakened in the interpersonal context (McLeod, Fitzpatrick, Glynn, and Fallis 1982). There is some evidence to suggest that the impact of influences outside the family, such as television advertising, is greater under conditions of parental restrictiveness (Atkin, Reeves, and Gibson 1979). Similarly, Hawkins and Pingree (1982) found reduced effects of television for youngsters in families that are low in conflict and parental control. These findings might be attributed to family communication patterns. For example, it has been found that protective families stress obedience and social harmony and make a conscious effort to protect the child from controversy within the home. Since parental control using restrictiveness is likely to be present in these families, parental efforts to protect the child within the home might leave the youngster unprotected from outside influences (McLeod and Chaffee 1972). Thus, it is not surprising that studies find children from protective homes to be susceptible to the influence of external sources such as peers and television advertising (Moore and Moschis 1978b).

To summarize, the evidence indicates that the family mediates the effects of socialization agents on consumer learning. Such mediation is the result of the opportunity for mediation, such as parent-child television coviewing behavior. The specific effects of parental mediation on consumer socialization are not clear and have been examined mainly in the context of television advertising. These appear to be a function of parent-child relations, including family communication processes.

Proposition 5.11: Family communication processes modify and channel the influence of information from nonfamily sources.

(a) Television advertising viewing stimulates parent-child communication about consumption.

(b) Parent-child communication about consumption weakens the effects of television advertising.

(c) A protective family communication pattern contributes to the youth's susceptibility to television advertising more than any other family communication pattern.

(d) A protective family communication pattern contributes to the youth's susceptibility to peer groups more than any other family communication pattern.

The evidence presented regarding the effects of family communication in the consumer socialization of youths suggests the model shown in figure 5-1. Specifically, the findings suggest that parent-child communication directly affects the youth's acquisition of consumer-related properties. It also indirectly affects consumer socialization because family relations affect levels of, types of, and motivations for interactions with the mass media and peer groups, and such interactions are likely to result in the acquisition of additional aspects of consumer behavior. Finally, family members (parents in particular) mediate the effects of other socialization agents by modifying and channeling the interpretation the youth makes of the information received from the mass media and peers; family members act as gatekeepers, filtering the information the youth receives from these sources.

Adulthood

Consumer learning appears to be a continuous process. It does not appear to stop when the child matures, but it continues throughout a person's life cycle (Moschis 1981b). The consumer learning of the adult is likely to be affected by a large number of socialization agents. Many types of consumer decisions are made within the family, and various family members are likely to influence the adult consumer. The socialization agents exerting such influence might include the spouse as well as the children (Riesman and Roseborough 1955; Davis 1976; Murphy and Staples 1979). Such influences are likely to vary over the family life cycle. For example,

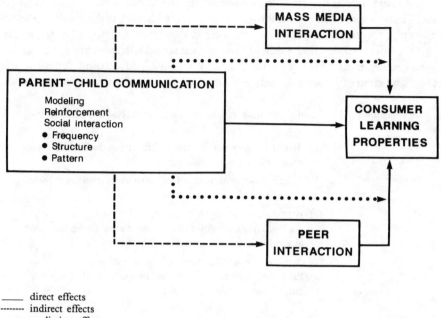

_____ direct effects
------- indirect effects
.... mediating effects

Figure 5–1. A Model of Family Communication Influences on Children's Consumer Socialization

joint involvement in decision making decreases with the presence of children (Kenkel 1961) and generally decreases over the family life cycle (Engel et al. 1978).

One important aspect of socialization in later life derives from the reciprocal relationship between parent and offspring. This reciprocal relationship may play a part in socializing the parent during his or her later years (Riley et al. 1969). Riesman and Roseborough (1955) called this retroactive socialization. It is important to recognize the reciprocal nature of socialization, particularly as it relates to the family. Riley et al. (1969) posit that:

> As the socializing agent interacts with the individual he is training, he himself may thereby learn new or modified norms and attitudes—rather than merely reinforcing old ones . . . As the parent socializes the child, he almost certainly as a consequence both teaches certain things to himself and also learns from the growing child . . . Training the child to adapt to a changing world or a higher status may require the parent himself to seek new understandings (from the mass media, e.g., or from friends) . . . So too, the parent who helps his child to apply family norms outside the family (such as honesty in testing situations in school) may have to revise his expectations in line with the child's reports of revised norms applied to new situations. (p. 961)

Margaret Mead (1970) observed that today's adolescents have more influence on their parents than at any other time in the past. She noted that society is approaching a "prefigurative culture" (rather than configurative) in which adults are socialized by the young, offering specific examples such as clothing styles, hairstyles, and music.

Adult socialization often is considered resocialization. Resocialization occurs because a new situation or a new role requires a person to replace established patterns of thoughts and actions with new ones. In one study, children and adolescents were found to play an important role in the resocialization of the parent, influencing both attitudes and behaviors in areas such as sports, leisure, minority groups, youth, drug use, and sexuality (Peters 1985). Such influences also might apply to consumer socialization. Baranowski's (1978) research shows that adolescents attempt to influence their parents' behavior. The study shows attempted influence in personal appearance, day-to-day activities, repairs and decorating, and car purchases. Attempts to influence were more frequently directed at the mother rather than the father. Fathers tended to be viewed as autocratic, while mothers were seen as permissive. Another example of the effects of child-initiated communication can be found in parental learning about home computers. On many occasions, parents have been found to purchase a home computer as a result of child-initiated communication, and they learn to use the product with the help of children (Pollack 1982).

Most of the research on the effects of children on adults has been in the context of the child's influence on specific family decisions (see, for example, Assael 1984). For example, research has suggested that the influence of the child varies by product class, decision stage, and subdivision area (Belch et al. 1985; Darley and Lim 1986; Moschis and Mitchell 1986). While such interactions might appear to have few direct implications for adult consumer socialization, the literature on the emergence and identity of self among symbolic interaction theorists supports the socialization perspective. Parents often look to their children for affirmation of successfully fulfilling their parenting role (Peters 1985). Thus, children's requests for products or suggestions about family purchases might help parents redefine their consumer role to incorporate their children's expectations, resulting in resocialization to a modified consumer role.

The role of a parent in relation to a growing child changes over time, gradually moving from disciplinarian, to counselor to friend. Through these developmental stages, the parent might shift his or her self-perception from parent-teacher to parent-friend. At the latter stage, the child is seen as independent and responsible, increasing the parent's likelihood of learning from the child.

Similar adjustments in self-perceptions are likely to occur after marriage. One spouse can act as a socialization agent to the other in redefining self-perceptions of the consumer role in the context of the family. Unfortunately, little socialization research exists on direct spousal influence processes and outcomes. The existing research focuses primarily on power relations rather than communication processes and examines influences in the context of husband-wife decision making rather than socialization (see, for example, Engle and Blackwell 1982; Schiffman and Kanuk 1983). Some recent research focusing on husband-wife interaction processes focused on patterns of interaction; it did not examine the consequences of these interactions for consumer socialization (Brinberg and Schwenk 1985).

Peters (1985) suggested that optimal parental socialization occurs in families in which affectivity remains mutually high, the members enjoy mutual respect, and parental power is not exercised. A democratic parent is expected to be more amenable to socialization from his child; an authoritarian parent is expected to be less amenable (Baranowski 1978). These observations are parallel to family communication patterns and processes, in which pluralistic families tend to have democratic patterns, while protective families tend to have authoritative tendencies.

One important aspect of interaction between child and parent is the indirect effect the child can have on adult socialization. Studies, for example, show that the interaction between spouses increases as a result of dealing with their child (see Peters 1985). Relatively little research seems to exist with respect to the process by which family members influence other members' consumer behavior, although some research suggests that a reinforcement mechanism (including, for example, affection or psychological punishment) might operate (Davis 1976).

Proposition 5.12: Adult consumer learning is influenced by communication processes with spouse and children.

(a) The communication effects of family members are specific to the life-cycle stage.

(b) Different learning mechanisms are involved in the consumer learning of adults than in the consumer learning of children and adolescents.

(c) The influence of children on parents is functionally related to family communication patterns.

(d) Children from pluralistic homes are likely to have more influence on the consumer socialization of their parents.

Late Adulthood

In later life socialization, major modifications of the familiar early learning model must be made, focusing on reciprocal communication between parent and offspring, which might play a part in socializing the parent during his or her later years (Riley et al. 1969). There appears to be ample opportunity for parents to learn from their offspring. Studies have found relatives to be important sources of consumer information for the elderly (Klippel and Sweeney 1974; Schiffman 1971). The child's influence on parental consumer socialization and consumer behavior is demonstrated in a study examining the decision of the elderly with regard to entering a nursing home. The study found significant participation by relatives in the decision-making process (Baumgarten et al. 1976).

A child's influence is likely to continue even during later stages in the parent's life cycle. For example, studies of elderly consumer socialization suggest that the development and change of elderly consumer orientations regarding consumption are related to the person's communication with other family members, including their children (see, for example, Smith 1982; Smith et al. 1982). The child's influence on elderly consumer behavior is in line with the social breakdown theory, which suggests that changes in behavior are the result of demands made by the person's immediate social environment (Kuypers and Bengston 1973). One perspective on changes in the consumer behavior of the elderly assumes the amount of communication with family and friends to be positively associated with high morale and self-perception among elderly people (Lemmon et al. 1972). In fact, general social interaction among the elderly and their family and friends has been found to be positively related to product-related social interaction (Schiffman 1972b). In another recent study of elderly consumer learning, the amount of consumption-related communication with family members was positively related to self-perception among the elderly (Smith et al. 1982). In fact, family communication about consumption was positively and significantly related to every criterion variable studied. Similar results were obtained from a more recent study in which exposure to and reliance on personal sources of information (including family members) was positively associated with economic motivations for consumption, social motivations for consumption, and traditional sex role perceptions regarding decision making; it was negatively associated with the ability to filter puffery in advertising (Smith et al. 1985).

Proposition 5.13: Reciprocal communication between elderly parents and offspring are likely to affect consumer learning of the parent during later years. They are likely to affect the parent's:

(a) consumption-related cognitions
(b) consumption-related attitudes
(c) consumption-related behaviors

Finally, the child's influence on the older person's consumer socialization might be indirect or mediated through other socialization processes. For example, in a recent study (Smith and Moschis 1985a), we found family interaction regarding consumption matters to be strongly ($r = .42$) associated with mass media advertising exposure. Fairly similar results were obtained from an earlier study in which exposure to personal sources of information was positively related to mass media advertising exposure (Smith et al. 1985). While the direction of causality cannot be determined from these cross-sectional studies, the findings appear to support the selective exposure hypothesis, and they are in line with the media uses and gratification perspective (see, for example, Katz et al. 1974).

Proposition 5.14: The older person's communication behavior with other sources of consumer information is functionally related to interaction with family members.

Summary and Discussion

The information presented in this chapter suggests some generalizations that are supported by reasonably adequate evidence and others that are more speculative and require additional research. Parents appear to play an important role in the consumer socialization of their offspring, and they are instrumental in teaching their offspring the rational aspects of consumption. In addition, youngsters appear to acquire a variety of other consumption-related orientations and skills from their parents. Parental influence on the consumer behavior of their offspring is situation specific; it varies across products, stages in the decision-making process, and consumer characteristics.

Parents can directly and indirectly influence the development of their children's consumer behaviors. Directly, parents influence the consumer learning of their offspring through several communication processes (both overt and cognitive), including overt interaction about consumption matters (such as purposive training), using reinforcement mechanisms (both positive and negative) and providing opportunities for the child to observe the parents' consumer behaviors. Apparently, different communication processes are involved in the direct transmission of specific values and behaviors from parent to child, and these processes vary by sociodemographic characteristics. Indirectly, the family can affect consumer learning by influencing the youngster's interaction with other sources of consumer influence. Family communication processes lead to rather different interaction patterns with other sources of consumer learning. Finally, the evidence indicates that the family mediates the effects of other socialization agents and that family communication processes play an important role in this mediation process. The findings concerning the role of children and spouses in the consumer socialization of adult individuals are still sketchy. It appears, however, that family influence on consumer socialization does not stop at the adolescent stage but continues throughout life.

Several avenues for future research are possible. Clearly, there is a need for better understanding of the nature of family influence—that is, what additional aspects of consumer behavior are acquired from parents and parental influence across situations. There also is a need for understanding the communication processes involved in the transmission and acquisition of certain values and behaviors from parent to child and how these vary by sociodemographic characteristics.

Another pressing need is evidenced by the findings showing that a great deal of the family influence in consumer socialization operates indirectly by affecting other sources of consumer learning. It would be useful to understand and separate the direct from the indirect effects of family communication processes.

The mediating effects of family also deserve some attention. It would be useful to know how out-of-home influences are modified and channeled in the context of specific family communication processes.

Research also is needed to provide additional insights into adult consumer socialization, including that of the elderly. There is a need for a better understanding of how parents acquire new information from their children and the specific types of attitudes, values, and behaviors acquired from children over the life cycle. Another pressing need is in adult socialization and the role spouses play in resocializing one another into new or different consumer roles. Such research would go beyond specific influences on consumption situations to include socialization processes operating in the transmission of values and behaviors. Finally, research is needed on the reciprocal influence of siblings within the family, as this type of research is almost nonexistent.

More recent research on family communication patterns also suggest the need for a more systematic examination of the antecedents and consequences of specific styles of family communication patterns (FCP). For example, we need to understand whether specific patterns grow out of specific social value systems and whether family communication patterns and specific consumer orientations are both outcomes of the more global sociocultural beliefs and value systems that prevail in our society (Tims and Masland 1985). Research could be facilitated by developing better conceptualizations and applying more rigorous methodologies. For example, one pressing need for research appears to be the need for studying the influence of family in the context of specific dyads, focusing on specific pairs. The research viewed here suggests that family communications have been examined only in the broad context of how parents affect the development of their children's consumer behaviors. Research also should address specific dyads and directions of influence, such as mother-son, mother-daughter, father-son, and father-daughter. The study of family communications in the context of specific parent-child dyads might be useful in understanding the effects of specific communication processes on the development of various types of consumer behaviors.

In addition, there appear to be methodological issues that must be addressed in measuring family communication processes and effects. Specifically, we need research that addresses family communication processes in a way that is somewhat similar to the manner in which communications researchers have examined mass communication processes. For example, communication processes conceptualized according to mass communication models recently have departed from the traditional assumption of "exposure equals effect," and they have included additional processes of interaction with the mass media such as "gratifications sought" and "gratifications received" from the source (see, for example, McLeod, Bybee, and Duvall 1982). In evaluating family communication effects, research could focus on methods for measuring such effects and developing meaningful criteria of consumer learning, both relational and absolute.

Much of the research needed in this area can be addressed only by using a certain research design. Because communication involves exchange of information and subsequent effects, cross-sectional designs might not be adequate for studying certain types of family communication processes. Rather, experimental and longitudinal designs could better enable the researcher to study such processes and their effects.

6
Peer Influences

Peer groups play an important role in consumer socialization at various stages in a person's life cycle. Humans need social interaction with various groups of people, including friends, co-workers, classmates, and members of formal organizations. The need for interaction stems from several sources, including inner biopsychological needs (such as aging, uncertainty, or reinforcement of values) sociological needs (such as conformity or status) and specific needs arising out of changes in the individual's social structure (such as family life cycle or employment). Interaction with peers results in needs gratification. Needs gratification, in turn, might involve changes in the individual's behaviors and attitudes. For example, the individual's desire to belong and be accepted by a reference group might require the performance of various types of behaviors. Laboratory studies and field surveys have demonstrated such group influences on consumer behaviors (see, for example, Assael 1984).

The extent of peer group influence on an individual's behaviors and subsequent socialization is a function of a complex interaction of characteristics of influencer(s) and influencee, influence processes and antecedents. For example, the nature of the peer group (including, for example, the power of the influencing agent) and the personality of the influencer (including, for example, social dependency) are likely to determine the extent to which the latter will be influenced by the former. Similarly, the nature of the peer group is likely to define the learning process(es) most likely to operate. For example, sociologists have distinguished between two types of reference groups: those significant others who hold expectations for ego and convey them directly to the individual (definers) and those who influence ego indirectly through their own aspirations or level of attainment (models) (Haller and Portes 1973). Reinforcement (positive and negative) and social interaction mechanisms such as purposive consumer training are most likely to operate from definer to learner, while modeling processes are most likely to operate in model-to-learner relationships. Obviously, with the several types of peer groups that can be identified for an individual (see, for example, Assael 1984), there are several opportunities for socialization during the course of interaction with these groups, providing a number of possibilities for studying peer group influence processes and effects.

One interesting typology of social influence that is relevant to socialization has been advanced by Kelman (1961). Building on the research traditions of social psychology, Kelman attempted to account for the qualitative differences in the acceptance of social influence. The typology is expressed in the conceptualization of three processes of social influence—compliance, identification, and internalization.

Compliance is the descriptor applied when an individual expresses behavior designed solely to elicit a favorable reaction from another person or group. The behavior does not represent the behaver's beliefs; it is expressed when it can be monitored by the person or group the individual is trying to satisfy, not when others cannot see. Thus, a concern for the social effects of behavior is a precondition for compliance, and the possibility of surveillance by the influencer through observation or informants is a condition for performance of the behavior.

Identification is the term applied to a behavior that expresses the existence of an individual's relationship with the influencing person or group. The identification process might indicate the existence of a reciprocal role relationship or an attempt to establish a linkage with an attractive person or group. The behavior is not innately satisfying to the performer, but it is carried on in both public and private situations. The behavior is consistent with the influencer's expectation of himself, and the influence acceptor acts in a manner congruent with the desired relationship between the parties. In sum, a concern with the social source of the behavior is a precondition for identification, and the institution of a salient relationship with the influencer is a condition for performing the behavior.

Internalization describes the acceptance of influence on behavior that expresses the values held by the actor. The behavior itself is intrinsically rewarding in this case because it is consistent with the individual's value system, not because of any potential or ongoing relationship with the influencer. A concern for behavior that is congruent with values held is a precondition for internalization, and the elicitation of relevant values is a condition for behavior execution.

Kelman (1961) supplies a few specific examples of influence sources that are typical of these processes. As examples of identification, he mentions friendship relationships, patient-doctor relationships, membership in informal groups, and socialization processes. There are fewer internalization source examples: experts or others with knowledge appropriate to the behavior. No examples of compliance influencers are presented; approval of the individual is the implied controlling mechanism in the compliance process.

One specific antecedent condition for a social influence process was suggested by Festinger (1954 in his initial formulation of the theory of social comparison. According to this theory, people must determine in various circumstances whether their opinions are correct and obtain accurate appraisal of their abilities. The existence of a drive to evaluate opinions and abilities implies that people will behave in ways that satisfy this need (Shaw and Costanzo 1970). Because of the important role peers can play in validating one's beliefs, as well as in helping one redefine or create new ones, peers can play an important role in socialization.

In the research literature, we can distinguish four broad types of propositions regarding the role of peers in consumer socialization:

1. The person's extent and pattern of interaction with peers determine levels and patterns of consumer learning.

2. The person's extent and pattern of interaction with peers are partly determined by other communication processes.

3. Antecedent variables affect the person's interaction with, and influence by, peers.

4. Peer communication processes modify and channel the person's interpretation of stimuli in the course of interaction with other socialization agents.

The evidence regarding the role of peers in consumer socialization is presented in line with these four broad propositions at various stages of the life cycle. Specific propositions are presented as they might apply to specific stages.

Childhood and Adolescence

The peer culture serves a valuable function for the young because it helps in renunciating dependence on the family by substituting peer group for family group. Peer group facilitates the young person's autonomy process and transformation into adulthood (Sebald 1968). It is believed that youth groups tend to arise in societies in which the family unit cannot ensure the attainment of full social status on the part of its members. When participation in family activities is inadequate for developing a full identity or full social maturity, the adolescent tends to seek in youth groups a framework for the development of his or her identity and effective transition into the adult world (Eisenstadt 1962).

By the time they are two or three years old, most children will have interacted with siblings, cousins, or neighborhood age-mates. For most young children, early peer combats come directly under parental surveillance or the surveillance of other family members or surrogates. At this early age, children are likely to become aware of the presence and wishes of others. Although social learning occurs much of the time during such interaction, peer pressure has little meaning. Not until a few years later does the emergence of structures of prestige and power within informal groups give these agents a special meaning in the socialization process (Clausen 1968b).

Joint parent-child activities tend to diminish in the later years of elementary school, and participation with peers increases. By the beginning of senior high school, most children are believed to be more preoccupied by activities with peers than by family activities, although this does not necessarily mean that parental values are replaced by peer values (Clausen 1968b). Although explicit socialization efforts tend to be minimal in peer relationships, the peer group exerts a great deal of pressure on the adolescent to break free from parental restrictions and conform to its definition of age-appropriate activities and norms. Peers can directly and indirectly affect consumer socialization; they also might mediate the effects of other socialization agents.

Direct Influences

Peers can influence a youth's consumer behaviors directly via several communication processes, including reinforcement, imitation, and social interaction processes. In this section, peer influences are discussed under two headings: consumer behavior (that is, what young people learn from their peers without reference to specific influence processes) and socialization processes (that is, how learning takes place).

Consumer Behavior. Sociologists have suggested that young people learn the symbolic meaning of goods from their peers (Riesman and Roseborough 1955; Parsons et al. 1953). Support for this view comes from a number of studies. In a study of 806 adolescents in Wisconsin, adolescents' communication with peers about consumption matters was associated with the strength of materialistic attitudes and social motivations for consumption (Moschis and Churchill 1978). Similarly, a longitudinal study among 211 adolescents in Georgia revealed a positive relationship between frequency of communication about consumption and materialistic attitudes (Moschis and Moore 1982).

Additional support for the notion that peers are instrumental in teaching expressive aspects of consumption comes from a number of studies examining youths' susceptibility to group norms. For example, Vener (1957) found that an adolescent's peers are salient referents in decisions dealing with dress selection. Similarly, Saunders, Samli, and Tozier (1973) reported high peer influence on female teens' decisions concerning the selection of clothing stores and clothing items. Finally, a study of adolescent decision making suggests that peers as a source of information are important in buying decisions concerning items important to peer acceptance, such as sunglasses and wallets (Moschis and Moore 1979b). The latter results were consistent with previous findings reported by Gilkison (1973).

In addition to the influence peers have on the development of a youth's orientations toward conspicuous consumption, research suggests that peer groups might play an important role in the development of general and specific decision-making patterns. For example, in analyzing data related to an adolescent's motivations for work, Moore and Moschis (1978a) found frequency of communication about consumption with peers to be associated with the need to work to satisfy day-to-day consumption motives. In another study of adolescent decision making, an adolescent's frequency of communication with peers about consumption was positively associated with preferences for information from peers and reliance on peer product preferences; it was negatively associated with the adolescent's propensity to prefer parental advice and product preference, as well as with reliance on price as a criterion in decision making (Moschis and Moore 1980).

Communication with peers is likely to increase brand awareness (Moschis and Moore 1978). In addition, peers appear to play an important role in the development of the youth's preferences for products and brands. A small-scale study of first-graders found peer groups to play an important role in the young child's development of product preferences and consumption patterns (Hawkins and Coney 1974). Similarly, the Moschis and Moore (1980) study found a significant linkage between peer communication about consumption and the existence of preferences for brands of selected products. Another study found a positive relationship between peer communication about consumption and brand preference formation and maintenance (Moschis, Moore, and Stanley 1984). McNeal (1964) also found peer recommendations to be influential in a young person's selection of stores. These findings suggest that peers might help the youth develop not only generic preferences but selective preferences as well.

Young people appear to discuss a variety of topics regarding consumption, resulting in the acquisition and processing of information about a variety of commercial stimuli. In an earlier study of 607 adolescents in Kentucky and North Carolina, we found that interaction with peers about consumption increases a youth's awareness of product price and knowledge about his or her legal rights as a consumer (Moschis and Moore 1978). The Wisconsin study also found a positive linkage between communication with peers about consumption and favorability of attitudes toward advertising, ability to filter puffery in commercials, and information seeking (Moschis 1978b).

To summarize, there appears to be reasonably good supportive evidence that young people acquire from peers the expressive aspects of consumption. In addition, peers might shape the youth's development of decision-making patterns and perception of commercial stimuli. The youth's susceptibility to peer influence appears to be conditioned by several factors. Some of them arise out of interpersonal relationships within the family and peer groups, while others are the result of family and learner characteristics, as well as situational factors.

The strength of peer group influence in general depends on the extent of peer group involvement vis-à-vis other types of involvement and commitment. When parents are available and on good terms with the child, reference group influence tends to diminish. Alternatively, children who are either without a stable home or at odds with their parents are likely to use peer groups as their primary source of reference and become assimilated into them. Such groups also tend to be less acceptable in the dominant peer groupings of the school and are very likely to engage in delinquent activities when opportunities arise (Clausen 1968b). Support for the theoretical propositions that significant others can be deviant socialization agents comes from a number of studies showing that juveniles are much more likely than adults to shoplift with companions (Cameron 1964; Klemke 1982; Robin 1963). In particular, Klemke's study of 1,189 high school students lends support to the deviant socialization hypothesis, showing a surprisingly strong relationship ($r = .82$) between shoplifting and having shoplifting siblings.

The notion that peer influence is contingent on family relations also appears to hold in the study of consumer socialization. For example, in two studies, the influence of peers was found to be greater on children whose parents spent little time discussing consumption with them (Churchill and Moschis 1979; Moschis and Moore 1982). Reliance on peers also is a function of family cohesiveness. In families where parents, especially mothers, dedicate their time to outside careers, youths tend to gravitate toward nonfamilial peer groups. Specifically, in homes where one or both parents frequently are absent, the child is likely not only to become more dependent on peers but also to become more alienated, a condition that might lead to the performance of activities disapproved by parents, including delinquent behaviors (Sebald 1968). In fact, the somewhat limited data available on social, psychological, and behavioral correlates of youthful drinking and driving problems indicate some association between feelings of rebellion, hostility, and alienation and an increased number of traffic violations and accidents (Cameron 1982). Similarly, data from our exploratory shoplifting study tend to be in line with this reasoning, showing that the degree to which parents are absent from home is positively associated ($p < .06$) with social motivations for shoplifting and favorability of attitudes toward shoplifting (Moschis et al. 1987).

Cohesiveness is not, however, a sufficient condition for reducing peer influence. A youth's susceptibility to peer groups is based in part on how well he gets along with his family. Peer influence is strongest on youths who find their parents unwilling to talk to them when they have a problem, difficult to talk to, and nonsupportive (Larson 1972). In addition, the use of power and restrictiveness is likely to alienate the child and to increase the amount of time spent away from home (with peers) and engaged in activities disapproved by the parents (Hartup 1970). In the context of family communication patterns, such relationships within the family appear to characterize a socio-oriented structure, especially a protective situation. Our small-scale adolescent shoplifting study was based on a small sample ($N = 143$) and did not allow meaningful analysis by family communication pattern (FCP). The data, did not support, however, the notion that a socio-oriented family communication structure will be positively related to shoplifting cognitions and behaviors (Moschis et al. 1987).

The preceding discussion suggests that frequency of interaction with peers might be associated with alienation toward consumption and delinquent behavior. Thus, it is not surprising to see findings, albeit cross-sectional, that peer communication is positively related to consumer discontent among youths (Moschis and Moore 1980; Moschis 1984); that frequency of communication with peers about shoplifting is positively and significantly related to both favorability of attitudes toward shoplifting and frequency of shoplifting (Moschis et al. 1987); and that youths are more likely to shoplift in the presence of peers than to shoplift alone (Powell and Moschis 1986).

To summarize, there appears to be reasonably good supportive evidence that young people acquire from their peers the expressive aspects of consumption. In addition, peers might shape the youth's development of decision-making patterns, and they might be a source of deviant socialization. Finally, the influence of peers appears to be contingent on family relations. The available evidence suggests the following propositions:

Proposition 6.1: Peers are likely to influence the development of the decision-making patterns of the young. They are likely to influence the:

(a) development of needs for products

(b) development of patterns of use of information sources

(c) perceptions of commercial stimuli

(d) development of generic and selective preferences for commercial stimuli

(e) formation of postpurchase orientations toward products and stores

Proposition 6.2: Peers play a significant role in deviant socialization and the development of delinquent consumption-related orientations.

Proposition 6.3: Peer influence is contingent on a youth's relationship with his or her family:

(a) It is lower among families that are cohesive and on good terms.

(b) It is greater among families in which parents spend little time interacting with their children.

(c) It is greater among families characterized by a protective family communication pattern (FCP) than in families characterized by other patterns.

The influence of peers also appears to be conditioned by select family and child characteristics. Family size can effect children's orientation toward their peers. Children in large families tend to be more strongly oriented toward their peers than children from small families. Inkeles (1968) suggests that in high-tensity families, peers rather than adults often are more likely to be the most important models. For example, Bowerman and Kinch (1959) found that children from large families shifted their orientation toward peers much more rapidly during middle childhood than did children from small families. Similar findings are reported by Rose (1956), who found that rural high school students with no or few siblings were more likely to choose a single chum as their primary reference group in comparison with children from large families, who tended to choose more organized and larger groups. Again, the findings of our exploratory shoplifting study (Moschis et al. 1987) show a positive relationship between family size and shoplifting frequency, suggesting that the relationship might be mediated by deviant socialization processes with peers. Thus, the effect of family characteristic (size) on deviant socialization might be indirect via peer interaction.

Thus, the presence of children within the family appears to serve as a basis for orientation toward peers. This might be due to the child's effort to compensate for lack of parental attention, family warmth, and supportiveness. For example, the Bowerman and Kinch (1959) study found the degree of peer orientation to be directly related to the adequacy of family adjustment. Generally, the findings of previous research suggest that firstborn children respond more readily to normative peer influences than do later-born children, but later-born children are particularly responsive to informational influence (Hartup 1970).

> Proposition 6.4: Family characteristics condition the degree of influence peers exert on a youth's consumer socialization.
>
> (a) Children from smaller families are less likely to be susceptible to peer influence than children from larger families.
>
> (b) Children with older siblings are more likely to be susceptible to peer influence than firstborn children.
>
> (c) Firstborn children are more likely to be susceptible to normative social influence than later-born children.
>
> (d) Later-born children are more likely to be susceptible to informational social influence than firstborn children.

Finally, a youth's susceptibility to peer influence appears to be affected by select characteristics of the youth. For example, whether firstborn children are more susceptible to peer influence than later-borns also might depend on the child's sex and the context in which group pressure is exerted. Brittain (1963) examined ninth- and tenth-grade girls using the age and sex of the child's siblings as independent variables. He found that the sex, but not the birth order, of siblings had a significant effect on conformity. Specifically, girls with brothers tended to lean toward parental conformity, while girls with sisters tended toward peer conformity. It has been suggested that girls with sisters manifest greater sibling rivalry and hostility to parents than girls with brothers, creating conditions for using peers as a primary reference group (Hartup 1970). Additional data presented by Schmuck (1963) concerning college women are supportive of this line of reasoning.

In general, females are believed to be more likely to conform to peer pressure than males. This might reflect a greater need for social approval in girls than in boys (Hartup 1970). Specifically, girls in their need for subjective indexes of their potential exhibit stronger peer orientation, and this orientation leads to higher degrees of conformity than occurs among boys (Campbell 1964). With most deviant norms acquired from peers, and delinquent behavior occurring in a social context (Miller 1979), girls might be more apt to perform delinquent behaviors when accompanied by a peer. In fact, a study of 7,328 juveniles in Georgia found female juveniles to shoplift more frequently with peers than male juveniles (Powell and Moschis 1986), although these findings also might reflect a greater tendency by females to shop with peers.

Martin (1975b) suggested that children exhibit greater resistance to temptation if they are treated in a warm and reasoning manner rather than a power-assertive fashion. The girls' greater likelihood to shoplift on impulse found in the Powell and Moschis (1986) study might be due to the different ways parents treat children based on their sex. Boys generally have more freedom than girls because of a more permissive parental climate. The adolescent girl's greater susceptibility to peer influence might be attributed to family reaction toward her. In attempting to cope with the "modern girl" (free, sexual, independent), parents might be placing more restrictions on the adolescent girl, who might be less responsive to enhanced parental regulations and requirements, substituting peer norms for parental support (Larson 1972). Given that a socio-oriented family communication structure imposes greater restrictions, one would expect girls from protective homes to be more responsive to peers and to be more concerned with the perceived effects of their behaviors on others.

Peer characteristics related to susceptibility to peer influence also can include a youth's perceived similarity with peer groups—that is, a measure of perceived congruency in line with the general co-orientation model discussed in chapter 3. Such co-orientation (similarity) with peers appears to influence the extent to which a young person seeks information about products or services. Clarke (1971 and 1973), for example, showed that information seeking about music is functionally related to a youth's level of knowledge of how others evaluate an entertainment, using levels of perceived similarity as a measure of co-orientation. Similarly, Kline, Miller, and Morrison (1974) used perceived knowledge congruency of family planning as a measure of co-orientation, a predictor of information seeking and processing in messages, including message discrimination, and a predictor of actual knowledge about family planning methods. These findings can be interpreted in the context of social comparison theory.

Personality correlates of yielding to peer influence also have been identified. Personality characteristics are likely to develop early in life. As early as middle childhood and adolescence, the peer-conforming child tends to resemble the conformity-prone adult. Specifically, the conformity-prone individual manifests low ego strength and self-esteem, repression of impulses, and social sensitivity. Such personality traits, however, are likely to interact with situational factors in determining conformity behavior in older children and adolescents (Hartup 1970).

To summarize the effects of learner characteristics on the learner's interaction with and susceptibility to peers, not only birth order but also sex seems to play an important role in the youth's susceptibility to peer influence. The limited data presented suggest:

Proposition 6.5: Peers are the most important reference group among later-born female children.

Proposition 6.6: In comparison with their firstborn male counterparts, female youths with older female siblings are more susceptible to peer influence than male youths with older male siblings.

Proposition 6.7:   Female youths are more likely than male youths to be susceptible to peer influence.

Most of what is known about situational factors in determining conformity
has been derived from studies of college students. Generally, several factors appear
to be associated with group conformity, including group size, uniformity of values,
task difficulty, competence, and attractiveness of the influence source, as well as
a variety of incentive factors (see Hartup 1970).

In the context of adolescent decision making, peers were found to be more
important referents than parents in situations concerning decisions dealing with
personal appearance—that is, uniformity of values. Parents were more important
in decisions regarding personal finances, personal problems, and political issues
(Remmers and Radler 1957). Within the framework of consumer decision making,
Moschis and Moore (1979b) presented findings suggesting that peers might be more
important referents in decisions concerning items of social significance, such as
clothing (see also Saunders et al. 1973; Vener 1957).

Proposition 6.8:   Peer influence on a youth's consumer behavior is situation
specific. It is more likely to be significant in consumer decisions concerning items of social significance than in decisions
concerning items of little social significance.

The influence of peers also has been evaluated at the interpersonal level within
the family decision-making context. In one study, for example, Moschis and Mitchell
(1986) examined the adolescent's propensity to participate in various stages of the
decision process concerning a wide range of products, some for the adolescent's
use (such as school supplies or clothing) and others for the family's or adults' use
(such as small appliances or car repairs). It was found that the more frequently
the youth interacted with peers about consumption matters, the more likely the
youth was to mention the need for these products or services within the family,
discuss their purchase, and actually decide what or whether to buy. Although the
relationship between peer communication and the last stage of the decision process (actual purchase) was not significant, the data do seem to suggest that peer
influences are likely to be carried into the family decision process and might affect
family decisions. Lack of a significant relationship between a youth's low propensity to purchase products and level of communication with peers might simply
be due to the youth's inability to purchase such products (caused, for example,
by inaccessibility to credit, transportation, and retailers). It also is possible that
the child might influence generic product or service decisions but that parents might
have more influence on brand decisions.

Proposition 6.9:   Peer influences on the young consumer are carried into the
youth's family, influencing adult consumer socialization and consumer behavior.

Socialization Processes. Researchers have used a variety of concepts to study peer influence processes. These efforts have been summarized as follows:

> Research dealing with peer influences has been dominated by such concepts as *conformity, suggestibility, yielding persuasibility, imitation, behavior contagion,* and *social facilitation.* All of these terms refer to instances in which the child's behavior becomes, over time, similar to the behavior of some other person. Each of these terms refers to an outcome of social interaction, but this interaction may not have been initiated with the intent of evoking behavior change. (Hartup 1970, 405)

Because similarity in behavior is a common operational definition for modeling or imitation, the latter term commonly is used to tap peer influence. For example, Hartup (1970) uses the term *imitation* to subsume all the other terms related to peer influence. The extent to which a young person will imitate a model's behavior is a function of several factors, including frequency of reinforcement received from peers for imitating rewarding models, perceived similarity with the model, and incentives for imitating a model (Hartup 1970).

Some early theorists have discussed the origins of imitation in the infant and young child in the context of instinct theory, while others have recognized the environmental impact on imitative behavior (see Hartup 1970). A more popular theory of imitation proposed by Miller and Dollard (1941) accounts for the acquisition of imitative behavior in terms of contingent reinforcement. Social learning theory, in general, offers a rather weak basis for predicting a youth's susceptibility to reference group influence with increasing age (Hartup 1970).

Piaget (1932), in his general theory of social development, made more explicit predictions concerning responsiveness to peer influence with increasing age. Although he discussed changes in responsiveness to peers in the broader context of changes in the youth's perception of the "rules of the game," he believed that the child's consciousness of such social rules evolved through three stages. Briefly, Piaget posited a curvilinear relationship between chronological age and conformity to peer influence among children. Conformity to peer influence should increase until preadolescence and then decline. Thus, contrary to the conventional wisdom that peer influence increases throughout adolescence, Piaget's formulation suggests decline in social conformity beginning in early adolescence.

The results of several studies support Piaget's theory (see Hartup 1970). Generally, these studies show that conformity to peer influences tends to increase following the preschool years and tends to decrease with the onset of adolescence. The precise age at which conformity is greatest varies, however, with the peak occurring as early as nine years and as late as fifteen. Situational and cultural factors are likely to be responsible for these inconsistencies, suggesting that peer influence might peak by high school.

Few studies of consumer socialization provide support for Piaget's theory. For example, McNeal (1969) reported significant peer influence on a child upon reaching age seven. Another study by Shaak, Annes, and Rossiter (1975) found stronger peer influence operating among fifth-graders than among second-graders. In a study of adolescent consumer socialization (Moschis 1976a), however, no significant differences in peer influence (indicated by social motivations for consumption) emerged between younger (twelve to fourteen years) and older (fifteen to nineteen years) adolescents.

More convincing evidence in support of Piaget's theory comes from studies of shoplifting, where peer influence is believed to be particularly strong (Miller 1979; Klemke 1982). Our study of 7,328 juveniles in Georgia found that among the 2,432 respondents who indicated that they had shoplifted, the largest percentage had done so prior to reaching adolescence (Powell and Moschis 1986). Similar results were reported by Klemke (1982), whose findings clash with the prevailing view that delinquency begins to increase during early adolescence and peaks in middle adolescence. Klemke's model suggests that delinquency begins at a much earlier stage and parallels the increase in peer influence.

To summarize, several processes that have been linked to modeling appear to be involved in the transmission of norms, values, and behaviors from the influencer to the learner. A youth's susceptibility to peer influence might be curvilinear, becoming strongest in late childhood and early adolescence.

> Proposition 6.10: Modeling processes account for much of the acquisition of skills, attitudes, and values from peers during childhood and adolescence. Modeling processes are involved in:
>
> (a) the acquisition of desirable skills
> (b) deviant socialization
>
> Proposition 6.11: Peer influence during childhood and adolescence is curvilinear, becoming strongest in late childhood and early adolescence.

Indirect Influences

In addition to direct effects peers might have on a youth's consumer behavior, such groups might affect consumer learning indirectly. Indirect influences can take place when a youth's interaction with peers affects his or her interaction with other socialization agents, which, in turn, directly (or indirectly) affect the development of consumer behavior. Several studies have established a relationship between peer interaction and interaction with other socialization agents, including the mass media and the family (see, for example, Moschis and Moore 1982).

One of the more common assertions about mass media use by children and adolescents is that it is closely linked to their social relations (Chaffee and Tims 1976). It is generally accepted that as youths spend more time with peers, they spend less time interacting with the mass media. Lyle and Hoffman (1972), for example, found that among their sample of first-graders, those who infrequently played with other children often turned on television to find companionship. Rossiter and Robertson (1974) found that peer integration was inversely related to television exposure among children. Similarly, our studies of adolescent consumer socialization found an inverse relationship between frequency of communicating with peers about consumption and frequency of television viewing (see, for example, Moore and Moschis 1978a; Churchill and Moschis 1979). These patterns of interaction have been linked to age as well.

Perhaps of greater importance is the differential impact on mass media use and the perception of stimuli in the mass media as a result of peer interaction. For example, findings suggest that interpersonal interaction with peers about consumption matters might make the adolescent aware of goods and services in the marketplace and of the buying process. This greater awareness of the consumer environment apparently contributes to active interaction about consumption matters with other socialization agents, such as the mass media, which results in additional learning (Moschis 1976a; Moschis and Churchill 1977). Specifically, the same study of adolescents found peer communication about consumption to be positively associated with the adolescent's motivations for viewing television shows and ads as well as for reading the newspaper (Moschis and Churchill 1978). Similarly, in a smaller sample of adolescents and their parents in Georgia ($N = 166$), Moschis and Mitchell (1986) found a variety of motives for advertising viewing to be positively associated with peer communication about consumption. Finally, the child's interpersonal context within a peer group appears to influence his or her perception of the usefulness of the mass media.

For example, Greenberg and Reeves (1976) found that a youth's relations with peers influence his or her perception of televised stimuli. In the Kline et al. (1974) study, a youth's perceived knowledge about family planning in relation to that of his or her peers predicted the youth's propensity to seek information in messages, process that information, and discriminate among messages. Specifically, it was found that the youth's interaction with the mass media is likely to be greater when his or her perceived knowledge is greater than that of peer groups; it is lower when peers are perceived to be more knowledgeable. The authors interpreted these findings in the context of social comparison theory.

> Proposition 6.12: Mass media use and the interpretation of stimuli in the media are functionally related to a youth's social relations. The youth's social relations affect the following:
>
> (a) amount of mass media used
> (b) types of mass media used
> (c) perception of mass media stimuli
> (d) ability to discriminate stimuli in the message

It also is likely that consumer-related cognitions learned from interacting with peers will influence the parents' consumption. Riesman and Roseborough (1955) have termed this influence *retroactive socialization*. Under such conditions, the child may be viewed, in Stone's (1955) terms, as an "agent of his peers" (p. 23), communicating the acquired information to his parents. One contemporary example of the effects of child-initiated communication can be found in parental learning about home computers. On many occasions, parents purchased a home computer as a result of child-initiated communication, and they have learned to use the product with the help of their children (Pollack 1982).

Additional support for these speculations has been revealed in several studies. One study found that an adolescent's interaction with peers creates opportunities for positive parent-child interaction and consumer learning (Churchill and Moschis 1979). Similarly, Moore, Moschis, and Stephens (1975) reported a positive relationship between an adolescent's frequency of communication about consumption with peers and the individual's frequency of initiating discussions about consumption with parents. In another study of 784 adolescents, the relationship between the two variables was very strong ($r = .51$) (Moore and Moschis 1979a). Finally, the results of a study of 166 pairs of adolescents and their mothers show that communication with peers is likely to influence parental decisions concerning products for adolescent use as well as for family use (Moschis and Mitchell 1986).

> Proposition 6.13: A child's interaction about consumption with parents is determined by his or her social relations with peers.

Mediating Effects

Peers might mediate the effects of other socialization agents. While the evidence is not as convincing as in the case of family interactions, some research shows that peer interaction is likely to increase children's positive reaction to advertising messages, to predispose the selection of an advertised toy, and to affect the level of happiness ascribed to the central character in the message (Laughlin and Desmond 1981). A study by Moschis and Moore (1982), however, provided little evidence that peers play a mediating role in an adolescent's reaction to television advertising.

> Proposition 6.14: Peers mediate the effects of other socialization agents on a youth's consumer behavior.

Adulthood

Although many patterns of consumer behavior are likely to be learned during preadult years and persist well into adulthood, the relatively long period that defines adult stages in the life cycle creates several opportunities for additional socialization and resocialization. As the individual encounters new situations such as relocation and changes in employment, financial status, and life cycle, the salience of various reference groups (such as neighbors, co-workers, and club members) is likely to change as well. These groups are likely to serve as reference groups that probably will influence the individual's behavior. Thus, ongoing interactions with different reference groups is likely to play an important role in the person's socialization and resocialization during the adult years.

Direct Influences

Consumer Behavior. Although the influence of peers on adult consumer behavior is documented in a number of studies on reference group influence, these studies traditionally have examined peer influence in the context of purchase situations rather than from a socialization perspective (see, for example, Engel et al. 1978). In recent years, however, researchers have examined susceptibility to reference group influence from a socialization perspective. For example, Park and Lessig (1977) attributed differences in reference group influence between students and housewives to the different stages in which these groups are found in the socialization process, recognizing that socialization is a lifelong process. They attributed the greater susceptibility to reference group influence found among students regarding the purchase of products (brands) to the individual's continuous socialization process, which is stronger at earlier stages (among students) than at later stages (among housewives) in the person's life cycle. This, in turn, is due to young people's need to express themselves, form an ego, and test their acceptability to others (p. 104).

Other researchers have attributed differences in susceptibility to reference groups to the nature of the influence processes. Moschis (1976b), for example, found that an individual's propensity to seek information from informal groups, to rely upon informal reference groups, and to take peer preferences into account in choosing products is related to the degree of perceived similarity (co-orientation) with these groups. These results were replicated in another study (Becherer and Morgan 1982) and are in line with social comparison theory.

In a similar vein, Bellenger and Moschis (1981) summarized findings of studies that support their contention that consumer patronage behavior can be viewed from a socialization perspective, with peers playing a significant role in the formation of patronage patterns. For example, research shows that store-loyal consumers show moderate to heavy socialization with their neighbors (Woodside 1973). An earlier study by Kelly (1967) also examined the role of information in the patronage decision. The manner in which both formal and informal information flows among prospective customer groups was found to have a profound influence on the patronage decision process associated with new retail outlets. This exploratory research suggested that there is a hierarchy of influence in the determination of patronage decision outcomes: in-store experiences were found to be most influential, followed by personal influences and newspaper advertising. Similarly, a study reported by Woodside (1973) investigating the linkage of store patronage and promotion found direct experience and personal contacts to have the greatest impact. Peer group influence also is likely to affect an individual's preferences for alternative modes of distribution. Peer expectations, for example, often mediated through perceived social risk, are likely to influence an individual's preferences for type of stores—for example, discount stores versus department stores (Prasad 1975; Korgaonkar and Moschis 1986).

The development of information-seeking patterns is likely to be affected by peer relations. Specifically, the development of patterns of information use with respect to the amount, type, and sources of information are functionally related to a person's interpersonal relations. For example, an individual's tendency to seek information from peers and rely on their judgment is functionally related to the consumer's co-orientation with group members (Moschis 1976b; Becherer and Morgan 1982). These findings have been explained in line with the theory of social comparison. Similarly, the amount and type of information sought in a specific situation is likely to be an outgrowth of the person's social relations. In analyzing data from a study of cosmetics buyers, it was found that the information a person seeks is likely to fulfill social needs beyond the need for resolving purchasing-related problems. For example, a buyer might seek information about products to be able to discuss certain consumption situations with others, manipulate others' impressions, and share the information with peer groups (Moschis 1980). Similarly, Chaffee and McLeod (1973) found that information on politics often is sought not only to reach a decision but also to be able to share it with others by reinforcing the views of peers. Such tendencies, whether they can be explained in the context of social comparison or reinforcement theory, are likely to be rewarded by peers; they are likely to be repeated and, as a result, become learned patterns of behavior during adulthood.

Thus, although peer group influence on consumer learning has been speculated to apply only to affective behaviors (styles and moods of consumption) (Riesman and Roseborough 1955), it also might apply to the learning of other consumption-related orientations as well.

> Proposition 6.15: Peers play a significant role in the consumer socialization and resocialization of adults. They influence the adult consumer's development and change of:
>
> (a) social and nonsocial consumption needs
> (b) patterns of information acquisition and use
> (c) evaluation and perception of marketing stimuli
> (d) preferences for products, brands, and stores

Socialization Processes. While some work has addressed the type of orientations adults might develop as a result of peer interaction, there are almost no studies that have explicitly examined learning processes in the context of the socialization of adult consumers. Implicit in several studies of word-of-mouth communications and informational influences is the assumption that the social interaction mechanism might operate (Assael 1984; Engel et al. 1978), while studies of social comparison process suggest that modeling (as in the case of comparative appraisal) and reinforcement (such as reflective appraisal) are likely to operate as well (Moschis 1976b; Becherer and Morgan 1982; Chaffee and McLeod 1973).

> Proposition 6.16: During adulthood, socialization influences from peers operate via processes of modeling, reinforcement, and social interaction.

Indirect Influences

Finally, peer influence in socialization might operate indirectly through other socialization agents. For example, the amount, type, and content of mass media the adult person uses is determined partly by interaction with peers (see, for example, Moschis 1980; Chaffee and McLeod 1973; McLeod, Bybee, and Duvall 1982; McLeod, Fitzpatrick, Glynn, and Fallis 1982). Similarly, information acquired from peers is likely to be shared with other family members, especially in the context of purchase decisions (see, for example, Engel et al. 1978), thus providing opportunities for socialization.

> Proposition 6.17: Peer influences in adult socialization operate indirectly by affecting the adult person's relations with other sources of consumer information.
>
> (a) Peer relations affect the adult person's use of the mass media.
>
> (b) Peer relations affect the adult person's interaction with family members.

Late Adulthood

Friends and neighbors are important sources of primary relationships in later life; they also provide help and contact with the outside world (Atchley 1972). The role of a friend is one the aging individual might retain indefinitely (Clark and Anderson 1967). Most older people have at least fifteen friends who provide companionship, support, and information (Smith 1982). Older people also might join clubs and groups to supply themselves with human relationships and emotional support lost in the relinquishment of their roles as parent or worker (Riley et al. 1969).

Rosow identifies peers and organized groups as agents of change in elderly socialization (Rosow 1970 and 1974). The elderly's learning of appropriate behaviors might occur through interaction with peers (Ahammer 1973). Klippel and Sweeney (1974) identified friends and neighbors as specific information sources for older consumers, as did Schiffman (1972a), who used level of social interaction as an explanatory variable for the degree of perceived risk in purchasing a new product.

Older people might acquire from their peers a variety of cognitions and norms appropriate to roles in later life (Smith et al. 1982 and 1985; Smith and Moschis 1985a). For example, one study found exposure to personal sources of information to be positively associated with traditional sex role perceptions and economic and social motivations for consumption; exposure was negatively associated with the elderly's ability to filter puffery in advertising (Smith et al. 1982). With respect to the relative influence of peers in comparison with other socialization agents, peers were found to be stronger than mass media exposure as a socialization agent but weaker than family communication (Smith 1982).

Proposition 6.18: Peers play an important role in the consumer socialization of older adults.

(a) They influence the development of cognitions and behaviors regarding the consumer role.

(n) They influence the older person's perceptions and interpretation of marketing stimuli.

Indirectly, peers can influence the consumer socialization of older adults by affecting their interaction with other socialization agents. In a study of 286 elderly in Atlanta, Smith and Moschis (1985b) found a significant relationship ($r = .66$) between personal interaction (hearing about products from significant others, including friends and neighbors, and relying on their opinions) and mass media exposure and reliance. While this strong relationship was confounded with the presence of more than just peers in the personal interaction scale used, as well as with the relative importance of exposure versus reliance, the findings lend credence to the notion that mass media interaction and personal interaction are functionally related in later stages of the life cycle. In another study of 317 senior citizens, Smith, Moschis, and Moore (1985) demonstrated the interdependence of reliance and exposure measures, for both the mass media and personal sources, and shed light on the relationship between mass media and interpersonal interaction. Specifically, exposure to personal sources (that is, hearing others talking about twelve different products) was related ($r = .24$) to mass media exposure (that is, hearing about or seeing the same products in television, newspaper, magazine, and radio ads) but not to reliance on the mass media for decisions regarding purchasing these products. Similarly, reliance on personal sources of information was related only to mass media advertising exposure ($r = .38$).

While the results show no directionality of influence, two plausible explanations are in line with previous theory and research. First, older people are likely to discuss the products they see or hear advertised in the mass media with significant others, suggesting that the media might play an informing role, while personal sources might play a legitimizing one. The results are not necessarily in line with the two-step flow hypothesis because exposure to and reliance on the mass media and personal sources were not related, suggesting that opinion leaders who first hear about products in the mass media do not rely on these sources; nonleaders who hear about products from others do not rely on others in making purchase decisions.

Alternatively, the products a person discusses with others are likely to be noticed in the mass media, a view that is in line with the selective exposure hypothesis. Support for the latter view (that use of mass media advertising is a function of personal interaction) is provided by Schiffman's (1972b) findings, suggesting that more socially involved elderly individuals might rely on mass media "as a source of information to make themselves more interesting and knowledgeable in their social encounters" (pp. 448–49).

> Proposition 6.19: Mass media use and interpretation of stimuli are functionally related to an older person's social relations.
>
> (a) Interaction with peers increases the likelihood of mass media advertising awareness and evaluation.
>
> (b) Interaction with peers increases the likelihood of an older person's actively seeking and using mass media advertising information.

Summary and Discussion

In this chapter, the literature reviewed centered on four broad propositions regarding the role of peers in consumer socialization. The first type of proposition was concerned with the effects of the extent and pattern of interaction with peers on levels and pattern of consumer learning. The data presented suggest that both extent and type of influence might affect the acquisition of various orientations among youths. The evidence is less clear or direct regarding the effects of specific processes in the consumer socialization of adults and the elderly.

The second broad type of proposition—that a person's extent and pattern of interaction with peers are determined partly by other communication processes—appears to be justified by substantial evidence, mostly from studies concerning the socialization of young people. Little information appears to be available to justify the proposition for socialization in later life.

The third proposition dealt with the role of antecedent variables in a person's interaction processes and the influence of peers. Several types of variables appear to play a role in this influence process among youths, but few were uncovered concerning adult socialization in general and consumer socialization in later life in particular.

The final proposition—that peer communication processes modify and channel a person's interpretation of stimuli in the course of interaction with other socialization agents—was justified over a person's life cycle. The data presented, albeit limited, seem to provide justification for this last proposition.

In summary, we know relatively little about how peers affect the consumer learning of individuals over the life cycle. Research on influence processes is particularly lacking. One challenging avenue of future research would be to delineate the effects of various social influence processes, since such processes currently are treated very broadly in consumer socialization research. Another avenue would be to examine a person's interaction with, and subsequent consumer socialization by, other agents as a result of his or her relations with peers. For example, it might be that susceptibility to the mass media is related to a person's low evaluation of his or her peers' knowledge and skills as consumers or to low interaction with peers, rather than merely to individual characteristics. Finally, researchers must guard against the possibility that the observed patterns and interactions with peers, and subsequent consumer socialization, could reflect broader cultural orientations, which are responsible (as third variables) for our causal relationships.

7
Mass Media Influences

No other agent of consumer socialization has received more attention than the mass media. Because much consumer socialization research has focused on issues surrounding the effects of advertising on youths and their families, mass media advertising (television in particular) has been the focus of much of that research. This chapter examines the role of the mass media in the development of consumer orientations. Specifically, models of mass media effects are presented to provide theoretical and conceptual bases for evaluating and interpreting research findings. Next, the results of studies relating to the effects, both direct and indirect, of television and other media on consumer learning over the life cycle are presented. Finally, a number of propositions are developed on the basis of previous theory and research related to specific effects and stages in the life cycle.

Models of Mass Media Influence

The evaluation of media performance can be approached from two different perspectives: from the researcher's perspective and from the audience's. When the media are evaluated from the researcher's point of view, the effectiveness of the medium or message is assessed on the basis of relationships between exposure and effects, with the latter being a change in audience, cognitions, attitudes, or behaviors. The second perspective, referred to as the uses and gratifications perspective (Katz et al. 1974), is evaluated on the basis of the individual's subjective report of what she or he receives or wants from a medium or a message.

First, from the researcher's standpoint, media effects have been evaluated at three different levels: individual, interpersonal, and social system. The first level, *individual,* has its roots in the stimulus-response behavioristic theory of attitude and opinion change guided by the psychological audience model. The model assumes that atomistic audiences who receive media messages are likely to be affected at cognitive, affective, and behavioral levels, producing corresponding short-term immediate and measurable changes.

When the effects of the media are evaluated at the *interpersonal* level, the audience members are viewed as collections of interactants within the social structure. This sociological influence model emphasizes the role of social structure and interpersonal relations in the mass communication influence process, shifting the focus of media effects from direct to indirect influence.

At the *social-system* level, mass media effects are evaluated at the aggregate (societal) level, with little attention paid to how the mass media affect individuals or interpersonal relations. Examples of this type of evaluation include the role of the mass media in a country's economic development and relationships between advertising expenditures and gross national product (GNP) or company sales and market share.

Finally, mass media effects have been evaluated at more than one level or at a combination of levels (intrapersonal, interpersonal, or societal). Hornik, Gonzalez, and Gould (1980) developed and empirically tested a theory of susceptibility to mass media. The theory is based on the premise that the mass media (and other sources of information) are most effective when the audience (individuals, small groups, or large collectivities) has the least amount of contact with or knowledge about the object of communication—that is, when the audience deals with distant environments. Distant environments are defined as environments on which we can make no firsthand reality tests. They can be distant over time, over geography, and over culture.

The media uses and gratifications perspective shifts conceptual inquiries from "what media do to people" to "what people do with the media." It attempts to understand the role of the media in the lives of the audience by emphasizing the role of the audience as active seekers, selectors, and users of messages and by seeking to explain motivations for specific media use behavior. More recent uses and gratifications researchers have been concerned with identifying specific functions of the mass media (see, for example, Blumler and Katz 1974; Katz et al. 1974; Lull 1980a; McQuail and Gurevitch 1974).

The uses and gratifications perspective views psychological and sociological dimensions as intervening variables in the mass communication process. Media consumption is viewed as goal-directed and purposive behavior and as an outgrowth of the audience's needs. Emphasis is placed on audience initiative in selecting appropriate media and media content to satisfy these needs (Katz et al. 1974).

One of the unique virtues of the uses and gratifications approach is its ability to reach out "effectively to a wide range of new theoretical developments in other disciplines" (Blumler and Katz 1974, 15). The uses and gratifications paradigm implies that changes in patterns of uses and gratifications could derive from changes in biophysical or sociopsychological states, which in turn result in changes in the individual's need structure, and from changes in the available media and nonmedia sources of need satisfaction (Dimmick et al. 1979). For example, Dimmick and his associates portrayed stages in the life span associated with changes in sociopsychological and biophysical states. Such changes result in changes in the need structure, resulting in a reorganization of need-satisfying activities, including the mass media.

Katz, Blumler, and Gurevitch (1974) summarized the uses and gratifications approach to the study of mass media audiences as being "concerned with (1) the social and psychological origins of (2) needs, which generate (3) expectations of (4) the mass media and other sources which lead to (5) differential patterns of media exposure (or engagement in other activities), resulting in (6) need gratifications and (7) other consequences, perhaps mostly unintended ones" (p. 20).

In comparison with the psychological and sociological perspectives, the functional model of mass media use allows for a more direct investigation of the information-seeking and processing behavior of the audience by linking its communication behavior to the motivations and gratifications of human needs.

Research has shown that gratification orientations are related to media effects, suggesting that such orientations might mediate the effects of mass media exposure. Researchers are still uncertain about the exact nature of the influence of these mediating variables and how they interact with exposure or effects variables. For example, McLeod and Becker (1974) showed that gratifications might supplement exposure effects, while Kline and his colleagues (1974) found gratifications to interact with effects.

McLeod, Bybee, and Duvall (1982) recently suggested that audience needs might be necessary but not sufficient for media evaluation because what is needed or sought from the media might not be received. They pointed out the need for separating measures of gratifications sought and gratifications received, and they showed that the two measures (based on two different theoretical models, drive reduction and exposure learning) should be used together rather than separately. Specifically, the drive reduction model can be indexed by the degree of fit between each gratification sought and its level of perceived provision by the media source. For the exposure learning model, media use is seen as a habitual activity rather than a planned search for specific content.

The effects of the mass media also can be evaluated at the interpersonal level. The agenda-setting assertion is that the media suggest the topics about which the public thinks or concerns itself. Although the media might not tell people what to think about those topics, it is successful in focusing public attention on them. It is known from agenda-setting research that prominence in the media leads to some form of salience in the public mind; salience in the public mind is correlated with purchase outcomes (Sutherland and Galloway 1981). As far as communication strategy is concerned, the agenda-setting theory suggests that the major goal of the message should be to focus attention on what values, issues, products, or attributes to think about rather than to try to persuade the audience what to think of these. McGuire (1974) suggests a number of psychological explanations for the media's agenda-setting function. In addition, McGuire suggests that the mass media provide a sense of participation for consumers and provide individuals with a starting point for interaction with others.

Several explanations for the agenda-setting function of the media have been offered. Some of these are psychological, while others are sociological. For example, McCombs and Weaver (1973) offer motivational explanations, stating that the individual needs to be familiar with his or her surroundings and that the media serve an orientation function for the consumer by suggesting topics that then become part of the personal agenda of individuals. Similarly, McGuire (1974) suggests a number of psychological explanations, some of which derive from the individual's need for interacting with others.

Attempts to test the agenda-setting hypothesis in cross-sectional studies have been limited because they cannot show direction of causality. For example, a recent longitudinal study provided no support for the idea that local newspapers are effective in setting the reading agenda and only limited support for the assertion that they set the local talking agenda for respondents. Rather, the study showed that what respondents talk about might prompt newspaper reading (Sohn 1978). Generally, however, the empirical evidence shows that the mass media have some influence on the public's agenda of who and what is important. The evidence is somewhat stronger for newspapers than for television (see Comstock 1978).

Models of Advertising Effects

High Involvement Model

The traditional view of how advertising works is exemplified in a limited effects model, known to marketers and advertisers as the high involvement model. The consumer is viewed to be actively involved in the communication process, selectively perceiving messages (critically evaluating its content, ignoring some appeals, and challenging arguments made in the ad) before developing thoughts and feelings about the product and acting favorably. The effects of advertising are evaluated at cognitive, affective, and behavioral levels, with the consumer expected to go through these stages hierarchically in that order.

According to the limited effects model (Klapper 1960; Bauer 1964), the mass media reinforce existing predispositions through selective exposure, and mass media effects are neutralized largely by interpersonal processes in a two-step flow process. While the reinforcement point of view has been attacked on several counts by socialization researchers (Chaffee et al. 1970), the two-step-flow process seems to be more directly related to consumer socialization. Research findings suggest that the mass media might induce youngsters to discuss consumption matters among themselves or with their parents and peers (see, for example, Ward and Wackman 1971; Moore and Stephens 1975; Churchill and Moschis 1979). Such mediation is more likely to result in attitude formation and change than in reinforcement of existing attitudes (Ward and Wackman 1971; Chaffee et al. 1970).

Low Involvement Model

When the purchase is not very important to the consumer, he or she is expected to be passive in the communication process. The decision simply is not important enough to justify expenditure of mental or physical effort on the part of the consumer. Under such low involvement conditions, Krugman's (1965) passive learning theory has been offered as an explanation of how advertising works. Consumers tend to let down their cognitive defense mechanisms, and the message through constant repetition is likely to get through—that is, the ads are passively processed with little critical resistance, and attitude change occurs in the long run through familiarity. Mere exposure to a stimulus is a necessary and sufficient condition for effects, which are not likely to be hierarchical but most likely occur at the cognitive level (for example, awareness) and action stage (for example, trial). For this type of learning, the more a person sees a stimulus, the more he or she likes it (see, for example, Carter 1965; Zajonc 1968).

Bandura's (1971a) social learning theory proposes that modeled behavior such as eating or drinking portrayed on television will lead to greater consumption of corresponding products. Bandura also argues that this rather simple stimulus-response model explains how material objects acquire social meaning through mass media advertising:

> As a rule, observed rewards increase, and observed punishments decrease imitative behavior. This principle is widely applied in advertising appeals. In positive appeals, following the recommended action results in a host of rewarding outcomes. Smoking a brand of cigarettes or using a particular hair lotion wins the loving admiration of voluptuous belles, enhances job performance, masculinizes one's self-concept, tranquilizes irritable nerves, invites social recognition and amicable responsiveness from total strangers. (cited in Ward 1974a, 7)

The model views advertising effects as very powerful, with mere exposure to advertising being persuasive per se (Krugman 1965; Robertson 1976). Furthermore, mere exposure theory suggests that repeated exposure to a novel, simple stimulus will lead to increased liking of the object (Zajonc 1968; Krugman 1965; Stang 1974). As people interact with the mass media, they are exposed to a variety of advertisements and might develop favorable orientations toward advertised products. It is not surprising, therefore, that brand preferences have been shown to be linked to television viewing and newspaper reading (Resnik and Stern 1977; Gorn and Goldberg 1980; Moschis, Moore, and Stanley 1984; Teel et al. 1979).

Transactional Model

The transactional model (Bauer 1964) combines frequency of exposure to the medium with the receiver-oriented cognitive and need states. The model makes the assumption that exposure alone might not be sufficient for learning and seeks additional explanations for the influence of the media on an individual's motives and uses of the information to which he or she is exposed. This model is in line with the uses and gratifications perspective discussed earlier (McLeod and Becker 1974) and recently has been applied to consumer socialization research (Moschis and Churchill 1977 and 1978; Moschis and Moore 1982).

Mass Media Effects on Young Consumers

Television Effects

Television generally is considered one of the more important consumer socialization agents (Adler et al. 1977). Although television programming effects cannot be ignored (see, for example, Moschis and Churchill 1978; Vener and Hoffer 1959), television advertising appears to have the greatest influence on consumer learning among the young (Adler et al. 1977). Perhaps this is because programming effects often are unintended, while advertising attempts to generate a specific consumer response. Unfortunately, many studies of television effects on children and adolescents do not attempt to separate the medium's content and its subsequent effects, assuming that the exposure or use of the programs or ads produces a specific response. Comstock (1978) summarized the effects of television on children:

> It captures children's attention for long periods, and presents them with information and portrayals not duplicated or readily testable in their real-life environment. It is turned to by children for information not available to them in real life. It provides models of behavior children may emulate. It can alter the level of behavior and such alterations may shape the future pattern of behavior through the positive or negative reinforcement children receive. (p. 16)

While Comstock does not give us specific information on how television affects the consumer socialization of children, he does suggest the general dimensions of advertising effects.

For theory development and policy purposes, it is desirable to separate the effects of programming from those of advertising, although both are likely to produce similar types of effects in some instances. Unless there is theory to suggest that a given response is a function of specific content, one would be safer to assume that the effect might be due to either program content, advertising content, or both.

Studies of television effects on young consumers can be classified on a continuum ranging from very broad to very specific, depending on the focus of television influence. For example, some studies focus on the effects of television on a youth's self-concept, and others address a child's reaction to specific stimuli in advertising ads. Some researchers have been explicit in suggesting the specific types of television influence. For example, Faber, Brown, and McLeod (1979) suggest that entertainment programs might help the adolescent achieve affective and economic independence from the family by providing young role models who are on their own. Similarly, the same authors suggest that television might provide information about future career options by portraying a wide range of occupational roles.

Previous research also suggests that young people who watch a great deal of television are likely to be aware of occupations traditionally portrayed on television (DeFleur and DeFleur 1967, 785). In addition, television viewing has been linked to the development of certain occupational aspirations (Himmelweit et al. 1958). Such occupational aspirations might be acquired from television role models (Christiansen 1979). In addition to occupational stereotyping, television might serve as a source of sex role acquisition. Research suggests that sex role conceptions might be acquired from television programs by children and adolescents (Sternglanz and Serbin 1974; White and Brown 1981).

Proposition 7.1: Viewing of television programs by young people contributes to the development of occupational orientations.

    (a) Viewing of television programs increases young people's awareness of occupations.

    (b) Viewing of television programs creates desires for occupations in youths.

    (c) Viewing of television programs creates occupational stereotypes in youths.

    (d) Viewing of television programs affects the formation of youths' sex role perceptions.

In addition to programming, advertising also might affect the youth's conception of occupational role. Commercials provide occupational models such as athletes and movie stars, with most of the latter being portrayed by women. Content analysis of advertisements has shown that women in commercials traditionally have been stereotyped as housewives and mothers, with such stereotyping remaining relatively constant over the years (Courtney and Whipple 1979). Research suggests that youths are likely to develop occupational stereotypes by viewing television commercials (Courtney and Whipple 1979). Similarly, a more recent study found television viewing to be associated with occupational aspirations among adolescents (Moschis and Moore 1984).

Viewing television commercials in which the portrayal of traditional sex roles regarding consumption is frequent might lead to the development of stereotyped sex role conceptions regarding consumer decisions among children (Freuth and McGhee 1975; Mayes and Valentine 1979; Dominick and Rauch 1972; Culley and Bennett 1976; Welch et al. 1979; Chiles-Miller 1975) and adolescents (Tan 1980; Moschis and Moore 1982). Young people might acquire these and other similar conceptions about future roles from television. For example, early sociologists (see, for example, Riesman and Roseborough 1955) speculated that people learn anticipatory consumer cognitions from the mass media. Recent research in consumer socialization indicates that motivations for television viewing might be important in the acquisition of a variety of consumer orientations (Moschis and Churchill 1977 and 1978). More specifically, one study found television viewing motives to be positively related to consumer role perceptions (Moore and Moschis 1983), although a longitudinal study suggests a reverse causality (Moschis and Moore 1982).

Sociologists also have speculated that television contributes to the development of knowledge about and need for products in the consumer's "standard package" (Riesman and Roseborough 1955). For example, one study found television viewing to be associated with expectations about the purchase of major consumer products (Moschis and Moore 1984). Such television effects might be the result of both programming and advertising (Vener 1957; Rubin 1979; Adler et al. 1977).

In another study, exposure to television advertising was found to be associated with rather undesirable consumer learning. It decreases the youth's ability to distinguish facts from exaggerations in advertising; it increases the level of dissatisfaction with products the youth buys or uses, suggesting that discontent might be due to increasing expectations about the performance of products advertised; it appears to contribute to the development of positive general attitudes toward marketing stimuli; and in the longer run, it might hamper the development of cognitions about consumer-related matters (Moschis 1984). In addition, nearly all studies examining the negative effects of advertising on children and adolescents have found correlations between the amount of television viewing and several "undesirable" consumer orientations, such as materialistic attitudes and social motivations for consumption (see, for example, Atkin 1975g; Ward et al. 1977; Moschis and Churchill 1978; Moschis and Moore 1982). Specifically, one study found that motivations for advertising (but not programming) viewing were related to social motivations (Moschis 1976a), while research by Ward, Wackman, and Wartella (1977) provided little evidence that frequent exposure to commercials facilitates the acquisition of consumer skills by children. On the contrary, heavy exposure to commercials was associated with poorer acquisition of consumer skills. With respect to the effects of television on delinquent behavior, the findings presented by Schramm et al. (1961) suggest that very little delinquency can be traced directly to television. Rather, the authors view television to be at least a contributory cause (p. 174).

To summarize the effects of television advertising viewing on young people's acquisition of general consumer orientations, television advertising appears to be associated with the acquisition of a wide variety of both desirable and undesirable consumer orientations. These associations often are confounded with possible effects of television programming with respect to the acquisition of these general orientations. The possible effect of television advertising can be summarized in the following propositions:

Proposition 7.2:   Television advertising contributes to the development of young
                   people's perceptions related to several consumer-related roles.

(a) Television advertising affects the development of occupation role perceptions.

(b) Television advertising contributes to the acquisition of traditional sex roles.

(c) Television advertising affects the acquisition of consumer role perceptions.

Proposition 7.3:   Television advertising viewing affects the development of young people's consumption-related motives.

(a) Television advertising viewing increases the desire for material possessions and conspicuous consumption in children and adolescents.

(b) Television advertising viewing decreases the desire for nonsocial, nonimpulse consumer decisions in youths.

Proposition 7.4:   Viewing television commercials affects young people's general knowledge about and attitudes toward consumption.

(a) It increases their knowledge about the purchase of major consumer products.

(b) It creates more positive attitudes toward the marketplace among the young.

Proposition 7.5:   Television advertising hampers the development of consumer skills in young people.

(a) It decreases their ability to process information efficiently.

(b) It decreases their ability to develop realistic expectations about product performance.

The effects of advertising on youths' responses to products and brands can be assessed at three levels: cognitive, affective, and behavioral.

Cognitive Responses. Several studies across different situations suggest that advertising increases youths' awareness and knowledge of products, as well as their perceptions of these products and the people who use them. Specifically, young people, especially children, become aware of new products and brands by watching television ads. A study by the Gene Reilly Group (1973b) suggests that children acquire information from food commercials, as was shown by their high awareness of nationally advertised brand names. More explicit evidence of television influence is provided by Donohue (1975a), who found black elementary school children naming television as a source of awareness of their favorite toy. In a similar kind of research, Caron and Ward (1975) found that one-third of the kindergarteners and more than half of the third- and sixth-graders studied mentioned television as a source of gift ideas for toys and snack foods. These findings are in line with reports from parents of young consumers. For example, Howard et al. (1973) and Barry and Sheikh (1977) interviewed mothers of young children who cited television as the most important information source for products in general and cereal and toy products in particular.

The degree of youths' learning of brand names also is affected by exposure to commercials. For example, Gorn and Goldberg (1976) used commercials for a brand of ice cream unknown to 151 eight- to ten-year-olds and found that any exposure to the commercials resulted in increasing recall of brand name and number of flavors of the product. Alternatively, several surveys of adolescent consumers presented mixed results regarding the relationship between advertising exposure and acquisition of brand and product awareness. For example, in a study of alcohol advertising, Atkin et al. (1980) reported findings linking actual viewing of ads to awareness of the slogans, symbols, and content of these ads, but there was a moderate relationship between advertising exposure and general product knowledge. Several studies assessing adolescents' ability to link brands to appropriate product categories produced contradictory results (see, for example, Moschis and Moore 1978; Moore and Stephens 1975; Moore and Moschis 1979b; Robertson et al. 1979), while adolescents' ability to recall brand slogans as a function of television viewing was rather weak (Moore and Moschis 1979b; Moore and Stephens 1975; Ward and Wackman 1971).

Several researchers have investigated the effects of youths' exposure to advertised products and their perceptions of users of such products. For example, the more television commercials adolescents watch about products such as proprietary medicine, alcohol, mouthwash, and deodorants, the more likely they are to think that more people need or use these products (Atkin 1982).

Besides making youths aware of the products available in the marketplace, television advertising also appears to have some influence on children's perceptions of reality and beliefs about products. For example, previous reviews of the literature suggest that children's conceptions of illness and medicine are affected to some extent by exposure to medicine advertising (Adler et al. 1977). Similarly, Sharaga (1974) reported findings showing a negative relationship between accuracy of perceptions held by children regarding the validity of nutrition claims in food commercials and amount of television viewing. Atkin, Reeves, and Gibson (1979) found that children who were heavy viewers of television ads were more likely than their light-viewing counterparts to say that sugared cereals were highly nutritious. Similarly, Atkin (1975d) interviewed mothers of four- to twelve-year-olds about the main factors affecting children's cereal selection. He found a slight positive relationship between Saturday morning advertising exposure and citing nutrition when asking for cereal. In another study of 256 five- to seven-year-olds, Atkin (1975e) found those children with high exposure to medicine advertising to be more likely to think that people are sick more often and that they take medicine more often. The relationship between exposure to commercials and the adolescent's belief that medicine and hygiene products are effective also has been tested and found to be positive (Robertson et al. 1979; Atkin 1975g and 1978b).

Advertising can influence the basic beliefs of the child. An extensive amount of research shows that exposure to advertising is likely to affect the youth's expectations and beliefs about the advertised products (Adler et al. 1977; Atkin 1982). Haefner, Leckenby, and Goldman (1975) investigated the persuasiveness of four commercials among children in the second, seventh, and eighth grades and found changes in their level of acceptance of the specific product claims made in all four ads. Atkin and Gibson (1978) exposed four- to seven-year-old children to a cereal ad featuring a circus strongman lifting a playhouse and eating the cereal. Children who were the heaviest viewers of Saturday morning cereal advertising were much more likely to express beliefs concerning the effects of the cereal on their own strength.

Another study of the effects of cereal advertising on five- to twelve-year-olds (Poulos 1975) depicted the edibility of wild vegetation. After viewing the commercial, children were more likely to rate similar-looking toxic plants as edible. Atkin (1975e) investigated the relationship between children's exposure to medicine advertising and their beliefs about medicine. He found a positive relationship between exposure to medicine advertising, the child's belief in quick relief after taking medicine, and concern with getting sick. Finally, studies conducted by Robertson, Rossiter, and Ward (1985) and Atkin (1975g) show that heavy exposure to commercials for toys and games is likely to raise the child's expectations about such products.

Research also suggests that commercials might alter the perceived importance attached to the attributes young people use in selecting products (or asking for them). Atkin, Reeves, and Gibson (1979) asked children to evaluate the importance of the attributes of various food products. They found moderate positive correlation between food commercial viewing and the importance of attributes emphasized in messages, such as sweetness, chewiness, and "fun of eating."

To summarize the effects of advertising on young people's cognitions, heavy exposure to television commercials tends to have a favorable effect toward the advertised product. The effects of television advertising viewing often are confounded with the effects of advertising programming. Specific possible effects of advertising on youth's cognitions can be summarized in the following propositions:

Proposition 7.6: Television advertising makes young people aware of products and brands in the marketplace.

   (a) Television advertising affects perceived reality about consumption in life.

   (b) Television advertising affects youths' perceptions, beliefs, and expectations about product performance.

Proposition 7.7: Television advertising effects on the development of cognitions about products and brands is greater among younger than among older youths.

Affective Responses. The most pertinent affective variables are expressed in terms of preferences or liking for advertised brands, approval of advertised products, and satisfaction or disappointment with advertised products. Unlike the effects of advertising on youths' cognitions, the effects of advertising on affective variables do not appear to be as conclusive. First, we have studies that show a significant relationship between advertising exposure and affective variables. Experimental studies show that exposure to television commercials increases preference and liking for the advertised product. For example, Gorn and Goldberg (1977) exposed low-income boys between eight and ten years of age to an ad for a new (unfamiliar) toy product. In comparison to a nonexposed control group, the exposed group was more likely to develop positive attitudes toward the toy. Goldberg and Gorn (1978) also exposed children to a toy commercial and compared them with a nonexposed group. They found that exposed children were significantly more likely to want to play with the toy than the nonexposed group.

Similar results have been reported by other investigators. For example, Atkin and Gibson (1978) found that a larger proportion of children exposed to a Pebbles cereal commercial, as opposed to children in a control group, wanted to eat that cereal. Similarly, in an experimental study, Atkin (1975c) found young adolescents exposed to an acne cream commercial to like the advertised brand more than the nonexposed group.

However, a similar experiment with Honeycombs cereal produced no significant impact, perhaps because of less effective ad execution (Atkin 1982). In another experimental study, Haefner, Leckenby, and Goldman (1975) tested second-, seventh-, and eighth-graders' preferences for a product shown in a commercial, which was inserted in a short film. Exposure to the commercial was not found to be associated with preference and liking for the product.

More convincing results concerning the effects of advertising on young people's attitudes come from cross-sectional surveys. In a correlational study, Atkin, Reeves, and Gibson (1979) found preferences for various food brands to be associated with television commercial viewing among five- to twelve-year-olds. Similarly, Atkin and Block (cited in Atkin 1982) found a positive relationship between watching beer and wine commercials and citing the same brands as favorites among a sample of adolescents.

Another group of studies have found a positive relationship between exposure to television and other media and youths' preferences for brands (see, for example, Moschis and Moore 1979b; Moschis 1978b; Moschis, Moore, and Stanley 1984). Although these studies do not measure exposure to ads per se, they suggest that heavier exposure to the medium also will involve heavier exposure to ads in that medium. Programming effects are assumed to be minimal, since brand names of most products used in programs seldom are identified. More convincing evidence of advertising effects on brand preferences was found in a study that analyzed teenagers' affective responses to brands of varying advertising intensity and level of involvement (Moschis and Moore 1981c). Generally, the data indicated that brand preferences and loyalty varied by advertising intensity and product relevance; they were more likely to exist for heavily advertised and more relevant products than for lightly advertised and less relevant products. These results suggest that although brand preferences are likely to be developed earlier for relevant products, advertising might play an important role in establishing preferences and loyalty for brands of less relevant products among adolescents. Thus, advertising effects on the young consumer might be conditioned by situational variables.

Television ads also are likely to affect youths' attitudes toward product use. For example, approval of medicine was positively associated with exposure to medicine advertising among 256 fifth-, sixth-, and seventh-graders (Atkin 1975e). Similarly, television advertising exposure was associated with the favorability of attitudes toward teenagers' use of certain restricted products such as alcohol (Atkin and Block 1984) and proprietary drugs (Atkin 1978b; Robertson et al. 1979). Finally, Ward and his colleagues (1977), using self-reported measures of advertising influence in their study of children's desires for brands, found a preference for advertised products.

With respect to television advertising effects on children's (dis)satisfaction or disappointment with advertised products, research by Robertson and Rossiter (1976a) and by Atkin (1975g and 1982) suggests that under heavy advertising conditions, such as during the Christmas season, heavy viewers among younger children are likely to have their expectations about products raised by advertising; accordingly, they are more likely to experience less satisfaction with the products they receive and more disappointment over those they do not receive. A study of adolescent consumer socialization, however, found no relationship between television exposure and general consumer dissatisfaction with the marketplace (Moschis and Moore 1980).

To summarize, there appears to be reasonably good supportive evidence that television advertising influences young people's acquisition of affective orientations toward products and brands. Considerably less is known about conditions that facilitate or hamper television advertising influences on the formation of such affective orientations.

Proposition 7.8: Television advertising is more likely to influence the development of affective orientations toward products and brands when the advertised product is relevant to the child's needs than when it is not relevant.

Proposition 7.9: Television advertising increases the level of expectations about product performance.

Proposition 7.10: A youth's dissatisfaction and disappointment is greater when expectations about product performance is higher than when expectations are lower.

Proposition 7.11: A youth's dissatisfaction and disappointment with the advertised products are greater when the person is exposed to heavy television advertising than when he or she is exposed to light television advertising.

Behavioral Responses. The effects of advertising on young people's consumer behavior can be evaluated at two levels: intrapersonal and interpersonal. Some studies show the effects of advertising on the individual's own behavior in terms of actual purchase, while other studies assess advertising effects in terms of parent-child relationships (such as product requests) and subsequent consequences of such requests (such as parental yielding, parent-child conflict, and disappointment). Another way of assessing advertising effects is by looking at several aspects of children's consumer behavior. Wells (1965) posits the following actions of children as consumers: making personal purchases, making direct requests at home, giving passive dictation (that is, parents buying what they know their children like and avoiding what they do not like).

Several studies have investigated the relationship between exposure to advertising and actual consumption. Atkin (1975e) measured consumption of heavily and lightly advertised brands of cereals among 506 fourth- to seventh-graders and found greater consumption of the heavily advertised products. The same findings were revealed in another survey (Atkin, Reeves, and Gibson 1979). Similarly, Duesere (1976) found that television viewing was positively associated with the consumption of heavily sugared cereal. A similar relationship was found between television viewing and eating heavily advertised food products. In the only study assessing self-reported measures of the affects of advertising on young people's consumer behavior, Ward and Robertson (1972) found that half their teenage sample had purchased products as a result of advertising. Poulos's (1975) study revealed findings suggesting that cereal commercials are likely to influence children's behavior. In an experimental study conducted by Resnik and Stern (1977), children were asked to choose between two unfamiliar brands of potato chips. Those children who were exposed to an ad for one brand of potato chips were more likely to choose the advertised product.

While these studies of children show a positive association between advertising and consumption of food products, studies of teenagers concerning the effects of advertising on nonfood items present a rather different picture. For example, use of proprietary drugs was only marginally related to advertising exposure in three studies (Atkin 1978b; Milavsky et al. 1975–1976; Robertson et al. 1979). Moderate associations have been reported between exposure to alcohol commercials (beer and wine) and actual consumption (Atkin and Block 1984). Similarly, survey and experimental research by Atkin (1975c) indicate a moderate relationship between advertising exposure to hygiene products such as deodorants and acne cream and actual consumption. One study, however, found that although exposure to alcohol commercials had no effect on consumption of alcohol by teenagers, a social utility orientation (involving normative expectations about drinking) and a vicarious utility orientation (involving identification with models in alcohol beverage commercials) were found to mediate the impact of advertising exposure (Strickland 1982).

The effects of advertising on product use by youths appear to be conditioned by social and structural factors. For example, the relationship between advertising exposure and the consumption of cereal and candy products is reduced when parents impose restrictions on their children's eating habits (Atkin 1975e). Similarly, Hulbert (1974) found that illicit drugs were used less by those college students who lived at home. Apparently, the presence of parents at home or the child's relationship with them played an important role. As Coles (1986) has suggested, the child most likely to be affected by television stimuli is" a child who is having a rough time personally—whose parents, for instance, are mostly absent, or indifferent to him or her, or unstable . . . [this child] will be much more vulnerable to the emotional and moral power of television" (p. 7). Other factors such as peer group relations and availability of products also are likely to affect behavior (see Adler et al. 1977).

In sum, television advertising affects children's acquisition of consumption patterns. Television advertising effects might not be as strong on the development of behavioral consumption patterns of adolescents, and they might be conditioned by social and structural factors.

Proposition 7.12: Television advertising effects on the acquisition of behavioral orientations are conditioned by individual characteristics and social and structural factors. They are stronger when:

(a) the youth is younger

(b) parents do not impose restrictions on the youth's consumer behavior

(c) parents do not interact with the child about consumption matters

(d) the youth has opportunities and the ability to purchase and use the advertised products

(e) consumption of advertised products is reinforced by peer groups

Because children do not always have enough money to buy many products advertised and they usually have difficulty getting to the store, they are likely to express their desires in terms of requests to parents. In evaluating advertising effects in terms of children's requests, the unit of analysis shifts from the individual child to parent-child relationships. This interpersonal unit of analysis is rather complex because of many factors that can influence parent-child relationships. First, mere opportunity for the child to make the request, either at the store or at home, appears to be an important factor. For example, Atkin (1975f) found two-thirds of the 516 families observed in supermarkets to select cereal because of children's initiation. Clancy-Hepburn et al. (1974) found that children who frequently accompanied their mothers on grocery trips made the most purchase demands. Similarly, coviewing provides more opportunities for requesting the advertised product. Thus, it is not surprising that frequency of requests declines with age (Adler et al. 1977), since older children tend to spend less time at home viewing television with their parents.

Second, parental acquiescence or reinforcement exerts a significant influence on children's request frequencies (Adler et al. 1977). Thus, the child's inclination to request advertised products depends on the extent to which parents are likely to respond favorably to the request. Sheikh and Moleski (1977) found that children exercise discretion in expressing desires to parents. Similarly, the Gene Reilly Group (1973b) study found children admitting to parental restrictions on their eating habits. Finally, because children make a large number of requests for products, the task of isolating those requests that result from advertising is rather difficult. One must demonstrate that attempts are more frequent for advertised than for nonadvertised products. Furthermore, requests or expression of desires to parents assumes that parents are unaware of such preferences. This assumption probably is the exception rather than the rule. For example, the Gene Reilly Group (1973b) study found that of the 82 percent of children who reported ever wanting ready-to-eat cereal, 56 percent said that their mothers knew which cereal they wanted without having to ask (passive dictation). Other characteristics of the parent are likely to affect frequency of requests. For example, in a study conducted by Clancy-Hepburn et al. (1974), children of mothers with a high knowledge of the validity of nutritional product claims expressed significantly fewer requests and preferences for advertised foods.

An impressive number of studies show a positive linkage between exposure to advertising and requests for products advertised. Galst and White (1976) studied three- to eleven-year-olds in a laboratory setting. Exposure to commercials was positively related to purchase attempts. In the same study, request frequency was moderately related to amount of home viewing of commercial programming but was not related to public television programming. Sheikh and Moleski (1977) used a scenario to measure children's likelihood of requesting advertised toys, food, and clothing, finding that the likelihood was rather high. Clancy-Hepburn et al. (1974) found a positive relationship between television viewing on Saturday morning and frequency of food requests reported by mothers of eight- to thirteen-year-old children.

Caron and Ward (1975) studied eighty-four third- and fifth-grade mother-child pairs and found that children cited television as a source of gift requests in 27 percent of the cases. Atkin (1975d) studied three- to twelve-year-olds and found that those who watched Saturday morning commercials and were heavy television viewers in general were more likely to ask their mothers to buy toys and breakfast cereals. In another study, Atkin (1975g) surveyed 738 children, from preschoolers to fifth-graders, and found that one-fifth of them asked "a lot" for cereals after viewing cereal commercials on television. Atkin, Reeves, and Gibson (1979) also surveyed children and found that heavy viewers of Saturday commercials were almost twice as likely to request nine food products as light viewers.

Additional evidence of children's requests for advertised products was found by the Gene Reilly Group (1973b) in a national study of 1,053 children and 591 of their mothers, who completed self-administered questionnaires. Twenty categories of products were examined, and 75 percent of the mothers who purchased these products indicated that they were influenced in their selection by their children's requests.

Children's requests as a result of advertising appear to be affected by several factors. Requests tend to decrease with increasing age (see, for example, Ward and Wackman 1972; Caron and Ward 1975; Clancy-Hepburn et al. 1974; Robertson and Rossiter 1976a) and with parental restrictions on children's consumption behaviors; they increase with social class level (Atkin 1975a; Caron and Ward 1975; Wells and LoSciuto 1966). For products relevant to the child's consumption, the requests tend to be more frequent than for less relevant products (see, for example, Ward and Wackman 1972; Ward et al. 1977). Moschis and Mitchell (1986) studied the relationship between exposure to televison advertising and the adolescent's propensity to participate at various stages in the family decision process concerning products of various levels of relevance to the adolescent versus that of his or her family. Self-reported measures of television advertising viewing were not related with the mother's perceptions of her child's influence (in relation to parental influence) at each stage. These findings suggest that the second-order consequences of television advertising effects found in previous studies (see, for example, Adler et al. 1977) might apply only to young children or products specifically for the child's use (such as toys or candy); they might not apply to older children or to products purchased for family use. Such findings are in line with the results of a study by Henderson and others (1980).

Thus, although there is ample evidence to suggest that television advertising increases a child's likelihood of requesting advertised products, the data seem to indicate that the frequency of such requests might depend on a host of other factors related to child and family characteristics, as well as to structural and situational factors.

Proposition 7.13: Television advertising is most likely to affect a child's requests for advertised products:

 (a) during childhood rather than during adolescence

 (b) when the youth is of a higher socioeconomic background

Proposition 7.14: Television advertising is more likely to affect a youth's likelihood of requesting advertised products from his or her parents when the parents provide opportunities for such requests:

 (a) when they do not restrict the child's consumer behavior

 (b) when they spend time watching television with their child

 (c) when they are accompanied by their child on shopping trips

Proposition 7.15: The effects of television advertising on a child's likelihood of requesting advertised products are greater for products of higher relevance than for products of lower relevance to the child's individual consumption.

Second-Order Consequences. With respect to second-order consequences of television advertising effects, research suggests that a child's influence attempts are likely to lead to parental yielding or denial of the requested product or service. Denial, in turn, is likely to lead to a host of desirable and undesirable outcomes, including the child's dissatisfaction, frustration, and anger; parent-child conflict; and negative feelings on the part of the child toward the parent. On the positive side, parental denial might provide opportunities for consumer socialization.

Many parents respond to a child's requests by yielding to them. In an observational study of 516 families in supermarkets, Atkin (1975f) found that 62 percent of parents yielded to the child's cereal requests. Ward and Wackman (1972) reported yielding levels ranging from 87 percent for cereals to 16 percent for shampoo and 7 percent for pet food. Wells and LoSciuto (1966) found that parents acquiesced to 69 percent of their children's requests for cereal and 57 percent for candy. For products such as toys and children's Christmas gifts, the percentage of requests to which parents yielded were between 31 percent (Caron and Ward 1975) and 54 percent (Ward and Wackman 1972). Only the study by Berey and Pollay (1968) found the mother to be a strong gatekeeper in children's selections, but this study has been criticized on methodological grounds (Adler et al. 1977).

In a study of adolescent purchasing patterns, Moschis, Moore, and Stephens (1977) found differences in parents' participation in teenagers' shopping trips, with higher participation for products of high socioeconomic risk (such as clothes). Such participation is likely to provide opportunities for parental intervention in the purchase or denial when a request is made. In another study of 734 adolescents, Moschis and Moore (1979b) found greater parental influence on youths' decisions for products of high socioeconomic risk. These findings suggest that yielding levels vary by product category. They are substantial for products of low socioeconomic risk of relevance to the child but are lower for products of high socioeconomic and performance risk.

Besides the nature of the product, yielding is likely to be affected by other factors, some of which are related to the child, some to the parent, and some to the family's social structure. Although several researchers have found a positive relationship between a child's social class, age, and parental yielding levels, some research has failed to find such a relationship, and it has been speculated that the strength of the relationship might be contingent on specific social structures (Adler et al. 1977). For example, Berey and Pollay (1968) found child-centered mothers to yield less frequently to cereal requests and have speculated that this might be due to the mother's overriding concern for the child's well-being, which would result in her ignoring the child and purchasing what she thinks is best. Such concern might be highest among mothers of middle social class than among mothers of lower and upper social classes, as the findings of another survey of adolescent consumers suggest; it might be higher for products relevant to the youth's well-being and appearance (Moschis et al. 1977).

Finally, parental yielding to a child's request might be affected by variables related to the parents' knowledge and attitudes. For example, Clancy-Hepburn et al. (1974) found that children whose mothers have a good understanding of the validity of nutritional claims tend to make fewer requests for advertised products and that the mothers yield less to such requests. In sum, parental yielding to a child's requests for advertised products is likely to be affected by several characteristics of the child and the parent, as well as by situational factors.

Proposition 7.16: Parental yielding to a child's requests for advertised products is likely to be less frequent when:

(a) the product is of higher socioeconomic and performance risk

(b) the child is of the middle class rather of than the lower or upper class

(c) the parents are relatively less capable of evaluating the validity of claims in ads

Research also has investigated the outcomes of parental denials of children's requests. Such outcomes can be classified roughly into undesirable and desirable. Denial of the requested products is likely to produce conflict, disappointment, and in some cases anger. Atkin (1975f) found conflict and disappointment over parental denials (conflict occurred in 65 percent of the instances, while unhappiness was recorded nearly half the time). The level of conflict and disappointment over parental denials has a lot to do with the way parents relate to their children. In a study of seventy-two mothers with children ages three to six, Donohue and Sheehan (1980) concluded: "Conflict in the home over product request denials is a function of the manner in which the parents discipline their children, and the manner in which the parent monitors the child's reality with respect to character identification and exposure" (p. 14). Unfortunately, the authors are far from being explicit about the specific monitoring activities and processes leading to less conflict.

Robertson et al. (1985) measured children's disappointment upon not receiving Christmas presents requested and found that 35 percent of the children indicated disappointment after denial. Disappointment was more likely to be greater among children with high television viewing frequency, among younger children, and among children from homes with high parent-child interaction. In studies by Atkin (1975f) and Ward et al. (1977), children's dissatisfaction and disappointment also was found to decline with age. It is not clear, however, whether disappointment declines because of fewer requests associated with increasing age or whether children become more capable of coping with denial (Atkin 1982).

An experimental study conducted by Goldberg and Gorn (1976) sought to determine whether there was a significant relationship between exposure to a television commercial for a toy and a child's feelings toward parents who deny a request for the advertised product. The findings suggest that denial might contribute to negative feelings toward the parent. Unpleasant consequences of a parent's refusal to yield appear to differ by characteristics of the child. Sheikh and Moleski (1977), for example, studied 144 first-, third-, and fifth-graders and found such unpleasant consequences to decline with age and to be fewer among males than among females. Similarly, Robertson, Rossiter, and Ward (1985), in their study of children's (dis)satisfaction with toys, found that younger children experience less satisfaction, as do children with high media exposure and high parent-child interaction. Dissatisfaction was expressed mainly in terms of disappointment over not receiving presents requested. Disappointment measures were negatively associated with the child's age, low television viewing, and, contrary to the researchers' expectations, frequency of parent-child interaction. Apparently conflict and disappointment is more likely to occur when parents and children have greater opportunities for interaction about consumption. In sum, the limited evidence suggests that undesirable consequences of parental denial, expressed either in terms of disappointment or parent-child conflict, are likely to be greater under similar conditions.

> Proposition 7.17: Dissatisfaction or disappointment over not receiving an advertised product is likely among youths who:
>
> (a) are heavy television viewers
>
> (b) are younger
>
> (c) tend to interact frequently with their parents about consumption

Parents' responses to childrens' requests might provide opportunities for consumer socialization, as parents very seldom deny their children's requests without an explanation (Atkin 1975g). Since parental purposive training appears to be rare (see, for example, Ward and Wackman 1973; Moschis, Moore, and Smith 1984), television might serve as a catalyst in children's consumer learning as a result of interpersonal communications with parents at home. The results of a longitudinal study appear to support this line of reasoning. The relationship between television advertising and prosocial consumer role perceptions in the short run was much higher ($r = .37$) among families in which interpersonal communication about consumption was frequent than among families in which it was infrequent ($r = .20$), after taking into account the effects of age, sex, race, and social class (Moschis and Moore 1982).

Thus, it has been found that parental denial, of children's requests for advertised products provide opportunities for socialization, but the degree to which these opportunities produce desirable outcomes might depend on the parents' willingness to interact with their children about consumption.

> Proposition 7.18: Television advertising viewing is likely to have more positive effects on youths' consumer learning among parents who interact frequently with their children about consumption than among those who do not.

The preceding discussion of television effects on youths suggests the model outlined in figure 7–1. Specifically, these findings suggest that television advertising affects the cognitions, attitudes, and behaviors of young viewers. Such effects tend to be stronger on cognitions than on preferences or behaviors, and they tend to be related to one another in line with the hierarchy of effects model. Parents tend to mediate advertising effects, resulting in several unintended consequences, many of which are undesirable, while others might result in effective socialization.

Effects of Conditional Variables. Studies also have investigated conditions under which commercials have the greatest impact on the young consumer. These studies can be grouped into those that have focused on specific characteristics of the ads, the medium, and the intended audience.

Advertising characteristics investigated relate to source and message. Source characteristics have been confined to source credibility. For example, Atkin, Reeves, and Gibson (1979) surveyed five- to twelve-year-olds about the competence of Cookie Jarvis as a source of cereal information. They found that the competence of the source of product information in ads was positively related to television viewing among five- to twelve-year-olds. Similarly, Atkin and Gibson (1978) found four- to seven-year-olds who were heavy viewers of cereal ads to be more likely than light viewers to attribute credibility to the animated figures.

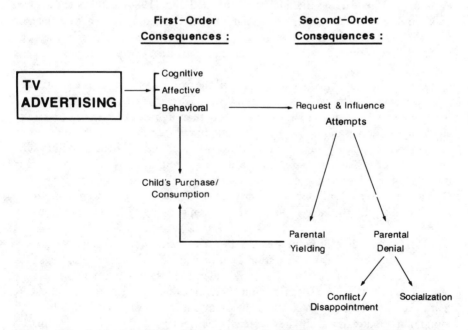

Figure 7–1. A Model of Television Advertising Effects on Youths' Consumer Behavior

Message characteristics include cluttering, brand name repetition, appeal, time compression, and premium. After reviewing extensive research, Adler et al. (1977) concluded that the evidence on cluttering as a volume phenomenon was inconclusive. Similar conclusions were reached with respect to repetition of the brand name in commercials. Atkin (1975b) tested the effectiveness of two appeals (a rational and an emotional message) on five hundred three- to ten-year-old children and found no significant differences between the two messages in children's overall recall of the two commercials and preferences for the advertised product. The potential effectiveness of emotional messages, however, has received some support in a study by Gorn and Goldberg (1982a). The researchers placed the product (orange juice) in an attractive context within the commercial (using music and vivid colors) rather than providing information on the taste or health benefits of drinking orange juice. The researchers found that children were influenced to drink more orange juice by messages previously judged to be emotional in nature.

Young people's attention to, and learning from, television is affected by the time alteration of the visual presentation—that is, the rate at which the material is viewed, either faster (time-compressed) or slower (time-extended). Research suggests that the activity levels and perhaps the information abilities of viewers influence the impact of time compression (Flessati and Fouts 1985). Specifically, time compression is likely to result in poorer learning because of the time available for encoding and rehearsing the televised content. Fouts (1984) also has shown that children might prefer different presentation rates depending on whether they are viewing for entertainment or learning. Other viewer characteristics such as age and experience with time-altered materials are likely to affect learning (see Flessati and Fouts 1985).

One of the more effective message attributes appears to be the premium offer. The survey of five- to twelve-year-olds by Atkin, Reeves, and Gibson (1979) found heavy viewers to be more than twice as likely than light viewers to cite premiums as an important reason for cereal preferences. In another experimental study, Atkin (1975b) exposed two groups of children to two ads, one with the premium offer and the other without it. Those exposed to the premium offer showed a greater desire for the advertised product. In the mother-child study reported by Atkin (1975g), mothers of children who were heavy televison viewers were more likely than mothers of light viewers to report children's asking for products because of premiums.

It is very likely that premiums children see in commercials play a major role in product selection. In an observational study of parent-child interactions in supermarkets, one-tenth of the children studied identified the premium as the primary reason for their wanting a specific brand of cereal (Atkin 1975f; Atkin 1978a). About half the children seemed to consider the premium in choosing a cereal. The study found that about half the children selected a particular cereal from the supermarket shelves because of the premium, based on observer opinion and actual mentions. In another study by the Gene Reilly Group (1973a), a hypothetical choice technique provided more direct evidence of the importance of premiums shown in television commercials. More than half the six- to ten-year-olds and one-third the eleven- to fifteen-year-olds chose the premium attribute over nutrition as a reason for preferring the advertised products.

In addition, a small amount of empirical research has attempted to determine the effects of nonadvertising television content. Atkin (1975c), for example, assessed children's reactions toward public service announcements advocating the use of seat belts, avoidance of littering, and emphasis on nutrition vis-à-vis sugar in foods. The results showed that heavy viewers were not more likely than their light viewer counterparts to endorse the positions advocated in these commercials. A series of studies commissioned by the Council on Children, Media, and Merchandising investigated the use of graphic materials to convey nutritional information to children (Feshbach et al. 1976). The majority of the six- to ten-year-old children used as subjects were able to recall the nutritional information, but only the oldest children could do so without prior orientation.

Another group of studies investigated the effectiveness of public service announcements (PSAs). PSAs about nutrition and food consumption were effective in influencing children's attitudes and behaviors (Goldberg, Gorn, and Gibson 1978; Atkin 1975b; Scammon and Christopher 1981), but antidrug and antismoking PSAs had limited success (Gorn and Goldberg 1982b; Ray and Ward 1976; Smart and Fejer 1974). Similarly, a campaign in Australia aimed at increasing young people's knowledge about alcohol and traffic accidents resulted in a dramatic increase in knowledge and in small but statistically significant changes in attitude in the desired direction (Freedman and Rothman 1979). Thus, studies in this area are not sufficient to suggest whether exposure to prosocial messages has the same effect as exposure to commercial messages.

Finally, certain characteristics of young people influence their susceptibility to television advertising. Research on attitudes toward advertising, which has been fairly extensive, shows that the more experience a youth has with advertising in general, the less favorable his or her attitudes toward it (James 1971; Moore and Stephens 1975). For example, while Breen and Powell (1973) found that second- through fifth-graders both like and believe television commercials, Haller (1974) found that college students generally find advertising irritating, misleading, unnecessary, and insulting to their intelligence. Such differences in responses might be due to differences in experiences or to cognitive development factors (Rossiter 1979). A rather similar explanation is suggested by Campbell (1974), who examined the development of illness concepts among six- to twelve-year-olds. He found that the child's development of illness concepts was related to the child's history and age.

The effect of advertising on young people is likely to depend on various other characteristics. Many studies show that advertising and other commercial and noncommercial sources of consumer information are likely to have a greater impact if the youth is black (or from another minority background), of lower socioeconomic status, younger, female, or from a rural rather than an urban area (Busby 1975;

Moschis 1976a; Gerson 1966; White and Brown 1981; Christiansen 1979). Other factors likely to influence children's cognitive defenses, and therefore their susceptibility to commercial messages, include state of cognitive development, knowledge about advertising, knowledge about the product, spontaneous information-processing abilities, emotional involvement with the ad or product being advertised, and verbal ability (Brucks et al. 1986). These findings collectively suggest that young people possessing such characteristics are likely to be more isolated from "paths of experience," and that this lack of information might make the individual susceptible to exploitation by commercial sources of information (Hess 1970). It is not clear, however, from the available research whether greater susceptibility is due to such characteristics per se or to other factors associated with those characteristics (third variables). For example, culturally deprived or underprivileged children might have fewer opportunities for interaction with their parents, which might increase their susceptibility to television (see, for example, Comstock et al. 1978; Moschis and Moore 1982). The findings also can be interpreted in the context of the theory of distant environments (Hornick et al. 1980), which posits that mass media are most effective when the audience has little or no contact with, or knowledge about, the object of communication. When youths do not have the opportunity or ability to acquire information about consumption from other sources, they are likely to acquire such information from the mass media, including advertisements (Adler et al. 1980).

To summarize the conditions under which commercials have the greatest impact on young consumers, the effects of prosocial advertising content might not be similar to those of commercial messages. Relatively little is known regarding factors relating to the source. There is some evidence that emotional and time-extended messages might be more effective than rational and time-compressed messages, respectively. A premium might be a very important message attribute, possibly affecting awareness of the advertised product, desire for it, and actual purchase. Although several characteristics of the child have been found to relate to his or her susceptibility to television advertising, the reasons for the linkages are not clear.

Proposition 7.19: The effects of prosocial television messages are different from those of commercial messages.

Proposition 7.20: Television advertising messages are more effective when the message:

(a) has an emotional appeal rather than a rational one
(b) is slower (time-extended) rather than faster (time-compressed)

Proposition 7.21: The use of premiums in television advertisements are likely to be effective. They are likely to:

(a) increase awareness of the advertised product
(b) create a desire for the advertised product
(c) result in purchase of the advertised product

Proposition 7.22: The effects of television advertising messages on consumer socialization are greatest when the youth has fewer opportunities or less ability to acquire information about advertised products from other sources. Such conditions are most likely to be present when the youth:

(a) is younger
(b) is black (or a member of another ethnic group)
(c) is of low rather than high socioeconomic background
(d) lives in a rural rather than an urban area
(e) has limited knowledge about the advertised product
(f) has a limited ability to process information and evaluate advertising messages

Print Media Effects

Since children are not heavy users of the print media, the effects of print advertising and editorial content are confined mainly to adolescents or young adults. Findings suggest that newspapers play an important role in the acquisition of consumer behaviors during adolescence. Information in the newspaper is likely to create generic as well as selective demand for products (that is, the formation of purchase expectations regarding generic classes of products) and brand preferences (Moore and Moschis 1981a; Moschis, Moore, and Stanley 1984). Similarly, the results of a study of adolescent decision making indicate that newspaper advertising might significantly affect the formation of brand preferences, even though this agent was perceived as low in credibility in decision making (Moschis and Moore 1979b).

Several studies also have inferred the effects of print ads (mainly newspaper advertising) on adolescents' consumer role conceptions. Such studies have shown a positive association between amount of newspaper reading and the teen's level of competence on various positive consumer skills (Moschis and Moore 1978a; Moschis 1978a). In another study, adolescent newspaper reading was not significantly correlated with materialistic values, but it was significantly related to consumer competency, including consumer affairs knowledge, consumer role perceptions, ability to manage consumer finances, and propensity to perform positive consumer activities (Moore and Moschis 1981a).

Newspaper reading appears to foster the development of positive consumer skills useful in the adolescent's effective and efficient interaction with the marketplace. Thus, contrary to television viewing, which has been found to contribute to the development of primarily nonrational consumer orientations among adolescents, newspapers appear to contribute to the acquisition of primarily rational consumer skills (Moore and Moschis 1981a). It is not clear, however, whether these effects are due to newspaper ads, editorial content in newspapers, or both.

Proposition 7.23: Newspaper reading by youths fosters the development of skills useful in the person's effective and efficient functioning as a consumer in the marketplace. It affects:

    (a) formation of positive consumer norms and behaviors
    (b) development of knowledge about consumer matters
    (c) formation of generic and selective preferences for products

Indirect Influences

Television viewing and newspaper reading also might indirectly affect consumer behavior by affecting youths' frequency of communication about consumption with others. The mass media usually set the agenda for interpersonal discussions (see, for example, Comstock 1978; McCombs and Shaw 1972). This notion is consistent with the two-step flow portion of the limited effects view of the mass media and is supported by some empirical findings (see, for example, Murray and Kippax 1978; Churchill and Moschis 1979).

Television viewing might spur interpersonal discussions about consumption with significant others. Research findings of several studies show that young people are likely to discuss with their parents products they have seen advertised on television (Ward and Wackman 1972; Caron and Ward 1975; Frideres 1973; Burr and Burr 1977). Research also suggests that young people might pay attention to television commercials and discuss them with their peers (Ward and Wackman 1971; Moore and Stephens 1975). The data from one study, however, indicate that television might indirectly affect the acquisition of consumer-related properties by stimulating interaction about consumption with parents and decreasing it with peers (Churchill and Moschis 1979). A comprehensive review of research on parental mediation of television advertising effects (Robertson 1979) found the evidence scattered and incomplete but suggested that parents are "instrumental in the socialization of the child and the values brought to TV viewing" (p. 24) and that a more complex model incorporating family, child, and situational factors might explain relationships better than the traditional linear flow model.

Although it has been suggested that television advertising might lead directly to the development of materialistic attitudes, some findings strongly suggest that family communication processes might condition children's susceptibility to such influence (Moore and Moschis 1981b). The consumer socialization process apparently involves more than mediation of media effects; the data indicate that this learning also might be conditioned by the family communication environment.

On the question of whether television advertising has a direct effect or is mediated through interpersonal processes, the Moschis and Moore (1982) study found that the family communication environment might perform such a mediating function. Specifically, television advertising appears to have some effect on the development of materialism and traditional sex roles when parents do not discuss consumption matters with their children, apparently placing children at the mercy of advertising, a finding consistent with research reported by Churchill and Moschis (1979) and Comstock et al. (1978). The results of the studies generally show that the prowess of television appears to depend on the presence (or lack) of intervention by nonvicarious agents, such as parents.

Moschis and Moore (1982) also noticed short-term television advertising effects on adolescents' interaction with their peers, but these results cast some doubt on the direction of such influence. Apparently, peers play a minor mediating role in learning from mass communication, at least in the long run (Moschis and Moore 1982). Generally, the results from the Moschis and Moore (1982) study were not consistent with the exposure/perception hypothesis advanced in studies of television violence and aggression (Murray 1980) but were consistent with findings in the related area of political socialization (Atkin and Gantz 1978).

In summary, the data suggest that television advertising viewing and newspaper reading might affect the level of youths' interaction with other socialization agents, which, in turn, might affect consumer learning. The mediating role of television ads appears to be more complex, and the data are far from being conclusive. The available evidence suggests that interpersonal processes might condition the youths' attention to and learning from television commercials, resulting in both negative and positive socialization (Moschis and Moore 1982).

Proposition 7.24: Television advertising viewing increases youths' likelihood of interaction with other socialization agents about consumption.

    (a) Television advertising viewing increases youths' likelihood of interaction with family members about consumption matters.

    (b) Television advertising viewing increases youths' likelihood of interaction with peers about consumption matters.

Proposition 7.25: Newspaper reading increases youths' likelihood of interaction with other socialization agents about consumption matters.

    (a) Newspaper reading increases youths' likelihood of interaction with family members about consumption matters.

    (b) Newspaper reading increases youths' likelihood of interaction with peers about consumption.

Mass Media Effects on Adults

Direct Influences

Very little is known concerning the role of the mass media as agents of adult socialization. With respect to the direct effects of specific media, one major group of researchers (Comstock et al. 1978) has hypothesized that since older individuals go to television for much of their information, this medium in particular might have a definite impact on norms, values, and knowledge. Kubey (1980) has hypothesized that since adult socialization is thought to occur most readily when it builds on previously established socializing agents, television (and presumably other mass media) might have a more profound impact on future cohorts of the aged, who will have a more extensive history of exposure to mass communication and its influences. For example, if present trends hold, by the time today's children reach sixty-five, they will have watched television an average of more than nine full years.

Although the role of television and other mass media on the adult socialization process has been left virtually unstudied (Davis and Kubey 1982), some researchers have suggested that the mass media might play a significant role in the consumer acculturation process (O'Guinn, Lee, and Faber 1986). Adult media use can be related to particular need states that might exist not only for adults but other life cycle groups as well (Morrison 1979). While most of the uses and gratifications research advanced in the field of mass communication deals with usage of programming or editorial content by adults, some research has direct implications for consumer socialization. Specifically, Becker (1979) found motivations for using advertising to be a major and distinct aspect of newspaper reading. The primary newspaper gratifications sought by adults are entertainment and advertising information (Morrison 1979).

The effectiveness of mass media advertising is a function of a complex set of variables related to the source, message, media environment, and audience. With respect to source effects, previous research shows that source credibility, likability, power, attractiveness, expertise, and source-audience similarity enhance advertising effectiveness (see, for example, Gelb et al. 1985; Joseph 1982; Assael 1984). Message-related factors include message content (for example, informative versus persuasive) and message structure (the method of presentation and the specific appeal). The effectiveness of specific content appears to be dependent on the situation (including the type of product), circumstances (such as source characteristics), and several audience characteristics (such as race, age, income, and education). (For an updated review of the communication effects of specific advertising content, see Gelb et al. 1985). Message structure includes method of presentation (for instance, one-sided versus two-sided arguments) and specific appeals (such as fear or humor). The effectiveness of specific methods of presentation and specific appeals varies by situation and audience characteristics (see, for example, Assael 1984; Gelb et al. 1985; Belch and Belch 1984; Madden and Weinberger 1984). Message structure also includes time alteration of visual presentation, either faster (time-compressed) or slower (time-extended). Time compression was found to have a significant effect on cognitive orientations. Specifically, time compression is likely to increase attention to and recall of television commercials, and the commercials are likely to be perceived as more interesting (see Gelb and Pickett 1983; Flessati and Fouts 1985).

With respect to the effects of advertising clutter, the existing evidence suggests that heavy clutter conditions and internal placement within a string of advertisements result in a decrement in advertising effects (Webb 1979; Cobb 1985). However, research on message repetition, based on the mere exposure hypothesis (Zajonc 1968), has produced contradictory findings (see, for example, Gelb et al. 1985). The effects of repetition might be curvilinear, or repetition might be effective under certain conditions, such as in ads for low involvement products (Gelb et al. 1985). Other manipulations of variables tested (for example, subliminal advertising) produced inconclusive evidence (Gelb et al. 1985).

Music and visual imagery appears to affect consumer learning. Background music appears to affect product preferences (Gorn 1982), in-store traffic flow, and dollar sales volume (Milliman 1982), while findings in visual imagery show that pictures are better than words in affecting recall and attitude formation (Gelb et al. 1985). The effect of any stimulus is influenced by the environment in which it is presented. Such environments might include editorial or programming content, product fit, technical capabilities, competitive advertising strategy, target population receptiveness, and product distribution system (Gensch 1970). Finally, the effects of advertising source, message, and medium are likely to have a varying impact on individuals having different characteristics (such as personality, demographics, attitudes, and values). Most of these factors have been examined in the context of specific media (especially television) and short-term learning rather than long-term changes in patterns of behavior and cognition.

With respect to specific effects of television advertising, previous research shows that advertising is likely to influence cognitions, attitudes, and behaviors. For example, researchers report high levels of awareness of heavily promoted slogans (Larson and Wales 1970), brands (Atkin et al. 1980) and specific product attributes (Bogart 1967), while a plethora of studies and models show a relationship between commercial messages and attitude formation and change (see, for example, Howard and Sheth 1969; Engel et al. 1978; Assael 1984). Studies also show a mild to strong association between television advertising exposure and the purchase of advertised items (Gorney et al. 1977; Benson 1967). Similar findings are revealed in studies of advertising effectiveness in other media (Atkin and Block 1984). Similarly, aggregate analyses of television advertising expenditures and sales suggest a positive relationship. While it is difficult to infer causality from cross-sectional and aggregate data, field experiments provide more convincing evidence (see Atkin 1982). Advertising, for example, appears to shape the adult's cognitions by providing product information and often affecting his or her purchase decision, especially in the case of unimportant consumer decisions (Robertson 1976).

Thus, it appears from the available data that the influence of television might have different influences on the acquisition of product orientations based on product characteristics, consumer attributes, and a multiplicity of source-message factors. Again, these conclusions are based on the results of studies designed to assess short-term rather than long-term reactions to product or brand advertising in the mass media.

Mass media advertising also might play an important role in learning other types of consumer behaviors, including general and specific patronage habits. For example, Kelly (1967) found advertising to play a role in making consumers aware of a new dairy products outlet. Similarly, Bearden, Teel, and Durand (1978) reported a study of the differences in demographics, psychographics, and media usage of patrons versus nonpatrons of four different types of retail institutions (convenience stores, department stores, discount stores, and fast-food outlets). They found several significant differences in the media usage patterns of patrons and nonpatrons of the four different types of retail institutions. Another study by Darden, Lennon, and Darden (1978) showed that out-shoppers (that is, consumers shopping outside their trading areas) have different media behavior than in-shoppers (those shopping inside their trading means). Different types of out-shoppers also used significantly different information sources, suggesting a possible influence on general shopping patterns by mass communication variables.

To summarize the effects of mass media advertising on adult consumer socialization, the available evidence suggests possible effects of a host of factors on short-term cognitive, affective, and behavioral orientations toward brands, products, and retail stimuli. Most of the causal factors have been examined in the context of television advertising, ignoring possible long-term socialization effects of these and other types of media programming or editorial content and advertising.

> Proposition 7.26: Exposure to and use of advertising in various media contributes to the consumer socialization of adults. The media help form and change cognitive, affective, and behavioral orientations toward:
>
> (a) brands
> (b) products
> (c) stores

Indirect Influences

Besides the direct effects on adult socialization, the mass media also might indirectly affect adult consumer learning by affecting a person's interaction with other sources of consumer information. A great deal of information on diffusion of innovations and the two-step flow hypothesis suggest indirect influences of mass media advertising through interpersonal sources (see, for example, Assael 1984; Engel and Blackwell 1982). Similarly, much of the research in mass communications suggests media uses in interpersonal contexts and the agenda-setting function. The mass media might fulfill a social need, as many people are likely to turn to them for information they can share with others (see, for example, Katz et al. 1974). Similarly, the proposition about the agenda-setting function of the mass media argues that the mass media suggest topics about which the public thinks and concerns itself. Although the mass media might not tell people what to think about those topics, they are successful in focusing public attention on them (Sutherland and Galloway 1981). Thus, although the limited data do not differentiate between programming or editorial content and advertising effects or among types of media, they suggest that the mass media might affect the adult person's interaction with significant others who are likely to serve as socialization agents for the adult consumer.

Proposition 7.27: Use of the mass media increases the adult person's likelihood of interaction with family members and peers about consumption matters.

Proposition 7.28: The mass media suggest topics adult consumers are likely to discuss with significant others.

Mass Media Effects on Older Adults

Several researchers have found the elderly to be heavy users of the mass media (Real et al. 1980; Samli 1967). Cowgill and Baulch (1962) found mass media use to be the dominant leisure activity of older persons. From the activity theory approach, Graney and Graney (1974) advanced the notion that the elderly substitute the mass media use for lost roles (for example, occupational or parental), while Schramm (1969) suggested that the elderly use the mass media to combat social disengagement. Samli and Palunbiskas (1972) reported that the elderly rely heavily on mass media sources of information. Young (1969) indicated that one way in which the aging individual might learn appropriate behaviors in later years is through observation of the mass media. Some studies also suggest that the elderly are more susceptible to pursuasion from consumer information sources when they are socially isolated and perceive themselves as lacking in decision-making competence (Smith et al. 1982; Smith and Moschis 1984b).

According to Graney and Graney (1974), the function of mass media use possibly can promote a new type of social integration. If the elderly substitute mass media content for personal communication, they should be more likely with age to learn consumption-related information from those sources. Indeed, Wenner (1976) found that the elderly view television for information acquisition, social engagement, and compensation.

Proposition 7.29: The mass media play an important role in the consumer socialization of older adults; they serve as sources of information and help older adults form and redefine the consumer role appropriate to their age.

Television

Television is the most widely used mass medium among the aging (fifty-five to sixty-four years) and the elderly (sixty-five years and up). More time is spent watching television than engaging in any other activity, except sleeping (see, for example, Schramm 1969; Rubin 1982; Rubin and Rubin 1982). Research investigating the relationship between television and older viewers has focused on television usage (for example, amount of television viewing and program preference); viewing motivations (positive—information seeking, entertainment, scheduling of activities, topics of conversation; negative—alienation, escape, disengagement); portrayals of the elderly on television (for example, representativeness of older adults on television programs and commercials; images and stereotypes of the elderly presented on television); and effects of television on older viewers (Heatherton and Fouts 1985). The functions of television in the lives of older people vary. Davis and Kubey (1982) summarized research findings showing that television helps the older person obtain information that might otherwise have been missed because of sensory decline, serves as substitute for loss in companionship, offers a convenient way for marking time, and fills ideal time associated with retirement.

Programming Effects. Surveys suggest that television is the most important communication medium for the elderly (Davis 1971; Davis et al. 1976; Rubin and Rubin 1981). The older person watches television from three to five hours per day (see, for example, Stephens 1981; Rubin and Rubin 1982; Nielsen Report 1982), which is more than nonelderly viewers do. Studies of programming effects on the elderly generally have followed two different perspectives: those that view the audience as active and those that treat the audience as passive recipients of communication. With respect to the first type of studies, there have been surveys to determine the elderly's viewing preferences and behaviors. Specifically, Davis (1971) found that older persons prefer nonfictional programs such as news, public affairs broadcasts, quiz shows, and talk shows. Similarly, Schramm (1969) and Steiner (1963) report a higher interest in information than in entertainment among senior citizens. The reasons for such preferences are not clear. Use of television by mature persons fulfills several needs, such as those for information, entertainment, companionship, and relaxation (Rubin and Rubin 1982). Some researchers (such as Stephenson 1967) have suggested that entertainment is the main function of television because it serves a companionship function for the elderly by providing information in place of the loss of face-to-face social interaction that occurs with increasing age (Wenner 1976). Another group of researchers contended that television's major function for the elderly is to provide a link to society (Goldberg et al. 1985). Young (1979) suggested that because the importance of issues such as health, social security, housing, and finances is intensified with advancing age, mature persons (especially those over sixty-five) use television for information about these issues. Thus, the mature person's need for information from television may well represent increasing sensitivity to his or her environment.

Another group of researchers has examined the effects of television on older people from a passive audience perspective. This is the opposite of the active perspective, which views the elderly as being actively involved in the communication process, selectively seeking information to satisfy needs emerging with advancing age. According to the passive perspective, the older person's cognitions and behaviors tend to be influenced by selected television stimuli. It has been suggested, for example, that older persons who are relatively isolated might be especially vulnerable to television's influence on those aspects of their lives of which traditional roles leave them relatively uninformed, especially if persons cannot test the validity of their perceptions through interpersonal communication (Comstock et al. 1978). According to Charles Cooley (1912), social validation is crucial to the development of an individual's self-esteem. As major social institutions, the mass media might represent a significant factor in the formation of many elderly individuals' self-perceptions (Kubey 1980). One study found that among heavy television viewers, including those who were elderly, images of older people were considerably negative (Gerbner et al. 1980). Other studies show that television is an important agent of consumer socialization in the development of perceptions regarding age-related roles. Many of the expectations about roles related to later stages in the life cycle are likely to be affected by television (Greenberg 1982).

It should be noted that while prime-time (8:00 to 11:00 P.M.) television programming is lacking in older characters and presents a generally negative image of the elderly, daytime serial dramas differ in their portrayals. A recent study (Cassata et al. 1980) found that 15.9 percent of the characters appearing in thirteen daytime soap operas were judged to be fifty-five or older, with more than half these characters in their sixties. According to the researchers, the "overall physical appearance of the older characters portrayed was . . . positive . . . the profile of the older person that emerges . . . is one of an attractive individual, usually employed in an important position, who lives independently and makes up an important part of the soap opera world" (p. 49).

A recent study by the University of Pennsylvania's Annenberg School of Communication concluded that:

> More older characters are treated with disrespect than are characters in any other age group. About 70 percent of the older men and more than 80 percent of the older women are not held in high esteem or treated courteously, a very different pattern of treatment than that found for younger characters. Similarly, a much larger proportion of older characters than younger characters are portrayed as eccentric or foolish. (Gerbner et al. 1980, 45)

Even more interesting is that the Annenberg study found a significant positive relationship between amount of television viewing and negative and unfavorable perceptions of older people, especially among young viewers. This relationship held even with important demographic variables, such as education, income, sex, and age held constant. Furthermore, the more television an individual watches, the more likely it is that he or she believes that people (especially women) become old earlier in life. George Gerbner (director of the study) and his colleagues concluded: "In every case, heavier viewing makes a consistently negative contribution to the public's image of the personal characteristics of the elderly, and the quality of their lives. We did not find watching television to be associated with *any* [emphasis in original] positive images of older people" (p. 47).

The two views of how television viewing might affect people appear to be in line with the prevailing views of how the mass media in general and television in particular affect people. Further, they suggest the need for using measures derived from these models (exposure, gratifications sought, and gratifications received) in studying television programming effects on older adults. To summarize the evidence regarding programming effects of television on older adults, viewing of television programs might make older persons aware of age discrimination, and as a result they might develop negative stereotypes about older people in general and a negative self-image in particular. This might consequently have a negative effect upon their consumer role.

Proposition 7.30: Viewing of television programs by older adults is likely to create negative perceptions of older people and themselves. Such viewing:

(a) makes older adults aware of age discrimination

(b) contributes to negative self-perceptions

(c) negatively affects their role as consumers in the marketplace

Advertising Effects. Unlike programming effects, television advertising effects can be interpreted almost entirely in the context of the passive view of the mass media. Some (limited) research suggests that the elderly might use mass media advertising for consumer decisions, although the effects of television were not isolated from the effects of other forms of mass media advertising (Schreiber and Boyd 1980). More recently, Goldberg et al. (1986) extended findings of television programming effects on older people in line with the active perspective of mass media influence. They speculated that since older people use television to get information about important issues such as health, they also might be inclined to seek similar types of information from specific television messages. In spite of the small sample used, their experimental findings suggest that those exposed to information-oriented messages were more likely to recall the health-related information than those exposed to music-oriented (emotional) message.

The extent to which older adults learn from television is likely to depend on several factors related to the presentation of information. For example, time compression is believed to have an impact on their ability to obtain information from television advertisements (Stephens 1982). Older consumers need more time to process information, and time-compressed messages might have a negative effect on their consumer learning. Similarly, because older consumers are more likely than younger adults to experience short-term memory loss, repetition might be more effective in communicating with them. Finally, novelty appeals might not be as effective with older adults.

In viewing television advertising effects from the perspective of a passive audience, the research findings suggest that the consumer behavior of the elderly is affected by advertising in general (French and Crask 1977). More specifically, experience with the mass media appears to influence the elderly's "learning to associate need satisfaction with characteristics of products and services" (Mauldin

1976, 124). One study found significant favorable attitudes toward advertising among the elderly, although they were more likely to boycott products whose advertisements they found distasteful (Warwich et al. 1981). It is thus reasonable to assume that the elderly's attitudes toward advertising are affected by mass media advertising exposure, in line with mere exposure theory, which suggests that increased exposure to a simple stimulus can positively affect attitudes toward the stimulus (Zajonc 1968).

Because the elderly are heavy users of the mass media, including television, exposure to advertising in television might have a particularly strong impact on their norms, values, and knowledge (Comstock et al. 1978). For example, two studies found a negative correlation between amount of exposure to mass media advertising among the elderly and their perceptions of elderly people as being positively portrayed by advertising (Smith et al. 1981; Smith and Moschis 1984b). In another study, exposure to mass media advertising among the elderly was negatively related to self-perceptions, perceptions of old people in general, and perceptions of elderly people as being positively portrayed by advertising (Smith et al. 1986). These relationships become less significant, however, when the effects of age are held constant, suggesting that mass media advertising might have different effects on older people of different ages.

In addition, exposure to mass media advertising was found to be positively associated with economic and social motivations for consumption (Smith et al. 1982; Smith and Moschis 1985b; Smith et al. 1985), suggesting that advertising might increase the salience of product attributes or evaluative criteria. These findings tend to support the agenda-setting function of mass media advertising in the consumer behavior setting. The Smith et al. (1982) study also found mass media advertising exposure to be negatively associated with preferences for brands, suggesting that television advertising information might induce brand switching among older adults. Phillips and Sternthal concluded in their review of the research of the elderly that older people are influenced more by the media than are younger people (Phillips and Sternthal 1977). This might be partly because of increased influenceability and partly because the elderly interact with the mass media more than any other group (Nielsen Report 1982).

The influence of television is particularly noted among the elderly who are relatively socially isolated. These individuals are handicapped in making judgments about the validity of promotional information (Phillips and Sternthal 1977). For example, studies have shown that older people have a good deal of faith in the credibility of television, as opposed to younger people, who tend to be rather skeptical of television's validity as an information source (Stephens 1981). Schreiber and Boyd (1980) also report that television advertising is considered rather credible in relation to, for example, radio, magazines, and outdoor advertising, regardless of the educational background of the mature person.

One way in which the elderly might be affected by advertising is in their ability of differentiate between what Shimp and Preston call evaluative advertising (puffery) and factual advertising claims (Shimp and Preston 1981). Their literature review found solid support for the implication that evaluative advertising is decep-tive. As has been pointed out, irrelevant information might make the learning of in-formation difficult for all people (Slovic and Lichtenstein 1971), particularly the elderly (Bikson et al. 1976). Heavier exposure to mass media advertising might increase the amount of faulty learning because irrelevant information is frequently not recognized as irrelevant, increasing the likelihood of nonoptimal response (Bikson, et al. 1976).

Research findings of one study appear to be consistent with this line of reason-ing, showing a strong negative relationship ($p < .001$) between exposure to mass media advertising and ability to filter puffery in advertising (Smith et al. 1986), while another study using similar measures found a mild positive ($p < .05$) relationship (Smith and Moschis 1985a). Similarly, mass media advertising exposure was positively associated with an older person's frequency of interacting with others and reliance on personal sources of information, suggesting a two-step flow model of influence. Although the effects of television advertising were not singled out in these studies, the results suggest that mass media advertising might affect the manner in which elderly consumers gather, process, and use consumption-related information.

Another role-related aspect of the consumer behavior of the elderly that might be negatively affected by exposure to television advertising is the perception of sex roles in consumer decision making. Several researchers have suggested that televi-sion commercials reinforce stereotypic sex role expectations (Culley and Bennett 1976; Dominick and Rauch 1972). Freuth and McGhee (1975) in particular found a relationship between traditional sex role development and amount of time spent watching television while in another study (Smith and Moschis 1985a) the rela-tionship between exposure to mass media advertising and traditional consumer sex role perceptions among the elderly approached significance ($p < .07$).

To summarize the effects of television advertising on older adults, informa-tion in television advertising is likely to be attended to, and used by, the elderly, especially by those who are relatively isolated socially. Such commercial messages might alter their perceptions, provide reasons for purchase, and provide informa-tion for consumer decisions.

Proposition 7.31: The elderly's exposure to television advertising contributes to their consumer socialization. It affects their perceptions, motiva-tions for consumption, and patterns of information processing. In relation to older adults, television advertising is likely to create in older people stronger:

(a) negative stereotypes of the elderly in general
(b) negative self-perceptions
(c) motivations for consumption
(d) traditional sex role perceptions

Proposition 7.32: The older person's use of information in television adver-tisements differs from that of younger adults. Older individuals are more likely to:

(a) seek out information in television advertising

(b) favorably evaluate television advertising messages

(c) use television advertising information in consumer decisions

Proposition 7.33: The older person's use and interpretation of television advertising messages is more likely to be enhanced to the extent that the messages are:

(a) time-extended rather than time-compressed

(b) repetitive

(c) emphasize few key points

(d) short

(e) simple

(f) presenting information linked to previously learned (familiar) stimuli (such as situations, environments, and products)

Newspapers

Newspapers appear to serve as an important source of news information and of consumer decisions for the elderly (Dodge 1962; Phillips and Sternthal 1977). A study in Atlanta, for example, found that more than half the elderly surveyed read a daily newspaper, and almost 70 percent read the Sunday newspaper (Bernhardt and Kinnear 1976). Similarly, the Schreiber and Boyd (1980) study found that 65 percent of the elderly surveyed named newspapers as the most influential medium in affecting buying decisions. The authors attributed this finding to the importance of food shopping among the elderly and the featuring of supermarket coupons in local newspapers. Newspaper reading, however, appears to decline with age among older adults (Bodec 1980).

A study commissioned by the Newspaper Research Bureau (NRB) (1981) found that 79 percent of those 65 years of age and older read daily newspapers everyday. Males between sixty-five and sixty-nine years old, married individuals, and those who were better educated read most regularly. Seventy-two percent of those seventy-five years old or older read everyday. Men also were found to be heavier users than women in studies reported by Bartos (1980) and Bodec (1980).

Mature individuals read the newspaper for several reasons. Newspapers fulfill a very important information need for the older person, especially the need for local news and social events, including local meetings and shopping sales. The need for such information is reflected in the interest in various content items found in the NRB (1981) study. Although television and newspapers enjoy high credibility among mature consumers, their perceived influence on consumer decisions differs. For example, the Schreiber and Boyd (1980) study found the perceived influence on newspapers to be higher than that of any other medium.

Several reasons might account for the differences between the influence and credibility of television and newspapers. First, mature persons have difficulty processing information, and they do so at a slower pace than younger people. Newspapers allow the older person to control the speed of exposure. Thus, it is not surprising that older people were found to have difficulty in filtering puffery claims in television advertisements with age (Smith et al. 1985). It also is possible that older people who tend to show a relatively high thrifty buying style (Towle and Martin 1976) are more responsive to special promotions such as coupons or sales announcements, which most often appear in newspapers.

> Proposition 7.34: Newspapers play an important role in the consumer socialization of older adults. They affect the formation of decision-making patterns.

Magazines

Magazines also are popular media among the elderly, although they are not used as much as other types of mass media. Their usage varies by type, age, and sex of the individual (Axiom Market Research Bureau 1979). Because magazine advertising effects are confounded with other forms of mass media advertising in studies of the elderly consumer (see, for example, Smith et al. 1981, 1982, 1985), it is not clear how exposure to or use of magazines affects consumer learning of the elderly.

The portrayal of the elderly in magazine advertisements parallels their images on television. Gantz, Gartenberg, and Rainbow (1980) studied seven national magazines (*People, Reader's Digest, Time, Sports Illustrated, Ladies' Home Journal, Playboy,* and *Ms.*) and found that only 6 percent of all ads sampled contained older people, with little variation across magazines. Seventy-four percent of the elderly in the ads were men, suggesting that the elderly, especially women, "are not considered to play a major role in the consumer society" (p. 60).

> Proposition 7.35: Use of magazines by older adults is likely to affect the formation of traditional sex role stereotypes of the aged.

Radio

There is relatively little information regarding the effects of radio programming and advertising on the consumer socialization of older adults. Although mature consumers are not as heavy users of radio as teenagers, they are likely to listen to specific radio stations more regularly than younger adults. Older persons, regardless of sex, are heavy listeners of talk shows. This might be one way of substituting this type of "companionship" format for lost interpersonal interactions. Studies have shown that people who phone radio shows are substituting the contact with the talk show host for the face-to-face contact of which they are deprived (Dimmick et al. 1979). These findings support the activity theory.

Proposition 7.36: Radio listening is likely to be more frequent among older adults who interact infrequently with others than among those interacting frequently.

Indirect Effects

The indirect effects of the mass media also have received some attention in studies of elderly consumer socialization. One study found exposure to mass media advertising to be positively related to personal interaction (Smith et al. 1985). Similar findings were revealed in a different study (Smith and Moschis 1985a and 1985b). These findings suggest that mass media advertising exposure might increase personal interaction about consumption, which in turn might indirectly contribute to the socialization of the elderly.

Proposition 7.37: Mass media advertising is likely to affect the consumer socialization of older adults indirectly by affecting the person's frequency of interaction with friends and relatives.

 (a) Mass media advertising exposure is likely to increase the likelihood of communication about consumption with peers.

 (b) Mass media advertising is likely to increase the likelihood of communication about consumption with family members.

Summary and Discussion

The studies reviewed here suggest conclusions regarding the effects of the mass media and propositions requiring additional support. First, with respect to the effects of television on consumer socialization, the research appears to support this statement by Nicholas Johnson: "All television is educational television. The only question is, What is it teaching?" (Nicholas Johnson, U.S. federal communications commissioner, cited in Liebert et al. 1973, 170). The main implication of this statement is that most of the effects of television on consumer learning are unintended, since so little of television's content is meant to be educational (Williams 1981).

Bronfenbrenner has made the strongest statement regarding the negative effects of television viewing on people: "The major impact of television is not in the behavior it produces but the behavior it prevents" (quoted in McLeod, Fitzpatrick, Glynn, and Fallis 1981, 277). Because television viewing preempts other interpersonal and intrapersonal activities, according to Bronfenbrenner, an individual's development and growth stops while viewing television. Although this chapter did not address the negative effects of television from this perspective, the data seem to suggest that television viewing is associated with both desirable and undesirable consequences across age groups. Furthermore, contrary to Bronfenbrenner's argument, television viewing of specific content (such as advertisements) might stimulate interpersonal discussions, which can lead to consumer learning.

After reviewing the literature, Comstock et al. (1978) concluded that television most effectively influences social behavior when it reinforces attitudes and expectations derived from direct experiences or when it defines situations for which information is not available from other sources. They conclude that "the socialization process of television depends on the lack of intervention by non-vicarious agents, such as teachers and parents" (p. 71). The findings from the present review of studies appear to be in line with this conclusion.

While programming or editorial effects are unintentional, advertising effects are easier to assess. At the cognitive level, advertisements create product awareness and educate consumers about product attributes. At the affective level, ads might influence the development of general attitudes toward consumption (for example, attitudes toward spending or materialistic values) as well as specific orientations, such as brand preferences. At the behavioral level, advertising can play a role in influencing purchases.

The data presented here highlight the important role the mass media in general, and advertising in particular, play in the consumer socialization of people over the life cycle. It is interesting to note that mass media advertising (television advertising in particular) appear to have the greatest effects on people at the extreme stages in their life cycle—stages at which people are relatively less able to process information (Roedder-John and Cole 1986). Furthermore, advertising effects depend on the type of consumer decision.

Solow (1968) suggests that the effects of advertising are strongest on brand-choice behavior and they become weaker on more general types of consumer decisions (product, expenditure, and saving/spending). Since most advertising attempts to stimulate selective demand, one would expect to find more positive linkages between television viewing and cognitive and behavioral orientations toward products and brands than between viewing and orientations toward general types of consumer decisions. Partial support for this line of reasoning comes from the numerous studies of television advertising effects reviewed in this chapter.

The effectiveness of mass media advertising in consumer socialization comes primarily from studies designed to measure short-term effects. In this context, advertising communication via television involves a complex interplay of stimulus and audience variables. Stimulus variables include those related to the message, its source, and the medium itself. Examples of source-related variables include characteristics of the source (model) itself (including sex, race, age, source likability, and trustworthiness). Medium-related factors include advertising clutter and medium involvement. Audience variables include a variety of receiver characteristics and orientations. For example, the consumer is viewed as an information processor to the extent that the product advertised is important to him or her. The more important the decision, the more likely the consumer is to seek information actively and evaluate alternatives on a number of decisional criteria (Robertson 1976).

Future research could examine not only the effects of short-term learning from television advertising but long-term effects as well. Research also should distinguish between advertising and nonadvertising effects. Finally, research should focus on conditions that contribute to the power of mass media advertising in consumer socialization. The view of these data suggest that it is not a question of whether the mass media play an important role in consumer socialization but rather of understanding the processes by which, and the circumstances under which, advertising has its most powerful effects.

8

The Effects of Other Socialization Agents

Besides mass media, family, and peers, other socialization agents might play an important role in consumer socialization. These might include school, siblings, retailers, and church. Unfortunately, data on the effects of these socialization agents are rather limited. The purpose of this chapter is to present the existing research and suggest avenues for future research. When data are available for various age groups, information on the effects of these socialization agents is presented by age category.

School

Childhood and Adolescence

The school can be a potentially significant socialization agent for early and middle adolescence. A young person spends substantially more time in the presence of teachers and classmates than with family or neighbors (Campbell 1969).

Direct Effects. Schools are charged with the responsibility of preparing young people to assume adult roles in society by giving them the skills and knowledge necessary for good citizenship and economic self-sufficiency (Campbell 1969, 844). Economic competence is widely accepted as one of the goals of elementary school education, and this is shown in the courses offered. The typical course of study contains activities and topics that might help develop economic understanding. Among the areas of focus has been the emphasis on knowledge and skills related to consumer behavior, such as understanding business terms and practices and learning some basic vocabulary in economics, intelligent money management, and the ability to select and use goods and services wisely (see, for example, Gavian and Nanassy 1955).

Early sociologists (Parsons et al. 1953; Riesman and Roseborough 1955) speculated that children learn at school "something of the adaptive functions of consumption" (Riesman and Roseborough 1955, 4). Such learning properties are expected to be similar to those taught in consumer education classes and are considered to be necessary for the efficient functioning of the society's economic system.

Numerous studies attempting to assess the effectiveness of consumer-related courses on consumer competencies have concluded that such courses have little impact, if any (see, for example, Hawkins 1977; Langrehr and Mason 1977; Moschis 1978a). These findings are consistent with those in the area of political socialization, where civics courses were found to have little impact (see, for example, Langton 1969; Atkin and Greenberg 1974). It has been suggested that one reason for the poor results is that the courses are offered too late in the child's life to make a difference (Heinzerling 1984). Of interest, however, are the findings of more recent studies suggesting that consumer education might be effective under certain conditions. Conditions under which formal consumer education affects a youth's acquisition of consumer competencies can relate to variables that can be grouped into four categories: content of learning, measures of consumer education effects, time of measurement, and specific learner characteristics.

The content or criterion behavior examined is likely to affect the outcome of the analysis. Given the specific content of consumer education courses, researchers expect to find knowledge gain, for example, as a result of exposure to these materials. Consumer education materials are based on little research (see, for example, Ward 1974a), however, and reflect what young people should know rather than what they are able or ready to learn. During adolescence, students are expected to develop knowledge and skills by taking courses in consumer education, an assumption that is open to question, as a great deal of such knowledge might have been gained by the time they reach this level (see, for example, Moschis and Moore 1979b) or it might not be relevant to the youth (for example, skills in managing family finances).

Miller (1978) argued that the entire curriculum often can be incongruent with the developmental needs of adolescence and should be reexamined to take developmental considerations into account. He presents three theoretical conceptions of adolescence (Erikson, Piaget, and Kohlberg) in the context of educational environments that are conducive to development. Miller's argument has received some support. For example, Levine (1976) contended that adolescence is a period of occupational choices, and at least one study found a positive relationship between consumer-related courses taken at school and the adolescent's likelihood to indicate preference for occupation (Moschis and Moore 1984).

> Proposition 8.1: Consumer education courses at school are more effective when they teach skills relevant to present and immediate consumption needs than when they teach skills relevant to needs in the distant future.

The notion that educational materials should be tailored to the developmental stages in a person's life has been challenged by Ausubel (1960), who maintains that young people can be taught concepts and skills that cognitive developmental psychologists (such as Piaget) consider too complex for their age. Several researchers have demonstrated that when concepts are properly sequenced and translated to an appropriate vocabulary level, they can be learned by children who are not expected to have the cognitive abilities for such learning (see, for example, Lawton 1977). In the context of consumer socialization, our small-scale exploratory research with preschoolers showed that marketplace concepts, when translated to an appropriate vocabulary level, can be learned by these youths (Stampfl et al. 1978; Moschis et al. 1980), suggesting that Ausubel's formal structured approach to the presentation of consumer-related materials should be chosen over the more common open framework of Piaget's approach.

Proposition 8.2: Consumer education materials considered too advanced for youths' cognitive development stage can be effective if they are translated into the appropriate vocabulary level and are presented in line with Ausubel's structured approach.

Another reason for the absence of positive relationships might be the way consumer education is measured. In most studies, measures are taken or comparisons made that reflect exposure to courses related to consumer education. Such measures often include courses such as home economics or economic principles, which might not contain adequate information on consumer education. Langrehr (1979), for example, showed that improvement in economic competency will be achieved by taking consumer education rather than economic principles courses. Inconsistency in the types of courses (and, generally, the quality of education to which a person is exposed) used to assess the effects of formal consumer education in schools also might account for inconsistencies in the findings. For example, while a study of adolescent students from Kentucky and North Carolina found formal consumer education to be related to youths' propensity to perform several positive consumer behaviors (Moore and Moschis 1979b), a study of Wisconsin adolescents found no relationship (Moschis 1979).

Other conditions (requirements) for demonstrating the effectiveness of formal consumer education include appropriate measures of consumer education effects (competencies) and the time lag between course completion and measurement of competencies. When studies assess the effectiveness of formal consumer education, they usually compare subjects who have had such courses to those who have not. Most cross-sectional studies, for example, attempt to infer effectiveness by comparing measures of cognitive and behavioral competencies among subjects who have had certain types of courses and those who have not (see, for example, Langrehr and Mason 1977; Moschis 1984). In experimental or quasi-experimental studies, however, education effects are measured in terms of knowledge gain and/or behavior modification. For example, in a study of educating children about playground safety, a variety of educational materials were produced for playground safety, including a film and sound/slide presentation for schools and pamphlets for teachers, parents, and children. Several information distribution strategies were tested, including no materials distribution, distribution of all or some of the materials to homes only or teachers only, and distribution of all or some to both homes and teachers. Follow-up questioning of children about their knowledge of playground safety and observations of their playground behavior revealed a positive effect of the information. The greatest gains in knowledge and behavior resulted from distributing all materials to both homes and teachers, especially for young children (Reid and Preusser 1983).

It is possible, however, that instructional materials might not be effective until the youth has had the opportunity to interact with the marketplace and relate the acquired knowledge to real-life situations—that is, practice what is taught in the classroom. A longitudinal study of adolescents, for example, showed no relationship between formal consumer education and consumer knowledge in the short run, but the two variables were significantly related after a year's time lag, suggesting that certain activities after formal consumer education might be required for consumer learning to take place (Moschis 1984). While the specific nature of these activities are not explicitly known, Ausubel's theory suggests that participation in the purchasing and consumption process might be required for learning acquired in the classroom to be effective (Ausubel 1960; Ausubel and Robinson 1969). For example, a study by Turner and Brandt (1978) found that learning can be enhanced if parents follow up immediately after teaching takes place by providing their children with opportunities to interact with the marketplace and share family responsibilities. Similarly, Langton and Jennings (1973) suggested that there might be delayed consequences from course exposure, which suggests the importance of timing in measuring consumer education effects. One difficulty in measuring the effect of consumer education over time lies in specifying the time and order in which several courses were taken in the past, as well as pinpointing possible interactive effects of such timing and ordering of courses.

Proposition 8.3: Consumer education courses are likely to have a greater effect on youths who are provided with opportunities to apply what they learn in class to real-life consumption processes.

The last set of conditions for learning deals with the individual's characteristics. It is conceivable that subpopulations of students are differentially affected by the curriculum or consumer education courses. For example, Langton and Jennings (1973) examined the effects of civics courses on the acquisition of political orientations. Specifically, the researchers found black students to be affected more by taking such courses than were whites. These differences were attributed to the black students' lower likelihood to encounter information redundancy in these materials, with the implicit assumption that minority populations have less information. Findings in consumer socialization literature support this assumption, showing that lower-class and black adolescents know less about consumer matters than their upper-class and white counterparts. (Moschis and Moore 1981a; Langrehr and Mason 1977).

Proposition 8.4: Youths most likely to benefit from consumer education materials are those from minority backgrounds having little prior information about effective consumer behavior.

Indirect Effects. School might have stronger indirect than direct effects on consumer learning. Formal consumer education has been found to be related to a youth's interaction with other socialization agents. For example, Moschis (1976a) found a positive relationship between the number of consumer-related courses taken at school and the adolescent's propensity to discuss consumption with parents and read the newspaper. Although the relationship between consumer education and newspaper reading might be the effect of a third variable (specifically, age), the relationship between age and interaction with parents about consumption was, as expected, negatively associated with age.

Proposition 8.5: Consumer education materials to which youths are exposed at school affect their level of interaction with other socialization agents.

(a) Consumer education materials are likely to be discussed with parents at home.

(b) Consumer education materials increase youths' ability to understand, and their interest in reading, consumer-related information in newspapers.

Adulthood

The effects of school as a socialization agent are much more easily assessed among young people than among adults. This is because school might not serve as a socialization agent for the latter group since most high school graduates do not attend college. Furthermore, consumer education following high school is based on the individual's choice, whereas the subject is mandatory in nearly all high schools. It is possible, however, for one to acquire information about consumer matters in different courses (such as nutrition, marketing, finance, and economics), as well as from socializing with classmates, teachers, and peers while attending college. Thus, number of years of education following high school could be as good a measure of formal consumer education as actual number of courses taken in consumer education.

While relatively little is known about the effects of formal education on adult consumer socialization, research on consumer behavior suggests that education might affect the development of consumer cognitions and behaviors. Specifically, education has been linked to saving and spending patterns, budget allocation decisions, and specific aspects of consumer behavior such as information seeking and adoption of new products (see, for example, Engel et al. 1978; Bowen 1977). Generally, these findings suggest that the more educated consumers are, the higher their level of competency in the marketplace with respect to rationality.

Similar to the direct effects, the indirect effects of consumer education have not been examined in the context of consumer socialization. Of special significance are the effects of education on the individual's use of the mass media. Specifically, use of the print media increases with education, while use of the electronic media decreases (see, for example, Allen and Clarke 1980; Wade and Schramm 1969). Of greater interest and importance from a socialization standpoint are the functional relationships between education and gratifications sought in these media, since receiving such gratifications is likely to affect learning.

Wade and Schramm (1969) were among the first to point out the role of education in socialization via the mass media. By analyzing surveys based on national samples, they investigated patterns of information seeking and levels of public knowledge with respect to public affairs, science, and health. The authors concluded:

> It seems evident that an interaction between education and mass media use helps explain how much and what kind of current knowledge an individual has, and to some extent where he seeks it . . . the more education a person has, the more likely he is to use print as his major source of news and information . . . from the parade of events through TV, which is the most vivid and dramatic carrier of events, we tend to fill in our cognitive ways with facts and findings, but to add concepts and understandings we turn to the slower print media which can somewhat more easily offer perspective and interpretation. (pp. 206 and 209).

McLeod, Ward, and Tancil (1965–1966) were more explicit in demonstrating specific functional relationships between education and reasons for reading newspapers. Their findings show that education is positively related to informational reasons for reading; it is negatively related to vicarious reasons. The relationship between education and mass media is likely to be different within specific subcultures. Allen and Clarke (1980) investigated the relationship between education and mass media use among blacks, Latinos, Chicanos, Puerto Ricans, and Cubans. They found that newspaper reading was positively related to education in all groups. Television viewing, however, was negatively related to education only among black and Latino adults; it was positively related to education among Chicanos. Radio listening was positively related to education only among Puerto Ricans.

To summarize the effects of formal education on the consumer learning of adults, little evidence is available regarding the direct effects of specific courses on adult consumer learning. Much more research suggests functional relationships between formal consumer education and the adult person's interaction with the mass media, although certain background characteristics might affect this relationship.

Proposition 8.6: Formal education contributes to the development of skills necessary for the adult person's efficient interaction with the marketplace.

Proposition 8.7:   The level of formal education affects the person's frequency of exposure to and use of the mass media.

    (a) Formal education increases the adult person's likelihood to use print media.

    (b) Formal education decreases the adult person's likelihood to use electronic media.

Proposition 8.8.:   Formal education increases the adult person's likelihood to seek information from the mass media.

Late Adulthood

A limited number of studies have addressed the role of formal education in the consumer socialization of older adults. Smith (1982) examined the effects of formal consumer education in consumer socialization and found no significant effects on select aspects of consumer behaviors. In the same study, formal education was positively associated with mass media exposure, peer interaction, and family interaction. Perhaps one of the reasons the number of consumer education courses taken by these older adults was not associated with the same variables was the small variance resulting from the limited number of respondents reporting exposure to these courses.

Proposition 8.9:   Formal education effects on the consumer socialization of older adults are indirect via the mature person's interaction with other socialization agents:

    (a) It increases the level of interaction about consumption with family members.

    (b) It increases the level of interaction about consumption with peers.

    (c) It increases the older person's likelihood of using the mass media.

Siblings

Siblings can play an important role in consumer socialization. Their influence is expected to be greater during childhood and adolescence than in later years because of their proximity and frequency of contact with the learner. The importance of siblings in the socialization of youths appears to be influenced by the sex characteristics and birth order position of the socializee and socializer. Research by Vener (1957) on the clothing behavior of adolescents suggests that older siblings might be important referents in decisions dealing with dress selection, suggesting that siblings might serve as a source of expressive orientations. Sibling rivalry, which is believed to be stronger among females than males (Hartup 1970), might diminish the importance of a similar-sex socializer sibling.

> Proposition 8.10: Siblings affect the young person's acquisition of expressive aspects of consumption. Siblings are likely to affect the development of:
>
> (a) social motivations for consumption
> (b) materialistic attitudes

The youth's relationship with siblings is likely to affect his or her relationship with other socialization agents. Chaffee and Tims (1976), for example, showed preferences for programming as a function of social context, including sibling interaction, although such preferences are likely to be influenced by specific family and peer communication patterns. Similarly, preschoolers' viewing patterns were found to be highly correlated to the viewing patterns of six- to eleven-year-old siblings (Valdez 1979).

> Proposition 8.11: A youth's relationship with siblings affects his or her relationship with other socialization agents; it affects interaction with:
>
> (a) the mass media
> (b) peers
> (c) parents

The influence of siblings on adult socialization in later life is confounded with the influence of other significant familial referents under the commonly used label *relatives* in studies of consumer behavior. For example, Katona and Mueller (1955) found that one-third of durable goods buyers bought a brand or model that they had seen at someone else's house, often at the house of a relative. Katz and Lazarsfeld (1955) reached a similar conclusion in their landmark study of physician selection.

Research regarding both direct and indirect effects of siblings on adult consumer socialization is lacking, as is research on how relations with siblings affect the adult individual's interaction with other sources of consumer information. Siblings might directly or indirectly affect the acquisition of consumer orientations, but very little is known regarding the specific skills individuals acquire from siblings and the effects of sex (dis)similarity on the sibling relationship over the life cycle.

Retailers

Retailers as agents of consumer socialization have received relatively little attention in the literature. The role of retailer in consumer socialization has been addressed by consumer researchers only in a broad context. For example, in their model for planned social change, Sheth and Frazier (1982) recognized marketers as agents of change, without specifically mentioning retailers. Similarly, Hirschman

(1986) recognized marketers as agents of socialization in subsistence subcultures. Researchers also have presented data suggesting that marketers can function as socialization agents because they can help modify or develop consumption patterns. For example, Matosian (1982) examined the effectiveness of free-ride coupons in increasing ridership. Similarly, Hirschman (1979) showed how credit card payment systems might relate to retail patronage behavior.

Retailers, in particular, appear to meet Brim's (1966) criterion of a socialization agent, as retail establishments are formal organizations with which a person interacts on a frequent basis, with the learner's role not specified (Talmon 1963). Two learning processes appear to be most relevant in transmitting norms and values to the learner: social interaction and reinforcement.

Salespeople and store personnel in general are in a position to affect the socialization of individuals into the consumer role. By interacting with them, a person can acquire information and form impressions about new situations, products, and other consumption-related orientations. Salespeople, for example, are believed to be an important source of new product information and are likely to affect the formation of cognitions and usage of new products (Engel and Blackwell 1982, 343–345).

Furthermore, retailers are in a position to create consumption habits by rewarding certain behaviors and punishing others. For example, specials, contests, coupons, and similar promotions are aimed at rewarding certain behaviors (such as shopping during the workday or off-season travel), while other policies, such as fees for returned checks, ticket cancelation, and shoplifting prevention and prosecution, can be viewed as punishment. Thus, the retailer, through various mechanisms (policies) and operation procedures, might very well contribute to the individual's formation of attitudes, values, and behavioral patterns. Unfortunately, data on the role of the retailer in the consumer socialization of people over the life cycle are sparse. The majority of studies investigating the individual's relationship with the retailer have focused on the person's attitudes and behaviors toward the store (such as store loyalty) rather than on the role of retailer in the socialization of the consumer.

Childhood and Adolescence

Additional analysis of our Wisconsin data (Moschis and Churchill 1978) shed light on the probable importance of salespeople as socialization agents. The survey contained information regarding adolescents' reliance on salespeople as a source of information and advice before buying five products. Salespeople were perceived as a more reliable source than the mass media and on some occasions (for the purchase of pocket calculators and watches) second in importance to parents and more important than peers, with approximately 40 percent of them indicating a preference for salespeople as a source of information and advice. The importance of salespeople as a source of information increased with age but did not differ by social class. Thus, salespeople might become more important as a source of consumer information as youths acquire independence from their parents and must make their own purchasing decisions.

More direct evidence of the importance of retailers in the consumer socialization of young people comes from our multistate study of adolescent consumer socialization (Moore et al. 1975; Moore et al. 1976; Moore and Moschis 1979b). Students were asked to rate the integrity of retail trade and service people with whom they came in contact when making purchase decisions (sources included sales clerks, doctors, television repairmen and car mechanics). In separate analyses of our Kentucky and North Dakota samples of 359 and 301 adolescents, respectively, the favorability of these individuals' perceptions was positively associated with the level of positive consumer activities and brand awareness; favorability was positively associated with slogan recall among Kentucky students (Moore and Moschis 1979b; Moore et al. 1976). These findings suggest that youths' reliance on information they receive from these individuals might affect their consumer socialization Information on how other retail stimuli, besides advertising, affect the consumer socialization of young people is almost nonexistent. Some research suggests that free samples might induce the initial trial and brand purchase, resulting in brand loyalty development (Madison Avenue 1980).

With respect to the indirect effects retailers might have on the consumer socialization of young people, our Kentucky data showed that the favorability of evaluations of retailers was strongly associated in a positive sense with television viewing and newspaper reading, as well as with discussions with friends about consumer matters (Moore et al. 1975). Since these data show relationships and not causality, it is difficult to draw conclusions regarding cause and effect relationships between specific socialization agents.

Adulthood

Retailer influences in the consumer socialization of adults can only be inferred from studies of consumer behavior, as no study of consumer socialization has yet to address this area. Salespeople appear to play an important role in informing adult consumers about products, especially in situations where the consumer lacks the knowledge and ability to evaluate the purchase (see, for example, Engel and Blackwell 1982, 344–345). Such information might result in the formation of beliefs and behavioral patterns regarding the use of products.

Other retailer-initiated efforts might affect the consumer socialization of adults. Such efforts include retail strategies such as free samples, sweepstakes, coupons, and other deals; in-store stimuli aimed at creating product awareness, such as promotional literature on use of products (for instance, vitamins) and services (such as health care); and even direct-mail material, including mail-order catalogs. These mass promotions serve a role fairly similar to the one the mass media play, as they too are dispensers of product information. The effects of retailer-related variables on other socialization agents, their interaction, and the subsequent indirect effect on consumer socialization have received no attention by researchers.

Late Adulthood

Studies of the consumer behavior of older adults provide more direct evidence regarding the retailer's role in the consumer socialization of older people than do studies of adult consumers. There are at least two reasons for this. First, the consumer behavior of older persons recently has been approached from a socialization perspective (see, for example, Smith et al. 1982 and 1985). Second, the retailer's awareness of the importance of the mature market (fifty-five and up age group) has resulted in specific courses of action and the implementation of retail strategies (such as discount programs) aimed at the older consumer. In so doing, the retailer satisfies the needs and reinforces the attitudes of some older customers and socializes others by, for example, making them aware of the consumer "rights" associated with the transition into the role of senior citizen.

Salespeople might play a very important role in the consumer socialization of older adults. For example, a study by Klippel and Sweeney (1974) found salespeople to be among the more important sources of consumer information, along with neighbors, friends, and family members. In another study of 317 senior citizens in metro Atlanta, Smith et al. (1982) found personal interaction, which included interaction with salespeople, to be positively associated with traditional consumer sex role perceptions ($r = .35$) and social and economic motives; they found personal interaction to be negatively associated with the ability to filter puffery. Hoy and Fisk (1985) attributed the older person's focus on interpersonal trust to the geographic area in which older persons lived, which involved buying and selling based on personal relationships and interpersonal judgments.

Other in-store stimuli and retail strategies are likely to affect the consumer socialization of older adults, but the influence of these factors has not been examined in the context of consumer socialization. For example, it is not clear whether the availability of discounts for senior citizens makes these individuals discount prone (see, for example, Lumpkin et al. 1985) or whether they reflect the existing needs of older consumers.

Similar to the case of adult consumers, the indirect influence of retailers on the socialization of older adults remains unexplored. Only the study by Smith and Moschis (1985b) reported a personal interaction variable, which included interaction with significant others and salespeople, to be positively correlated with mass media interaction. Unlike the speculation regarding the directionality of influence in the case of interaction with peers, the influence is more likely to be interpreted in the content of flow from mass media awareness to interaction with salespeople rather than the reverse—that is, older people are more likely to interact with salespeople (for example, ask for products they have seen advertised) than pay attention to advertised products as a result of their interaction with sales people.

In sum, retailers and retail personnel are likely to affect the consumer socialization of a person over the life cycle. They might be particularly important in the development of the person's decision-making patterns and consumer role perceptions related to specific stages in the life cycle.

Proposition 8.12: Retail personnel influence consumer learning over a person's life cycle. They are likely to affect the development of orientations related to the main stages of the decision-making process:

    (a) needs and motives
    (b) information seeking and utilization
    (c) use of criteria in product evaluation
    (d) product and brand preferences
    (e) product (dis)satisfaction

Proposition 8.13: Retail personnel help shape consumer role perceptions appropriate to a person's behavior at various stages in the life cycle.

Church

Although there is limited evidence that religion, in the form of an organized church or synagogue, affects consumer behavior (Engel and Blackwell 1982), there is some evidence that youths find in their religious groups socialization goals that they cannot find in their schools or even families (McCandless 1969). Similarly, research by Burton and Hennon (1980) suggests that church might serve as an agent of consumer socialization for the older person. The most significant effects of religious affiliation are believed to be conflict, guilt, and shame, especially in the social-sexual area.

Church and church-related education is believed to be successful in teaching children the *verbal* distinction between right and wrong, although there seems to be little internalization of truth (McCandless 1969). Consistent with religious and cultural standards, one would expect church as a socialization agent to affect the development of behaviors and values that are morally right and wrong. While there appear to be no right behaviors regarding the consumer role, with perhaps the exception of charitable contributions, there do appear to be consumer behaviors that can be considered wrong from a moral and ethical standpoint. For example, delinquent behaviors such as shoplifting would be considered undesirable by most religious standards. Similarly, self-indulgence, hedonism, and material possessions are likely to be deemphasized by most religious groups as desirable goals in life.

Interaction with church groups is likely to affect the individual's relationship with other socialization agents. For example, children who spend their time preparing for and attending church instead of watching television or interacting with friends are likely to be affected less by these socialization agents. Certainly, these speculations deserve future study.

Proposition 8.14: Church is likely to affect the development of morally right and wrong consumer behaviors. People who attend church frequently, in relation to those who do not, are less likely to:

(a) engage in delinquent consumer behavior
(b) possess materialistic values
(c) buy products promoted via sex appeal

Summary and Discussion

Birren and Woodruff (1973) have summarized the role of formal education in socialization over the life cycle. First, according to the researchers, development does not end with biological maturity but continues until death, providing opportunities for education to help individuals meet the challenge of developmental tasks throughout the life span. Second, formal education has focused on youths rather than on individuals of all ages. This, along with the increase in life expectancy, are expected to create a greater need for providing education to older adults. Third, as social and psychological progress continues to accelerate and individuals are forced out of careers, and as their skills become obsolete, there will be opportunities for education to play an important role in the resocialization of adults. Finally, education is expected to play a significant role in the future, as more women are pursuing careers and the amount of leisure time increases.

One of the difficulties in studying the school as a socialization agent stems from the fact that in itself, the school can be viewed as a separate social system within which socialization occurs. Thus, curricula and course objectives define the desirable outcome of socialization (content or criterion behavior); socialization agents might include teachers, classmates, and peer groups with whom the individual interacts during school hours; and, finally, the school, through various policies, creates a unique environment (social structure) within which the person is expected to learn. For example, bused-in children and minority groups often impose social structures on the person within which learning is expected to take place. Similarly, some religious groups cut their children off from any after-school extracurricular activities (McCandless 1969). And, as in the case of minority group children, these individuals might have no functional peer group in the school setting.

Siblings also might play an important role in the consumer socialization of individuals, but the specific effects and socialization processes operating are unclear. There is some indication that the sex and birth order characteristics of siblings might determine their importance as socialization agents and the manner in which they influence the socializee. Retailers and retail personnel also seem to be in a position to, and apparently do, affect the development of consumption-related orientations at various stages in the life cycle. Finally, other socialization agents might play an important role in the acquisition of consumer values, norms, and behaviors, but data are too sparse to suggest the specific skills acquired from these agents and the processes of skill acquisition.

Future research could investigate the effects of these socialization agents in a more systematic fashion. We need to know the types of consumer skills individuals acquire from these agents over the life cycle, the processes of skill acquisition, and the circumstances under which siblings, school, retailers, and other agents are most effective. Research also is needed in addressing the indirect effects of these agents on consumer socialization.

9
The Effects of Age and Life Cycle

The notion that consumer behavior patterns change during the course of a person's life cycle was first presented by social scientists (Clark 1955) and a decade later by consumer researchers (Wells and Gubar 1966). Initial efforts to study consumer behavior over the life cycle have focused primarily on descriptive differences in consumer behavior among age groups (see, for example, Reynolds and Wells 1977; Scanzoni 1975). More recently, researchers have systematically begun examining changes in consumer behavior using socialization perspectives. In addition to consumer socialization researchers who focused on young people (see, for example, Ward and Wackman 1971; Ward 1974a; Moschis and Churchill 1978; Moschis et al. 1980), an increasing number of consumer researchers have used socialization perspectives to understand differences in consumer behavior over the life span. For example, Smith and Moschis (1985a) used socialization theories to study the consumer behavior of the elderly. Similarly, Belk (1985) emphasized the importance of studying materialism over the life cycle, and Rook (1985) approached the ritual dimensions of consumer behavior from a socialization perspective.

It already has been empirically demonstrated that the family life cycle concept is a good predictor of a wide range of consumer behaviors ranging from broad expenditure decisions to choices of specific products (see, for example, Arndt 1979; Wells and Gubar 1966; Murphy and Staples 1979). Utsey and Cook (1984) traced the origins of the family life cycle variable as a predictor of several aspects of consumer behavior, ranging from residence and economic decisions to telephone usage and deal proneness. In addition, they used Simmons Market Research Bureau data to analyze product consumption over the life cycle. Their results clearly indicate the importance of life-cycle variables in predicting general and specific aspects of consumer behavior.

Since most of the research in consumer socialization and consumer behavior has used age as an explanatory variable, with less emphasis on other time- or life-span-related concepts, information on consumer behavior differences and socialization processes is presented as it might relate to age for broad age groupings (childhood, adolescence, adulthood, and late adulthood).

Childhood

Consumer Behavior

The most striking feature of children's consumer socialization is that it begins at a very young age. Long before children are able to purchase products, they are already dictating product preferences to their parents (Reynolds and Wells 1977). An exploratory study by McNeal (1969) found that there is significant involvement with the consumption process as early as age five. By the time the child reaches the age of nine, he or she has acquired fairly sophisticated consumption orientations. The child's participation in the consumption process is greatly facilitated by the availability of income. Common sources of income for children include receiving money as a gift, an allowance, and outside earnings (Belk et al. 1985).

A great deal of consumer socialization appears to take place during childhood. During this period, consumer learning involves the acquisition of general and specific orientations, as well as simple and complex consumer skills. General consumption orientations include the acquisition of concepts such as materialism and consumption stereotypes. Specific orientations include orientations such as preferences for brands and understanding the meaning of money.

At least three studies suggest that materialistic attitudes are acquired early in life. Ward et al. (1977) and Atkin (1975c) found a significant negative relationship between materialism and age during childhood. Similarly, Belk, Rice, and Harvey (1985) found that children's wishes for material possessions declined with age. The decline in materialistic attitudes suggests that materialistic values might be acquired by middle childhood.

Belk, Bahn, and Mayer (1982), as well as Belk, Mayer, and Driscoll (1984), examined children's ability to recognize consumption symbolism. They found an increasing ability with age, but they suggested that differences might be due to both age and experience. While the development of cognitive skills can be interpreted in the context of Piaget's theory, the experiential perspective is more in line with Ausubel's formulation.

Specific consumption orientations also are likely to undergo formation and change during childhood. For example, the Ward, Wackman, and Wartella (1977) study found that children's familiarity with brands and sources of information increased with age. Such simple skills are likely to be acquired during childhood, but other, more complex skills are not likely to be acquired prior to adolescence. A developmental study of consumer information-processing strategies among four age levels (kindergarten, fourth grade, eighth grade, and college) suggested that certain information-processing skills might not begin developing until late adolescence, and they might not even become fully developed during adulthood (Capon and Kuhn 1980).

Research also suggests that older children use more sophisticated consumer skills and strategies than younger children as they acquire additional information and accumulate more experience in the marketplace (Roedder-John and Whitney 1986). In fact, the Ward et al. (1977) study shows an increase in the awareness of multiple sources of consumer information about new products and in the importance of television as a source of product information. Some age-related differences, however, could reflect ability to recall rather than merely awareness, both of which seem to be related to age. For example, Atkin (1975b) found that brand name recall among children increases about 100 percent with age.

Since most early consumer socialization research focused on the effects of television on children, the available evidence on age-related differences in children's consumer behavior is concerned with orientations toward television commercials. Rossiter (1979) has summarized the results of studies dealing with the effects of age on children's responses to television commercials. The evidence suggests that with age, children become more capable of understanding the nature and purpose of television, and they develop more negative attitudes toward television advertising. Children's desires for advertised products and their requests to parents are not affected with increasing age. Fairly similar conclusions were reached in another literature review by Atkin (1982).

Although television advertising has little effect on children's requests to parents as the children age, requests to parents in general tend to decrease as children grow older (Isler et al. 1977). This decline is due partly to the child's understanding of the persuasive intent of various marketing efforts and partly to the child's acquisition of economic independence. For example, the Ward et al. (1977) study showed a decline in children's desires for most products shown on television with advancing age, while Reece (1986) found independence in shopping to increase with age among kindergarten students and third- and sixth-graders. Children's acquisition of economic independence from their parents often is combined with parental permissiveness. McNeal (1969) found that with increasing age, there is not only an increasing desire among children to assume independent purchasing activities but also an increasing parental permissiveness in children's independent consumer behavior.

Consumption orientations are likely to undergo formation and change during childhood, in line with cognitive development theory, which postulates successive stages in the development of cognitive ability with age. Some research, however, has found that some children displayed consumer-related skills beyond what would be expected from theoretical descriptions of their cognitive-stage abilities (Ward et al. 1977). Another study found that preschoolers can, with appropriate teaching procedures, develop consumer skills that normally can be acquired only by children older than eight years of age (Moschis et al. 1980).

In a more recent study, Soldow (1983) analyzed children's responses to radio and print advertising to determine how much children of different ages actually retain from these modes of communication. The children were exposed to the same advertisement in television, radio, and print forms. After exposure to the ad, they were asked to pick out the previously described product package from five different packages offered. Contrary to expectations, preoperational children (two- to seven-year-olds) were as good at selecting the right package from the radio ad as they were from the television print ads.

To summarize, children acquire a variety of consumer orientations (skills) with increasing age. Simple skills such as desires for products are likely to be acquired earlier than more complex skills (such as information processing). Skills not related to the actual purchasing process—that is, indirect skills (see chapter 2) such as attitudes toward material possessions—appear to be acquired earlier than skills directly related to the purchasing process. This might be due to the youth's involvement in purchasing activities in late childhood rather than to the cognitive-stage abilities of the child.

Proposition 9.1: Children acquire simple consumer orientations earlier than complex consumer orientations. Specifically, children in early childhood are likely to acquire affective orientations, including:

(a) preferences for marketing stimuli

(b) attitudes toward marketing stimuli and the consumption process

Proposition 9.2: Children are more likely to acquire complex cognititive consumer skills in late childhood than in early childhood years. Older children are more likely than their younger counterparts to possess cognitive consumer skills, including:

(a) knowledge about marketing stimuli

(b) the ability to discriminate between marketing stimuli

(c) the ability to complete purchasing transactions

Proposition 9.3: Children acquire consumption orientations that are indirectly related to the purchasing process before they develop skills that are directly related to the purchasing process.

Proposition 9.4: Children's skill-acquisition process depends on their cognitive abilities to the extent that they are exposed to uniform teaching methods or structural factors affecting learning.

Proposition 9.5: With appropriate teaching methods, children's acquisition of consumer-related skills can be enhanced beyond expectations based on cognitive-stage abilities. Children can acquire skills that normally can be acquired only by children with more developed cognitive abilities.

Socialization Processes

The early school years find children changing in the way they interact with socialization agents. Television viewing increases throughout childhood years, as does its use as a source of consumer information (Alder et al. 1980). Similarly, the use of newspapers, magazines, and books appears to increase between the first and sixth grades as the child becomes increasingly capable of reading printed information (Wartella et al. 1979). Peer influence seems to begin in about middle childhood (McNeal 1969). Parents also seem to treat their children differently according to the child's age. The limited research data available suggest that overt parent-child interaction about consumption is likely to be of importance during early childhood; it might be supplemented or followed by observation of parental behaviors in later childhood (Ward et al. 1977).

Proposition 9.6:   With increasing age, the child's relationship with socialization agents changes in line with an increase in cognitive developmental abilities. With age:

(a) Children use more mass media.

(b) Children interact more with peers about consumption matters.

(c) Children begin learning consumption skills by observing parental behaviors.

Adolescence

Consumer Behavior

Several patterns of consumer behavior appear to undergo formation and change during the adolescent years. During adolescence, a person generally acquires several consumption-related skills and is transformed into a fairly sophisticated consumer (see, for example, Moschis 1978a and 1981a; Moschis and Moore 1979b). Furthermore, several of the consumption-related orientations adolescents acquire are likely to persist well into adulthood. For example, a recent brand-loyalty study prepared by Yankelovich, Skelly, and White for *Seventeen* magazine found that a significant percentage of adult women were using the same brands they chose as teenagers (Madison Avenue 1980).

An adolescent's discretionary income and expenditures constantly rise with age (see, for example, Moore and Moschis 1978a and 1979b). Older teenagers generally have more money, and they earn most of it. For example, a study by the Youth Research Institute found that older teenagers (sixteen- to nineteen-year-olds) had more than three times as much discretionary income as younger teenagers (thirteen- to fifteen-year-olds) (Youth Research Institute 1967).

Maturation is believed to be a major factor in the development of future role expectations (see, for example, Thorton and Nardi 1975). Role knowledge in general increases linearly with age (DeFleur and DeFleur 1967). With respect to the development of cognitions regarding anticipatory consumption, some sociologists have suggested that during adolescence, people are likely to develop expectations regarding the purchase of some key items that make up the family's "standard package"

(Riesman and Roseborough 1955). Research also has found that aspirations (including aspirations for material possessions and impatience for their acquisition) vary by age (Cobb 1954). Similarly, older adolescents were found to be more interested in family consumption matters, including planning of finances (Moore and Holtzman 1965), and to have more accurate consumer role perceptions than their younger counterparts (Moschis and Moore 1978; Moore et al. 1976). A more recent study of anticipatory consumer socialization found that as adolescents grow older, they are more likely to develop accurate consumer role perceptions and expectations for purchasing products, and they are less likely to defer gratifications regarding the purchase of products (Moschis and Moore 1984).

Although several orientations regarding cognitions for present and future consumption are likely to develop during adolescence, many such orientations are likely to be formed by the time a person reaches adolescence. For example, Mayer and Belk (1982) found that acquisition of consumption stereotypes occurred prior to reaching early adolescence. Specifically, impressions formed by sixth- and eighth-graders were similar to those of college students and adults. Similarly, Moschis and Moore (1979b) found that by the time a person reaches adolescence, he or she has formed accurate sex role perceptions regarding consumer decisions.

It is likely, however, that many orientations that develop during childhood or adolescence are tentative and might undergo further formation and change in later life. For example, Moschis and Moore (1981a) examined the development of desires for items in a family's "standard package" (including house, car, and furniture). The findings highlight the notion that the development of desires for consumer products occurs throughout a person's life cycle, with cognitions likely to change at various stages. The findings further suggest that young people develop tentative expectations regarding the purchase of major household products at a fairly young age. These expectations are likely to change at a later stage. Such modifications might not necessarily occur at every stage in the person's life cycle because changes in purchase expectations for some products do not seem to occur during adolescence (Moschis and Moore 1981a). Thus, adolescence appears to be a period characterized by development and changes in purchase expectations and in expectations regarding the role of the consumer, which they will be called upon to enact in later life.

Proposition 9.7: During adolescence, youths develop perceptions regarding consumption and the roles they are likely to acquire in later life. With increasing age, adolescents are likely to:

(a) develop expectations regarding the time horizon for acquiring certain major products

(b) develop perceptions regarding normative consumer behaviors

(c) acquire greater knowledge about adult consumer roles

Proposition 9.8:   Many role perceptions and expectations regarding product acquisition are tentative and are likely to undergo changes in later life. Adolescents are most likely to revise their expectations regarding the purchase of major household items.

Proposition 9.9:   Adolescents are least likely to modify stereotypes acquired. They are least likely to change:

    (a) sex role perceptions regarding family decisions
    (b) consumption stereotypes

Three studies that investigated the relationship between age and materialistic attitudes among children suggest that such orientations are developed by early childhood and decline with age during later childhood years (Belk et al. 1985; Atkin 1975c; Ward et al. 1977). During adolescence, changes in materialistic orientations appear to vary by socioeconomic characteristic. In the study reported by Moschis and Churchilll (1979), age and socioeconomic status by themselves had little influence on materialistic attitudes, but there was a crossover interaction between age and social class. Specifically, lower-class adolescents were found to develop less favorable materialistic attitudes with age, while youths from middle-class families were found to be more likely to develop stronger materialistic orientations with age.

Similar observations can be made with respect to the acquisition of desires for brands of products. In the Moschis and Moore (1981a) study, brand preferences were tracked over short time intervals. The data suggest that brand preferences for some products, such as toothpaste, softdrinks, and jeans begin early in childhood and are completed by the adolescent years, where brand preferences for products such as light bulbs, typewriters, and radios begin prior to and are continued during the adolescent years (although the formation of brand preferences does not necessarily stop at the end of this period). Brand preferences for products such as furniture might develop after adolescence, and brand preferences for products such as coffee and tires might develop or change before and after adolescence. Again, as in the case of materialism, such development or change appears to be affected by the youth's socioeconomic background. In a separate analysis, brand preferences were found to increase with socioeconomic status, as in the Moschis and Churchill (1979) study, after taking into account the race of the adolescent. Similarly, Guest (1964) found that brand loyalty increases somewhat among children of a higher socioeconomic status.

Apparently adolescence is a period during which youths become aware of their potential for fulfilling consumption wishes and desires acquired earlier in life. Youths from higher socioeconomic classes might recognize that such desires are within their reach and as a result, might develop even more optimistic expectations, resulting in a stronger desire for material possessions and products. Socioeconomically deprived youths might perceive a lower potential in product acquisition because

of their low socioeconomic status, and as a result, they might downplay the importance of material possessions and the ownership of products. This might explain
the decline in materialistic attitudes and brand preferences.

> Proposition 9.10: The development of desires for products and brands during
> adolescence is contingent on the youth's socioeconomic
> background. With age, desires for products and brand are likely to:
>
> (a) increase among adolescents from higher socioeconomic
> backgrounds
>
> (b) decrease among adolescents from lower socioeconomic
> backgrounds

Childhood and adolescence are periods during which many decision-making
patterns develop. The results of a study on consumer decision processes suggest
that children have acquired fairly sophisticated decision-making cognitions and skills
by the time they reach early adolescence (Moschis and Moore 79b). The findings
further suggest that adolescents tend to rely more on personal sources of information for products of high socioeconomic and performance risk; they rely on the
mass media for products perceived as being low according to such criteria. These
findings are similar to those from adult consumer research (see, for example, Engel
et al. 1978). The same study also revealed that although adolescents preferred to
consult with their parents or rely on information they received from them, parents
did not appear to be instrumental in the child's decision regarding which product
to buy. Rather, brand name and reduced price seemed to be the primary considerations in adolescent buying decisions. Surprisingly, peer influence was found to be
quite low at the product evaluation stage, nearly as significant as advertisements
and store reputation.

Finally, examination of the effects of maturation on youths' decision-making
patterns found significant differences in the number of information sources preferred, but age had no impact on the number of attributes used in decision making. The data do, however, show changes in the type of information sources preferred (peer versus parents). Similarly, although adolescents do not seem to use
an increasing number of attributes or criteria in decision making with age, they
might emphasize different available product attributes. For example, age correlated
with the respondent's tendency to evaluate a product by brand name, suggesting
that young people might be developing efficient shopping skills by using brand
name as a summary of a larger number of attributes, such as price, performance,
and warranty (Moschis and Moore 1979b).

Adolescence also is the period during which additional consumer skills are acquired. For example, Moschis and Churchill (1979) examined age-related differences
in a wide variety of consumption-related skills and found significant differences between younger and older adolescents. Specifically, older adolescents had greater
amounts of consumer affairs knowledge, were better able to cognitively differentiate

product attribute information in advertisements, manage consumer finances, and seek information from a variety of sources prior to decision making. They also were more likely to perform socially desirable consumer behaviors than their younger counterparts. Younger adolescents had more favorable attitudes toward advertising and prices than older adolescents.

The relationship between age and advertising responses also is documented in several other studies (Adler et al. 1977). In one study, older adolescents scored significantly higher on brand knowledge, price accuracy, legal knowledge, and role conception measures than did their younger counterparts (Moschis and Moore 1978). These findings suggest that with increasing age, adolescents tend to develop a greater resistance to persuasive advertising, understand marketing strategies relating to the pricing of products better, and become generally more sophisticated consumers. The results might further suggest the development of general discontent toward marketing stimuli and practices as young people acquire more experience with the marketplace.

Age-related differences in decision-making patterns, as well as other consumption-related attitudes, skills, and values, can be explained by cognitive developmental perspectives (see, for example, Moschis 1981a). For example, cognitive developmental theory suggests that a person's cognitions undergo formation and change during adolescence. Specifically, young adolescents (age eleven to fourteen) are believed to be at a formal operations stage of cognitive development, whereas older adolescents are assumed to have developed their cognitive skills more thoroughly (Piaget 1972). Unlike Piaget's stage notions of cognitive development, however, consumer learning might be facilitated or accelerated as a result of various experiences in the marketplace. This proposition would be in line with recent work on Piaget's theory placing more emphasis on the effects of experience (Flavell 1970).

It is interesting to note that older adolescents are somewhat more skeptical about the integrity of retail trade and service people with whom they come in contact when making purchase decisions. In one study (Moore et al. 1975), we asked respondents how honest or dishonest they believed the following were: radio ads, television repairmen, car mechanics, sales clerks, television ads, teachers, magazine ads, doctors, and newspaper ads. An honesty evaluation scale for media sources was constructed by summing the ratings given radio ads, television ads, magazine ads, and newspaper ads. The other sources were grouped into an honesty evaluation of personal sources scale and scored in a similar manner. The differences in mean evaluations of personal sources were significant, with the senior high school youngsters giving personal sources a more negative rating than the junior high school youngsters.

Older adolescents in this study were more skeptical about the integrity of the retail sales and service people with whom they interact in making purchase decisions. Both adolescent age groups were more skeptical about the information derived from media sources than they were about the consumer information derived from personal sources. The honesty ratings of older adolescents apparently were based on more frequent direct contact with retail sales and service people, since older students reported making more purchase decisions alone than did younger students.

Although personal sources were given higher ratings than media sources by both sample groups, the senior high school students were slightly more skeptical of media sources than were the junior high school students. These differences in evaluation might stem from the fact that older adolescents have had more direct experience in the marketplace and thus more direct personal contact with these sources. Hence, the older adolescents might base their evaluations on direct experience, while the younger adolescents might base their evaluations on expectations.

In sum, the evidence suggests that decision-making skills undergo formation during adolescence. With age, young people acquire a variety of orientations related to various stages in the decision-making process. Age affects the way adolescents go about using information and evaluating products, as well as the extent to which they understand the consumption process and can function efficiently in the marketplace.

> Proposition 9.11: An adolescent's ability to function as an efficient and independent buyer in the marketplace is functionally related to age. With increasing age, the adolescent:
>
> (a) uses a larger variety of information sources
>
> (b) uses more objective (rather than subjective) criteria in evaluating products
>
> (c) develops greater resistance to persuasive stimuli
>
> (d) develops a better understanding of marketing practices and policies
>
> (e) develops a greater discontent toward marketing stimuli and practices
>
> (f) acquires greater independence from his or her family in purchasing products

The opportunity to learn from direct experience appears to be a function of the degree of purchasing independence acquired during childhood and adolescence. For example, Moschis, Moore, and Stephens (1977) found significant differences in the degree of purchasing independence between younger and older adolescents for various types of products. Their findings further suggest that opportunities to learn from direct experience are different in various subcultures. For example, significant differences in purchasing independence among younger and older adolescents were found for upper-class adolescent consumers, but only for the purchase of six of the eleven types of products studied (health care, school supplies, shoes, shirts and jeans, socks and underwear, and records or tapes). Middle-class adolescents appear to attain relatively less independence in purchasing as they grow older than do adolescent consumers in the other two social classes.

Not only do adolescents acquire greater independence in purchasing with age, but they also influence the family decision-making process. In the Moschis and Mitchell (1986) study, for example, age was positively related to the youths' involvement at all stages in the family decision process. Although age differences were not analyzed by socioeconomic status, the data show that the influence in purchase decisions declined with increasing socioeconomic status.

The Moschis and Churchill (1979) study also found age-related differences in consumer behavior by socioeconomic status. Specifically, younger, lower-class adolescents were found to hold more favorable attitudes toward advertising than their middle-class counterparts. They held less favorable attitudes when they were older. While the attitudes of middle-class adolescents toward advertising remained relativley stable with age, those of lower-class adolescents tended to decline. These findings suggest that various levels of opportunities for consumption in social classes might affect the development of consumer-related orientations during adolescence, with the upper classes having more opportunities than the lower classes. These notions are in line with Lewin's (1951) life-space theory and are supported by additional data (Ward 1974a). Thus, the findings suggest that middle- and upper-class families might make a more conscious effort to socialize their children into their class norms by closely supervising their purchases, helping them better understand marketing stimuli, and providing opportunities for consumption.

Proposition 9.12: Social class norms mediate youths' acquisition of independence in purchasing and involvement in family decisions. Adolescents from higher-class families, in comparison to those from lower-class families, are:

(a) less likely to acquire independence in purchasing with age

(b) more likely to participate in family decisions with age

(c) more likely to be exposed to opportunities for consumption with age

One of the difficulties is assessing developmental differences in consumer socialization stems from the difficulty in specifying the direction of the development or change of many consumption-related orientations, especially attitudes and values. This is partly because many attitudes and values are culturally bound. For example, one culture might stress conspicuous consumption as a measure of success, while another might recognize the individual's contributions to the community. In such instances, youths are likely to develop the attitudes held by their culture or subculture.

Maturation also helps us understand certain aspects of the development and change of dysfunctional consumer behaviors. Kohlberg (1976) focused on adolescence as a period of moral development during which a person develops the ability to engage in moral reasoning. During this period, the youth is expected to lose the egocentric orientations developed during childhood and to begin considering relevant others and society. Beginning in early adolescence, the child becomes increasingly concerned with the mandates of society and the internalization of the belief that morality is defined by law and moral codes. This process is believed to be completed by the time the adolescent has entered adulthood, at which stage the importance of laws and rules to the functioning of society has been completely internalized.

Support for Kohlberg's (1976) contention comes from two studies of shoplifting behavior among youths. Specifically, Klemke (1982) and Powell and Moschis (1986) presented data based on large-scale surveys suggesting that shoplifting is highest during early adolescence and declines thereafter. These data also support a model of delinquency that Klemke (1982) calls declining adolescent crime (DAC).

Thus, the general process of moral development outlined by ego and moral judgment theories involves the increasing maturity of moral thinking and impulse control. A developmental view of impulse control is inferred largely from a theoretical curve developed by Anna Freud (Elder 1968). Such a curve shows the fourteen-year-old as having reached about 65 percent of mature development in impulse control; by nineteen years old, the control has reached nearly 95 percent. Based on these notions, Powell and Moschis (1986) tested the hypothesis that shoplifting on impulse declines with age. Their data, based on reponses from 7,379 juveniles (age seven to nineteen), supported this hypothesis.

> Proposition 9.13: Delinquency declines during adolescence with respect to shoplifting behavior.
>
> (a) Adolescents shoplift less with age.
> (b) Adolescents shoplift less on impulse as they grow older.

Socialization Processes

Adolescence is a period of rapid change in interaction patterns with socialization agents. With respect to the adolescent's interaction with the mass media, research shows that television viewing (including uses of television content, both programming and advertising) and use of books and comic books declines, whereas radio listening, record playing, and newspaper reading increase (see, for example, Lyle and Hoffman 1972; Avery 1979; Moschis and Churchill 1978; Moore and Moschis 1981a).

The adolescent's interaction with and use of the mass media might be interpreted in the context of developmental perspectives. The need for real-world situations begins to displace the fantasies of early childhood as long-term goals, career objectives, and consumption needs enter the adolescent's value system. This is attested to by the gradual shift toward more news and public affairs program preference during late adolescence (Avery 1979).

Although television viewing appears to decrease with age, motivations for viewing remain constant during adolescence, with teenagers at all age levels reporting use of television as a means of passing time, relaxation, entertainment, relieving loneliness, or simply forgetting (Avery 1979). By the age of sixteen, the teenagers' viewing patterns are likely to be similar to those they will display as adults (Schramm et al. 1961).

Record listening and record playing increase during adolescence, and listening to music is most likely to be a source of relaxation, entertainment, and relief from loneliness (Avery 1979). Given that music listening is a way of coping with anger and hurt feelings arising from parent-child conflicts (Lyle and Hoffman 1972) and that these motivations are similar to those of television viewing, one might speculate that consumption preferences for electronic media arise out of interactions with parents at home. The increasing use of the radio also might reflect the teenager's need to spend more time with peers and be accepted by them. Knowledge of contemporary performers and their music is a necessary prerequisite to many interpersonal relationships (Avery 1979; Clarke 1971 and 1973).

During this period, adolescents' need for independence from their parents leads them to establish a dependence on peers (Coleman 1961), causing them to spend more time outside the family context. This seems to affect their frequency of interaction with parents and peers, and thus it is not surprising that age has been found to be negatively associated with frequency of communication about consumption with parents and positively associated with peers (see, for example, Moschis and Churchill 1978). While the frequency of communication with peers and parents seems to change, it is not clear whether the actual influence of these agents undergoes corresponding change with age. One study found that although older adolescents spend more time communicating with friends on consumer matters, both adolescent age groups are more inclined consistently to rate parents as good consumers than they are to rate friends, brothers and sisters, or other adults as good consumers (Moore et al. 1975). Some studies have shown that parents are still the main influence (agent) affecting buying decisions (see, for example, Gilkison 1965; Moschis and Moore 1979b), although their significance might be declining (Gilkison 1973). The evidence also suggests that such influence might be situation specific (see, for example, Moschis and Moore 1979b; Brittain 1963).

In sum, there is reasonably adequate evidence to suggest that during adolescence, television viewing and book reading decline, while radio listening, record playing, and newspaper reading increase. Furthermore, adolescents spend less time interacting with their parents but more time with peers regarding consumption matters. Motivations for mass media use might be related to the youths' interpersonal relationships.

Proposition 9.14: Parent-child conflict declines with increasing age, resulting in lower usage of television and radio listening to escape from reality.

Proposition 9.15: The degree of parental and peer influence on youths' consumer learning becomes situation specific with age.

Adulthood

Consumer Behavior

The completion of adolescence is followed by the long life span of adulthood, roughly between the ages of eighteen and fifty-five. During this time, many activities, especially consumption behaviors, are more related to the individual's position in the life cycle or planes of life-span progression than to chronological age. For example, product usage differs considerably between Baby Boomers and older adults (Time Inc. 1985). Progressive changes in a person's life cycle are related to important changes in purchasing behavior as well as to communication behavior (Wells and Gubar 1966).

Several aspects of the individual's consumption behavior are likely to be affected as he or she moves into different stages of the life cycle. They vary from changes in the person's available income to changes in aggregate consumption categories and specific products (Wells and Gubar 1966). It should be noted, however, that these changes in consumption-related cognitions and behaviors do not necessarily occur at the time of the actual change in the person's life cycle. They might be acquired before the person reaches a particular stage through anticipatory socialization. In our recent adolescent consumer socialization study, for example, we found that a great deal of learning concerning adult consumer roles consisting of cognitions related to rational consumer behaviors occurs during the adolescent years and that the learning of such role perceptions determines how the person behaves in the marketplace (Moore and Moschis 1983). Similarly, anticipatory socialization might occur during adult and later years in the life cycle (Riley et al. 1969). Thus, acquisition, and perhaps enactment, of skills, values, attitudes, and norms related to a given role might occur at an earlier stage than is expected.

The importance of needs are likely to change over the life span in response to changes in sociopsychological states, and changes in need structure often result in the reorganization of need-satisfying activities (Dimmick et al. 1979). As a result, the life cycle is likely to be a better predictor of consumer behavior than age, although the latter is likely to discriminate better than the former in some cases (Wells and Gubar 1966). For example, in a literature survey, Fritzche (1981) found that the family life cycle construct, as compared to other approaches, satisfactorily explains household energy consumption patterns. Similarly, Belk (1985) demonstrated the importance of studying changes in consumer values and perceptions over the life cycle. Life cycle appears to be a strong predictor of consumer behavior with regard to needs and preferences for products or services and general shopping patterns, rather than specific preferences or consumer skills. For example, a great amount of research suggests the link between the consumption of durable goods and stages in the life cycle (see, for example, Berkman and Gilson 1978; Assael 1984). Similarly, Granbois et al. (1986) found the family life cycle to be negatively related to the family's propensity to use a written budget, pointing to the importance of experience in planning consumer expenditures.

With respect to developmental variables, previous theory and research suggest changes in cognitive and behavioral orientations as people approach the middle and later years, during which they accumulate experience and become more committed to norms, people, and ways of doing things (Riley et al. 1969). The positive relationship found between store loyalty and age (Reynolds et al. 1974) might be a reflection of such changes. Similarly, maturational factors might account for differences with respect to store patronage patterns. For example, previous research by Bellenger, Hirschman, and Robertson (1976–1977) found age to have a strong relationship with store selection among female shoppers. Age also has been found to have some effect on cognitive orientations toward shopping (Cort and Dominguez 1977–1978). Finally, age has been shown to be positively related to store loyalty (Reynolds et al. 1974), suggesting that with age, people become increasingly committed to ways of doing things.

It should be noted that not all changes in consumer behavior variables during adulthood can be explained in terms of maturational or life-cycle factors. It also is possible that such developmental explanations might reflect cohort effects or even period effects. Chronological age and life-cycle stages are devoid of any historical influences, which can account for differences between age groups in cross-sectional studies (Jaworski and Sauer 1985). Support for this argument is provided by a study that measured the value patterns of two groups representing different generations and growing to maturity under different social and historical conditions (Penn 1977). Unfortunately, cohort and time explanations are less specific in theoretically describing expected functional relationships between various cohorts, times, and consumer behaviors, suggesting their use as control variables in socialization research.

Thus, the evidence provides adequate support for the contention that consumer socialization is an ongoing process occurring through the adult years. During adulthood, changes in consumer behaviors and the reestablishment of consumption patterns are associated with changes in the need structure due to changes (both sociological and psychological) taking place in the person's life. Such changes are likely to affect general consumption orientations as well as specific aspects of the person's consumer behavior. Changes in such orientations (mostly cognitive) might occur prior to reaching the stage at which changes in consumer behaviors are likely to occur. These earlier acquired cognitive orientations, in turn, are likely to affect subsequent consumer behaviors.

Proposition 9.16: Stages in a person's life cycle are associated with unique behavioral patterns of consumption.

Proposition 9.17: The development of behavior patterns about consumption at each stage of the life cycle is preceded by the development of corresponding cognitive patterns—that is, anticipatory orientations.

Proposition 9.18: Anticipatory orientations determine how a person behaves as a consumer at a given stage in the life cycle.

Proposition 9.19: Life cycle is a better explanatory factor than age of development and changes in general consumption patterns; it is a more viable predictor of the development of:

(a) general consumption needs

(b) orientations toward general consumption patterns, values, and perceptions

(c) saving and spending patterns

(d) major expenditure patterns

Proposition 9.20: Age is a better predictor than life cycle of the development and change of the person's specific consumption orientations.

(a) Age is positively related to behavioral consistencies (such as loyalty to brands and stores).

(b) Age is negatively related to innovativeness.

(c) Age is positively related to traditional values and perceptions (such as sex roles).

Socialization Processes

An individual's age or life-cycle position also is likely to affect communication behavior. While media use for adults might be more stable than for children and adolescents, some evidence of changes in media use within the adult life cycle does seem to exist. For example, newspaper readership seems to increase with age (Kline 1971; Samuelson et al. 1963) and decline at very late stages in life (Chaffee and Wilson 1975), while television viewing seems to be related to age in a curvilinear fashion with middle-age categories showing the lowest amount of time spent with this medium (Greenberg and Kumata 1968; Mendelsohn 1968). In comparison with other stages in the life cycle, however, few studies have focused on mass media use by adults, while the study of adult media use is almost nonexistent in the life-span literature (Dimmick et al. 1979). While media use for adults might be more stable than for children, adolescents, and older adults, changes in media use within the adult life cycle do occur (Morrison 1979). Such changes often are the result of changes in the life cycle as a result of major events (such as career choice or marriage) rather than specific age-related changes. Specifically, differences in media use are likely to reflect the psychosocial needs associated with major events that can be satisfied by the mass media. Thus, the uses and gratifications perspective has become one of the more popular approaches to the explanation of adults' use of the mass media (Morrison 1979).

Proposition 9.21: A person's interaction with socialization agents undergoes changes during adulthood. These changes are reflective of changes in the life cycle as a result of major events. During adulthood:

(a) Newspaper reading increases with age.

(b) Television viewing declines until middle adulthood and then increases.

Late Adulthood

Consumer Behavior

Consumer behavior among older adults, as in other age groups, differs in two important ways: First, it is different from the consumer behavior of younger adults; second, it differs across age groups of older individuals. Differences in consumer behavior between older and younger adults were noted several decades ago. Hepner (1949) was among the first to predict changes in the tastes, preferences, and demand of products among the growing number of elderly.

Most research on the consumer behavior of older adults has found differences not only between younger adults (under fifty-five) and older adults, but also within age groups of the latter group, especially between the fifty-five to sixty-four and the sixty-five and over age groups (see, for example, Lumpkin et al. 1985; Smith 1982). It should be noted, however, that such age-related differences are not only attributed to age but also might be the effects of cohort and period (Jaworski and Sauer 1985). For example, because the educational level achieved by each cohort is progressively different, it is recognized that declining intelligence scores with age found in cross-sectional studies might be misleading (Smith 1982). Similarly, the effects of television (as a socialization agent) on older adults is expected to have a greater impact on future aged cohorts than on present or previous aged groups as a result of a greater cumulative exposure to and experience with television. Thus, age-related differences in the consumer behavior of the aging person might not apply to successive groups of the elderly, and they might not be attributable to age per se.

Most explanations of differences in the behavior of the elderly are closely tied to theories of alterations in the sociopsychological and biophysical stages of life-span development. Sociopsychological perspectives include both sociological and psychological theories. Examples of the first type are the disengagement, activity, social breakdown, and subculturation theories. Psychological approaches include mostly personality theories. Biophysical theories derive from developmental perspectives.

Role Perceptions. Whereas most significant life roles (for example, spouse, parent, or employee) have rather clear role norms, role models, and even rites of passage (such as a wedding), socialization into old age exhibits none of these, with the possible exception of the retirement ceremony (Rosow 1970). Role-related aspects of behavior have been found by some researchers to be related to advancing age (Streib 1968; Fulgraff 1978). Neugarten, Moore, and Lowe (1968) found that "as the individual ages he becomes increasingly aware of age discriminations in adult behavior and of the system of social sanctions that operate with regard to age appropriateness" (p. 27–28). One of the few consumer role prescriptions for the older consumer appears to be the maintenance of economic independence, often in the face of a fixed or shrinking income (Riley et al. 1969). The desire for economic independence might explain the elderly's propensity to use deals, special offers, and coupons (Schewe 1985).

Aging is accompanied by the increasing interiority of the individual (Neugarten, Havighurst, and Tobin 1968) and greater susceptibility to influence, especially in areas in which self-confidence is lacking (Phillips and Sternthal 1977). According to the social breakdown theory, the elderly internalize the negative stereotypes of the aged advanced by society, resulting in lowered self-esteem and self-perceptions (Kuypers and Bengston 1973). "People in later life seem to become less resilient and more sensitive to socially mediated stereotypes. Information on 'the old' that is loaded with negative evaluations easily affects their self-concept and their feelings of social and personal competence" (Olbrich and Thomas 1978, 69).

The consumer role is likely to change significantly for aging individuals (Mauldin 1976), and it might be affected by negative prescriptions leading older consumers to perceive their consumption roles in the marketplace as less significant than those of younger people. For example, one study found the elderly's perception of themselves and their consumer role to decline with age (Smith et al. 1986). Research also suggests that older people might lack adequate socialization into roles assumed in later life. For example, Lambert (1980) found many older people to be ill-prepared to assess their medical protection needs and to choose wisely among alternative insurance policies.

Age also might affect sex role perceptions in general and sex roles related to family decisions in particular. Specifically, advancing age might have what Sherman and Schiffman (1984) call an "equalizing effect"—that is, a man's life situation deteriorates at a more rapid rate than that of a woman, resulting in male-female equalities that were absent during middle age. According to this view, from a developmental perspective, aging men and women become more like each other (more androgynous) psychologically (Neugarten 1972). After retirement, in particular, males and females may have less clearly defined sex roles, sharing household chores and other tasks (Finch and Hayflick 1977), including decision-making (Neugarten 1968). Traditional sex role boundaries gradually might fade as a result of the reduction of differences between roles and the sharing of household chores (Lipman 1961; Finch and Hayflick 1977). The result is that in terms of decision making, there is more egalitarianism (Lipman 1961; Neugarten 1968 and 1972). In two studies, for example, age was negatively related to egalitarian sex role perceptions among the elderly (Smith et al. 1982; Smith and Moschis 1985a).

The fact that older men and women become more alike with increasing age also might be based partly on the hormonal changes that occur during aging (Finch and Hayflick 1977). Thus, biologically as well as psychosocially, men and women become more like each other (Birren 1964).

On the other hand, the jeopardy hypothesis suggests that with advancing age comes a worsening of inequalities existing between males and females in earlier life stages. While the research cited by Sherman and Schiffman (1984) comes from areas other than consumer behavior, it does suggest that the jeopardy hypothesis might help explain select aspects of the aging consumer household. Some studies support the view that older adults have more traditional sex role perceptions than younger adults, based on cross-sectional age-group comparisons, and these perceptions might be attributed partly to cohort effects. For example, one would expect older adults to have more traditional attitudes than their younger counterparts because younger women have more egalitarian attitudes than older women, probably as a result of higher educational levels and rates of labor force participation (Mason et al. 1976; Scanzoni 1975, 1976, 1977).

To summarize age differences up to this point, older people's perceptions regarding consumer roles are likely to change in later years. These changes in perceptions reflect changes in the older person's sociopsychological and biological states and, perhaps, inadequate socialization for consumption roles assumed in later life.

Proposition 9.22: Increasing age is associated with general negative perceptions of the older person's consumer role. It is associated with:

(a) negative perceptions of their consumer role
(b) negative stereotypes of the consumer behavior of older adults
(c) increasing concern with maintaining economic independence

Proposition 9.23: Older people's sex roles regarding family decisions are likely to become egalitarian. With age:

(a) Sex role perceptions regarding family decisions become more egalitarian.
(b) Joint decision making increases.

General Consumption Patterns. Consumption patterns and orientations vary across age groups of mature adults. Such differences often reflect changes in need structure, reflecting changes in biopsychological, sociopsychological, and life-style characteristics.

Beginning with saving and spending patterns, older adults show differences in financial services and products used. For example, popular investments among older consumers include IRAs, CDs, property, vacation homes, stocks, and mutual funds (Gilson 1982). Preferences for conservative investments might indeed reflect the need for security and risk avoidance. Similarly, older people have a relatively greater need for leisure- and convenience-related products, health-related products and services, and housing facilities (McMahon 1976). Such preferences might reflect intensified sensitivity to health, convenience, and housing issues (Young 1979). For example, statistics show that up to 66 percent of the elderly's total expenditures are for food and housing (Moroz 1979). Proportionately more money is spent on medical care and household operations, whereas expenditures for household furnishings, transportation, clothing, personal care, and vacations have been found to decrease with age (Dodge 1962; Media Decisions 1977; Goldstein 1968). Thus, it appears that the consumption patterns of older consumers do not always reflect their needs, perhaps because of income constraints.

> Proposition 9.24: The general consumption patterns of older consumers reflect intensified sensitivity to needs due to aging when income is not a constraint. These consumption patterns are likely to focus on products and services related to:
>
> (a) leisure
> (b) convenience
> (c) health
> (d) housing
> (e) financial services

> Proposition 9.25: The general consumption patterns of older consumers reflect basic consumption needs where income is a constraint. These consumption patterns focus on products and services related to:
>
> (a) food
> (b) medical care
> (c) housing

Information Processing. Other changes in the consumer behavior of the elderly might be explained by developmental (biological) factors. The elderly have been reported to process information less efficiently than younger people, requiring more time, slower pacing of stimuli, and fewer distracting influences (Phillips and Sternthal 1977). This might be due to the deterioration of the eye-movement mechanism that controls pursuit—that is, the ability to follow an object that moves quickly across the visual field. It also might reflect a decline in the individual's ability to process new information due to loss of fluid intelligence—that is, the ability to see and use abstract relationships and patterns—less ability to screen out irrelevant information, and the physical aging of the nervous system. Such a deficiency in information-processing capabilities might explain the elderly's greater susceptibility to advertising. The effect of advertising in general has been found to have a significant impact on the consumer behavior of the elderly (French and Crask 1977). One way in which the elderly might be affected by advertising is in terms of their inability to differentiate between what Shimp and Preston (1981) call evaluative advertising (puffery) and factual claims. All of the Shimp and Preston (1981) research implies that evaluative advertising is deceptive. The findings of three other studies support this line of reasoning. Specifically, the ability to filter puffery was negatively related to age among the elderly (Smith et al. 1981 and 1985; Smith and Moschis 1985a).

Another age decrement in consumption problem-solving situations concerns data integration. It has been acknowledged that the consumer is presented with a distressing abundance of information, not all of which can or will be used (Zedek et al. 1974). Many elderly people have poor eyesight because of deterioration of focusing ability, light sensitivity, and light-level attention, which results in changes in color perception. Some of this information is irrelevant and redundant, creating difficulties for most decision makers (Slovic and Lichtenstein 1971), including the elderly (Bikson et al. 1976). Some aging persons experience short-term memory loss. A great deal of the information gathered about a purchase cannot be recalled, creating a reluctance to gather and evaluate (integrate) information. Elderly consumers might make less than average use of open-code dating, product components, warnings, nutritional labeling, and unit pricing because this information is hard for them to read or comprehend (Reinecke 1975; Bearden et al. 1979; Silvenus 1979). The distractibility of older consumers might affect the effectiveness of product messages because distractions might decrease their ability to understand auditory information (Bergman 1980). Furthermore, because a person's ability to understand and learn abstract information declines with age, Hoy and Fisk (1985) postulate that older consumers have more difficulty than their younger counterparts comprehending benefits associated with services. It should be noted, however, that although most research has found age-related differences in information-processing abilities, Capon, Kuhn, and Gurucharri (1981) found minor differences in the ability to process information and make judgments among age groups in middle and later years. Such differences in findings might be due to different aspects of information processing studied or different methodologies used.

Proposition 9.26: The information-processing abilities of the aging consumer undergo significant changes as a result of biological changes common in later stages of the person's life. With increasing age, older persons process information less efficiently because they:

(a) need more time to follow stimuli that cross the visual field quickly

(b) are becoming unable to see and use concrete information, abstract relationships, and patterns

(c) have a decreasing ability to screen out irrelevant information

(d) are becoming increasingly unable to differentiate between stimuli

(e) are becoming less able to recall newly gathered information

(f) are becoming less able to integrate newly gathered information into a previously established cognitive structure

Proposition 9.27: Decreasing information-processing abilities due to aging affect the way consumers respond to marketing stimuli. With advancing age, the older consumer is:

(a) less likely to use product information
(b) less likely to understand commercial messages
(c) more likely to need personal in-store assistance in locating and evaluating products
(d) more likely to exhibit brand and store loyalty

Purchasing Patterns. Mature consumers, like all other types of consumers, have several methods of shopping available to them: in-store, door-to-door, mail-order, telephone-order, and to a limited extent electronic. Studies show that shopping at stores becomes a major outlet and social activity for the older consumer (Mason and Smith 1974). Mature consumers not only increasingly use retail outlets with age (see, for example, Barnes and Peters 1982), but they also spend more time searching for products than the average consumer (Mason and Smith 1974).

In-home shopping enjoys limited popularity among mature consumers (Mason and Smith 1974; Barnes and Peters 1982). Nonstore alternatives, especially mail, telephone, and electronic shopping, are associated with a high degree of risk in the minds of many older consumers (Barnes and Peters 1982), as well as low trust (Schewe 1984). Because physical impairments often make use of automobiles or public transportation unavailable, new technologies (such as videotex or cable TV shopping) have been suggested as methods to meet the needs of the elderly, particularly shut-ins and those unable to shop effectively (Exter 1985). In several studies, however, mature consumers were found to be less likely to be early adopters of such technologies (Moschis et al. 1985; McMillan and Moschis 1985; Gilly and Zeithaml 1985).

The commonly held belief among practitioners and scholars is that the older population is technologically averse. This stereotype has been attributed to a number of things, including the older person's hesitation to be an early adopter of new concepts, limited physical mobility, sensory loss, and the gradual separation (disengagement) from contemporary society. Other conventional wisdom about the elderly includes notions that older people are more traditional and more rigid, being less likely to accept new products and ideas (Prisuta and Kriner 1985). While these notions might be attributed to the older person's inability to ignore distracting information (Phillips and Sternthal 1977), one finds little data showing that older people are low users of high-tech innovations or the extent to which they have negative attitudes toward new technology (Prisuta and Kriner 1985).

A recent national telephone survey sponsored by the American Association of Retired Persons (AARP) provides some information regarding new technology adoption among older persons and their attitudes toward technology in general. The study used a probability sample of 1,300 and tested the hypothesis that lower use of technology and negative attitudes toward communication technology are a function of age (one sample of 600 was surveyed in 1981 and another of 700 in 1983). Generally, attitudes were split, explaining previous contradictory research findings. The stability of the diversity of opinions was noted over a two-year period in the follow-up study. These findings suggest that attitudes toward technology are diverse and rather stable. The study also found that older age was not a significant factor in explaining negative attitudes. Rather, lower income and less formal education (both characteristics of older adults) were strongly associated with negative attitudes. The study generally found a technologically active, rather than a technologically averse, older population.

A more recent study investigated adoption of several key consumer-related technologies in elderly and nonelderly samples, including scanner-equipped grocery stores, electronic funds transfers, automated teller machines, and custom telephone calling services. Although the elderly group was less likely to adopt most innovations, they were more likely to adopt electronic funds transfers (Gilly and Zeithaml 1985). The author of this book also is aware of several proprietary studies showing that older consumers are willing to accept new technologies and products when these are likely to benefit them. This is particularly the case among consumers with high incomes.

These data suggest that acceptance of new technologies by mature adults might depend on perceived benefits associated with their adoption. Thus, contrary to the conventional wisdom that older people are negatively predisposed toward various technologies, there are sufficient data to support the opposite belief. Thus, differences in the adoption process might not be due to age but to factors associated with older age, such as lower income and education, as well as lower perceived benefits of the new technologies.

To summarize, with increasing age, the older person is less likely to use nonstore shopping methods, perhaps because of a high perceived risk, their need for special assistance in shopping, and the fact that shopping can be a major social activity. Older consumers might be technologically averse to new products not only because of their age but also because they perceive lower benefits in using new products and have lower incomes and less formal education.

Proposition 9.28: Older consumers increasingly prefer shopping in retail outlets with age. The relationship between age and shopping at stores is higher to the extent that the older person:

(a) perceives the risks associated with a purchase

(b) needs assistance in locating and evaluating merchandise or services

(c) views shopping as an important social activity

Proposition 9.29: The older person's increasingly negative disposition toward new and existing technologies is moderated by socioeconomic factors and perceptions of these technologies. Older consumers are less likely to develop negative dispositions, with age when they:

(a) perceive the benefits of adopting new technologies

(b) have high socioeconomic status

Store Selection. Although mature consumers use criteria similar to those used by younger consumers in evaluating and selecting stores to patronize the importance of these criteria varies with age. One of the more interesting findings is that older consumers, especially those age sixty-five and older, are attracted to stores and marketers that actively seek their business. For example, one study found that 57 percent of mature consumers are attracted to stores with "Welcome Senior Citizens" signs. The older consumer tends to view such actions on the part of the retailer as respect for longtime patronage (Gelb 1982). Alternatively, in line with activity or engagement theory, the older person's perception of the retailer's efforts might convey a feeling of acceptance by society, which could be important if the individual chooses to remain "engaged" with the marketplace.

Although mature consumers use a variety of criteria in choosing among stores, services offered appear to be of primary importance (Mason and Bearden 1978). Such services include courteous, patient treatment by store employees, assistance in locating products, transportation to and from shopping areas, and places to rest when they become tired (Lambert 1979; Mason and Bearden 1978). Similarly, another study suggests that special treatment (such as carry-out service for packages), special considerations (such as assistance in product selection), and similar-aged clerks affect the mature person's patronage habits (Schewe 1984). The importance of such services increases with the age of the older consumer (Lumpkin et al. 1985). Desire for these services might indeed reflect cognitive and biological changes (such as information-processing skills and immobility) due to aging.

The Lumpkin et al. (1985) study of 3,000 mature consumers (age fifty and older, including 1,720 respondents younger than sixty years of age) provided more detailed information about the shopping needs and habits of older adults. Again, discounts for senior citizens were rated relatively high, as were several other attributes, including convenient entrance and exit and a comfortable physical environment. Of greater importance, however, was the variation of attribute importance across age groups. For example, older consumers were more likely than their younger counterparts to perceive store attributes such as in-store rest areas, ease of locating items, width of aisles, and transportation to store to be important. Discounts were found to be an important attribute that older people used in the retail vendor selection process, with more than half the respondents in the study expressing a desire for discounts. This might reflect concern with prices, resulting from a fixed income or the elderly's effort to behave in line with their consumer role perceptions.

Shopping styles and orientations, as well as the perceived importance of store attributes in the older person's store-choice behavior, is likely to be affected by the type of purchase involved. For example, older consumers enjoy shopping for apparel where they are known by the store personnel, and they tend to shop for social reasons rather than just to make a purchase. They are not price, brand, or energy conscious, however, and they do not check advertising specials more than younger consumers (Lumpkin and Greenberg 1982).

Older people tend to shop less frequently than their younger counterparts. The elderly, like all other age groups, tend to shop more often at department stores than discount stores (Bernhardt and Kinnear 1976; Lumpkin and Greenberg 1982). Unlike other age groups, older people shop more often at specialty stores than at discount stores (Lumpkin and Greenberg 1982).

Changing patterns of the elderly's shopping behaviors and motivations for shopping might be part of an effort to substitute for previous role behaviors. For example, data reported by Mason and Smith (1974) show that the elderly shop as part of a life-style, not just for particular purchases. Similarly, Mason and Bearden (1978) found that the elderly shop for a variety of reasons, including exercise, leisure, and recreation. Increasing isolation from significant others, increasing environmental constraints (such as reduced income), and a greater focus on self might lead the elderly to evaluate consumption decisions more on economic, and less on social, bases. One study, however, hypothesized that economic motivations for consumption would be positively related to age among the elderly and found a significant inverse relationship between the two variables (Smith et al. 1985).

> Proposition 9.30: Older consumers' store patronage behavior is influenced by store attributes perceived to be important. Such perceptions reflect sociopsychological and biological changes as a result of aging. With increasing age, the older person becomes more likely to choose a store that:
>
> (a) provides a wide variety of convenience-related services
>
> (b) conveys the feeling to older individuals that they are important customers
>
> (c) adopts strategies appealing to the older person's perception of his or her consumer role

Sources of Information Used. Sources of information used by mature consumers in making consumer decisions might not be similar to those used by younger people. For example, Gilly and Zeithaml (1985) found that the elderly use information sources differently than the nonelderly to learn about innovations. There are at least two reasons for these differences. First, unavailability of some sources (such as relatives and friends) prohibits the older person from frequent interaction with them as a result of the social withdrawal or isolation associated with aging. Second, the individual's ability to use certain sources of information is likely to be affected as a result of aging. For example, aging is likely to create vision problems, which might hamper the individual's ability to read print advertisements in the newspaper.

Sources of information can be classified into two broad categories: formal and informal. The first category includes commercial sources such as the mass media and salespeople, while the second category includes word-of-mouth communications from relatives and friends. When available, informal sources of information are likely to play an important role in the mature person's decision. In fact, some major decisions often are made by significant others in the aging person's social environment. For example, a study examining decisions with regard to entering a nursing home found significant participation by others (relatives) in the decision-making process (Baumgarten et al. 1976).

Another investigation into the elderly consumer's preference for formal versus informal information sources showed that formal sources—particularly neighbors, friends, family, and salespeople—were significantly more important than informal sources, such as radio, television, and newspapers (Klippel and Sweeney 1974). According to several other studies reported by Phillips and Sternthal (1977), extended family members and friends are the two most important informal sources of information.

While mature consumers consider informal sources as most important, they often are influenced by formal sources. In our study, for example, age and cognitive age were positively associated with frequency of interaction with (exposure to) advertisements in the mass media and favorability of attitudes toward advertising, respectively (Smith and Moschis 1984a). Susceptibility to formal sources is a characteristic particularly noted among those mature consumers who are relatively socially isolated. Such individuals are handicapped in making judgments about the validity of promotional information (Phillips and Sternthal 1977).

Martin (1975a) and Phillips and Sternthal (1977) found that older people use the mass media more than their younger counterparts, while other researchers (Lumpkin and Greenberg 1982; Reid et al. 1980) found that older consumers perceive various information sources, including the mass media, to be less important in the decision-making process. Thus, older adults might use the mass media to gather information but rely less on them in evaluating alternative solutions to their consumption needs.

With respect to the influence of specific media, studies show that older people have a good deal of faith in the credibility of television, even though other age groups tend to be rather skeptical of television's validity as an information source (Stephens 1981). One study found television and newspapers to be far more credible information sources than radio, magazines, or outdoor advertising, regardless of the education background of the mature respondent (Schreiber and Boyd 1980). Although television and newspapers enjoy a high degree of credibility among mature consumers, the perceived influence of these media on the decisions of older people differs. Schreiber and Boyd found the perceived influence of newspapers to be higher than any other medium.

Several reasons might account for the differences between the credibility and perceived influence of television versus newspapers. First, mature persons have difficulty processing information, and they do so at a slower pace than younger people. Newspapers allow the mature person to control the speed of exposure. It also is possible that older people, who are likely to live on fixed incomes, tend to be more responsive to special promotions such as coupons or sales announcements, which most often appear in newspapers.

The yellow pages as source of information is not very popular among mature consumers, although younger mature individuals are heavier users than older adults. According to one source, approximately 31 percent of adults age fifty-five to fifty-nine report using the yellow pages more than once a week. The figure drops to approximately 18 percent after age seventy (Fannin 1985). Several reasons might account for low usage, including contraction of one's consumption activities and, therefore, less need for information (Smith and Moschis 1984b and 1985a), the diminishing ability to read and generally use the yellow pages, and perhaps the substitution of more effective sources of information such as newspapers or other directories designed for the aged.

Thus, mature consumers are fairly similar to younger consumers with respect to the types of information sources they use; they differ in terms of exposure and the trust they place in these sources. Information sources in the person's external environment are not the only sources that can affect behavior. Rather, past experience tends to serve as a strong internal source of information for the older consumer. For example, a survey showed that the elderly tend to deal with buying-decision pressures by using their own consumer knowledge and experience (Friedman and Wasserman 1978). Similarly, another study found mature consumers to rely on personal judgment more heavily than any other consumer age group. As people age, the study found, they become more dependent on past experience as an information source (Schiffman 1971).

To summarize, a person's social isolation might result in lower exposure to personal information sources, but personal sources might become more important because of the person's decreasing ability to evaluate consumption alternatives. The replacement of scarce informal personal sources with commercial sources also might result in greater reliance on such sources for consumer information when informal personal sources are not readily available, in spite of the aging person's increasing difficulty to use these commercial sources of information.

> Proposition 9.31: An older person's use of information sources for consumer decisions is functionally related to his or her social environment, as well as to physical and cognitive abilities to use the available sources. With increasing age, the older consumer is:
>
> (a) more likely to be exposed to formal sources of information
>
> (b) less likely to be exposed to informal personal sources of information
>
> (c) more likely to rely on informal sources
>
> (d) more likely to rely on formal sources when informal personal sources are not available

Product Selection. The selection of products by mature consumers is likely to be affected by two rather unrelated factors: general consumption patterns and specific product attributes. General consumption patterns are closely tied to a person's need structure, which often is the result of changes in life-cycle stages. For example, food consumption and clothing purchases decline with age, while consumption of medical services increases (Gilson 1982). Thus, specific products are likely to enjoy various levels of demand depending on the age of the older person. Of greater importance, however, in choosing specific brands or generic products or services within a certain category are the perceptions of product attributes and the environment in which products are sold. For example, because mature consumers are heavier coupon users than their younger counterparts, coupon offerings are likely to be important determinants of product selection, especially among female consumers (Fannin 1985).

Although mature consumers are brand loyal and become even more so with age, they often rely on store reputation rather than brand reputation in their selection of merchandise (Martin 1975a; Lumpkin et al. 1985). This might be due in part to increased store loyalty (Schewe 1985), to the mature person's tendency to use brand name as a summary or umbrella attribute for product evaluation, or to a greater commitment to a certain way of doing things (Riley et al. 1969), resulting from their increasing difficulty to learn when distracting (new) stimuli are presented. The older person's decreasing ability to learn when irrelevant information or distracting stimuli are presented might explain the resistance to change and the lower likelihood of new product adoption (Gilly and Zeithaml 1985). Thus, in relation to younger people, older consumers use fewer attributes to evaluate products. For example, older people were found to make less use of informational aids such as open-code dating and nutritional labeling (Schewe 1985) but more use of general attributes such as brand name and store reputation.

Studies addressing the relative importance of product attributes among mature consumers generally reveal mixed results regarding the importance of price, quality, store reputation, functionality, and coupon and stamp offerings (Schewe 1985). It is possible that the perception of these attributes varies by other characteristics of the older person besides age.

The activity perspective implies that the elderly substitute age-relevant activities for those lost through role attrition (Lemmon et al. 1972). One of the few clear role prescriptions for the elderly is the maintenance of economic independence (Smith 1982). Increasing age, usually accompanied by a fixed or shrinking income, might be associated with economic motivations for consumption and the propensity to use money-saving sales promotion offers. LaForge, French, and Crask (1981) found aging to be positively related to proneness to deals, while others (for example, Lambert 1979; Lumpkin et al. 1985) found the availability of discounts to be important in choosing among vendors. In the Smith and Moschis (1985a) study, proneness to deals was not related to age. Perhaps economic orientations and motivations for consumption are not manifested in behavior because of the physical and biological changes that can hamper a person's ability to use economic information and take advantage of special deals.

Not only are mature consumers likely to have different buying styles than their younger counterparts, but buying styles do not appear to be uniform among older adults. For example, a study using data from Axiom Market Research (Target Group Index) identified six clusters of mature consumers based on their life-styles (Towle and Martin 1976). The most significant segment was a conspicuous consumer segment, with approximately 35 percent of older adults falling into this category. The saver/planner segment (25 percent) also was significant, while each of the remaining segments included approximately 10 percent of the elderly sample.

> Proposition 9.32: With increasing age, older persons evaluate products using attributes reflecting the desire to maintain economic independence and their ability to process information. With age, the older person is:
>
> (a) more likely to choose a product on the basis of its brand name
>
> (b) more likely to choose a product on the basis of the store that sells it
>
> (c) more likely to select a product on the basis of money-saving sales promotion offers

Payment Method. Mature consumers differ from their younger counterparts with respect to the method used to pay for products and services. Generally, the older consumer uses cash as the method of payment. In a national study of 1,800 adults selected on a probability basis, it was found that approximately 25 percent of the retired mature consumers paid only cash for products and services; approximately 40 percent preferred using mostly cash, as opposed to other methods of payment (Stanley et al. 1982). Thus, mature consumers generally make little use of credit cards.

Payment method preference differs across types of products and services purchased. For example, a study showed that for groceries, up to 87 percent of the sixty-five and older shoppers used cash (Zbytniewski 1979). Other methods of payment for products and services also vary by type of product or service. For example, a national study found age differences in preauthorized payment across a variety of services. Generally, older individuals are less likely to use preauthorized payment services, with the exception of paying for their utilities (Payment Systems 1982).

Differences in payment methods used are difficult to explain in line with the available theories. Perhaps differences reflect previous experiences older people had at earlier stages in their life cycle due to historical events (for example, the Depression). If this is the case, when newer generations are in the same age brackets, they should exhibit preferences for payment methods different from those currently exhibited by older adults.

Dissatisfaction and Complaining. Although older consumers readily recognize shabby practices, they tend to avoid direct action to correct the wrong. The work of

Zaltman et al. (1978) and Bernhardt (1981) found that older consumers were less aware of unfair practices and less likely to complain than their younger counterparts. Rather, they usually resolved the problem indirectly by shopping elsewhere (McMahon 1976; Bernhardt 1981). Reasons for the low propensity to complain include the perception that complaining will not accomplish anything or that it is simply not worth the trouble. Some elderly consumers do not know where to go to voice their complaints. In addition, a higher proportion of mature consumers complain about services than about actual physical products. Bernhardt (1981) found that 45 percent of the older respondents attributed responsibility for their dissatisfaction to the source of the service. This might be due to the older person's lower ability to understand and learn abstract information (Hoy and Fisk 1985), which might result in greater expectations about services than about product performance.

> Proposition 9.33: An older person's propensity to experience dissatisfaction with products and services is affected by the declining ability to process information. With increasing age, older people become:
>
> (a) more dissatisfied with services than with products
> (b) less aware of options available to them for remedy

Dysfunctional Consumer Behavior. While older adults are not as likely to engage in deviant consumer behavior in the same manner juveniles do, they are likely to exhibit consumer behaviors that are relatively more dysfunctional (from a societal perspective) than those of younger adults. These usually are due to the decline of physical and mental abilities. For example, declines in sensory capability, reaction time, and short-term memory have been offered as explanations for an increased number of traffic accidents and violations among the aged (Valentine et al. 1978).

Socialization Processes

As people in this age group grow older, they tend to interact rather differently with various sources of consumer information. In later years, the importance of some socialization agents might diminish and that of others, including new ones, might increase. For example, senior citizen centers and other social institutions are likely to become important agents for the aged person in much the same manner the school is an agent for young people. In fact, a study by Burton and Hennon (1980) found senior citizen centers to be the third most preferred source of consumer information, behind television and newspapers, even though their importance is likely to vary by social structural factors such as residence status. As individuals grow older, they experience role attrition—through retirement, children leaving home, the death of friends or spouse—their life space contracts, and they are less involved with others. Thus, there is a decrease in informal information sources (such as family and co-workers) and a compensating increase in formal information sources (such as television and newspapers).

Several studies have found a negative relationship between age and interaction with others regarding consumption-related matters (Schiffman 1971; LaForge et al. 1981), suggesting that with increasing age, the mass media and other commercial sources of consumer information might play an increasingly important role in the consumer socialization of older adults. For example, studies show that with increasing age, there appears to be less interaction with friends and family and less reliance on such sources of consumer information among the elderly, but there is a greater reliance on mass media advertising (Smith et al. 1986; Smith et al. 1985). The mass media help older persons compensate for other kinds of loss—financial, physical, or social—and they provide a socially acceptable substitution for previous activities (Young 1979). Older persons in general tend to use less radio, but they are heavier users of newspapers and television than younger groups. In particular, there appears to be a marked increase in exposure to newspapers and television past the age of sixty, which declines after the age of seventy (see, for example, Real et al. 1980). Interestingly, the criteria for media use preference also seem to change with age. Starting at about age sixty, older people use the mass media more for information than entertainment purposes (Bernhardt and Kinnear 1976; Phillips and Sternthal 1977; Schramm 1969; Morrison 1979).

Television fulfills several needs. Rubin and Rubin (1982), for example, reported that motivations for television viewing include information, entertainment, companionship, and relaxation. Mature persons, especially those over sixty-five, show a marked preference for news and public affairs programming, suggesting that they need more information about their environment than younger people (Young 1979). Because the importance of issues such as health, Social Security, housing, and finances is intensified with advancing age, the older person's sensitivity to his or her environment increases, as does the need for practical information about such issues, resulting in the mature person's use of television for information about them (Young 1979).

Newspapers appear to meet an important information need of the elderly, especially the need for local news, including shopping sales (Young 1969). The older person's need for information from newspapers increases sharply with age (Newspaper Research Bureau 1981). Magazine and book reading remains relatively stable among the aging population and is rather high among high-income and high-education groups. It tends to decline at the very late stages of the life cycle because of vision loss (Young 1979).

Radio listening declines with advancing age, with major reasons being the elderly's inability to find programming tailored to their needs (Young 1979). Although mature consumers are not as heavy users of radio as, for example, teenagers, they are likely to listen to a specific radio station more regularly than younger adults. Older persons are particularly heavy listeners of talk shows, perhaps substituting this type of companionship format for lost interpersonal interactions. Studies have shown that people who phone radio shows are substituting the contact with the talk show host for the face-to-face contact of which they are deprived (Dimmick et al. 1979).

As people age, they become more dependent on past experience as an information source (Schiffman 1971; Friedman and Wasserman 1978). This might be due to the unavailability of informal personal sources as a result of the person's social isolation. The reliance on and influence of various sources of consumer information appear to be functions of the psychological and sociological changes associated with advancing age. The influence of formal sources is a characteristic particularly noted among older adults, who are relatively more handicapped in making judgments about the validity of promotional information than their younger counterparts (Phillips and Sternthal 1977). Studies, for example, show that older people have a good deal of faith in the credibility of television, even though other age groups tend to be rather skeptical of television's validity as an information source (Stephens 1981). One study also found television and newspapers to be far more credible information sources than radio, magazines, or outdoor advertising regardless of educational background (Schreiber and Boyd 1980).

Older people seem to prefer different entertainment programming than the rest of the adult population. Research summarized by Young (1969) shows that older people prefer variety shows, "old-time" music, and quiz shows, but they are not particularly attracted to action and adventure shows. Avoidance of action and adventure shows has been attributed to deterioration of the eye-movement mechanism that controls pursuit, producing muscular fatigue due to the effort to locate fast-moving images in these types of shows (Heatherton and Fouts 1985).

Changes in sensory abilities during later years might limit the amount of television viewing and influence the viewer's uses and gratifications, program preferences, perceptions of portrayals of older people on television, and the effects of television (Heatherton and Fouts 1985). For instance, as a result of hearing loss, older people find it difficult to follow and understand conversations, predisposing them to replace interpersonal settings with interaction with mass media such as television and radio, in which the variance is controllable (Kubey 1980; Heatherton and Fouts 1985). Heatherton and Fouts (1985) speculate that older viewers' difficulty in understanding speech is likely to affect their program preferences. They contend that a preference for news over other kinds of programming might be due to the additional visual cues (mouth movements) provided by anchorpersons in close-ups, which aid the comprehension of those with auditory deficiencies. Their suggestion is supported by research showing that the elderly find speakers with poor diction more difficult to understand (House et al. 1965).

The decline in television viewing very late in life also might be due to a reduction in contrast sensitivity. Owsley, Sekuler, and Boldt (1981) found that elderly subjects required three times more contrast to detect and discriminate between faces. Similarly, Davis and Edwards (1975) found that the elderly prefer greater contrast in television pictures than younger viewers. Loss of acuity results in a decrease in the ability to read standard-size print media (Doolittle 1979). Use of the print media is likely to wane with aging and be replaced by television. Even with television, larger images often are required for older adults. Heatherton and Fouts (1985) argue that program preferences, especially news and public affairs programs, might be due partly to a decline in acuity, since news and public affairs programs use close-up views, which present the human face as a large image.

In sum, with increasing age, older adults interact rather differently with socialization agents. These differences reflect changes in opportunities for interaction, changes in motivations for interaction, and changes in abilities due to biophysical changes. With increasing age, older people are more likely to use the mass media for information rather than entertainment.

Proposition 9.34: Television viewing increases with increasing age as a result of an intensified need for information. With increasing age, television is most likely to be used by those adults who:

(a) are socially isolated

(b) remain physically and cognitively healthy

(c) need information about issues related to their stage in their life cycle

Proposition 9.35: Changes in the older person's interaction with television reflect changes in sensory abilities. Those who are the heaviest users of television are:

(a) less likely to experience auditory deficiencies

(b) less likely to experience reduction in contrast sensitivity

(c) less likely to experience loss of the ability to control eye movement (control pursuit)

(d) less likely to experience loss in acuity

Proposition 9.36: The time an older person spends listening to the radio declines with advancing age, but the time he or she spends listening to talk shows increases.

Proposition 9.37: Newspaper reading by older adults increases initially but declines at later stages because of vision loss. Older people who are the heaviest users of newspapers tend to:

(a) need information about issues relevant to their stage in the life cycle

(b) experience the least loss of vision

Proposition 9.38: The older person's interaction with personal sources of information declines with age. The aged person is less likely to interact with personal sources when he or she:

(a) is socially isolated

(b) experiences hearing loss

Summary and Discussion

Consumer behavior and consumer socialization processes and effects appear to undergo constant formation and change throughout a person's life cycle. These changes can be explained by theories drawn from several fields. Quite often two or more competing theories might be offered as alternative or complementary explanations. Certain theories might be more relevant than others in explaining differences at specific stages in the life cycle. When the stage is characterized by a short time span, differences in consumer socialization and behavior might be more amenable to theoretical explanations than stages characterized by longer time intervals. For example, while age is strongly related to the emergence of cognitive and communicative abilities, especially during the formative years (and to a lesser extent in later life), the relationship of age to life events (such as marriage, employment, and parenthood) weakens considerably, suggesting that age might not be a useful variable, even as a marker of life events (Dimmick et al. 1979). More recent efforts to mark changes over the life cycle include Veroff's (1978) developmental approach to social motivation based on the premise that different life stages introduce new motivations in the same way that different points in a life cycle evoke new types of cognitive organization.

In studying behavior over long time spans, the researcher must take into account period and cohort effects, whose functional relationship with consumer socialization tends to be void of theoretical explanations. In addition, the specification of the length of a meaningful cohort might be different across age groups and time. For example, previous researchers have reported cohorts as short as one year (Jaworski and Sauer 1985). Furthermore, as cohorts move through time, they become different because of social and cultural changes, age norms, and cumulative effects of previous life experiences. Being a certain age carries with it certain normative expectations, which are defined by society and are unique to a given historical period. Similarly, the impact of cumulative life experiences cannot be ignored as explanatory factors (Jaworski and Sauer 1985).

One difficulty in using the family life cycle as a variable to predict consumer behavior stems from the researcher's failure to control for socioeconomic variables associated with different stages. This problem was demonstrated empirically in a study of family clothing expenditures. When the effects of income and other demographic variables were controlled, life cycle had a rather weak influence on household family expenditures (Wagner and Hanna 1983).

Perhaps one of the greatest difficulties in studying consumer socialization and consumer behavior over the life cycle is in understanding where certain changes in behavior, as well as influences of socialization agents, are likely to occur. Individuals are likely to acquire patterns of cognitions and behaviors prior to reaching certain stages where theoretical explanations might account for differences in their thoughts and actions. Similarly, consumer socialization agents might have delaying effects.

One of the greatest challenges for consumer socialization researchers would be to develop specific measures of events that have taken place at various stages in a person's life cycle and attempt to understand their functional relationships to consumer behavior development or change. Also, specifying conditions, aside from age or life-cycle stage, under which one would expect the development of certain consumer behaviors could be useful in helping explain anticipatory consumer socialization. While cohort analysis could help separate developmental effects from period and cohort effects, the functional relationship between variables characterizing specific time spans and cohorts should be established. For example, it is recognized that comparisons of the intelligence scores of different age groups based on cross-sectional data are misleading in their implications that intelligence declines with age because the educational level achieved by each cohort is progressively lower from younger to older cohorts (Blau 1956). Such a cohort effect also could include a host of other factors, and differences cannot be attributed only to education. Removing cohort effects through cohort analysis would not necessarily help us isolate possible causal variables, but longitudinal studies could help us establish specific causal relationships.

10
The Effects of Gender and Birth Order

Sex Differences

Sex differences in consumer socialization appear to stem from two broad perspectives: biological and sociological. Sex differences due to biological factors reflect changes in physical appearance and biological functions, while sex differences due to sociological factors stem from sex role relationships and social influence processes. Given that both biological and psychosociological processes are ongoing phenomena, they are likely to have a different impact on the individual's behaviors at different stages in the life cycle. This section presents information on sex differences at three stages in the life cycle: childhood and adolescence, adulthood, and late adulthood. At each stage, findings are presented and interpreted in the context of specific theoretical frameworks.

Childhood and Adolescence

Consumer Behavior. Sex differences in consumer behavior become evident early in life. For example, McNeal (1969) found sex differences in children's consumer behavior starting at around age seven, while Belk and his colleagues (1984) found sex differences in consumption stereotyping among fourth- and sixth-graders.

One of the sex differences in consumer behavior that emerges early in childhood is in consumption orientations regarding physical appearance in general and clothing in particular. A large number of studies have found girls to be more aware of, and interested in, clothing than boys (see, for example, Vener 1957; Hurlock 1955). Such differences in orientations might reflect differences in physical and psychosocial maturation. For example, it has been suggested that these changes might be due to changes in body shape and the parallel development of the belief that other people also are preoccupied with the youth's appearance (Elkind 1967). The great emphasis on physical attractiveness and the need to be accepted by one's peers, especially during early adolescence, is believed to contribute to the youth's concern with decisions such as what clothes to buy (Avery 1979). Girls in particular at a very early age become aware of the symbolic meaning of apparel in achieving group status. To them clothing signifies peer group identification, conformity to group norms, individuality, and maturity. Such differences between boys and girls might be due partly to emotional maturity, since girls are believed to reach maturity faster than boys (Avery 1979).

Differences in orientations toward consumption in boys and girls also is likely to affect the way these young people go about spending their money. For example, studies show that teenage girls spend a greater portion of the money they have available on clothes than their male counterparts (Powell 1963; Youth Research Institute 1967).

By early adolescence, several differences can be observed with respect to the acquisition of certain consumer skills, many of which are likely to remain throughout life. General orientations toward, and use of, advertising messages begin appearing during adolescence. Specifically, females show stronger positive orientations toward television advertising, as is shown by their greater ability to discriminate cognitively and retain information in messages (Moschis and Churchill 1979), along with their more favorable attitudes and greater susceptibility to advertising in general (Moore and Moschis 1978a; Moschis and Churchill 1979).

Male youngsters, however, are likely to develop other consumer skills better or faster than their female counterparts. For example, Moschis and Moore (1978) found male adolescents to possess a greater ability to price products and services accurately, to have more knowledge about legal matters, and to have better conceptions of what a socially desirable consumer role consists of than their female counterparts. This might be due to the greater independence the male adolescent acquires from his or her parents in purchasing products of relevance to the adolescent's own use (Moschis et al. 1977). These sex differences also might be the result of different socialization processes, and they could reflect differences in values stressed by families. For example, boys are socialized to place more value on competence, whereas girls learn to place relatively more value on interpersonal relationships (Bush et al. 1977–1978).

The decision-making patterns of young people begin to show marked sex differences at a rather young age. These differences can be observed at each main stage of the decision-making process, including motivations for consumption, purchase planning, information seeking and use, product evaluation, and purchasing patterns.

With respect to motivations for consumption and general consumption orientations, product desires are likely to differ as a result of the differences in psychosocial development between girls and boys. Girls are believed to have a greater need for subjective index of their potential, and as a result, they develop a stronger peer orientation than do boys. This peer orientation leads to girls' displaying higher degrees of conformity than boys (Campbell 1964). This also might account for differences in social orientations and conformity to peer norms and potential expectations. Research by Cobb (1954), however, suggests that social orientations might be a broad concept that should be viewed separately from orientations such as material possessions. Specifically, in this study, adolescent girls in all grade groups exceeded boys in wishes relating to family, and in junior high and high school, girls exceeded boys in personal social wishes. Boys exceeded girls in elementary and junior high in wishes relating to personal achievement, and in all age groups, boys exceeded girls in wishes for possessions (Cobb 1954).

The findings of another study also suggest that social orientations might be a broad concept that should be viewed differently than consumption motives and material possessions. Specifically, Churchill and Moschis (1979) expected females to have stronger social motivations for consumption than males. Contrary to this expectation, the study found male adolescents to have stronger expressive orientations toward consumption (materialistic attitudes and social motivations) than did their female counterparts. The researchers reasoned that perhaps the adolescent's sex affects aspects of his or her social orientations other than consumption, perhaps such orientations are of a broader nature, or perhaps conspicuous consumption provides the male more than the female adolescent with a means of establishing status, power, and respect among his peers (Churchill and Moschis 1979).

Proposition 10.1: Social orientations toward consumption are likely to be stronger for male than female youths. Males are more likely than females to:

(a) have stronger social motivations for consumption
(b) have stronger materialistic attitudes

With respect to prepurchase activities, sex differences have been noted in the amount of information sought, purchase planning, and sources of information used. Differences in purchase planning appear to depend on the type of product or service involved. For example, Gibbs (1963) found that boys made planned decisions before buying grooming products, but they made more impulsive decisions when buying clothing items. The opposite was found with girls. Powell (1963) also found girls to be more likely than boys to shop around before purchasing in general. These differences do not, however, take into account the purchasing social environment. For example, it is possible that girls shop around more because they are more likely to shop with their parents, while boys tend to shop more frequently with their friends or alone (Samli and Windeshausen 1965). Sex differences also might reflect girls' greater propensity to participate in family decisions (Moschis and Mitchell 1986; Oppenheim 1969).

Because females are more likely than boys to be involved in family decisions, they have more opportunities to rely on their parents as a source of product information. Additional analysis of our Wisconsin data (Moschis and Churchill 1978) based on a sample of 1,002 adolescents found sex differences with respect to information seeking from parents across five products (bicycle, watch, hair dryer, pocket calculator, and camera), with females being more likely to consult parents than their male counterparts ($p < .0001$). No significant sex differences emerged for other sources of information examined (friends, television ads, salespersons, *Consumer Reports*, newspaper or magazine ads). Similarly, we examined sex differences in information source utilization using our Georgia data ($N = 734$, Moschis and Moore 1979b). The results of the analysis by product and information source are shown in table 10–1.

The results in table 10–1 suggest that parents might serve as a source of information to a significantly greater extent among female than male adolescents, but this might depend on the type of product. The data in table 10–1 also show the female's greater propensity to rely on mass media advertising, reflecting her greater susceptibility to these commercial stimuli. These results are consistent with findings of previous studies. For example, Emmerich (1978) found that the relative influence of parents and peers on adolescents is determined by the situation and sex of the adolescent. Furthermore, boys appear to change their orientation from ninth to twelfth grades; girls' responses remain constant over the same period; and ninth-grade boys rely on parents' opinions more than older boys and ninth-grade girls. These results suggest that in this respect, girls mature faster than boys.

The development of inner controls and moral autonomy is markedly slower among girls than among boys. This can be interpreted in terms of the stronger autonomy and identity pressures experienced by boys (Elder 1968). Boys express less unquestioned identification and acceptance of parental restraint and thus can be expected to conform less to parent-approved behavior. Thus, it is not surprising to find research showing that male youths acquire greater independence in purchasing (Moschis et al. 1977); that males shoplift more than their female

Table 10–1
Information Sources Used by Sex of Adolescent
(percentages)

	Friends		TV Ads		Consumer Reports		One or Both Parents		Newspaper or Magazine Ads	
	M	F	M	F	M	F	M	F	M	F
Wristwatch	26.1	29.0	15.8	16.2	23.6	17.9	71.2	81.3*	17.7	14.2
Hair dryer	21.2	38.6*	28.8	31.0	21.7	13.9*	47.6	54.0	17.4	24.4*
Flash cubes	15.5	13.6	28.8	37.0*	16.6	14.2	42.1	42.0	25.3	27.0
Sunglasses	45.4	46.6	25.3	33.2*	10.6	5.7*	29.6	28.7	20.1	27.8*
Calculator	21.2	17.9	19.8	22.2	26.9	29.3	56.0	64.2*	21.5	19.6
Batteries	16.3	9.1*	35.3	36.1	19.3	14.2	40.5	50.0*	22.6	21.6
Dress shoes	26.1	52.6*	14.7	13.6	7.3	4.8	70.1	59.9*	17.1	21.6
Wallet	42.1	37.6	11.7	20.8*	10.6	5.1*	46.7	46.2	20.4	29.1*

* Significant difference at .05 level.

counterparts (Klemke 1982); and that female juveniles shoplift more on impulse than males (Powell and Moschis 1986).

Sex also appears to influence other aspects of the decision process, including awareness and evaluation of available alternatives. For example, Moschis and Moore (1978) found female adolescents to be more aware of brands than their male counterparts. Male adolescents, however, were found to have a greater ability to price products and services accurately. Using our Georgia data (Moschis and Moore 1979b) ($N = 734$), we analyzed sex differences in six criteria used to evaluate several products. Table 10–2 shows the results of this analysis. Again, the data suggest that males are less likely to take parental preferences into account in buying products, a finding that reflects higher conformity to parent-approved behaviors among girls than among boys. The female's propensity to take peer preferences into account in deciding what product to purchase suggests that females might have a higher degree of conformity than males, a finding consistent with previous speculations (Campbell 1964). The data also show the female adolescent's relatively greater susceptibility to advertising.

> Proposition 10.2: A youth's sex affects the types of information he or she is likely to use in decision making. Females are more likely than their male counterparts to:
>
> (a) rely more on parents
> (b) rely more on peers
> (c) rely more on advertising messages

One also might pose the question: What kinds of criteria do males use in evaluating products? The data in table 10–2 do not seem to show any distinct pattern. To answer this question, our Wisconsin data ($N = 1,002$, Moschis and Churchill

Table 10–2
Use of Criteria in Decision Making by Sex of Adolescent
(percentages)

	On Sale		Advertised		Friends Like		Well-known		Parents Like		Store	
	M	F	M	F	M	F	M	F	M	F	M	F
Calculator	46.9	41.3	9.9	15.6*	4.3	14.2	58.4	52.8	20.9	32.1*	14.5	19.6
Flash cubes	50.9	45.8	13.9	21.2*	2.4	3.1	43.7	39.7	10.2	14.8	8.0	7.3
Hair dryer	36.7	31.6	19.6	16.8	7.8	16.8*	45.3	54.7*	20.6	26.3	13.7	15.1
Batteries	49.1	48.6	18.2	19.6	2.7	1.4	40.5	34.1	8.3	14.2*	7.5	7.0
Wallet	44.2	45.3	7.5	9.5	12.3	21.8*	34.9	26.5*	18.0	17.0	16.4	12.3
Dress shoes	32.2	29.6	7.5	8.9	13.9	31.0*	39.9	34.9	30.8	33.8	21.4	24.6
Sunglases	47.2	41.9	12.6	17.3	21.4	31.6*	33.0	27.9	11.8	14.2	8.8	8.7
Wristwatch	37.0	28.5*	14.7	14.5	11.3	15.4	60.3	60.3	24.4	37.4*	17.7	22.9

* Significant difference at .05 level.

1978) on specific motivations for purchasing five products were analyzed by sex. The results of this analysis are shown in table 10–3. The data in table 10–3 appear to suggest that male adolescents, in comparison to their female counterparts, are more concerned with what others might think of them as persons and the general associations others make between purchasing specific products or brands and the life-styles of the people using them—that is, the image they might project. The data in tables 10–2 and 10–3 collectively suggest that both males and females might be susceptible to social influence, but males might be more susceptible to normative social influence, while females might be more susceptible to informational social

Table 10–3
Perceived Importance of Select Types of Information by Product among Male and Female Adolescents
(*percentages*)

					Before buying a:					
	Bicycle		*Watch*		*Camera*		*Pocket Calculator*		*Hair Dryer*	
It is important to know:	M	F	M	F	M	F	M	F	M	F
a. What friends think of different brands or products	70.0	66.1*	39.2	31.2*	37.8	35.6	36.7	20.1*	28.2	44.6*
b. Guarantees on different brands	71.3	73.8	78.7	82.4	69.1	78.5*	74.3	79.1	57.7	76.5*
c. What kinds of people buy certain brands or products	34.5	35.5	33.7	29.7	37.0	27.8*	31.2	21.7*	20.4	23.7
d. The name of the company that makes the product	76.2	72.5	66.0	71.3	69.3	68.9	56.1	53.2	40.9	54.2*
e. Whether any brands are on sale	66.9	68.4	54.1	57.9	55.8	62.6*	64.4	63.1	52.2	63.2*
f. What others think of people who use certain brands of products	40.9	33.3*	35.9	27.3*	35.1	27.6*	32.3	19.6*	20.4	23.7
g. Kinds of materials different brands are made of	72.9	66.2*	61.9	62.2	58.0	53.5	52.5	45.4*	41.7	51.5*
h. What brands or products to buy to make good impressions on others	44.8	41.6	42.8	36.1*	35.1	27.8*	28.5	14.8*	15.7	14.0
i. Quality of the store selling a particular brand	66.9	67.7	59.7	61.5	59.7	60.1	55.8	54.9	59.4	45.4*

* Significant difference at .05 level.

influence. This might explain the differences found between the two sexes in regard to expressive orientations (Churchill and Moschis 1979; Cobb 1954).

> Proposition 10.3: Sex differences exist in young people's susceptibility to social influence.
>
> (a) Males are more susceptible to normative social influence.
>
> (b) Females are more susceptible to informational social influence.

Sex differences also have been observed with respect to general purchase orientations. For example, the Simmons Teenaged Research Study (Adweek 1981) found that males were more brand loyal (name conscious) and cautious than their female counterparts, while females were more likely to experiment and shop around than males. Although female youths appear to be more likely to take fewer risks in trying new products, they are not necessarily likely to take other (greater) types of risks. For example, in reviewing studies of youths and traffic safety, Clayton (1985) concluded that males have a worse driving record than females because of a higher propensity to take risks associated with driving.

Similarly, Powell and Moschis (1986) found that male juveniles shoplift more than female juveniles. Of greater importance in the latter study is the demonstrated variance in shoplifting behavior, which reflects the different socialization patterns of males and females. Females were found to be more likely than males to shoplift with others, suggesting that peer pressure to shoplift might operate differently among boys and girls. The findings that planned shoplifting is infrequent and that it tends to take place in the presence of peers suggests that peer pressure might be important in activating the major motivations for theft. Various writers also have pointed to the gamelike aspects of shoplifting (see, for example, Cameron 1964; Gold 1970; Klemke 1982), which offer the potential for excitement and trophies, and have suggested that peer pressure might be the main reason for such "sporting" and "economic" motivations. This pattern apparently is more likely to exist among females, who tend to shoplift more frequently with others with increasing age than their male counterparts (Powell and Moschis 1986).

> Proposition 10.4: The adolescent's sex is likely to affect involvement in delinquent activities. In comparison to their female counterparts:
>
> (a) Males are more likely to shoplift.
>
> (b) Males are more likely to have a bad driving record.

> Proposition 10.5: Delinquent activities are more likely to be committed on impulse by females than by males.

Evidence further suggests that in father-absent or female-centered homes, boys lack a clear male figure with whom to identify, and "he later is likely to become panicked by fear of his female identification, and therefore acts in an excessively aggressive, assertive, and often antisocial manner to prove his maleness to himself and others" (Inkeles 1968, 120).

> Proposition 10.6: Boys living with only their mother are more likely to shoplift than boys living with both parents.

Although the youth's sex is likely to affect conformity to peers, sex influence appears to be contingent on the presence and sex of siblings. Theory and research suggest that girls, especially later-born, with sisters manifest greater sibling rivalry and hostility to parents than girls with brothers, creating conditions favoring use of peers as a primary frame of reference and engaging in activities of which parents do not approve—that is, antisocial behaviors (Hartup 1970).

> Proposition 10.7: Female youths who shoplift with peers are likely to have older sisters.

Finally, sex differences were found in the way young people go about purchasing products and services. For example, one study examined the extent to which purchasing role structures vary by sex of the adolescent consumer (Moschis et al. 1977). Because previous studies found that female adolescents were more susceptible to peer influence than males for products important to overall personal appearance and that they would not buy clothes that peers did not approve (Cannon et al. 1952; Saunders et al. 1973), the researchers had expected this group conformity to be reflected in their purchasing patterns through greater family independence in purchasing products relevant to physical appearance. The data partly confirmed this expectation.

Analysis of our Georgia data (Moschis and Moore 1979b) also leads to a similar conclusion, since males reported greater independence in purchasing three of the eight products examined (see tables 10–1 and 10–2). Females reported greater independence only in purchasing dress shoes. In further analyzing sex differences by age, we found that males tended to acquire greater independence in purchasing with age as compared to their female counterparts. These findings were consistent with those reported by Moschis et al. (1977) using samples from Kentucky and North Carolina. The finding that females can purchase relatively expensive items (such as clothing) without parental supervision, given that such products are reflective of class norms (see Moschis et al. 1977), suggests that the female's greater orientation toward parents and peers might reflect a greater dependence on them rather than parental permissiveness. In fact, Hoffman (1972) suggested that parents, especially mothers, might provide girls with too little encouragement for independence and autonomy. These parental behaviors could result in lower self-confidence and expectancies, along with excessive dependency and affiliation needs in females (Parsons et al. 1976).

Proposition 10.8:   A youth's independence in purchasing products consumed by him or her varies by sex and product type.

      (a) Parental involvement in purchasing is lower among males than females.

      (b) Parental involvement in purchasing products related to personal appearance is lower among males than females.

Not only do females seem to acquire independence in purchasing products relevant to their appearance, but they also tend to participate in decisions concerning products for their own as well as their family's use. In a study of 166 teenagers and their mothers, female adolescents were found to be more likely than their male counterparts to participate in these types of consumer decisions (Moschis and Mitchell 1986). Sex role conceptions about family decisions also might differ among young people by sex. Some research, for example, suggests that male adolescents are likely to develop sexist views and more traditional attitudes about sexual stereotypes and career and family roles than females (Bayer 1975; Dunn 1960). Similarly, a study by Angrist and her colleagues (1977) found males to have more sexist attitudes than female adolescents.

Sex role perceptions of adolescents also were analyzed by sex in a study of consumer socialization. While adolescents of both sexes had accurate sex role perceptions regarding the responsibility for decision making on traditional male or female activities, the sex of the respondent did have some effect on his or her perception of spouse involvement in household decisions regarding economic, social, and common household activities, areas of less specialization (Moschis and Moore 1979b).

Proposition 10.9:   Female youths are more likely to participate in family decisions than male youths.

Proposition 10.10: Male youths are more likely to acquire traditional sex role perceptions regarding family decisions.

Socialization Processes. Sex also appears to affect the formation of a youth's consumer behavior indirectly by affecting consumer socialization processes. The child's differential interaction with socialization agents on the basis of sex begins at an early age when parents begin treating girls differently than they treat boys, for example, with respect to consumer training (McNeal 1969). In his exploratory study, Cateora (1963) reported sex differences not only in the shopping behavior of adolescents but also in the way adolescents interact with family members. Specifically, female subjects were found to be more likely to model themselves after their parents than their male counterparts.

Similar significant sex differences emerged in another study in which female adolescents were found to talk with their parents about consumption matters more frequently and to report a greater use of positive reinforcement by parents; males reported a greater use of negative reinforcement by parents (Moschis, Moore, and Smith 1984). In two other studies, female adolescents were found to talk to their mothers about consumption matters more frequently than did their male counterparts (Moschis and Mitchell 1986; Vener 1957), while analysis of our Wisconsin data (Moschis and Churchill 1978) suggested that adolescent girls might be more likely to model themselves after their parents than adolescent boys. Again, these differences might reflect the female's greater dependency on her parents and her need for affiliation (Hoffman 1972).

Because sex influences might be contingent on the youth's birth order position (Schmuck 1963; Hartup 1970), the effects of sex on socialization processes were analyzed controlling for birth order. Additional analysis of our Georgia data ($N = 734$, Moschis and Moore 1979b) found females to be more likely to talk to their parents about consumption and to report parental use of positive reinforcement practices; they were less likely to report negative interaction than their male counterparts. No sex–birth order interaction effects on these socialization processes emerged.

Proposition 10.11: Parents' use of consumer socialization practices depends on the youth's sex characteristic.

   (a) Parents are more likely to discuss consumption with a female rather than a male child.

   (b) Parents are more likely to use positive reinforcement with a female rather than a male child.

   (c) Parents are more likely to use negative reinforcement with a male rather than a female child.

Proposition 10.12: Sex affects the extent to which children model themselves after their parents. Female youths are more likely to model themselves after their parents than male youths.

Studies generally have shown that females have a stronger orientation toward their peers than do males (see, for example, Millson 1966; Hamilton and Warden 1966; Solomon 1963). Sociologists have speculated that this greater dependence might result from the desire to clarify and boost an unsatisfactory role identification and feel more certain of their competence in future roles (Parsons 1949; Lynn 1959). Females also wish to learn the standards and criteria for the various elements of attractiveness that are expected to be of crucial importance in competing for a husband (Solomon 1963). Peers are not as important to boys because they have more objective indexes of their potential to which they can turn (for exmaple, education or occupation). The findings of a study of the wishes of older children and adolescents appear to be in line with these speculations. Boys' wishes for personal aggrandizement and achievement exceeded those of girls, while girls' wishes about social and family relations and personal characteristics exceeded those of boys

(Solomon 1963). On the basis of these speculations and research findings, previous researchers (Churchill and Moschis 1979) expected girls to interact more frequently with their peers about consumption matters and to be more susceptible to social influence (possess stronger social motivations for consumption and value products on the basis of their perceived effects on others) than their male counterparts. The data, however, did not support these expectations, suggesting that peer influence might operate through mechanisms other than social interaction.

Proposition 10.13: A youth's sex affects peer socialization processes. In comparison with their male counterparts, female youths are more likely to:

(a) discuss consumption with peers

(b) model themselves after peer consumer behaviors

Sex differences in mass media use can be noted in early life, although few sex differences have been noted regarding the amount of television viewing, except that girls tend to watch more television immediately after school and somewhat less around the dinner hour (5:00 to 7:00 P.M.) (Avery 1979). Sex differences in program preferences are evident throughout adolescence. Boys are more likely to prefer action, adventure, sports, and public affairs telecasts, while girls show stronger preferences for situation comedy shows (Chaffee and McLeod 1972; Prisuta 1979). Differences in these viewing patterns and program preferences among adolescents have been attributed to emerging adult sex roles and reflect emotional and psychological maturation, which is believed to occur earlier for girls than for boys (Avery 1979).

Sex differences also have been noted with respect to newspaper content preference. Specifically, Mauro (1979) found that male adolescents were most interested in news items about sports, movies, local news, and other entertainment, in rank order. News and features of interest to girls were those concerning movies, people, entertainment, and fashion. The girls' greater preoccupation with their social environment might reflect their stronger orientation toward their peers and their greater need for identification (Parsons 1949; Lynn 1959; Solomon 1963).

Finally, sex differences have been noted with respect to use of other print media. Although teenage boys and girls report about the same level of magazine consumption, they show distinct differences in magazine preference. Boys prefer men's magazines (such as *Playboy* and *Esquire*) and sports magazines (such as *Sports Illustrated* and *Sports Afield*), whereas girls enjoy teenage and women's magazines (such as *Seventeen, McCalls,* and *Redbook*) (Avery 1979). Similar patterns are reported for adolescent book consumption. Specifically, girls appear to prefer love stories, mysteries, and popular novels, whereas boys prefer mysteries, science fiction, biographies, and popular novels (Lyle and Hoffman 1972). Reasons for reading books have been attributed to the need for entertainment and to escape from everyday problems, which are fairly similar to reasons for going to the movies, according to the functional analysis (Elliott and Quattlebaum 1979).

Proposition 10.14: A youth's sex characteristic affects his or her use of the mass media. It affects preferences for:

(a) television programs
(b) newspaper content
(c) magazine content

Adulthood

Several sex differences in orientations developed during formative years are likely to persist well into adulthood. For example, greater persuadability among females has been found in psychological and marketing literature (see, for example, Alexander 1947; McGuire 1969). Similarly, Scanzoni (1976) presented evidence suggesting that men are more traditional in sex role orientations than women. Because women are the subordinate group, he argued, they experience fewer privileges, rights, and benefits. As a result, they tend not to try to maintain a status quo regarding gender differences but to seek change instead. Men, however, prefer to maintain status differentiation because it is in their own best interest.

The relatively higher maturity exhibited by female youths also appears to be prevalent among younger adults. A study among graduate students age twenty-five to thirty-four showed that emotional maturity was higher among females. Emotional maturity was in turn related to drunk-driving behavior and involvement in accidents. Respondents with high maturity exhibited an internal locus of control and a greater risk consciousness than the other group (Boyd and Huffman 1984).

Sex differences in the consumer behavior of adults have been widely cited in literature and practitioner sources (for example, Simmons Market Research Bureau) and they range from food preferences (Kahle and Homer 1985) to blood donation (Burnett 1981). Such differences, however, have not been interpreted in the context of socialization theories. Furthermore, sex differences are confounded with the presence of other factors, such as work overload as a result of working status, which has been found to be causally related to consumer behavior (Reily 1982) as well as to the frequency of interaction with various socialization agents, including personal and commercial sources of information (McCall 1977).

Besides factors that are likely to affect opportunities for interaction with socialization agents, the available evidence seems to suggest sex differences with respect to mass media use. Not only is the amount of time females spend with television different from the time spent by males, but it also changes over the life cycle (*Nielsen Report* 1982). Since little research has focused on the socialization of adults, information is lacking as to how the two sex groups use the mass media and the subsequent effects on consumer socialization. The limited data do suggest sex differences in mass media exposure and use, suggesting the indirect role of sex in the consumer socialization of adults. For example, a study comparing sex differences in newspaper content interests highlights the possible role of newspapers in the socialization process (Newspaper Advertising Bureau 1977).

Proposition 10.15: The sex characteristic of adults affects their use of the mass media. It affects their preferences for:

(a) television programs
(b) newspaper content
(c) magazine content

Late Adulthood

Both developmental and sociopsychological theories suggest that sex differences are important in the aging process. It has been suggested, for example, that sex differences in elderly friendship patterns might represent a stronger effect on outcomes than cohort differences (Baltes 1978). Neugarten suggests that sex differences might diminish with age because of a variety of biological and sociological factors (Neugarten 1972).

Consumer Behavior. Sex differences in the elderly's consumption-related roles regarding decision making have been reported. Specifically, the data seem to suggest that the female becomes more dominant in decision making, especially upon the retirement of her husband (Neugarten 1964). This dominance appears to be reflected in her perceptions of roles regarding decision making. In one study, for example, female respondents were found to hold less egalitarian perceptions regarding decision making (Smith et al. 1981). A more recent study found no sex differences in sex role perceptions and other criterion variables except self-perception and proneness to deals (Smith 1982).

Proposition 10.16: Older females are more likely than their male counterparts to hold egalitarian sex role perceptions about family decisions.

Socialization Processes. Sex differences in interaction with socialization agents developed during childhood and adolescence appear to persist throughout life and be noticeable even during the older years. Older females were found to interact more frequently with family and peers than their male counterparts (Smith 1982; Smith and Moschis 1985a). Similarly, sex differences in mass media use have been reported among older adults. Several studies have reported that television viewing is heavier among elderly women than among older men (Young 1979; Newspaper Research Bureau 1981). Older males also were found to be more likely than older females to read newspapers, but there were few differences regarding radio listening between the two groups (Newspaper Research Bureau 1981). Apparently, older women are less interested than older men in keeping up with current events. Older women seem to rely on television, while older men rely more on newspapers as a source of information (Newspaper Research Bureau 1981).

Proposition 10.17: An older person's sex affects the way he or she interacts with socialization agents. In comparison with their older male counterparts, older females are:

(a) more likely to discuss consumption with their peers
(b) more likely to discuss consumption with family members
(c) more likely to watch television
(d) less likely to read newspapers

Birth Order

Birth order generally appears to be a significant factor in socialization and also might play a significant role in consumer socialization. Unfortunately, research on the effects of birth order on socialization is sparse, while research on the effects of birth order on consumer socialization is almost nonexistent. This section summarizes the limited evidence available.

First, with respect to the direct effects of birth order, firstborn individuals (children and adults) were found to be less cautious than their later-born counterparts (Kagan 1977). Firstborns also have been found to be more dependent, more suggestible, more likely to volunteer to take part in volunteer activities, and more likely to be affiliated (that is, to have their behaviors guided by a need to find love) than later-borns (McCandless 1969).

Furthermore, previous theory and research suggest that firstborn and only children are superior to later-born children in achievement motivation and educational aspirations (Glass et al. 1974). To secure more education, firstborn adolescents might delay entry into the labor force and thus postpone the acquisition of major consumption items (Straus 1962a). In contrast, the results of one study found that firstborn and only children, compared to later-borns, have higher occupational aspirations, but they were not likely to defer consumption gratifications (Moschis and Moore 1984). Another study of consumer socialization found children with older siblings (that is, later-borns) to be less likely to exhibit cognitive defenses toward advertisements on television than children without older siblings (Rossiter and Robertson 1974). Similar results emerged from a longitudinal study of adolescents, which found both short-run and longer-run effects on the ability to filter puffery in advertising messages (Moschis 1984). Additional analysis of our Wisconsin data (Moschis and Churchill 1978) containing a supplementary sample ($N = 1,002$) found significant differences between firstborn and later-born adolescents, with the latter group being more likely to have negative attitudes toward savings ($p < .007$), stronger materialistic attitudes ($p < .005$), and positive attitudes toward advertising and stores ($p < .05$). They also were more likely to rely on print ads for consumer information ($p < .02$).

Proposition 10.18: Firstborn individuals acquire better consumer skills than their later-born counterparts. They are more likely to have:

(a) aspirations for better occupations
(b) greater ability to evaluate commercial stimuli

Proposition 10.19: Later-borns are more likely than their firstborn counterparts to have positive orientations toward commercial stimuli. They are more likely to have stronger attitudes toward:

(a) products and brands
(b) advertising messages
(c) stores
(d) salespeople
(e) promotional stimuli

Birth order position appears to have indirect effects on socialization operating via socialization agents and processes. In a review of the literature, for example, Kagan (1977) suggested that the firstborn has a stronger tendency than the later-born to turn to parents, rather than peers, for values and to use parents as models. "The combination of identification with parental models, perception of 'privileged' status which the child wants to maintain and apprehension over rejection by adult authority leads the firstborn to adopt higher standards surrounding the competences and attributes that are valued by the parents" (Kagan 1977, 51).

Parents tend to award a firstborn a position of privilege, and the child becomes accustomed to the exclusive affection of the parents. The arrival of a second child poses a threat to the firstborn's relationship with the parents and becomes an incentive to differentiate himself or herself from the younger. This often is done by modeling after parental values or standards valued by the family (Kagan 1977; Schachter 1959). The later-born is likely to feel resentment toward older siblings because they are aggressive and domineering and enjoy privileges the later-born does not, causing him or her to turn to peers for values (Kagan 1977). These differences in orientation toward parents and peers might result in differential interaction and influence regarding consumption. In one study (Churchill and Moschis 1979), later-born adolescents were found to interact more frequently than firstborns with their peers regarding consumption matters.

Proposition 10.20: Different socialization processes operate among firstborns than among later-borns.

(a) Firstborns are more likely to interact with their parents than later-borns.

(b) Firstborns are more likely to model themselves after their parents than later-borns.

(c) Later-borns are more likely to interact with peers than firstborns.

(d) Later-borns are more likely to model themselves after peers than firstborns.

Because firstborns are expected to be more dependent, as well as more verbal and more conforming (albeit more anxious and aggressive), there should be fewer opportunities for parent-child conflict (McCandless 1969). In addition, birth order effects often are confounded with the presence of several other variables and processes. For example, later-borns have more opportunities to use older siblings as socialization agents than firstborns. In fact, research by Vener (1957) found older brothers and sisters to be significant referents in dress selection decisions.

Finally, birth order effects are more evident in certain groupings of population than in others. For example, Glass et al. (1974) argue that birth order effects occur only among populations from higher socioeconomic backgrounds. Similarly, the sex characteristic of the older sibling(s) is likely to affect the later-born's propensity to model after the firstborn, parents, or other socialization agents (such as peers). Specifically, later-born females with older sisters are more likely to experience greater sibling rivalry and hostility toward parents than girls with older brothers, and as a result, they are more likely to use peers as the primary frame of reference (Hartup 1970; Schmuck 1963). The results of additional analyses of our Georgia data ($N = 961$, Moschis and Moore 1981a) appear to support this line of reasoning in consumer socialization. Specifically, we correlated self-reported measures of parental modeling (that is, the adolescent's frequency of observing parents performing certain normative consumer behaviors) with the adolescent's perceptions of the desirability of performing similar normative behaviors among two groups: later-born females with older sisters and later-born females with older brothers (but not older sisters). The correlation between the two measures for the first group was .09 (not significant); for the second group, it was .43 ($p < 01$). The two correlations were significantly different (Z transformations).

> Proposition 10.21: Later-born girls with older sisters are more likely to model after peers than later-born girls with older brothers.

Summary and Discussion

The findings presented in this chapter, albeit limited, suggest the importance of sex and birth order as antecedent variables in consumer socialization. The evidence is stronger for sex than it is for birth order. Specifically, sex differences seem to be rather significant in terms of having a direct impact on a person over the life cycle. Of greater importance, however, is the evidence showing that once sex differences develop, they tend to persist throughout the life cycle. The same goes for the indirect influences of sex. Thus, for example, girls at a very young age begin developing social orientations that affect not only their consumer behavior in the remaining stages of the life cycle but also their patterns of interaction with other socialization agents, such as family members and peers.

One of the difficulties in studying the effects of sex in consumer socialization is the lack of adequate understanding of sex differences in the absence of theory. It would be rather naive to assume that such differences are due to genetic factors or that they are attributable to other psychosocial processes. Even of greater suspicion is the assumption that these differences are due to individual characteristics, when in fact they might reflect differences in socialization practices and processes used by agents because of the person's sex. Finally, these differences might be rooted in cultural and subcultural values and norms. For example, in a culture where both spouses are likely to work, a youth might be expected to assume certain responsibilities regarding household decisions. Similarly, older adults might be expected to look after an aging spouse, whereas in a different culture, this responsibility might be left to the aging person's children. Such differences in cultural values and expectations might be reflected in sex differences in the person's perception of his or her role and the consumption skills the person is likely to acquire.

The effects of birth order are even more unclear and complex. We have little information on how specific relationships between siblings (defined beyond sex and birth order positions according to number and sex of other siblings and age differences between siblings) and parents affect consumer learning. Thus, birth order effects might be confounded with the presence of other characteristics related to siblings and parents and, perhaps most important, with relationships between these persons. Furthermore, unlike sex differences, we know very little about whether differences in consumer behavior and socialization processes developed in the early years persist into adulthood or the extent to which these are likely to be modified by other socialization agents, such as children and spouse.

11

Socioeconomic Influences

Social class differences in consumer behavior appear to develop early in life. Once they are developed, they tend to persist throughout the person's life cycle. Because social class differences are developed early, most of the research has focused on understanding the formation of various orientations during childhood and adolescence. As a result, socialization research examining the development of cognitions and behaviors, including consumption, during adulthood is rather scarce. In this chapter, social class differences in consumer behavior and socialization are presented, with heavy emphasis placed on childhood and adolescence.

Childhood and Adolescence

One of the firmest facts in psychology is the positive relationship between a child's social class and his or her cognitive functioning. Youths from higher social classes are socialized to develop greater skills such as memory and inferential ability (Kagan 1977). In addition, youths from higher social classes are socialized into roles that are different from those acquired by lower-class children. For example, youths from high-status families are socialized into a gender role differentiation that is relatively less rigid than that learned by youths in lower-status homes (Scanzoni 1976), as shown by the less sexist attitudes held by higher-class youths (see, for example, Bayer 1975; Angrist et al. 1977; Osmond and Martin 1975).

Consumer Behavior

The effects of social class on children's consumer behavior become evident in the very early years of consumption. Ward and his associates (1977), for example, found socioeconomic differences in consumer behavior even among kindergarten children. Similarly, Williams (1970) found that knowledge of economic concepts for children from first through sixth grades was greater among children from upper socioeconomic family backgrounds than among children from lower socioeconomic backgrounds. It is evident from the available data that upper-class adolescents are socialized better and faster into the consumer role than their lower-class counterparts (see, for example, Moschis and Churchill 1979; Moschis and Moore 1981b). What is not clear is why and how such differences in consumer behavior develop. Explanations for social class differences have been traced to four possible sources: social class values, self-perception, socialization processes, and environmental factors.

Differences in the consumer behavior of young people often are the result of *values* held by various social classes. The different values stem from differences in the conditions of life (Kohn 1963). For example, Katz (1964) presented evidence of considerable variation in the concept of success for adolescents of different socioeconomic classes, suggesting the presence of cultural prescriptions and subcultural or class variations in the frame of aspirational reference, which is internalized in the process of socialization. In fact, the Katz study found that success can be judged in terms of accumulation of possessions and wealth, attainment of a secure job, and achievement of status—that is, a favorable position in a vocational or educational hierarchy. This orientation appears to be consistent with findings showing the father's occupational status to be the strongest factor related to the son's occupational status, which suggests that the son might be unwilling to accept an occupation of lesser status than that of his father (Corcoran et al. 1976). Furthermore, there are social class variations in perceptions of the acquisition of symbols of success (for example, material possessions). Studies show that middle-class children are likely to believe that success and failure is a matter of personal effort, while lower-class children attribute success to chance and circumstances beyond their control (Kagan 1977). These orientations might explain the decline in desires for material possessions among lower-class youths and the increase in materialism among higher-class youngsters during their adolescent years (Moschis and Churchill 1979).

> Proposition 11.1: Higher-class youths are likely to have higher aspirations than lower-class youths. They are more likely to have:
>
> (a) higher occupational aspirations
>
> (b) higher aspirations for acquisition of products perceived to be symbols of success

Many differences in the consumer behavior of young people can be attributed to the youths' *self-perceptions* of their social class position and the cultural prescriptions or aspirational references in terms of consumption behavior associated with maintaining or moving into a social class status. Awareness of social class distinctions appear by the fifth or sixth grade. Such awareness might come from observation of impersonal sources, including the mass media (Hess 1970).

Awareness of one's present or aspirational social class position is more likely to develop earlier among higher-class youths than among lower-class youths. DeFleur and DeFleur (1967) found lower-class children to have less knowledge of the characteristics of occupational roles than upper- and middle-class children. Similarly, Moschis and Moore (1984) found higher-class adolescents to be more likely to have occupational aspirations than their lower-class counterparts. These differences in awareness and aspirations might reflect differences in the youths' perceptions of present and aspirational social class positions and requirements for moving into or maintaining relatively high social status. Thus, it is not surprising to find studies showing social class to be an important factor in determining levels of aspirations. Of greater importance, however, appears to be the consequences of the youths' self-perceptions and status aspirations for present and future consumer role enactment, including the perception of material goods and consumption gratifications. Apparently, materialism increases throughout childhood (see, for example, Ward et al. 1977; Atkin 1975c), but upon entering adolescence, lower-class youths become aware of the requirements necessary for acquiring material possessions and the limitations of being from a lower socioeconomic background. This might explain the decline in materialistic attitudes of lower-class adolescents (Moschis and Churchill 1979). Upper-class adolescents, however, might become aware of their opportunities, capabilities, and class norms, and as a result, they are likely to develop stronger materialistic values with age (Moschis and Churchill 1979).

The effort to achieve or maintain the desirable class status often requires the attainment of higher levels of education, delaying entry into the labor force, and deferment of consumption gratifications (Straus 1962a; Scanzoni 1976). Lower-class youths are less likely to aspire to a higher social status and to perceive work, rather than education, to be associated with their present social class position (Straus 1962b).

Proposition 11.2: Youths from higher social classes are more likely than youths from lower social classes to have a better understanding of the requirements for achieving high social status. In comparison with their lower-class counterparts, higher-class youths are more likely to:

(a) acquire consumer role perceptions

(b) have materialistic attitudes

(c) make associations between the product consumption and life-styles associated with different social classes

Proposition 11.3: Lower-class youths are less willing to defer consumption gratifications than youths from higher social classes.

Other differences in the consumer behavior of young people are due to *socialization processes*, which differ across social classes. For example, studies show that working-class mothers use normative control to a greater extent than do middle-class mothers and that this type of control is negatively related to the development of various skills, including cognitive skills (Hess 1970). Furthermore, it has been suggested that purposive consumer training will be more likely to be present in upper-middle-class families than in working- or lower-middle-class families (Aldous 1974). The results of several studies appear to support this contention, showing purposive consumer training to be present in higher-class families (Ward and Wackman 1973; Ward et al. 1977). Part of the explanation for different socialization processes across social classes stems from the values held by higher-class families regarding the desirable consumer skills their children should possess. Higher value similarity has been found among middle-class than among lower-class mothers and sons (Rosen 1964). Value similarity between parents and children also might be present in consumer behavior.

While purposive consumer training is expected to occur most frequently in high-class families, parents often attempt to socialize their children by acting as role models, expecting them to learn through observation (Ward 1974a; Ward et al. 1977). Observation of parental behavior might not result in adequate socialization, however, as some data show that youths are likely to acquire behavioral patterns but not cognitive skills through observation (Moore and Moschis 1983).

To summarize the effects of socialization processes on youths' acquisition of consumer competencies among social classes, the different socialization processes that operate in various social classes lead to differential acquisition of consumer competencies. Upper-class families make more of an effort to socialize their children into the consumer role. Thus, we can speculate that the higher parent-child value similarity among middle-class families is acquired through modeling processes, which are supplemented with purposive training. In lower social classes, where purposive training is likely to be a rare occurrence, the transmission of skills and values from parent to child might take place only through observation, resulting in less effective learning.

Proposition 11.4: A youth's consumer competencies are more likely to resemble those of his or her parents in higher classes than in lower classes.

Social class variations in socialization processes also are found in the opportunities parents provide to their children for participation in the consumption process (Ward et al. 1977) and the independence they grant in purchasing. There is some evidence suggesting that parents in upper social classes are more likely to supervise closely their offspring's consumption activities than are parents in lower socioeconomic classes. Moschis et al. (1977) examined the relationship between the adolescent's independence in purchasing eleven types of products and social class. A major consideration in this study was to determine the extent to which adolescent independence in purchasing varies by social class. Previous research suggested that upper- and middle-class families, as opposed to lower-class families, are more conscious of the normative standards of their class and that parents are more likely to supervise their children's activities (including buying clothes) closely in an effort to socialize them into the class norms (Psathas 1957). Thus, the researchers reasoned that lower-class adolescents would have greater independence in purchasing than middle- and upper-class adolescents.

A significant negative relationship was found between social class and degree of adolescent independence for purchases of health care items, shoes, coats, and sports equipment. The tendency toward greater involvement by members of upper-class families in purchases of these types of products might indeed reflect the parents' desire for their child's competence, social acceptance, and well-being (Engel et al. 1973), since further analysis of the data showed no significant relationship between the adolescent's social class and available spending money. Social class also was a significant factor affecting the extent to which adolescents attained family independence in purchasing with age. In analyzing age differences in purchasing independence, a curvilinear relationship was found between social class and the extent to which older adolescent consumers had greater independence in purchasing than younger adolescents. Lower-class adolescent consumers appeared to acquire greater independence from family members in purchasing activities with age than did adolescent consumers in other social classes. Specifically, these data showed that with increasing age, lower-class adolescents had significantly ($p < .05$) greater independence in shopping than did adolescents from middle- or upper-class families for all eleven products examined except health care items, shoes, and film (Moschis et al. 1977).

The influence of social class on youths' consumer behavior also is shown in a study that examined adolescents' influence on various stages of the decision-making process involving not only products for the adoelscents' use but those for the family's use as well (Moschis and Mitchell 1986). Specifically, it was found that lower-class youths, as compared with their upper-class counterparts, were less likely to mention the need for products to other members of their family but were more likely to purchase them on their own.

Proposition 11.5: The level of independence in purchasing acquired by youths and their involvement in the family decision-making process are mediated by social class norms. In comparison to youths from the upper and lower social classes, youths from the middle classes, where purposive training is most common, have:

(a) less independence in purchasing products for their own use

(b) a greater likelihood of participation in family decisions

While different socialization processes operating in social classes are likely to affect the acquisition of consumer competencies, such processes also might affect the acquisition of dysfunctional consumer behaviors. For example, data show that involvement in delinquency is more likely to occur among lower-class children than among middle-class children, although this relationship is more likely to exist among youths in urban areas than youths in rural areas or small cities (Hess 1970). Hess also suggests that these differences might be due to higher divorce rates among the lower classes, in spite of the lack of evidence regarding the relationship between broken homes and delinquency. Shoplifting as a delinquent (dysfunctional) consumer behavior has been shown to have a moderate relationship with social class (see, for example, Won and Yamamoto 1968; Klemke 1982). Recent research, however, shows that social class differences in shoplifting frequency might be due to different socialization processes. For example, it has been argued that children in families that lack parental attention and warmth are more likely to become alienated and exhibit behaviors not approved by parents or to join peer groups likely to exhibit delinquent behaviors (Moschis et al. 1987). The same study, however, found no direct relationship between the presence of parents in the home and shoplifting orientations, a finding that is in line with those of previous studies showing a weak relationship between broken homes and delinquency (Hess 1970). It might be that deviant peers serve as catalysts encouraging delinquent behaviors. Alternatively, children from homes where parents are present and spend time with them are less likely to be neglected, alienated, and motivated to undertake dysfunctional activities.

Social class also has been linked to other dysfunctional behaviors. For example, it has been found that low educational level and poor educational achievement are characteristics related to the person's tendency to seek danger on the road (Maki et al. 1975).

Proposition 11.6: Lower-class youths are more likely than higher-class youths to engage in dysfunctional behaviors. They are more likely to:

(a) shoplift

(b) have automobile accidents

Proposition 11.7: The presence of deviant peers enhances the possibilities of exhibiting dysfunctional behaviors. The presence of deviant peers among lower-class youths, in comparison with the prsence of such peers among higher-class youths, is likely to result in:

(a) more frequent shoplifting behavior

(b) a greater likelihood of automobile accidents

A final cause for social class differences in consumer behavior among young people might be *environmental factors*. Such factors might provide different opportunities for consumer learning, in line with Lewin's (1951) life-space theory.

It has been argued from a learning theory point of view that adolescents of low socioeconomic status have less experience with money and might be less aware of the range of consumer goods compared to youths from upper socioeconomic backgrounds, who have more opportunities for, and experiences with, consumption (Ward 1974a; Riesman et al. 1956).

A great deal of research supports socioeconomic effects on the consumer behavior of adolescents from a learning theory point of view. For example, a significant positive relationship appears to exist between the adolescent's social class and the extent to which he or she is aware of available brands in the marketplace (Moschis and Moore 1978; Keiser and Kuehl 1972); seeks information (Moschis 1976a); can price products and services and understands consumer-legal matters (Moore and Stephens 1975; Moschis and Moore 1978); understands economic concepts (Williams 1970); and knows socially desirable consumer role expectations (Moschis and Moore 1978). These findings appear to support the contention that young people from low-income homes are less knowledgeable about their consumer environment than youngsters from high-income homes, who have more opportunities for consumption.

In addition, socialization theory suggests that lower-class persons are relatively isolated from the "paths of experience of dominant middle class" (Hess 1970, 468) and that this lack of information makes the individual susceptible to exploitation by commercial sources of information, such as sales people and television advertising. "The lower-blue-collar worker has few independent criteria for evaluating the content of the message, little awareness of specific alternatives, and little disposition to weigh evidence" (p. 468). Previous research in consumer socialization seems to support these contentions, showing that lower-class youths, compared with their middle-class counterparts, are less able to filter puffery in advertising, are less likely to use objective (rational) criteria in evaluating products, and are less able to price selected items accurately in a typical family budget (Moschis and Churchill 1979).

Further, it has been suggested that the cognitive field of the lower-class youngster is unstructured, increasing the possibility for eventual disappointment and frustration (Hess 1970). The latter notion might explain the inverse relationship found in consumer socialization studies between social class and attitudes toward advertising and business in general among children, adolescents, and college students (see, for example, Ferguson 1975; Ward and Robertson 1972; Rossiter and Robertson 1975; Ward and Reale 1972).

Finally, sex stereotyping is more likely to be present among children in higher social classes (see Belk et al. 1984). This might be due to a greater exposure to a variety of product uses resulting in more opportunities to observe relationships between consumption and life-styles. While these findings can be interpreted in the context of learning theory (see, for example, Ward 1974a), they are consistent with the life-space notion advanced by Lewin (1951).

Thus, youths from higher socioeconomic classes have more opportunities for consumption and wider experiences with the marketplace, which might result in better acquisition of consumer competencies. Youths from lower classes have less experiences and as a result might not only develop fewer consumer competencies but also be more susceptible to marketing practices.

Proposition 11.8: Upper-class youths are more likely than their lower-class counterparts to possess consumer competencies; they are more likely to:

(a) possess greater knowledge about the marketplace (brands, prices, consumer rights, economic knowledge)

(b) have acquired socially desirable consumer role expectations

(c) use more information in decision making

(d) evaluate alternatives based on objective evidence (attributes)

(e) make associations between consumption and life-styles—that is, stereotyping

Proposition 11.9: Lower-class youths are more likely than their upper-class counterparts to:

(a) be susceptible to marketing stimuli

(b) be dissatisfied with products and services they buy

(c) have negative attitudes toward marketing practices

Socialization Processes

Social class differences also have been noted with respect to parent-child interactions, peer interactions, and mass media use. Generally, upper-class parents are more likely to make a conscious effort to socialize their children than are parents from lower classes. Not only do they spend more time with them than other parents, but they also spend relatively more money in ways that foster the personal development of their children (Bowen 1977).

Theory and research suggest that upper- and middle-class families, as opposed to lower-class families, are more conscious of the normative standards of their class, and they are more likely to supervise their children's consumption activities closely in an effort to socialize them into the class norms (Psathas 1957; Moschis et al. 1977; Robertson and Rossiter 1975). This parental involvement in adolescent consumer behavior might result in more frequent discussions about consumption with the child. Ward and his associates (1977) found that high-status mothers are more likely to initiate discussions with their children about products and television commercials than middle-status or lower-status mothers. Similarly, Ward and Wackman (1973) found that purposive consumer training of children was likely to be present only among high-class families.

Although lower-class parents are more likely to intrude into the activities of their children, they are less likely than middle-class parents to explain punishments or give reasons for these prohibitions (Kagan 1977). Such activities tend to define the socio-oriented family communication structure (McLeod and Chaffee 1972). Thus, it is not surprising to find that a socio-oriented family communication structure is more prevalent among lower-class families than among higher-class families (McLeod and Chaffee 1972). In addition, Kagan (1977) reported that lower-middle-class caucasian mothers talked less to their children, suggesting that the laissez-faire pattern of family communication might be present in lower-class families more than in other classes.

It has been suggested that the relatively greater effectiveness of high-class parents in the socialization of their children can be attributed to the close-knit nature of the family structure. Specifically, the relatively loose family structure of lower-class families might be due to a combination of autocratic control and low influence (McCandless 1969). The lower-class father, especially the minority group father, has very little socially valued power, and this is likely to come to the child's attention early in life.

Peers are expected to play a more important role in the socialization of lower-class children than in that of middle-class children (McCandless 1969). The combination of the child's perception of the parents' low socially valued power along with greater autonomy and independence, create opportunities for interaction with peers and using peers as a frame of reference. With respect to the influence of peers on the consumer socialization of young people, research has found that upper-class adolescents interact more frequently with peers about consumption matters than lower-class youths (Moschis and Churchill 1978), but few studies have assessed the effect of the frequency of interaction with peers on consumer learning in different social classes. In a study of 608 adolescents from Kentucky and North Carolina, Moschis and Moore (1979a) found consumption interaction with peers to be related to the youth's ability to price products accurately, to higher levels of knowledge among middle-class adolescents, and to undesirable role perceptions among upper-class adolescents. The effects of social class on the youth's interaction with parents and peers can be summarized in the following propositions:

Proposition 11.10: Parent-child consumer socialization processes are more likely to operate among higher-class than among lower-class families. Upper-class youths are more likely than their lower-class counterparts to:

(a) discuss consumption with their parents

(b) use parents as role models regarding consumption

(c) come from families stressing a concept-oriented family communication pattern

Proposition 11.11: A laissez-faire family communication pattern is more likely to prevail among lower-class families than among upper-class families.

Proposition 11.12: A socio-oriented family communication pattern is inversely related to social class.

Proposition 11.13: Youths from lower social classes are more likely than youths from upper classes to:

(a) discuss consumption with peers

(b) model themselves after peer consumer behavior

Whereas there is a limited amount of research regarding socioeconomic influences on family socialization practices and peer interactions, there is a considerable amount of evidence regarding the connection between social class and media use behavior among children and adolescents. The data generally show that youngsters from blue-collar families watch more television and read newspapers less than do those from white-collar families (see, for example, Schramm et al. 1961; Lyle and Hoffman 1972; Greenberg and Dervin 1970; Greenberg and Dominick 1969). Socioeconomic differences in the youth's use of television as a learning device also have been found in other studies (see, for example, Greenberg and Dominick 1969; Christiansen 1979). Specifically, one study of consumer socialization found adolescents from lower socioeconomic backgrounds, in relation to their middle-class counterparts, to watch television ads and programs more for social reasons and for making consumer decisions (Moschis and Churchill 1978).

Of greater importance, however, from a socialization perspective is the learning that takes place during the youths' interaction with television. Lower-class youths are more likely to use television role models than their upper-class counterparts (see, for example, Christiansen 1979), and this might be explained in terms of learning theory. Miller and Dollard (1941) indicated that it is more rewarding to imitate those who are superior, for example, with respect to social status, suggesting that lower-class youths might attempt to emulate models perceived to be of a higher social status.

Schramm and his colleagues (1961) proposed that class norms mediate a change in youths' relationships to the mass media. Specifically, during adolescence, the children of white-collar families turned toward reality-oriented media such as newspapers (a finding that can be explained by the life-space perspective), while children of working-class families remained committed to fantasy-oriented media such as television. Such orientations toward the mass media might result in knowledge gain.

Communication researchers have used the life-space notion to explain the positive relationship between print media use and public affairs knowledge with increasing education and socioeconomic status (see, for example, Wade and Schramm 1969; Tichenor et al. 1970). Recently Ward and his associates (1977) used this notion to explain the individual's propensity to consult mass media sources. In sum, while there is overwhelming evidence to suggest the level of young people's interaction with the mass media, considerably less is known about how young people use the mass media, including the learning processes operating in consumer socialization.

Proposition 11.14: Television is used as a learning device about consumer matters during the youth's viewing time. In relation to their upper-class counterparts, youths from lower classes are more likely to:

(a) use television advertisements in making consumer decisions

(b) use television programs to get information about consumption

(c) imitate the consumer behavior of television role models

Proposition 11.15: Learning from newspapers is likely to occur primarily among upper- and middle-class youths. In comparison with their lower-class counterparts, youths from higher classes are more likely to:

(a) read advertisements for consumer information
(b) read editorials or news items for consumer information

Adulthood

Consumer Behavior

Social class differences in the consumer behavior of adults have been documented by several studies. These differences emerge across a wide spectrum of consumption orientations, including occupational choice, spending patterns, product ownership, consumption motives, purchasing patterns, and evaluative criteria. Because criteria for defining social class include income, education, and occupational status, these criteria are used in the context of social class to present evidence of socioeconomic status effects on consumer socialization and behavior.

First, with respect to occupational choice, Levine (1976) concluded, after summarizing much of the existing literature, that "knowledge about a range of occupations, aspirations, and expectations for reaching various occupational and educational goals differ by social class" (p. 132). Family studies relating household income to savings and household expenditures on various categories of consumption have been available since the work of Ernst Engel and Irving Fisher around the turn of this century. Greater refinement of these efforts is reflected in later works by Keynes, who recognized both the force of consumption habits and the relevance of expected income for current consumption decisions. These efforts, in turn, led to the development of the relative income hypothesis, which specifies that the household's consumption ratio is a function of income position within a reference group (Crockett 1976).

Individuals possessing different levels of education differ with respect to the manner in which they spend their income and behave in the marketplace. Specifically, better-educated individuals tend to allocate a higher portion of their income to housing, print media, education, and travel; they spend a lower portion on socially conspicuous products (clothing, cars, and personal care), food, tobacco, and alcoholic beverages (Bowen 1977). Such differences might reflect efforts on the part of higher-status (educated) consumers to maintain status differences. Specifically, the work of Segal and Felson (1973) suggests that as income and class consciousness distinctions among social classes are narrowing, material life-styles are converging, while status differences are maintained by different proportional saving/spending patterns, with white-collar workers emphasizing credit mobilization and blue-collar workers emphasizing consumption. Thus, it is not surprising to find data showing materialistic attitudes and orientations to be more relevant among blue-collar workers (Chinoy 1955; Goldthorpe et al. 1969).

Although social class is not believed to have an impact on what Riesman and Roseborough (1955) call "anticipatory buying," previous research suggests that social class origins might affect the perception of the time horizons associated with the purchase of items that might be included in the family's "standard" package." The tendency to postpone the acquisition of major items—that is, "deferred gratification"—appears to be more common among upper-class families than among lower-class families (Riesman and Roseborough 1955; Straus 1962a). Such deferment might be related to delayed entry into the labor force to secure higher education (Straus 1962a).

Social class also appears to affect other consumer decision patterns, including selection of specific products and brands, information source utilization, and perception of commercial stimuli in general. Specifically, upper-class families, in relation to their lower-class counterparts, appear to be more health conscious (Bowen 1977) and in a better position to select among food products (Abedl-Ghany and Bivens 1976); they are less likely to rely on national brands as a criterion in product selection; and they are less likely to shop on impulse (Levy 1966). Alternatively, lower-class adult consumers tend to limit shopping to a few stores and use interpersonal sources of information in making decisions (Engel et al. 1973). The reason for a greater reliance on informal sources of information has been attributed to the relatively limited number of alternative information sources available to lower-class consumers. In a study of 3,440 adults, Warwick, Walsh, and Miller (1981) found that individuals with lower education and income tend to have more favorable impressions of television advertising, suggesting that greater reliance on interpersonal sources versus the mass media might be due to differences in availability of these sources of consumer information. Another reason might be that lower-class consumers have not developed skills in using information from different sources, and they might prefer information from interpersonal sources because these sources can provide the information in a decisional form.

Finally, a number of studies have found certain socioeconomic variables to be associated with store selection. Tate (1961) reports a relationship between education and one-store grocery shopping. Enis and Paul (1970) also found education to be linked to customer loyalty to grocery stores. Similarly, in a study of female shoppers, Bellenger, Hirschman, and Robertson (1976–1977) found education to be strongly related to store selection. In another study of the image of the store-loyal customer, education was negatively related to store loyalty (Reynolds et al. 1974).

Similar social class variables have been found to be related to vendor or institutional-type loyalty. For example, consumers who are loyal to department stores have the following characteristics: they are white-collar workers, have higher incomes, and have more education (Rich and Jain 1968). Similarly, shoppers who tend to patronize discount stores normally are blue-collar workers.

In addition to their relationship to patronage behaviors, social class variables have been shown to relate to cognitive orientations, such as shopping orientation. Bellenger, Robertson, and Greenberg (1977) found that various demographic variables, such as income and occupation, related to women's shopping orientations. Finally, social class variables are likely to affect the respondent's general shopping patterns. For example, a person who is an in-home buyer tends to have a lower educational background, a lower level of income, and a lower-status occupation (Peters and Ford 1972).

Other social class differences are found in value orientations. For example, in comparison with their lower-class counterparts, middle- and upper-class husbands have been reported to be more permissive and egalitarian in their ideology and values, although they are likely to have greater authority over their wives and children (Engel et al. 1973, 146). It has been argued that individuals with more education are less traditional, having more egalitarian sex role perceptions than those who are less educated (see, for example, Bowen 1977; Scanzoni 1976). One explanation for this is that education tends to have a modernizing or liberalizing influence on various beliefs and actions, including gender differentiation.

It is possible to view sex role norms and their correlates from the diffusionistic model—that is, as a means of illuminating aspects of individual differences in readiness to accept innovations and to describe the succession of norms or expectations (Bernard 1976). Because socioeconomic variables are positively related to innovativeness, it is not surprising that the emerging sex roles are more common among upper-class consumers than among lower-class consumers.

To summarize, the consumer orientations and skills possessed by youths in various social classes also are possessed by adult consumers. The values and skills acquired by youths regarding consumption appear to persist in the adult years and influence consumer behavior. Generally, a reasonable amount of evidence is available to help us conclude that upper-class consumers are more competent in the marketplace than lower-class consumers. The remaining evidence suggests the following propositions:

Proposition 11.16: Upper-class adults are *relatively* less likely to emphasize conspicuous consumption than lower-class adults. Upper-class consumers are less likely than their lower-class counterparts to:

(a) spend lower proportions of their income on conspicous products

(b) hold materialistic attitudes

(c) defer consumption gratifications

Proposition 11.17: Social class affects several aspects of the adult person's patronage behavior. The individual's socioeconomic status is related to:

(a) store loyalty

(b) preferences for types of retail institutions

(c) general shopping patterns

(d) shopping orientations

Proposition 11.18: The upper-class consumer's tendency to hold more egalitarian sex role attitudes reflects a higher propensity to adopt new ideas earlier than lower-class consumers.

Socialization Processes

The adult person's interaction patterns with socialization agents are fairly similar to those observed for children and adolescents. Dervin and Greenberg (1972) found that middle-class residents were more likely to use institutional sources of information (including the media) than were lower-class residents. Lower-class persons were more likely to rely on interpersonal sources, particularly friends and relatives. Generally, the electronic media are more likely to be consumed by lower-class adults than middle- and upper-class adults. The print media, however, are more likely to be consumed by those individuals having higher incomes and education (see, for example, Greenberg and Kumata 1968; Kline 1971; Burgoon and Burgoon 1980; Schramm et al. 1961; Wade and Schramm 1969).

Late Adulthood

The effects of social class on older adults have been extensively documented in several disciplines. For example, when education is considered as a measure of social class, we find differences in cognitive functioning among older adults based upon their educational background. For example, Chap and Sinnot (1977–1978) found that level of education was correlated to the development of logical thinking, while Thibodeau (1980) related education to the performance of developmental tasks among the aged.

Consumer Behavior

Relatively less is known about the effects of social class on the consumer behavior of older adults. Although younger elderly (fifty-five to sixty-four years old) are likely to enjoy the highest economic status in their lifetime (Berger 1985; McMillan and Moschis 1985), the retired individual is likely to enter a state of status maintenance because of a reduction in income. When possible, the older person is likely to attempt to maintain the preretirement state in line with the activity theory (Lemmon et al. 1972). Thus, efforts to maintain one's socioeconomic status might reflect consumption activities, efforts that might not characterize the behavior of younger adults. Perhaps this is why some gerontologists (see, for example, Rosow 1974) believe that socioeconomic status is a powerful predictor of behavior in general. The findings of our recent studies appear to support this line of reasoning, showing that the middle-class elderly have greater economic motivations for consumption and tend to interact more frequently with friends and family about consumption matters than do the lower-class elderly; they also pay more attention to mass media advertising, which might stimulate conversations with others about consumption (Smith and Moschis 1985a). The middle-class elderly also were found to have more preferences for brands than their lower-class counterparts (Smith et al. 1981; Smith and Moschis 1985b). Thus, some consumption patterns and attitudes developed during earlier years among social class groups persist even into late adulthood, but the older person's consumption orientations might be affected by his or her social class norms.

Proposition 11.19: Older adults from upper classes are more likely than those from lower classes to attempt to maintain the economic status they experienced in earlier life. With increasing age:

  (a) The upper-class elderly are more likely than the lower-class elderly to develop economic motivations for consumption.

  (b) The lower-class elderly are more likely than the upper-class elderly to show declining consumption activity.

Socialization Processes

The relationship between social class and a person's interaction with socialization agents during childhood and adulthood is extended into the later stages of life. Clarke (1956) was among the first researchers to find a negative relationship between social class and the media exposure of the elderly. In a study by Schreiber and Boyd (1980), education was found to be related to choices of the most influential advertising medium in consumer decision making. As educational level increased, respondents were increasingly likely to choose magazines as the most influential advertising medium. Elderly with a low educational level chose television nearly as often as newspapers. The selection of television as the most influential source appears to decline as education increases. The same study found education to be negatively related to the amount of television viewing. In a more recent study, Rubin and Rubin (1982) found education and income to be inversely related to product advertising motivations for television viewing among older adults, suggesting that lower-class mature consumers might be using television as a source of information about consumer decisions.

Another significant finding of the Schreiber and Boyd (1980) study was the effect of occupation and social class on the older person's use of other media. The elderly in upper-status jobs were more likely to report that the print media had more influence on their consumer decisions than television. Some occupational effects on television viewing habits of the elderly also emerged. Professionals, clerical workers, and proprietors watched fewer hours of television each day than those in "less-skilled" occupations. Additional research also suggests that income and education are likely to affect the elderly's use of the print media. Those with a higher income and more education were found to be more likely to spend time reading newspapers than those with a lower income and less education (Harris and Associates, Inc. 1975). Similarly, book and magazine reading remained relatively high across life span for those with a high education and income (Schramm 1969; Louis Harris and Associates, Inc. 1975). Thus, the findings regarding the effects of socio-economic status on older people's interaction with, and use of, sources of consumer information are remarkably similar to those of people in younger age groups.

Summary and Discussion

The data presented in this chapter suggest several significant differences in the consumer behavior and consumer socialization of a person over the life cycle. Most of these differences in patterns of consumption and communication behavior develop at a relatively young age, and once developed, they tend to persist throughout the person's age.

There is overwhelming evidence to suggest that upper-class individuals are more competent consumers in the marketplace. These differences in consumer competencies might be due to cultural values, perception of social class norms, socialization processes, and environmental factors. The evidence also shows convincing patterns of interaction with socialization agents. Upper-class consumers generally discuss consumption with peers and family members more frequently than lower-class consumers, regardless of stage in the life cycle. They also tend to be heavier consumers of print media and consumer information in general, while lower-class consumers are heavier users of electronic media and entertainment content. Thus, it appears that if we could understand how different consumption patterns develop in youths from different social classes in early life, we would be able to predict the patterns they exhibit as consumers later in life.

12
Racial Influences

One of the more firmly established facts in consumer behavior is that the consumer behavior of whites differs from that of blacks. But while most marketers and consumer behavior researchers agree upon black/white differences, there appears to be less information available and, therefore less consensus on the cause of the differences. Explanations for these differences have included cultural factors, socioeconomic characteristics, role enactment, and socialization processes.

Many differences in consumer behavior reflect cultural differences. Such differences might be the result of values held by the two subcultures. Socioeconomic differences, however, are present due to a relatively large portion of black consumers from lower socioeconomic strata, with social class being responsible for such differences. Differences due to role enactment are attributed to the roles black and white consumers assume through socialization—that is, the development of expectations regarding the behavior associated with racial groups (see, for example, Greenberg 1982), with the mass media often cited as an important agent in racial socialization. Finally, socialization processes, which differ in the two cultures, can have different effects on the development of consumer behavior.

This chapter presents information on racial differences by age group, which is then discussed in the context of these potential explanations. The assumption is made that race is a nominal variable—that is, consumers can be classified into black and white categories—and that consumers display behavior unique to their racial class, although ample evidence suggests that part of the difficulty in studying and understanding consumer behavior stems from the fact that blacks, and to some extent whites, display multicultural behavior (Williams 1985).

Childhood and Adolescence

Consumer Behavior

Racial differences in consumer behavior are evident early in life. Williams (1970), for example, found that knowledge of economic concepts among elementary school children tended to be higher among white children than among black children.

Similarly, Wackman, Reale, and Ward (1972) found that black teenagers were more likely to hold materialistic attitudes than white children.

Children's aspirations for material possessions may well reflect cultural values (Kuhn 1954). It might be, for example, that black youths experience socioeconomic deprivation at a very young age, which is likely to affect their level of aspirations and desires for conspicuous consumption (Hess 1970). Such deprivation might lead blacks to develop high levels of occupational aspirations. For example, a study reported by Levine (1976) found that blacks had higher occupational aspirations than whites. A more recent study of adolescents, however, found no difference in occupational aspirations between black and white adolescents, suggesting that occupational socialization might take place in late adolescence and early adulthood (Moschis and Moore 1984).

Social deprivation also might lead blacks to strive toward upgrading their status by means of conspicuous consumption. Findings reported by Bauer and Cunningham (1970) as well as Bauer and others (1965) suggest that blacks, in comparison to their white counterparts, tend to overspend on items of personal display and immediate gratification. Impatience regarding consumption might further affect their time horizon regarding the purchase of goods and services used by adults. In fact, our study of anticipatory consumer socialization (Moschis and Moore 1984) found black adolescents to be less likely to defer consumption gratifications than their white counterparts.

> Proposition 12.1: Socioeconomic deprivation leads black youths to behave differently than whites in an effort to upgrade their status. Black youths, in relation to their white counterparts, are more likely to:
>
> (a) have higher occupational aspirations
>
> (b) have stronger desires for conspicuous consumption
>
> (c) be more impatient regarding acquisition of socially conspicuous items
>
> (d) be less likely to defer consumption gratifications

Similar cultural differences also might exist in lower socioeconomic classes (Hess 1970), confounding the effects of race. Socioeconomic status (SES), however, seldom is accounted for in examining racial differences in consumer behavior. For example, early studies of black and white youths' consumer behavior examined the youths' reactions to television commercials. Some of these studies found race to have an important effect on such responses, with black children being more likely to respond favorably to commercials (for example, to report purchasing products because of ads) than their white counterparts (Wackman et al. 1972; Donohue et al. 1978; Barry and Sheikh 1977). Because socioeconomic status was not controlled, however, it is not clear whether such differences are due to racial or socioeconomic characteristics (Richarde 1980). It might be that when socioeconomic characteristics are held constant, there is little difference in the consumer behavior of blacks and whites (Bennett and Kassarjian 1972, 110).

A more recent study examined the effects of race and SES simultaneously (Moschis and Moore 1981b). The findings suggest that black/white differences in consumer behavior might not be due solely to either socioeconomic or racial factors. Rather, both race and SES appear to affect consumer behavior independently, as well as in combination. Specifically, when the effects of SES were controlled, white adolescents were found to be better able to filter puffery in advertising than black adolescents. Ability to manage consumer finances and dissatisfaction with consumption were not affected by either variable.

Several effects of SES-race interaction also were observed beyond the independent effects of SES and race. The consumer knowledge gap between blacks and whites was found to widen with increasing socioeconomic status. Thus, whites are likely to know more about consumer matters with increasing level of SES, while blacks are likely to know less with increasing level of SES. Also evident was a crossover interaction of race and SES concerning attitudes toward marketing stimuli. Lower-class white and upper-class black adolescents were more likely to have favorable attitudes toward marketing stimuli than upper-class whites and lower-class blacks. Attitudes toward marketing stimuli became more negative with increasing SES among whites but more positive among blacks.

Thus, the limited data seem to suggest that racial differences in the consumer behavior of youths are due to both cultural and socioeconomic factors. When SES is controlled, black/white differences emerge on a number of aspects of consumer behavior. While some of these differences cannot be explained in terms of existing theory, differences in attitudes toward marketing stimuli might be due to family environment. Specifically, the black child's sheltering by his or her family does not last as long as in white families, resulting in earlier exposure to nonfamily socialization agents and thus more susceptibility to marketing practices. This could explain black youths' positive attitudes toward marketing stimuli and their greater susceptibility to advertising, particularly when they have more opportunities for consumption, such as a greater income and an expanded life-space field (Lewin 1951), which is more likely to be the case among higher-class blacks than among lower-class blacks.

Proposition 12.2: Black youths, compared to their white counterparts, are more likely to respond favorably to marketing stimuli. They tend to:

(a) have more positive attitudes toward marketing stimuli
(b) be more susceptible to marketing practices

An unexpected finding of the Moschis and Moore (1981b) study was the effect of race on brand preferences. With increasing SES, white adolescents expressed more brand preferences, while black adolescents indicated fewer brand preferences. One possible explanation of increasing brand preferences might be that blacks from lower-class backgrounds develop stronger preferences for brands as a strategy to avoid mistakes in purchasing. For example, Bauer and Cunningham (1970) argue that blacks have a greater difficulty in making decisions than whites, and they are more anxious about making a mistake. As a result, the researchers argue, blacks are likely to rely on brand name products to avoid a mistake. Some research has found blacks to be more aware of brands than whites and to know more about brands in general (King and DeManche 1969). These notions might apply only to lower-class blacks.

To gain better insights into these speculations, data used in the Moschis and Moore (1979b) study were analyzed with respect to criteria used in making purchasing decisions by race across eight different products. The results of this analysis are shown in table 12–1. Few differences emerged across products and criteria used. The most contrasting differences concerned the evaluation of two low involvement products (flash cubes and household batteries). Whites appear to use price, while blacks use reputable brand names, in judging which to buy. Lack of significant differences in the case of higher socioeconomic risk products suggest that both groups might use these criteria not to avoid mistakes but to simplify their purchase. If brand name was used as a way of avoiding mistakes or risks in purchases, blacks would have shown a greater propensity to rely on well-known brands in buying higher socioeconomic risk products.

These findings, taken together with those of Moschis and Moore, suggest an alternative explanation for black/white differences in brand orientations. Black youth, especially those from lower socioeconomic backgrounds, are deprived of opportunities to develop skills in buying products, and as a result they develop strategies to simplify the purchasing process when objective evidence is lacking, as in the case of low involvement products in which few discriminating attributes are perceived to be available (Robertson 1976). White adolescents might use other strategies, such as price, for purchase simplification.

Proposition 12.3: Black youths are more likely than white youths to use brand names when purchasing low involvement products.

Table 12–1
Use of Criteria in Decision Making by Race

	On Sale		Advertised		Friends Like		Well-known		Parents Like		Store	
	W	B	W	B	W	B	W	B	W	B	W	B
Calculator	44.3	43.1	12.2	18.5	4.8	0	56.0	49.2	27.3	16.9	17.6	9.2
Flash cubes	51.2	24.6*	16.8	18.5	2.8	3.1	40.0	60.0*	12.5	15.4	7.9	3.1
Hair dryer	34.9	24.6	18.2	16.9	13.0	4.6	49.8	49.2	23.5	24.6	15.0	9.2
Batteries	51.5	26.2*	17.9	21.5	2.2	1.5	35.3	53.8*	11.3	12.3	7.1	6.2
Wallet	44.6	50.8	8.3	7.7	17.3	9.2*	30.4	35.4	17.4	15.4	15.0	4.6*
Dress shoes	31.6	23.1	8.6	7.7	22.7	13.8	37.8	40.0	32.9	24.6	23.1	18.5
Sunglasses	45.7	33.8	14.0	23.1	27.5	15.4	29.6	33.8	13.4	9.2	9.3	4.6
Wristwatch	32.7	30.8	14.7	15.4	14.0	6.2	60.3	63.1	32.1	15.4*	21.1	9.2*

* Significant difference based on chi-square analysis ($p < .05$).

Proposition 12.4: The black youth's propensity to use brand name as a criterion in purchasing products declines with socioeconomic status.

Proposition 12.5: White youths are more likely than their black counterparts to use price as a criterion when purchasing low involvement products.

Researchers also addressed the question of whether these differences in consumer behavior between whites and blacks are the result of racial or socioeconomic influences—that is, whether differences are directly attributed to such characteristics or attributable to socialization processes operating differently in these subcultures (Moschis and Moore 1985). Race and SES produced independent effects on consumer socialization processes, which differentially affected the development of consumer orientations. Specifically, the impact of race and SES was assessed simultaneously with the impact of socialization processes, using multivariate analysis. The direct effects of SES disappeared, while racial effects remained strong. The impact of socialization processes on criterion variables was significant among blacks and whites, as well as among lower and upper social classes. These influences, however, did not appear to be as different among lower- and upper-class adolescents as among blacks and whites. Thus, the development of consumer orientations among black and white youths was found to be not only direct but also indirect via socialization processes operating differently in the two subcultures. Socioeconomic differences were mainly indirect via socialization processes, which affect consumer learning but do not operate very differently in the two social groups.

Although SES contributed to the understanding of differences in learning processes independent of race, fewer differences in the effectiveness of the learning processes were found among lower- and middle-class subjects. In addition, the direct effects of socioeconomic background tended to disappear when the effects of the learning process among blacks and whites were analyzed, suggesting that the influence of SES on the criterion variables might be indirect via the learning process. This did not appear, however, to be the case with race, since the main effects of race on the criterion variables tend to remain significant in separate analyses among middle- and lower-class youth (Moschis and Moore 1985).

One characteristic of black families that has implications for the consumer socialization of children is the high occurrence of divorce and the absence of a father. It is estimated that 55 percent of black children are born to unmarried mothers, and half of all black children have no father at home (McGhee 1984). The absence of a father, especially in lower-class black families, is believed to result in a less-extensive acquisition of independence and social responsibility in boys than in girls, as well as in greater conformity among black boys than among black girls (Hartup 1970).

Although the relationship between broken homes and delinquency has been found to be rather weak, broken home has been cited as an antecedent factor contributing to delinquency (Hess 1970). Perhaps the absence of a father is a necessary but not sufficient condition for delinquency; it also might require the presence of deviant peer group (Klemke 1982).

Proposition 12.6: Black girls in comparison with white girls are more likely to:
  (a) acquire greater independence than boys
  (b) participate more in family purchasing decisions that boys

Proposition 12.7: Black youths are more likely to shoplift with peers than white youths.

Proposition 12.8: Black youths are more likely to shoplift that white youths.

Socialization Processes

Several differences exist between black and white children with respect to their interaction with socialization agents and the extent to which they are affected by them. Black children generally watch more television, and they are more likely to evaluate television shows and ads as being more realistic and believable (see, for example, Christiansen 1979; Greenberg and Dervin 1970; Greenberg and Dominick 1969; Meyer et al. 1978). Not only do black children watch more television, but they also tend to view specific television characters as more realistic than do white children (Donohue et al. 1976). The same findings seem to hold for black and white adolescents (Moschis and Moore 1985; Prisuta 1979; Christiansen 1979).

Youths also differ in the way they respond to and use television. Black youths are more likely than white youths to use television as a source of information—that is, they are media socializees (Gerson 1966). Dominick and Greenberg (1970), for example, found that black adolescents were more likely than whites to watch television to learn "what life is really like," "how others solve the same problems they have," and so on. Similarly, Barry and Sheikh (1977) reported that blacks tended to use television as a learning device, while Moschis and Moore (1985) reported that blacks were more likely than whites to watch television ads and programs for social reasons.

While viewing television, black children are more likely to engage in fantasy behaviors and model themselves after television characters than are white children (Christiansen 1979; Greenberg and Dominick 1969). Specifically, "cross-race" modeling has been found only for black children (modeling after white characters) (Neeley et al. 1973; Atkin 1975b; Gerson 1966). The black youth's attempt to model after whites has been attributed to the fact that the black child is likely to perceive his or her peers as having less status and power and might think that their judgments are worth less simply because they are black (Hartup 1970, 410). This explanation is in line with Miller and Dollard's (1941) contention that it is more rewarding to imitate those who are "superior." The print media, are more likely to be used by white than by black youths. The findings might be due to differences in the availability of the print media as well as to differences in reading interests (Byrne 1969; Olson and Rosen 1967).

A commonly held belief among social scientists is that black children are sheltered by the family for a shorter period and exposed to peer interaction earlier than most white children (Hartup 1970, 409–10). Unfortunately, very little is known about the effect of race on a child's relationship with his or her parents, although some research suggests that black children are more likely to be mother-centered than white children (Stinnett et al. 1973). Similarly, research by Allen and Chaffee (1977) shows that family communication patterns differ between black and white families, suggesting that different communication processes also might operate. The effects of race on communication processes are shown in a study of the consumer socialization of black and white adolescents (Moschis and Moore 1985). Specifically, after controlling for socio-economic effects, it was found that white adolescents, as compared to their black counterparts, are more likely to report observations of parental behaviors.

Some data also indicate that different learning processes might operate among black and white adolescents in the acquisition of various consumer skills and that the effectiveness of such processes might vary by consumer learning property. For example, black youths seem to develop preferences for brands by observing their parents, while whites seem to develop such preferences by watching television. Another observation is that black adolescents tend to be affected more by such learning processes than white adolescents. The amount of variance accounted for among blacks is greater for nearly every consumer learning property examined, suggesting that whites might be socialized earlier than blacks (Moschis and Moore 1985).

To summarize the effects of race on youths' interaction with socialization agents, black youths interact rather differently than white youths with the mass media and informal sources of consumer information. These socialization processes are likely to have a different impact on youths based on race.

Proposition 12.9: Black youths are more likely to have favorable orientations toward television than their white counterparts. Black youths are more likely than white youths to:

(a) watch television
(b) evaluate television stimuli as being realistic
(c) use television for consumer information
(d) model after television characters

Proposition 12.10: White youths are more likely than black youths to use newspapers for information about consumption.

Proposition 12.11: Black youths are less likely than white youths to interact with parents about consumption matters.

(a) Black youths discuss consumption less frequently than white youths.
(b) Black youths are less likely to model after their parents' consumer behavior than white youths.

Proposition 12.12: White youths are socialized into the consumer role earlier than black youths.

Proposition 12.13: Different socialization processes operate among black and white youths.

Adulthood

Consumer Behavior

While racial differences in consumer behavior might be due to several other factors, such as income and education, most studies investigating racial differences have offered few explanations for the differences found. Robinson, Rao, and Mehta (1985) summarized most of the research on adult consumers. The appendix to this chapter reports these differences, which apply to consumer decisions, including selection of brands and products, shopping behaviors, and reactions to marketing stimuli in general.

The data in the appendix suggest that blacks are more likely to be innovators regarding products and services of social significance; have a stronger positive orientation toward brand names; are less likely to interact efficiently and effectively with the marketplace, as indicated by their low propensity to use information and consider a larger number of alternatives; and have a tendency to purchase socially conspicuous products. Thus, it appears that race accounts for several differences in the consumer behavior of adults. Such differences emerge across a wide variety of consumer behaviors related to a wide range of consumer decisions, as well as to saving and spending decisions (Alexis 1962), money spent on major expenditures, and perceptions of stores (Whipple and Neidell 1971–1972). This behavior is not unique to blacks, however but also applies to other lower-class consumers as well.

Minority groups in general are believed to be deprived of material goods; their status and the accompanying demand for majority advantages are believed to restrict both the acquisition and enjoyment of material goods (Young 1969), suggesting that material possessions might be valued relatively more by minority than majority groups. Specifically, while growing up, minority youths are believed to experience social deprivation, which might affect their consumer behavior as adults, leading them to strive toward upgrading their status by means of conspicuous consumption in early adulthood. Some research findings presented in the appendix appear to support this line of reasoning. Research by Straus (1962a) also suggests that blacks and lower-class consumers, as compared to their white and upper-class counterparts, are more likely to have materialistic attitudes.

Attempts to upgrade their status via conspicuous consumption are reflected in black consumers' tendency to spend less on nonconspicuous items such as medical care (see appendix) and life insurance (Hiltz 1971), to have higher occupational aspirations, and to experience impatience regarding the time horizons for the purchase of goods and services. Levine (1976) found that blacks have higher occupational aspirations than whites, but they seldom achieve higher occupational status, perhaps because of their unwillingness to defer gratifications.

To summarize up to this point, the available data overwhelmingly suggest significant black/white differences in consumer behavior among adults. The tendency of black consumers to value material possessions and socially visible items more than whites might reflect the desire to upgrade their status.

> Proposition 12.14: Black adult consumers are more likely than their white counterparts to emphasize consumption. Blacks are more likely than whites to:
>
> (a) hold materialistic values
>
> (b) spend a larger proportion of their available income on items of social status and social significance
>
> (c) be innovators of socially conspicuous products
>
> (d) have higher occupational aspirations

Blacks might be more likely than whites to experience not only social but economic deprivation as well. High unemployment rates among blacks (16 percent) and low family incomes (approximately 56 percent of white family incomes) (McGhee 1984) create considerably greater family instability among black consumers. The black poor adopt a variety of strategies for coping with such instability and desperation. One such strategy involves establishing socially recognized kin ties, which are aimed at expanding the number of people who are intimately obligated to care for one another. Hirschman (1985a) suggests that one strategy might involve trading goods and services among members of the extended family and close friends. She also notes that this trading of goods and services bears a remarkable resemblance to patterns of exchange characterizing reciprocal giving in non-Western societies.

> Proposition 12.15: Blacks are more likely than whites to trade goods and services among family members.

Economic deprivation also might limit the black individual's opportunities for interacting with the marketplace and with significant others about consumption, hampering opportunities for consumer learning. This might explain black consumers' tendency to consider fewer alternatives in the marketplace than white adults (see appendix).

> Proposition 12.16: Black consumers are not likely to interact with the marketplace as effectively and efficiently as white consumers. Blacks are less likely than whites to:

(a) seek information

(b) consider a large number of alternatives

(c) evaluate alternatives on a large number of objective attributes

Research suggests that black persons and black marriages might be more egalitarian than white persons and white marriages within a specific status level (Scanzoni 1976). Because black men have been given little or no opportunity to become more educated and attain meaningful occupations, Scanzoni (1975) argues, black women have been forced into the labor market. This might have resulted in greater husband/wife egalitarianism among blacks than among whites as a result of the black woman's access to economic resources. Results of other studies, however, cast doubt on this line of reasoning because they report blacks to have less egalitarian (more sexist) attitudes (Bayer 1975; Angrist et al. 1977). These contradictions in findings might be due to the fact that social class, which is positively associated with egalitarian attitudes, was not taken into account. In fact, black/white differences found in most studies of consumer behavior are confounded with differences due to social class.

Feldman and Star (1968) used *Chicago Tribune* data to determine whether the consumer behavior of blacks differs from that of whites because of cultural factors present in black and white racial subcultures, or whether the difference is "merely a manifestation of the low socioeconomic status of the Negro and thus not really distinctive" (p. 216). They concluded that the differences are a by-product of socioeconomic factors and not race per se.

Cicarelli (1974), using the same data, showed that black/white differences are a by-product of cultural factors and not relative socioeconomic status. Cicarelli's analysis was based on the relative income hypothesis, which emphasizes the imitative aspect of consumer behavior. Cicarelli compared blacks in one income bracket with whites whose absolute income was somewhat higher. The rationale for the relative income hypothesis is that the amount of a family's income devoted to consumption depends on the level of its income relative to the income of the peer group with which it identifies and not the absolute level of the family's income.

One interesting finding that emerged from Feldman's and Star's (1968) analysis was that black/white differences were greater among lower-income groups. This might be because upper-income blacks feel more pressure to conform to middle-class standards than lower-class blacks (see, for example, Williams 1985). As a result, the consumer behavior of blacks in higher-income groups is more likely that that of lower-income blacks to resemble the consumer behavior of whites (Williams 1985). This suggests that inconsistencies in the findings regarding differences between blacks and whites might be due to differences in the income levels of the samples examined.

Proposition 12.17: Black/white differences in consumer behavior are contingent on the adult person's socioeconomic status. When social class is taken into account:

(a) Blacks are more likely to hold egalitarian sex role perceptions about household decisions.

(b) Black/white differences in consumer behaviors are greater among lower-class than higher-class adults.

Socialization Processes

Patterns of interaction with socialization agents developed during the formative years are likely to persist into adulthood. Blacks are more likely than their white counterparts to be heavy television viewers (Broadcasting 1976) and radio listeners (Glasser and Metzger 1981), but they are less likely to use newspapers than white Americans (Burgoon and Burgoon 1980). Blacks also tend to rely on television for information (Allen and Chaffee 1979; Allen and Clarke 1980) and generally to use television as a learning device (Barry and Sheikh 1977).

Finally, research shows that blacks attempt to emulate the consumer behaviors of whites (Williams 1985). This is in line with the explanation offered by Miller and Dollard (1941) that it is more rewarding to imitate those who are "superior," for example, with respect to age, social status, intelligence, and so on. Minority groups (blacks) are likely to choose advantageous reference models to emulate. Because black reference models for emulation are in relatively short supply, blacks tend to find white models more rewarding (Young 1969).

Late Adulthood

Consumer Behavior

Relatively little research has been reported regarding the effects of race on the consumer behavior of older adults. Smith (1982) reports lower levels of consumption activity among black elderly than among white elderly. These findings do not seem to support Hirschman's (1985a) contention regarding the greater propensity to trade goods and services expected to exist among poor blacks, but these speculations might apply only to adults. Smith did not, however, control for socioeconomic status. Her findings are in line with the disengagement theory, suggesting that this theory might explain consumer behavior better among blacks than among white older adults.

Proposition 12.18: With increasing age, older black consumers are more likely to experience declining activity in consumption than older white consumers.

Socialization Processes

Smith (1982) examined the relationship between race and exposure to mass media advertising, consumer education, peer interaction about consumption, and family interaction about consumption among elderly consumers. Blacks were found to be less likely than their white counterparts to interact with family members about consumption and to have heard of products from various sources of mass media advertising; they were more likely to report exposure to consumer education courses. In another study, however, Schreiber and Boyd (1980) examined racial differences in the elderly's use of the mass media for consumer decisions and found that blacks were more likely than whites to choose television as the most influential medium in consumer decisions. Significantly more whites than blacks chose magazines as the most influential medium. The difference in the results of the two studies might be due to the measures used. The Schreiber and Boyd study used relative measures of influence of specific media, while the Smith study used absolute measures of exposure and reliance on all four types of mass media.

Summary and Discussion

The data presented in this chapter provide useful information for understanding black/white differences reported in consumer behavior literature. Racial differences appear early in life, and socialization processes that differ between the cultures might help us explain differences in the consumer behavior of adults. Apparently, consumer behaviors, especially values and attitudes acquired by youths, change rather little in later life. For example, the social significance of products is developed in early life, as are patterns of interaction with the mass media and significant others.

One of the limitations of most previous research examining black/white differences in consumer behavior has been the failure to isolate socioeconomic influences from racial influences. This shortcoming might account for inconsistencies in many of the findings. Apparently, social class is an important variable that might help us explain not only differences between black and white consumer behavior but also why such differences develop as they do—that is, socialization processes.

Future research should explore the racial differences of older adults, as little information appears to exist regarding the effects of race on consumer behavior in this age group. Perhaps the declining consumption levels of older black adults reported by Smith (1982) also can be observed among older consumers with a lower socioeconomic status.

Appendix:
Empirical Research Findings Relating to Black Consumer Behavior

		Blacks are			
Date	Researcher(s)	more likely to:	equally likely to:	less likely to:	
					Product Awareness and Adoption
1956	Kittles	X			Be innovative and fashion conscious when it comes to clothing
1965	Bauer et al.		X		Be fashion conscious
1966	Portis	X			(Same as Kittles 1956)
1969	King et al.	X			Be aware of both private and national brands
1969	Robertson et al.	X			Be innovators for socially visible products, particularly clothing
1970	Kindel	X			(same as Kittles 1956)
1971	Dalrymple et al.	X			(same as Kittles 1956)
1972	Sexton			X	Be innovators with respect to nonsocially visible items (appliances and food)
1972	Sexton	X			Be style-conscious, price conscious, and concerned with brand names
1975	Dietrich			X	Be risk-takers during the introduction of new products
1980	Harting	X			Be trend setters in fashion, hairstyles, shoes, and evening apparel
					Purchase Decisions
1971	Dalrymple et al.	X			Have female dominance
1980	Hirschman	X			Be innovators, possess fewer credit cards, place greater emphasis on credit and billing policies of retailers
					Shopping Behavior
					Brand
1959	Davis	X			Be Brand loyal
1966	Bauer	X			Prefer national brands

Date	Researcher(s)	Blacks are			
		more likely to:	equally likely to:	less likely to:	
					Brand (*continued*)
1966	*Printer's Ink*			X	Purchase brands with negative association
1968	Larson			X	Purchase brands with negative connotation
1968	*Marketing Insight*	X			Buy brands that are nationally advertised, those with prestigious connotation, and those about which they feel confident
1973	Larson et al.	X			Be brand loyal to substantially different brand preferences
1976	Soloman et al.		X		Purchase products that are promoted in displays by black, white, or integrated models
1981	Wellington	X			Be brand loyal to substantially different brand preferences
1981	Wellington			X	Switch toward private labels and generics as prices increase
1981	Whalen	X			Be loyal to national brand even when prices rise 45 percent or more
					Retail Institutions
1961	Bullock			X	Feel insecure when shopping in department stores because of the store atmosphere
1963	Caplovitz	X			Rely on small neighborhood stores and peddlers for the purchase of new durable goods
1966	Portis	X			Shop department stores if fashion conscious (women)
1968	Feldman et al.	X			Make fewer shopping trips
1968	Feldman et al.	X			Shop discount stores
1968	Feldman et al.			X	Shop by mail or phone
1971	Dixon et al.	X			Make more trips to grocery stores
1972	Cox et al.		X		Shop discount stores
1972	Gensch et al.	X			Emphasize attributes such as friendly atmosphere, convenience, price, service, quality, and shopping location
1972	Petrof	X			Complain about supermarket overcrowding, poor displays, cleanliness, and unfriendly employees
1974	Sexton	X			Shop at fewer stores
1979	Samli et al.	X			Shop department, discount, and specialty stores (women)

Date	Researcher(s)	Blacks are			
		more likely to:	equally likely to:	less likely to:	
					Prices
1968	Goodman	X			Pay more for products
1968	Braguglia et al.	X			Pay slightly more for clothing (low socioeconomic status women)
1969	King et al.	X			Be informed and concerned about prices with respect to food
1971	Petrof	X			Complain about prices
1971a	Sexton	X			Pay more for products
1975	Dietrich			X	Be concerned about lower prices
1975	Dietrich			X	Use coupons and premiums
1977	Sinha	X			Use coupons (younger blacks)
1977	Morse			X	Use coupons and premiums
1981	Yovovich			X	Use coupons and premiums
					Package Design
1966	Krugman			X	Respond as well to packages designed for whites as for packages designed for blacks
					Product Purchases
1962	Alexis			X	Spend less for housing, medical care, and automobile transportation
1962	Alexis	X			Spend more for clothing, personal care items, household furnishings, and tobacco
1968	Akers	X			Purchase larger and more luxury non-foreign cars
1970a,b	Bauer et al.			X	Spend less on medical care, food, and transportation
1970a,b	Bauer et al.	X			Spend more for clothing, personal care, and home furnishings
1973	Larson et al.	X			Own larger and more luxury non-foreign cars
1975	Andreason	X			Prefer carbohydrates
1979	Wall	X			Buy soft drinks that are sold outside of supermarkets
1981	Wellington			X	Purchase lower-priced private brands and generics
1981	Advertising Age	X			Spend more for record albums (twice as much)
1984	Assael	X			Use cosmetics and fragrances (women—spend twice as much)

Date	Researcher(s)	Blacks are more likely to:	equally likely to:	less likely to:	Models in Advertising
1964	Cundiff	X			Favor advertising that features all black models
1969	Barban	X			Prefer advertisements with all black models or with integrated groups of models than those with all white models
1970	Gould et al.	X			(same as Barban 1969)
1970	Gould et al.			X	React favorably to integrated ads if younger than 30 years old
1971	Tolley et al.	X			(same as Barban 1969)
1972	Schlinger et al.	X			Favor advertising that features all black models
1974	Choudhury et al.	X			(same as Barban 1969)
1976	Chapko			X	React favorably to integrated ads if younger than 30 years old
1980	Rozen	X			Purchase products featuring black ad models
					Impersonal Media Usage
1966	Carey	X			Watch television on weekends
1966	Carey			X	View programming emphasizing subjects such as family and organization
1966	Portis			X	Rely on information from newspapers
1970a,b	Bauer et al.	X			Rely on television and black-oriented radio for news and entertainment
1971	Tolley et al.	X			Respond favorably to radio advertising
1975	Glasser et al.	X			Listen to AM radio at home during the evening and on weekends
1977	Morse	X			Listen to black radio
1980	Hirschman	X			Prefer rock and jazz radio programming
1979	Shama et al.			X	Find humorous ethnic advertising depicting them to be funny

Source: Robinson, Rao, and Mehta (1985).

13
Cultural and Subcultural Influences

While socialization refers to the process of learning the norms, attitudes, and behaviors of the culture into which an individual is born, acculturation refers to the process of learning a culture that differs from the one in which the individual was raised. The latter can be thought of as a continuum along which a new entrant to a culture moves. One extreme represents the totally nonacculturated and the other those who have internalized the dominant culture yet still maintain some characteristics of their cultural heritage (Sturdivant 1973). For example, the first generation of immigrants tends to cling to its cultural heritage; the second generation usually discards the culture of its parents and absorbs the characteristics of the dominant culture; and the third generation tends to reevaluate its ethnic origins and to follow the more appealing features of it (Herberg 1955).

While acculturation refers to learning the patterns of behavior associated with the host culture, the effects of such processes on individuals native to the host culture often are neglected or assumed to be minimal. Rather, researchers prefer discussing assimilation—that is, the process of acceptance by the dominant culture—without assessing how the process affects the behaviors and values of the existing dominant society. Sociologists have identified components of assimilation into a new culture which can be grouped into six categories. These are used to determine the extent to which a person has taken on the identity of the new culture.

1. adjustment of behavioral patterns such as dress, food, place of residence, and language (also known as cultural assimilation)
2. involvement in the social structure through occupational and primary groups (structural assimilation)
3. choice of marriage partner, usually involving intermarriage between immigrants and members of the dominant culture (marital assimilation)
4. self-identity based on a particular culture or ethnic group (identificational assimilation)
5. being accepted (not discriminated against) by others in the ethnic group or culture (behavior-attitude-receptional assimilation)

6. adoption of values and power structures of the ethnic group or culture (Ellis et al. 1985; Wallendorf and Reilly 1983)

An important fact to take into account is that people can become assimilated without becoming acculturated, and vice versa. In fact, the Amish are more assimilated than acculturated, "whereas the Northern Negro is more acculturated than assimilated." (Berelson and Steiner 1964, 16–17). In addition, the degree of assimilation is not at the same rate in all aspects of life. For example, occupational or residential patterns may be better assimilated than marital patterns (Sturdivant 1973). Furthermore, it is possible that acculturation and assimilation might not result in a simple blending of two cultural patterns but in the emergence of a unique cultural style (Wallendorf and Reilly 1983).

Cultures

Elements of Culture

Several criteria have been used by researchers to define and measure cultures and subcultures. For example, Terpstra (1972) has synthesized the elements of culture into several categories that have direct effects on consumer behavior: material culture, language, esthetics, education, religion, attitudes, and social organization.

Material culture is represented by the tools, artifacts, and technology of a society. Common terms used to describe the stages of material culture found in a society are industrialized nations, agricultural nations, and less developed countries. For example, although the automobile is an important symbol of middle-class development throughout the world, perceptions of this product differ by stage of material culture found in various countries. In classless societies (such as the Scandinavian countries), for example, the car is strictly utilitarian, and showing off one's auto is not considered correct. In contrast, cars in transition countries (such as England, France, and Italy) are pampered as if they are an extension of the owner's personality. They are considered outward symbols of success (Dichter 1962).

Language is considered to be of particular importance to a culture. The words and phrases of a language are merely concepts and ideas reflecting the culture from which it was formed. *Esthetics* refers to a culture's ideas concerning beauty and good taste and the appreciation of color and form. For example, green is the national color of Egypt and Syria; purple is generally disapproved of in most Latin American markets because of its association with death; blue is the color for mourning in Iran; white is the color for mourning in Japan (Winick 1961). These cultural factors have effects on select aspects of consumer behavior (such as colors of automobiles).

The *education* level of people in a grouping is an implication of consumer socialization and behavior. Literacy rates affect the consumer's interaction with the print media and media substitution, which are likely to result in different socialization processes and outcomes. Furthermore, education is likely to determine the individual's social position (socioeconomic status) in an organization (culture), which is likely to be related to consumer behavior.

Religion influences consumer behavior directly as well as indirectly by affecting the socialization processes. For example, religious beliefs are related to the consumption of certain foods and the emphasis on certain norms by socialization agents such as the family.

Consumer *attitudes* toward nature, time, activity, and other value orientations have significant effects on consumer behavior. For example, one study found a correlation of such attitudes with the ownership of generic automobile categories. The categories studied were full-size, intermediate, compact, and subcompact cars (Henry 1976).

Social organization describes the way people relate to each other, the primary means being through family groups (Terpstra 1972). The nuclear family, consisting of a husband, wife, and their offspring, is a common family form in the United States. In many other cultures, the extended family concept is much more relevant. The existence of extended families means that consumption decisions are made in a larger unit, which makes it more difficult to determine the relevant consuming unit for some goods. One aspect of social organization related to decision-making patterns in a few cultures involves the redistribution of essential resources into networks via the process of reciprocal exchange (Stack 1974). What belongs to one belongs to all in a given time network. Such a redistribution of resources is likely to result in an egalitarian community, reinforcing group cohesion and hindering the development of consumption hierarchies, which promotes "a sense of oneness or sameness among group members" (Hirschman 1985a, 146).

Defining Cultures

Cultures often are equated with countries, and cross-cultural research is associated with cross-national research. Thus, differences between cultures tend to be inferred from differences between countries or groups of countries (see, for example, Sethi 1971). In cross-national research, countries tend to be the most common units of analysis in defining cultures. One of the reasons is that countries tend to define specific cultures, which can be used as a basis for segmentation. Operationally, the use of countries as units of analysis is much more appropriate in working with available data (such as economic indicators) than in combining data from different countries.

A key issue in defining a culture in a cross-national setting is the basis for such a definition. For example, researchers have used levels of economic development (measured by various economic indexes) to group countries into industrialized, developing, and less developed countries (Boddewyn 1981). Similarly, countries have been grouped into five geocultural clusters: the Anglo-American, Nordic,

Latin American, Latin European, and Central European, with four independent clusters not fitting into any of the five broad country clusters (Ronen and Kraut 1977). Geocultural segmentation often is based on social factors that supplement geographic characteristics, such as language and religion, because such variables are likely to define ethnicity, which often defines cultures beyond geographic boundaries (Hirschman 1981).

Unfortunately, the issue of whether geographic segmentation vis-à-vis segmentation based on ethnicity is more useful has not been adequately investigated. An ethnic group living in different countries might behave rather differently because of differences in structural factors such as product availability, government regulations, and the like. Another consideration in using ethnicity as a basis for defining a culture is deciding how to operationalize ethnicity, since this variable is likely to be continuous rather than categorical (Hirschman 1981).

While there is a tendency to define cultures and subcultures using socially based geocultural characteristics, recent research raises the question of whether subcultures should be confined to country or geographic criteria. For example, if countries are becoming more homogeneous, one would expect the world's population to develop more similarities in values, norms, and behaviors—that is, psychographic and life-style similarities. Such characteristics can be used to define subcultures at the international level and perhaps contribute to our understanding of cross-cultural consumer behavior. Psychographics have been used in connection with geographic characteristics to help us understand the dynamics of cultural changes across countries (Moschis and Bello 1987).

The usefulness of psychographics in cross-cultural research depends on the level of specificity used in the analysis. The more specific the psychographic or life-style measure, the more useful it is in defining a culture or subculture and differentiating it from others. For example, general life-style characteristics defining broad value systems are likely to overlap across countries and often are referred to as cultural universals (for example, status differentiation or cleanliness training). A researcher using cultural universals as a basis for defining cultures is likely to come up with homogeneous clusters. Specific life-styles might not be shared by several clusters, however, resulting in greater differentiation among countries. For example, research in three European countries (the United Kingdom, Germany, and France) revealed significant differences in product usage across cultural groups defined by psychographic characteristics (Boote 1982–1983).

Another typology of culture is based on societal development. For example Rodman (1972) hypothesized that there are four types of societies: *patriarchy*, characterized by little variation in strong patriarchal norms and overly stratified groups (such as India); *modified patriarchy*, where masculine authority is accompanied by rapid modernization (such as Greece); *transitional equalitarianism*, where equalitarian norms are replacing patriarchal norms (such as the United States); and *equalitarianism*, characterized by strong husband/wife sharing of power (such as Denmark). Green et al. (1983) tested this typology's applicability to understanding husband/wife involvement in purchasing by comparing respondents from the United States, France, Holland, Gabon, and Venezuela.

Comparisons between pairs of developed and less developed nations were performed. Some of the results provided support Rodman's classification. For example, in all comparisons, husbands in the less developed nations were reported to make significantly more decisions than husbands in the developed nations. This can be explained by the high level of paternal authority in the patriarchy and modified patriarchy societies. Similarly, there was significantly more joint decision making reported in the developed nations than in the less developed nations.

The findings of this study can be considered illustrative of the types of differences that might be found in family purchasing patterns across cultures. When a society moves from a traditional to a more modern culture, the husband/wife purchasing role goes from highly structured to less structured. This pattern also is observed at the individual family level. The economic level of the family unit affects the type of decision making (autonomous or joint). The low-income family holds a more traditional marital role; therefore, a more structured purchasing role is expected than in the high-income family (Green et al. 1983).

While factors related to the characteristics of the spouse, such as income, occupational status, and education, are likely to influence family decision making in some cultures, their importance or impact might be lessened or even negated by strong norms and role expectations within others. Rodman (1972), for instance, found Greece to be a highly inflexible patriarchal society in which the effect of relative resources is extremely limited by the strength of strong cultural norms. Similarly, Lambiri (1967) found Greeks to have a strong desire to conform to socially accepted standards. Due to the apparent strength of these cultural factors, Rodman reasoned that increased participation by women in family decision making would be more likely to be observed in more "modern" societies such as the United States, a contention supported by Green et al.'s (1983) study.

Results from such cross-cultural or cross-country analysis have several implications for consumer socialization. The most apparent seems to be the notion that differences between cultures might be due to some underlying variable (such as religion or value orientation) used to define the culture. Second, cultural differences might have an indirect impact on consumer socialization by affecting socialization processes. For example, in comparison with equalitarian societies, children brought up in patriarchical societies have little say in family consumption decisions, and they are greatly influenced by opinions expressed by their parents (Lambiri 1967), suggesting the presence of a socio-oriented family communication structure (McLeod and Chaffee 1972).

Finally, explanations for consumption-related differences might be due not only to differences in cultural values but also to the presence of several other structural factors. For instance, daily shopping by wives might be due to "stage of development characteristics such as the absence of home refrigeration facilities and differences in retail distribution structures, although preferences for personal relationships with neighborhood shopkeepers, a cultural factor, also might be important (Goldman 1974). Other factors to consider include the idea that shopping might serve as a desired social outlet or that consumers might be unable to finance extensive home inventories. These general observations suggest some broad propositions:

Proposition 13.1: Differences in consumer behavior between cultures are likely to be related to differences in variables used to define a culture. They can be attributed to:

(a) material culture
(b) language
(c) esthetics
(d) education
(e) religion
(f) attitude/value orientations
(g) social organization

Proposition 13.2: The socio-economic level of the members of a culture affects family member involvement and sex roles in family decisions. Lower socioeconomic levels are associated with:

(a) increased participation of family members in decision making
(b) egalitarian sex role perceptions in family decisions

Proposition 13.3: Children's consumer socialization varies by level of societal development. Parents in cultures characterized by egalitarianism, in comparison with those characterized by patriarchy, are:

(a) more likely to allow the participation of children in family decisions and conflict resolution processes
(b) less likely to emphasize a socio-oriented family communication structure
(c) more likely to stress a concept-oriented family communication structure

Subcultural and Cross-National Differences: Empirical Findings

Just as the term *culture* has been defined and measured using several criteria, the term *subculture* invariably is used to mean subdivisions of larger social groupings. Such subdivisions are based on fairly similar criteria. For example, Gordon (1947) defines a subculture as "a subdivison of a national culture, composed of a combination of favorable social situations such as class status, ethnic background, regional and rural or urban residence, and religious affiliation, but *forming in their combination a functioning unity which has an integrated impact on the participating individual"* (p. 40). This definition, allows one to speak of, for example, a black subculture or a Hispanic subculture to the extent that the component elements of that aggregate have some impact on individual behavior (Robertson et al. 1984).

The criteria for defining a subculture also tend to vary from very broad, which define large groupings (such as nationalities and ethnic groups) to very specific, which usually define smaller groupings (such as married working women). Another distinctive feature of research on subcultures is that most of it is atheoretical. It simply reports differences between two or more subcultures (for example, Hispanics versus non-Hispanics), or it describes a particular subculture. Subcultures also have different levels of impact on consumer behavior. The degree of influence is based on the individual's strength of identification and interaction with a particular subculture (Robertson et al. 1984). There often are strong ties when a person has a strong identification and interaction with a subculture and weak ties when identification and interaction are low. The final characteristic of the existing subcultural research is that it makes no distinction between age groups. Thus, differences are reported primarily for adults, with the assumption that the same findings apply to other age groups within that culture. Since data on age groups are not available, the findings presented in the following sections are not organized by age or life-cycle stage. Instead, information is presented for each specific subculture, in line with the general model of consumer socialization (chapter 2).

Hispanics

One of the more interesting aspects of the Hispanic culture is that it represents several rather heterogeneous groupings of people. Although there are several cultural and attitudinal similarities among Hispanics, such as language, religion, and family orientation (see, for example, Segal and Lionel 1983), there are enough differences within this subculture to justify its examination on a heterogeneous basis. Yankelovich et al. (1981), for example, found significant differences among subgroups of Hispanics with respect to value orientations.

Cervantes (1980) reached the same conclusions, suggesting that there is no such thing as a homogeneous Hispanic market. Rather, it is possible to establish the Mexican-American market as a pyramid structure with four main strata. The base is composed of recent immigrants and illegal aliens, who are well-off economically speaking, speak only Spanish, and are the least acculturated. The second strata is called the Radical Chicano. These people are native-born Americans, but they still have very close ties with their Mexican traditions. They are in the process of acculturation and speak a little English, but they are still deprived and discrimianted against. The third segment is the Conservative Chicano, consisting of native-born Americans who are beginning to lose some of their Mexican ties. Their achievement is due to higher education, feeling comfortable with the English language, and an identification with the American people. The fourth segment is the New Rich, consisting of individuals whose acculturation is almost complete and who have achieved a middle- or upper-middle-class status and have a high degree of education (Cervantes 1980). Valencia (1982) found similar major Hispanic groups to be heterogeneous in their shopping orientations.

Unfortunately, Hispanics have been treated as a homogeneous group in most research studies in which the emphasis has been on understanding the differences between Hispanics and non-Hispanics (usually Anglos) instead of the differences among Hispanics. I will use this orientation to report the research findings in this section.

Consumer Behavior. Hispanics tend to be conservative in nature, and this is reflected in their consumption patterns. Monetary outlays tend to be family-oriented, with the emphasis on food, beverages, and clothing (Segal and Lionel 1983; Strategy Research 1980). The Hispanic family spends almost one-fourth more of its income on groceries than does the non-Hispanic family (Strategy Research 1980). The average Hispanic family also spends more money than the non-Hispanic family on packaged goods and consumes more canned spaghetti, fruit nectar, malt liquor, and baby food. It consumes less dog food, diet soft drinks, frozen vegetables, and decaffeinated coffee.

Hispanics also prefer to shop at large department stores rather than smaller local stores (Sturdivant 1968), but their specific store patronage preferences vary. For example, a study conducted in Dade County (Florida) found differences in store selection, with Anglos patronizing Bardines, J.C. Penney, and Jordan Marsh and Hispanics patronizing Sears Roebuck and Zayre's more frequently (The Dade Latin Market 1980).

Furthermore, Berry and Solomon (1971) found that the most important factors for Mexican-American consumers in Denver, Colorado, when choosing a store were price and quality. Specifically, 55 percent mentioned price, and 32 percent mentioned quality. Interestingly, 77 percent of the respondents said that the ethnic background of the people working in the store was never important.

Additional findings show that, in comparison with their Anglo counterparts, Hispanics were more likely to be:

impulsive buyers (Bellenger and Valencia 1982; Velilla 1967; Messina and Reddick 1980)

non-innovators (Loudon and Della-Bitta 1979; Bellenger and Valencia 1982)

skeptical of marketing practices (Longman and Pruden 1972)

brand loyal and trusting of well-known or familiar brands (Messina and Reddick 1980; Watanabe 1981; Bellenger and Valencia 1982)

price-oriented (Gillet and Scott 1974; Boone et al. 1974)

uncertain about their shopping abilities (Gillet and Scott 1974) buyers of fresh rather than frozen prepared items (Berry and Solomon 1971; Velilla 1967)

shoppers at large supermarkets rather than closer smaller food stores (Berry and Solomon 1971; Gillet and Scott 1974; Sturdivant 1968; The Dade Latin Market 1980)

quality conscious (Strategy Research 1980)

These and other findings (see, for example, Valencia 1982) suggest that Hispanics and Anglos differ in their shopping orientations and that these differences are more likely to be attributable to ethnic cultural differences rather than socioeconomic status.

While little theory is available to help interpret these findings, some writers have offered plausible explanations. For instance, Alvarez believes that historical events have an effect on Mexican-Americans' attitudes toward their acceptance (or lack thereof) in the United States. He says, "Studies . . . are presenting those in the Chicano Generation with evidence that leads them to believe that they have been socially betrayed by the United States" (Alvarez 1971, 25). Andreasen (1982) has suggested that these feelings of rejection apply to Puerto Ricans and other Latin Americans, for they indicated similar feelings of rejection in New York in a 1966 study (Velilla 1967). More specifically, 94 percent thought that non-Hispanics did not greet them, and 70 percent thought that they were turned down for bank loans because of their ethnic status. According to Andreasen, Hispanics' beliefs about the dominant American society could be a reason for preferring to shop in their local communities (Andreasen 1982).

In a study concerning low-income Mexican-Americans in East Los Angeles, Sturdivant (1968) suggested that Mexican-Americans patronize certain stores because they need cultural reinforcement. Friendly personnel and Spanish-speaking clerks were mentioned as important factors in choosing a store. These characteristics tend to suggest that Mexican-Americans are more concerned with personal relations than with efficient shopping. Similarly, Kizilbash and Garman studied low-income Spanish-speaking persons in the Chicago area and found that grocery stores in the Spanish community are used as a place for gathering and social meetings (Kizilbash and Garman 1975–1976). At the same time, marketing practices such as price differentials for ghetto consumers and inferior product offerings and services to the poor can serve as a strong source of estrangement (Sturdivant 1968).

Sturdivant's (1969) findings of inadequacies in the marketplace serving minorities and low-income people are in line with Allison's (1978) study of alienation in the marketplace. An alienated person is one who "has been estranged from, made unfriendly toward, his society and the culture it carries" (Nettler 1967,870). The study was based on four concepts: powerlessness, normlessness, social isolation, and self-estrangement. The findings indicated that minority subjects (blacks and Hispanics) have higher consumer alienation scores than white subjects and that consumer alienation from the marketplace decreases as income increases (Allison 1978).

With respect to family decisions, some notable findings deserve discussion. Specifically, the Hispanic home is the center of the family, and the male is its focal point. This macho attitude still prevails, as the female's primary role involves childbearing, child rearing, and taking care of her husband and home. This family organization suggests a rather traditional approach in the buying decision process; that is, women are in charge of the groceries, home care products, and related items, while men are in charge of the car, financial decisions, and the like (Messina and Reddick 1980). Furthermore, the concept of the extended family is more relevant than the nuclear family in the buying decision process. Extended family members often serve as opinion leaders, and they influence the consumer behavior of other family members (Messina and Reddick 1980). Stronger patterns of husband dominance have been found in Mexican-American families than in Anglo families. Specifically, Mexican-American families engaged in less joint decision making than Anglo families, with differences going beyond those accounted for by income (O'Guinn, Faber, and Inperia 1986).

In sum, the Hispanic subculture does not appear to be a homogeneous one. Hispanics differ from non-Hispanics, or Anglos, with respect to various aspects of consumer behavior, but few theories are available to help us understand these differences. Being a minority group, Hispanics might experience socioeconomic deprivation, which might be reflected in their consumer behavior. Several theoretical notions used in explaining the consumer behavior of blacks and lower-class individuals very likely apply to Hispanics as well.

Proposition 13.4: Hispanics as a minority subculture exhibit consumer behaviors similar to other minority groups. In comparison with Anglos, they:

(a) express stronger economic motivations for consumption

(b) rely more on informal personal sources of consumer information

(c) rely more on brand names in evaluating products

(d) are more impulsive buyers rather than planners or deliberators

(e) are more brand loyal and store loyal

(f) seek out more "value" in products

(g) are more alienated from marketing practices

(h) are more susceptible to persuasive marketing stimuli

(i) are more likely to be non-innovators

(j) are more likely to patronize outlets appealing to minorities

(k) have more traditional sex role perceptions regarding family decisions

Socialization Processes. Hispanics are heavy users of television. On the average, adult Hispanics report spending nearly twenty hours a week watching television, with 70 percent of them watching Spanish-language programming (Yankelovich et al. 1981). The use of Spanish-language television surpasses the use of any other type of Spanish-language media. Not only do Hispanics appear to spend somewhat more time watching television than do Anglos, but they also express more positive attitudes toward television watching (Bellenger and Valencia 1982). In terms of programming preferences, Hispanics like variety shows and feature films significantly more than Anglos (Bellenger and Valencia 1982). Usage of Spanish television by Hispanics has been found to be related to several demographic characteristics. Specifically, Hispanic users of Spanish television are more likely to be older, female, and of a lower socioeconomic status (Yankelovich et al. 1981; Velilla 1967). Television usage among younger Hispanics is primarily for entertainment reasons (Tan and Gunter 1979).

Radio listening patterns of Hispanics parallel those of television viewing. Hispanics tend to listen to the radio more than Anglos (Roslow and Roslow 1980) where Hispanic radio stations are available (Bellenger and Valencia 1982). Velilla (1967) also reported that the radio seems to be the best medium to reach Hispanic consumers. Furthermore, Latin women seem to be heavy radio users, with a tune-in rate of 30 percent, compared with 19 percent for non-Latins. Regarding station format, "contemporary and country music" and "black and jazz oriented formats" deserve some consideration, in addition to the must of Spanish-language stations (Roslow and Roslow 1980). Hispanic radio stations tend to have a higher tune-in frequency, with 72 percent of the respondents reporting preferences for these stations and only 18 percent preferring English-language stations.

Hispanics are lighter users of the print media than their Anglo counterparts. Yankelovich, Skelly, and White (1981) estimated that Hispanics devote six and a half hours a week to reading magazines and newspapers. Hispanics generally read fewer magazines, although Spanish magazines such as *Vanidades* and *Selecciones* have a strong readership (Bellenger and Valencia 1982).

Hispanics are very light newspaper users. In a study in New York, 14 percent of the respondents read only Spanish newspapers, 7 percent read only English newspapers, and the great majority, 70 percent, did not read newspapers at all (Velilla 1967). This study suggests that although there is a lack of interest in reading newspapers, Hispanics tend to prefer a Spanish newspaper when they read one. A study of Hispanics in East and non–East Los Angeles, however, showed that the leading newspaper in both areas was the *Los Angeles Times*, with 27 percent and 36 percent readership rates, respectively. Furthermore, it was found that a Spanish newspaper was read by 26 percent of the Hispanics in East Los Angeles, compared with only 1.9 percent of Hispanics outside East Los Angeles (Messina and Reddick 1980). As in the case of television viewing, the main purpose of newspaper reading is entertainment (Tan and Gunter 1979).

Finally, with respect to the effects of these interactions with mass media, Hispanics appear to be more susceptible to mass media communications. For example, Hoyer and Deshpande (1982) report Hispanics to be more susceptible to advertisements. In sum, the evidence of the media use of Hispanics supports the notion that their communication behavior might be similar to that of other minority groups.

> Proposition 13.5: As a minority group, Hispanics, in relation to their Anglo counterparts, are more likely to use the mass media for entertainment rather than information. As a result, they are more likely to show a preference for "fantasy" rather than "reality" oriented media.
>
> (a) They are heavier users of the broadcast media (television and radio).
>
> (b) They are lighter users of the print media (newspapers and magazines).
>
> (c) They are more susceptible to mass media advertising.

With respect to the effects of interpersonal factors, Hispanics appear to be influenced by significant others a lot more than are Anglos. Family appears to play a major role in the socialization of this group. Evidence of a strong family influence comes from several studies (see, for example, Hoyer and Deshpande 1982). In addition, nonfamily informal groups can play an important role. Kizilbash and Garman (1975–1976), for example, reported a study where grocery store owners in the Chicago area were found to give advice and help not only on grocery products but also on other matters, such as finding an apartment, buying a car, getting a job, finding medical services, and translating from English to Spanish.

> Proposition 13.6: Interpersonal processes are more important in the consumer socialization of Hispanics than in the consumer socialization of Anglos. Hispanics are more likely to:
>
> (a) rely on peers for consumer information
>
> (b) rely on family members for consumer information

French

Consumer Behavior. A rather large number of studies have attempted to uncover differences between French (or French-speaking) and American (or English-speaking) consumers. Douglas (1976) compared working with nonworking wives in France and the United States across a wide variety of behaviors, including grocery purchasing, clothing purchasing, and attitudes toward female roles. The results showed that differences between the two national samples were more significant than between working status groups. This was true even after removing the effects of sociodemographic variables. The main difference between the two samples in grocery shopping was in the type of store they chose. American wives tended to patronize large supermarkets, while French housewives tended to patronize neighborhood stores. These differences were attributed to different retail environments, since large supermarkets are more prevalent in the United States and small neighborhood stores are more common in France. Alternatively, the availability of these retail environments might reflect underlying differences in preferences and attitudes (that is, cultural differences between the two countries).

In another somewhat similar study, Schaninger, Bourgeois, and Buss (1985) found significant differences in a wide variety of consumption behaviors, media usage, and durable goods ownership among French-speaking and English-speaking Canadian families. These differences remained after removing the effects of social class and income and appear to reflect cultural values that differ between the two groups.

Douglas (1979) also investigated cross-cultural differences in husband/wife involvement in various activities. The study involved five countries that can be divided into French- and English-speaking groups. Seventeen different household activities, including several related to consumption, were examined. Across all five samples (Chicago, Glasgow/London, Paris, Brussels, and Quebec City), Douglas found a significant similarity in terms of husband/wife involvement in various activities, and marital roles were seen as traditionally masculine or feminine. The relative participation of husbands and wives in the activities differed by language group. For example, in the French-speaking samples, there was greater participation by husbands and wives in the typically feminine tasks of supermarket shopping and vacuuming, as well as in some traditionally male responsibilities such as men's clothing decisions. Husband/wife participation in various decisions in all the samples tended to vary by type of activity, with socioeconomic variables affecting the degree of such participation across all samples (Douglas 1979).

Another study conducted by Green and Langeard (1975) examined innovator characteristics for groceries and other retail purchases. The study found many differences between French and American subjects with regard to word-of-mouth communications and a willingness to try new products and services, despite the economic similarities of the two countries. This study confirmed a well-recognized perception that Americans seem much less constrained by traditions and are, therefore, more apt to experiment with innovations. In fact, 84 percent of the Americans indicated a willingness to experiment when shopping for grocery products, compared with 71 percent of the more traditional French. Retail services showed the same pattern. Seventy-nine percent of the Americans indicated that they would try new retail services, contrasting with 69 percent of the French.

Several aspects of shopping habits can be attributed to the amount and type of the perceived risk. Americans are expected to shop in more different stores than are the French, since in France financial risk is negligible because of a fixed-pricing environment. This might explain why French families tend to be more store loyal than English-speaking families (Schaninger et al. 1985). The problem of psychosocial risk also is reduced by shopping at a neighborhood store where other neighbors traditionally also purchase their goods. In fact, according to an investigation by the Ecole Superieur de Commerce in Lyons, many patronize a certain store because doing so made them feel part of a privileged group or club whose loyalty reinforced their membership. Even a dress code prevails: no pin curls, no shorts, and no slacks are permitted for fear of compromising a shopper's image before other group members (Dunn 1962). Thus, shopping appears to be an integral part of the social life of many French housewives, whereas American women have become more time- and convenience-conscious (Green and Langeard 1975).

It would appear then that a French risk-reducing strategy would entail more store loyalty than brand loyalty, but it also might involve purchasing the most expensive brand. Buying only the most expensive brand was reflected in government experiment in France in which cheese slices of identical halves were labeled with different prices and distributed to various stores. Most shoppers chose the more expensive half, which demonstrated that the French seldom believe in a bargain but instead would agree that "you get what you pay for," even if this is not physically valid (Ardagh 1973).

Another experiment on a sample of American and French college students attempted to isolate the most important factors in determining product quality, using the dependent variables of price level, brand image, and nationality as independent variables. When price was the only available information, it was a major determinant of quality perception. When additional information such as brand image was available, however, pricing influences somewhat declined. By far the strongest influence on quality perception was nationality, which accounted for more than 56 percent of the variance indicated. Breaking the results down further, a monotonic relationship between price and quality existed for the French students, whereas a curvilinear relationship was perceived for the Americans. The researchers posited that perhaps the French use different cues, or use the same cues differently, than their American counterparts, or perhaps even the term *quality* can mean something differnt across cultures (Peterson and Jolibert 1976).

To summarize, consumer behavior differs between French and American consumers, but little theory is available to explain differences. Some of these differences might be due to structural factors, while others might be due to perceived risk.

Proposition 13.7: Risk perception in purchasing is greater among French than among American consumers. As a result, French consumers are more likely to be:

    (a) brand loyal
    (b) store loyal
    (c) dependent on a product's price
    (d) attracted to higher-quality products
    (e) non-innovators

Socialization Processes. With respect to differences in interaction with various sources of consumer information, the results of the relatively few studies appear to be mixed, primarily because of the different objectives, locations, and measures used in these studies. In terms of exposure to the mass media, a study by Schaninger et al. (1985) found that French-speaking families read newspapers less and watch more television than English-speaking families. Another study comparing the media exposure of French and American housewives revealed differences in sources of information about new products. American women tended to hear of new food products more through television advertisements, magazines, and newspapers. French women, in contrast, tended to learn more through exposure to billboards and point-of-sale promotions (Green and Langeard 1975).

These habits were explained by the breakdown in media consumption: Thirty-six percent of the French, in comparison with only 9 percent of the Americans, watched less than one hour of television per day; only 11 percent of French women watched three hours or more, compared with 48 percent of the Americans; Americans subscribed to 3.7 magazines per participant, while the French indicated an average of 2.4 magazine subscriptions. A downplay of the media's importance in exposing the French sample to new products is explained by more expensive print media, a lower rate of television set ownership, and the constraints of French television broadcasting due to government regulation. In fact, at the time of the study, broadcasting could take place only during lunchtime (normally a two-hour period) and between 6:00 and 8:00 P.M. (Green and Langeard 1975).

With respect to television use, although programming and format differ in each country, it is surprising how consumption behavior is similar. In fact, in a study conducted by Urban (1977), television was the only medium of the four investigated (television, radio, newspapers, and magazines) that was found to be sensitive to social class, level of education, and total household income. According to this study, both American and French women who are working full-time watched less television than nonworking women; French and American women with a college education watched less television and read more newspapers and magazines than less-educated women; and, finally, both American and French women with a higher income watched less television (Urban 1977).

Because the total consumption of newsprint is higher in France than in any other country in the European Economic Community (EEC), it is no wonder that the French spend most of their advertising dollars on newspapers. Newspapers in France, as in all of Europe, do not always have a high penetration of one geographic area as in the United States. Instead, their audiences are more clearly demographically or politically defined. According to a study by Lorimor and Dunn (1968–1969), 71 percent of the French questioned had read a newspaper the day before. Of that total, 7 percent fewer French men than women had read no newspapers the previous day, with no women reading more than two hours, while 4 percent of the men read two to three hours.

Magazines represent the second most important print medium. All periodicals are available on a national basis. A large percentage of French men (65 percent) reported having read no magazines the day before. Fifty-six percent of women classified themselves as nonmagazine readers, as compared with 75 percent of the men. Of the remaining percentage of female readers, 39 percent spent up to one hour reading, compared with only 25 percent of male readers (Lorimor and Dunn 1968–1969).

French women's magazine readership exhibits similar patterns. According to one study (Douglas 1977), French magazines were similar to American but were somewhat more interest-differentiated. Overall differences in readership between France and the United States were slight. The differences were seen in decreased reading frequency among working women with respect to general interest, fashion, and shelter magazines. Beyond this, working women apparently were more selective in readership patterns than nonworking women, concentrating less on home-oriented magazines.

Focusing on one specific segment of the population in both the United States and France—women, both working and nonworking—it would seem safe to assume that changes in the employment status of women would have an important impact on magazine readership. Working women have the dual responsibilities of a job and housekeeping, implying that there is less time to devote to the time-intensive activity of magazine readership. Because nonworking women center their lives on the home, their magazine readership should be quite high, as magazines often are one means of receiving outside information. Therefore, even the types of magazines used should differ among working and nonworking women (Douglas 1977).

A study by Urban (1977), however, found that overall, there are surprisingly similar national media usage patterns, except in the case of radio consumption. Heavy television viewing and radio usage are characteristics of lower-income Americans, and consumption of select radio programs is higher among higher-income groups. France shows similar television viewing habits, but radio listening is predominantly a characteristic of lower-class people. It is uncertain whether this difference is directly related to the material cultural disadvantage of poorer media coverage on both radio and television in France, life-style variations, or other factors.

Cinema advertising is an important medium in France because advertisers are restrictesd in television time allotment. In-theater advertising is shown for several minutes before a movie. The importance of this type of advertising is based on the fact that movies remain one of the world's foremost means of entertainment. Cinema advertising's impact varies inversely with the development of competitive media, especially television. With the spread of television broadcasting and set ownership, one can expect a decline in cinema advertising importance, but in the meantime, only about 56 percent of the French population even own a television set. Also, an interesting correlation to the importance of in-theater commercials is the fact that the French seem to be most attentive to this form of promotion, with 53 percent of them reporting attention, in comparison with 25 percent reporting attention to television commercials (Lorimor and Dunn 1968–1969).

Turning to interpersonal sources of information, most studies in the United States have uncovered a significant degree of innovator overlap across varying product categories. The French innovator does not exhibit such a strong profile across as many categories as his American counterpart. Therefore, innovators in both nations are identifiable to a certain degree in some product categories but not in others. In the Green and Langeard (1975) study, the consumption category in which innovators were more clearly defined were those characterized by less word-of-mouth communication. Most of these differences can be attributed to both social and environmental factors. To summarize, differences in communication processes between the two groups might reflect differences in environmental as well as cultural factors.

Orientals

Unlike research on Hispanics and the French, the available evidence regarding Oriental consumers is scattered and fragmented. A few studies in select Oriental countries provide limited empirical results and almost no theoretical interpretations. Many of these studies compare a particular Oriental culture with the U.S. culture, other studies compare the Oriental culture with non-U.S. cultures; and still other studies examine subcultures within a country.

With respect to studies examining U.S./Oriental differences in consumer behavior, Dalrymple, Robertson, and Yoshino (1971) compared whites, Japanese-Americans, and blacks in the West Los Angeles area with respect to their brand preferences, innovativeness, credit orientation, store preferences, and product information sources. The result of the study provided little support for the hypothesis that the three groups would show marked differences in their attitudes toward name brands or that minorities purchase name brands in an effort to be assimilated into society. Significant differences emerged in product information sources, suggesting differences in the importance of socialization agents as sources of consumer learning. The store preferences of Japanese-Americans were economy-oriented, and family decision making among the three groups was rather different.

Several studies have focused on Chinese consumers. Research by McCullough et al. (1986) has identified consumer segments in both Western and Oriental societies exhibiting attitudes and behaviors associated with traditional Chinese values. The findings suggest that Chineseness is more likely to exist in non-Asian than in Asian households. These findings raise questions regarding operational definitions of ethnicity and whether geocultural definitions are better than psychographic or lifestyle definitions.

In another study by Tan and McCullough (1985), high orientations toward Chinese values were associated with a higher reliance on price and quality; low orientation was associated with a higher preference for image. These findings suggest that general value orientations might affect specific consumption orientations. Finally, a study by Yau (1985) found that choice of products and sources by Chinese consumers is influenced by situational variables and environmental factors such as point-of-purchase displays. The same writer presents the results of several studies showing that the Chinese consumer has negative attitudes toward advertising.

Other studies of cultural values and consumption have examined respondents from other Oriental countries. Laurent (1985) found the Hong Kong population to have a strong family orientation, rather weak materialistic values, and a strong work ethic void of any success syndrome. In addition, they are willing to try new ideas and have liberal attitudes toward use of credit. In a study of materialism among Chinese adolescents in Singapore, materialism was found to be negatively associated with education and positively associated with achievement motivation (Mehta and Keng 1985).

The study of Singapore adolescents (Mehta and Keng 1985) replicated the findings of previous studies (Moschis and Churchill 1978). Family communication was found to overshadow the adolescent's ability to act as an independent consumer. Specifically, these adoelscents were found to enjoy a moderate level of independence in their purchase decisions, and they had stronger economic motivations than social motivations.

Marquez (1979) attempted to examine cultural differences in three diverse countries (the United States, the Philippines, and Thailand), using the cultural content of display advertisements. The results indicate a strong similarity in the portrayal of each culture. Other researchers have examined cultural differences among Orientals in the context of the country's economic development. Thorelli and Sentell (1982), for example, compared consumers in developed countries with consumers in less developed countries in an effort to explain differences in consumer behavior among Thai respondents. They found that consumers in developed countries sought more information than consumers in less developed countries (such as Thailand), partly because of the high illiteracy rates in less developed countries. Specifically, Thai consumers relied less on personal examination and recommendation. They were more satisfied with products and information, and they were more likely to perceive risks in purchasing products, which probably explains the high degree of brand loyalty exhibited by Thais. Thorelli and Sentell (1982) also observed intracultural differences in the consumer behavior of Thais.

Thus, consumer behavior might differ among Oriental cultures, and it might reflect cultural as well as environmental and developmental differences. Orientals apparently do not place as much emphasis on materialism as an indication of personal success as do Westerners.

Proposition 13.8: Orientals place less emphasis on material possessions than their Western counterparts.

Studies also suggest different patterns of interaction among Orientals and Americans. A recent study by Ward and his associates (1986) compared socialization practices and processes among American, British, and Japanese families. They found that Japanese parents were more indulgent of their children (agreeing to buy things children request) than are American or British parents. American children, however, were more likely to negotiate purchases with their parents than were British or Japanese children.

Several studies comparing American and Japanese families also suggest differences in socialization processes. Specifically, in comparison with American parents, Japanese parents show greater warmth, which is considered to be a broad definition of positive reinforcement; and they might place less emphasis on purposive consumer training, encouraging their children to learn consumption skills on their own, that is, by viewing ads, and through trial and error (see Ward et al. 1987).

> Proposition 13.9: Different consumer socialization processes operate among Oriental and American families. In comparison with their American counterparts Oriental youths are:
>
> (a) more likely to learn through observation
>
> (b) more likely to learn through positive reinforcement
>
> (c) less likely to be exposed to purposive consumer training from their parents
>
> (d) more likely to learn through trial and error

Although the mass media appear to play an important role in the socialization of Westerners, its effects are far from clear with regard to Orientals. Fujitake (1978) referred to surveys showing that the Japanese attach a greater importance to television than their American counterparts, a finding that implies the important role of the mass media in the socialization of Japanese consumers. Similarly, Thorelli and Sentell (1982) reported that most Thai respondents in their study felt that advertising was a viable source of information. Specifically, the responses indicate that villagers tended to believe that advertising paints a true picture more often than did respondents in Bangkok or the municipalities. Also, only 26 percent of the combined samples agreed that advertising results in better products, while 40 percent did not. Moreover, villagers were more likely to pay attention to the messages on the radio than did townspeople. The authors attributed this finding to the relative newness of the medium and the lack of alternative media. For similar reasons, rural viewers were much more likely to pay attention to ads than their urban counterparts. The evidence also suggests that television remains very much an urban medium, probably because of high price, urban access to nonbattery power sources, and geographic proximity to transmission towers.

> Proposition 13.10: The mass media play an important role in the socialization of Orientals. In comparison with their American counterparts, Orientals are more likely to:
>
> (a) rely on the mass media for consumer information
>
> (b) believe advertising claims

Other Subcultures

While the limited research available on other subcultures prohibits extensive examination of the effects of factors related to additional ethnic or cultural background characteristics, some general observations are in order. Groups that have been viewed as subcultures and have been subject to limited investigation include Jews, the Amish, various other ethnic and religious groups, and geographic subcultures.

Jews. The Jewish subculture is another example of how ethnicity (defined in terms of religion and nationality) affects values and consumer socialization in general. One writer states:

> When one is born a Jew, he/she is born into a culture and religion simultaneously. Although as an individual a Jew may choose to adhere to one, both, or neither of these two ethnic dimensions, the correlation between the two within Jewish populations has been found to be quite high. Jewish ethnicity is believed to exert a relatively stronger effect on the individual's behavior because it is multidimensional. One set of values is promulgated both by informal social interaction and religious instruction; therefore, the individual experiences greater normative consistency. (Hirschman 1981, 103)

McClelland (1961) suggests that "Jews should have high need for achievement on religious grounds" (p. 64). He attributes this to the emphasis on achievement in Jewish religious teachings. This thesis led Hirschman (1981) to propose some differences in the consumer behavior of Jews versus non-Jews, including the following:

1. Jews are more innovative (buy more new products) than non-Jews.
2. Jews exert more opinion leadership for new products than non-Jews (p. 108).

Research in fact has shown that American Jews are strongly competitive, eclectic, rational, innovative, cognitively complex, individualistic, information-seeking, and achievement-oriented (Hirschman 1981).

Research also suggests that such differences in consumer behavior are the result of different socialization processes operating within the Jewish subculture. Specifically, the need for achievement is transmitted by parents via exposure to special learning opportunities (such as magazines and special training and instruction), which might explain why Jews use more mass media information as adults than non-Jews (Hirschman 1981). Such selective exposure to information sources might account for differences in perceptions of advertisements between Israeli and American audiences (Hornik 1980). Thus, the need for achievement among Jews is likely to affect not only their behavior as consumers but also their levels and patterns of interaction with socialization agents, suggesting possible indirect effects on consumer socialization.

Proposition 13.11: The need for achievement among Jews affects those aspects of consumer behavior that relate to the process of acquisition and the expression of "successful" consumption. In relation to their non-Jews counterparts, Jews:

(a) aspire to a higher occupational status

(b) aspire to the acquisition of products whose usage symbolizes success

(c) are concerned with making rational decisions

(d) exhibit patterns of innovative behavior and opinion leadership

Proposition 13.12: Jews are more likely to make conscious efforts to socialize their children into successful consumer roles than their non-Jew counterparts. They are more likely to:

(a) use purposive consumer training

(b) encourage the use of information in the mass media

Amish. Whereas much of the Jewish innovative behavior can be attributed to their relatively high exposure to agents of change, specifically the mass media, the Amish subculture is relatively unexposed to such agents. Where agents of change are not readily available, one can observe an almost static social structure (Warner and Derlinger 1969). While it can be argued that the individual's interaction with (socialization) agents of change might reflect cultural values, it has been demonstrated that these agents can influence the development of values and behaviors (see chapters 5 through 8). Thus, it is not surprising to find non-innovative behavior to prevail among the Amish (Warner and Derlinger 1969).

Proposition 13.13: The Amish consumer's isolation and lack of interaction with agents of change provide few opportunities for socialization and resocialization. The Amish, in relation to the non-Amish, are less likely to be:

(a) innovators

(b) affected by nonsocial agents of change

Other Ethnic and Religious Subcultures. Several other studies have reported differences between subcultures. Most of these differences are in consumer behavior rather than socialization processes. For example, Hawes, Gromo, and Arndt (1978) examined differences in shopping time versus leisure time activities between nationwide samples of Norwegians and Americans. The results indicated very clear cross-cultural differences in the use of leisure time but not in shopping time.

In another study, Green, Verhage, and Cunningham (1981) compared American and Dutch wives in regard to their participation in family decisions. They found significant differences between the two nationalities, with American housewives reporting making more autonomous decisions and Dutch wives reporting a greater likelihood of having family roles structured by gender.

In a similar type of study, Kandel and Lesser (1972) compared Danish and American families. They found the wife's outside employment to be associated with marital power, a finding contradicting the results of Green et al.'s (1981) study, in which the wife's employment status was not a significant factor in family decision making. While there were significant cross-cultural differences in both these studies, there also were many similarities in consumer behavior. Such similarities have been attributed partly to the similar level of economic development that characterizes the United States and these European countries. To overcome this problem, Green and Cunningham (1980) compared the purchasing roles of samples drawn from Venezuela and the United States. Their findings suggested a greater variation in family purchasing roles, with Venezuelan husbands showing more power and influence than their American counterparts.

Studies also have uncovered similar consumer behavior patterns in the United States and other cultures. For example, Gans (1962) observed a high use of interpersonal sources in consumer decisions among lower-class families in an ethnic neighborhood in Boston. This finding is fairly similar to findings regarding the consumer behavior of underprivileged groups (see, for example, Engel et al. 1978). Similarly, a study of shopping and consumption patterns of individuals of various social classes in San Paulo, Brazil, revealed social class (subcultural) differences in the purchase of housewares and utensils. One important finding was that the lower classes purchased these items from itinerant street fairs rather than established stores (Cunningham et al. 1974), a finding that appears to parallel findings in the United States (see, for example, Engel et al. 1978). While few studies have examined the similarities and differences in consumer behavior between cultures defined at a national level (non-U.S. and U.S. subcultures), it has been observed that Italian-Americans exhibit many behavioral patterns similar to blacks (Hirschman 1985a). This suggests that some differences (cultural or cross-cultural) might be due to noncultural factors such as income.

> Proposition 13.14: The level of economic development of people comprising a culture affects the way they interact with the marketplace. The more economically advanced a culture is, the more likely its members are to:
>
> (a) have egalitarian sex role perceptions regarding family decisions
>
> (b) patronize large department stores
>
> (c) use more print media
>
> (d) use less broadcast media

Subcultural differences in consumer behavior also have been reported among religious groupings. For example, in attempting to explain differences in family decision-making processes, Scanzoni (1975) maintained that because of various theological and socioreligious reasons, egalitarianism is expected to prevail more among non-Catholics than among Catholics. This is because Catholics are more likely to consider marriage as a career for women, and anything outside the family role is considered incompatible. Catholic women were reported to be less egalitarian in outlook than non-Catholic women, and Jewish women were more egalitarian (Mason et al. 1976).

White Anglo-Saxon Protestants (WASPs) have exhibited consumption patterns that have changed very little over the past several decades. Their effort to focus on preserving their ancestral traditions seems to have some effect on their consumer behavior. For example, because of their desire to preserve certain clothing, WASPs are not likely to be style conscious (see Hirschman 1985a).

One study explored the role of the religious and personality characteristics of Nigerians in explaining differences in the extent of consumer acculturation. Although religious differences were related to the likelihood of accepting unfamiliar products, the effects were mediated by the personality trait characterized as close-mindedness and open-mindedness. Differences between religious subcultural groupings were revealed, with the tendency being that Moslems were more likely to be close-minded than their Christian counterparts (Schiffman et al. 1981).

Proposition 13.15: Subcultures defined in terms of religious beliefs are likely to exhibit consumer behaviors that reflect such beliefs.

(a) Catholics are more likely to possess traditional sex role perceptions regarding family consumer decisions than non-Catholics.

(b) WASPs are less likely to be innovators than non-WASPs.

(c) Christians are more likely than Moslems to be innovators.

Religious beliefs also are likely to affect individual's relationships with various socialization agents. One study, for example, investigated the relationship between religious subcultures and media content preferences among college students at a New York university (Hirschman 1985b). Although the sample characteristics do not allow for drawing generalizations on the basis of the findings, the study did support the general hypothesis that religious and national ethnicity are related to media content preference.

Proposition 13.16: The level and type of religious beliefs a person possesses affect his or her use of the mass media. Religious beliefs affect:

(a) types of mass media used

(b) content of mass media used

Finally, subcultures have been defined in terms of regional dimensions. A number of regional subcultural studies have been conducted on rural youths to determine whether they behave differently from urban youths. The findings show significant differences in the consumer behavior of the two regional groups, with rural youths being less likely to approve of teenage drinking and smoking. It is important to remember, however, that such differences might be due to factors other than geographic location (Copp 1965; Berkman and Gilson 1978). Straus (1962b) attributes some regional differences in the consumer behavior of high school students to the different socialization processes emphasized in rural versus urban areas. Apparently parents in rural areas attempt to provide meaningful work role learning experiences, especially for their sons (Straus 1962b). Similarly, rural youths lack the opportunity to interact with peers, and their attitudes are more likely to resemble those of their parents than urban youths (Bealer and Willits 1961), suggesting a stronger parental influence among rural youths.

Geographic and regional differences in consumer behavior and consumer socialization also have been reported among adult consumers. For example, Block and Kellerman (1978) reported differences in socialization processes between urban and rural adults. Specifically, those living in urban areas were reported to be heavier television viewers but less likely to be exposed to the print media and radio. The same study also reported differences in criteria used in making decisions, with urban shoppers being more concerned with the location of the outlet and rural shoppers with price. Again, these differences might reflect differences in income level and other structural factors (such as the availability of retail facilities). Similarly, recent research by Kahle (1986) shows differences in value orientations across regions of the United States that might have implications for consumer socialization.

In sum, subcultures defined geographically show different patterns of consumer behavior and interaction with socialization agents. These differences might be due to values that are likely to prevail in various regions or to different environments.

Proposition 13.17: Geographically defined subcultures exhibit different patterns of consumer behavior and interaction with sources of consumer information.

While other factors defining subcultures (such as marital status and work status) might not appear as important in explaining consumer behavior, they seem to play an important role in consumer socialization because they are likely to affect socialization processes. For example, in families where both parents work and in one-parent families, children have fewer opportunities to use parental models. As a result, they tend to be more susceptible to outside-the-house influences such as television and peers (Hur and Baran 1979; Comstock et al. 1978). One popular psychoanalytical theory, for example, holds that in father-absent homes, the young boys develop too close an identification with the mother (Inkeles 1969). Similarly, the widowed and single elderly are more likely to seek out companions and to interact with peers about consumption matters (Lambert 1979; Schiffman 1972b).

Summary and Discussion

While there appears to be ample evidence to suggest the importance of cultures and subcultures in consumer socialization, the effects of these social systems are not clearly understood. Part of the difficulty in understanding cultural and subcultural effects stems from the manner in which these concepts are defined and measured. Because cultures and subcultures often are defined in terms of similarities shared by large groups of people with respect to a host of factors ranging from values to geographic area, the causal variable is likely to be interwoven with several other factors. Furthermore, when cultures are defined geographically, the causal variable is likely to be in the individual's environment because of the laws and policies unique to a particular geographic area (for example, mass media availability or legal restrictions).

Another underlying assumption regarding the effects of cultures and subcultures is that individuals in such groupings exhibit uniform patterns of behaviors and attitudes as a result of the culture or subculture group to which they belong. Such an assumption is violated much of the time for at least two reasons: First, an individual might be a member of more than one culture (for example, as a result of having parents from two different cultures); second, belonging to a culture or subculture does not appear to be a question of group membership but rather a matter of degree of individual identification with the particular group. Thus, individuals believed to be part of a particular culture might identify with that culture in various degrees; they might strongly or weakly identify with one or more cultures; or they might not identify with any of the existing cultures or subcultures, as would be the case in unsuccessful socialization and acculturation (Brim 1968).

Better insight into the effects of subcultures on consumer behavior can be gained by separating direct effects on consumer learning from those that result from different socialization processes. Before undertaking such a task, the concept of culture must be explicated, operationally defined, and functionally related to consumer behavior and socialization processes. To gain a better understanding of cultural influences in consumer socialization, hypotheses regarding the relationship between consumer behavior and specific elements of culture (such as religion) must be developed and tested. It is very likely that specific elements in one culture or subculture might provide an explanation of specific aspects of consumer behavior and consumer socialization. It is also highly desirable to develop valid and reliable measures prior to undertaking any comparisons, since measures developed in one culture or subculture might not fit populations in other social settings as well (Allen and Chaffee 1977). A more challenging task would be to investigate the effects of the interaction of various elements of a subculture (such as value orientations and religion). It is likely, for example, that the individual might develop multiple consumption patterns and consumer behaviors as a result of conflicting cultural norms, which is likely to be the case when one wants to belong to two cultures (Hirschman 1985a).

Unfortunately, limited data are available by age group to suggest differences in cultural influences over the life cycle. Little information also is available on how consumer behavior and consumer socialization differ by generation. For example, one would expect different socialization processes to operate in the acculturation of immigrants, who might be lacking close family members to help them acquire consumption skills, as well as the ability to interact with specific mass media, (perhaps because of a language barrier). The socialization of second-generation immigrants might involve socialization into two different cultures and consumption behaviors that can be rather different from those in either culture. Such information would be useful not only in understanding socialization and acculturation processes but also in understanding the role socialization agents with select characteristics and experiences might play in the development of consumer behaviors.

14
Summary, Problems, and Prospects

The information presented in this book is based on the premise that consumer behavior can be studied and better understood in the context of socialization. Because the marketplace is characterized by dynamic changes, many of which reflect changes in consumer behavior, the need to understand the antecedent and processes underlying such changes would appear to be desirable. The socialization perspective was adopted for the study of consumer behavior because it can help us understand the dynamic aspects of human behavior acquisition and enactment.

Summary of Main Findings

The consumer socialization approach (model) presented here is supported by considerable empirical evidence, but the existing research often "fits" the model; it does not verify its specifics. Because the study of consumer socialization is relatively new and has evolved primarily as a result of public policy issues surrounding the effects of the marketing practices of young people, relatively little data are available on consumer socialization in later life.

The available data seem to support the consumer socialization perspective, at least empirically, as relationships between key variables in the model are supported with available research findings. Considerably less is known about the reasons for these relationships. Quite often, more than our theoretical interpretation is possible, but little alternative theory is available to help explain many of the empirical relationships reported. In spite of these deficiencies, certain general observations can be made based on the data presented.

First, several aspects of the individual's consumer behavior appear to undergo formation and change. Many of them are the result of interaction with specific socialization agents; others are due to internal biopsychological processes and experience. Parents play an important role in the consumer socialization of their offspring. They help the young person acquire a variety of consumer skills. Considerably less is known about the process of learning from these agents, as well as the specific effects of offspring on the socialization of parents. The role of family members in the socialization or resocialization of a spouse and older adult consumers is unclear, but the limited evidence suggests that these agents might be significant sources of consumer learning in early and late adulthood.

Peers as socialization agents also play a significant role in the socialization of younger people. The extent to which a young person acquires specific orientations by interacting with peers, as well as the learning process through which such orientations are acquired, appear to be conditioned by several family characteristics and antecedent variables. The role of peers of in the socialization of adults and older people is not very clear, although the evidence seems to suggest that peer relations modify and channel the interpretation of information received from other sources.

The vast amount of research related to consumer socialization has focused on the effects of the mass media on young people. The evidence suggests that young people learn a variety of consumer orientations from television advertising; some of them are desirable, but a great deal are not. The unintended consequences of television have received less attention in published research.

The mass media appear to play an important role in the socialization and resocialization of a person over the life cycle, particularly at the extreme stages. Considerably less is known about the process of influence and the second-order consequences of these agents. The evidence presented also suggests that there are circumstances under which the mass media (advertising in particular) can have more powerful effects. Other possible agents have been discussed, including school, siblings, retailers and retail personnel, and church, but evidence about the specific effects of these agents is sparse.

Consumer behavior undergoes constant formation and change over a person's life cycle. Certain orientations are learned earlier or better than others. Some aspects of the learned behavior are maintained throughout the life cycle, while others undergo further formation and development. Yet others are extincted later in life, and others are formed to supplement or replace acquired orientations. Explanations for changes in consumer orientation over the life cycle have been sparse, and those attempting to understand differences in consumer behavior must guard against alternative explanations, as well as cohort and period effects. What we seem to be able to conclude from studying consumer behavior over the life cycle is that consumption orientations undergo constant change, but little is known about the reasons for this change. Alternative explanations are possible, but the results often are questionable because they are confounded with the presence of possible cohort and period effects.

Perhaps one of the more interesting findings concerning the effects of structural factors (that is, variables placing individuals in specific subcultures) is that differences in consumer behavior and socialization processes emerge early in life.

Once these differences emerge, they tend to remain relatively unchanged throughout a person's life cycle, provided the person remains in the specific subculture experienced during the formative years. Unfortunately, our knowledge is limited in understanding why these patterns develop as they do. Little theory is available to help us understand subcultural differences. We seem to know very little about functional relationships between variables unique to a subculture and communication or consumer behavior. Often the causal variable is interwoven with other factors that are difficult to isolate and study in subcultural cross-sectional settings. We can observe and often predict the kind of behavior expected by individuals occupying a given social structure, but it becomes rather difficult to model functional relationships between the specific type of behavior and the causal variable in that subculture. Given that such functional relationships are hard to validate and test in cross-sectional or experimental settings, the differences in consumer behavior and consumer socialization are open to a great many alternative explanations.

Finally, the influence of socialization processes is likely to vary by stage in the person's life cycle, as well as by structural variable. For example, the effects of advertising appear to be greater to the extent that the individual is at either end of the life cycle and to the extent that the person comes from a lower socioeconomic background, has less education, is female, or is black.

Relationships in the model for which there is a reasonably adequate amount of evidence have been presented as conclusions, while relationships for which the support is less than adequate have been cast into propositions. On many occasions, the propositions are far from being specific, primarily because of a lack of knowledge in the area. The specificity of the propositions reflects the amount and specificity of the information available.

Consumer Socialization Issues

The reader probably has come across many problems and issues surrounding the use of the socialization perspective. These issues must be resolved before this perspective proves to be a desirable framework that would facilitate the accumulation of research findings.

One major issue focuses on the nature of the dependent variables that define a person's consumer role over the life cycle. The variable most relevant and desirable (from a societal perspective) must be identified and categorized to help accumulate research findings for a systematic and effective study. A conceptual framework for classifying consumer behavior is needed. While far from adequate in terms of classifying a wide variety of consumption-related orientations, frameworks such as the one presented might serve the purpose, particularly at an early stage of research.

Whereas conceptual issues seem to focus mostly on the dependent variables, measurement issues appear to focus primarily on the independent variables. One issue deals with the selection of age versus life cycle as a developmental variable.

Age might be a more powerful variable in explaining consumer socialization among children and adolescents, whereas life cycle might be a better predictor in later stages. Furthermore, the issue of how to categorize age groups and the life-cycle variable is not settled.

The specificity of independent variables, such as age, is a desirable goal. Age per se appears to have little value in consumer socialization research because it stands simply as an index of changes occurring over a person's life cycle, including changes in the person's cognitive structure, social relations, need structure, and other biophysical and psychosocial processes. It is the measurement of these underlying factors that might help us better understand changes in the person's consumer behavior. One difficulty in measuring age-related differences in consumer socialization and behavior is that there is little theory to suggest age-related differences in anticipatory consumer learning and processes. In terms of measuring other social structural variables, it has been argued that the variables should be treated as theoretical variables rather than as static categorical locators; they should be tied to specific learning processes.

The most perplexing measurement problem involves the need to establish functional patterns of communication and consumer behavior that cut across various discrete consumer orientations and socialization processes (McLeod and O'Keefe 1972). Measures focusing simply on time spent interacting with various socialization agents are not likely to produce meaningful results. Receiver-oriented categorizations of the agent's functions and ability to fulfill certain information needs, combined with specific use patterns, would seem to be the optimum strategy for measuring communication behavior (see, for example, McLeod, Bybee, and Duvall 1982; McLeod 1974; McLeod and O'Keefe 1972).

Because consumer socialization involves the study of specific agents and their effects, a measurement-related issue is the decision regarding the time lag between interaction with these agents and the learning of consumer orientations. Comparisons between short-term and long-term effects suggest possible differences in the effects of socialization agents as a function of time. In sum, the measurement issue must address the question of *what* to measure (content or criterion behavior) and *how* and *when* to measure consumer socialization processes and effects.

Another issue deals with the appropriate sampling units. Much analysis of consumer behavior is conducted by locator variables such as occupation, income, and social class. The socialization perspective implies that the organizational structure and structural relations at work in the community and in the neighborhood might be as important as the more general societal location in determining, for example, a person's communication with socialization agents (McLeod and O'Keefe 1972), which in turn might influence consumer behavior. This often requires sampling the social units of which the person is a part rather than the individual.

The development of research designs appropriate to the socialization model must meet at least two requirements: They must be capable of handling the large number of variables contained in the socialization model; they must deal with change over time and sequences of cause and effect (McLeod and O'Keefe 1972). Causal modeling using nonexperimental data gathered at a single point in time is one promising approach. When causal modeling is used, care must be taken in separating the effects of socialization processes whenever reciprocal causality exists. This can be accomplished in a number of ways, including the use of instrumental variables and maximum likelihood estimates.

The ideal research design is believed to be the panel design, which often has been advocated but seldom used in consumer socialization studies. Using this design, data can be obtained from the person being socialized as well from socialization agents such as parents and peers. Over long periods of time, the same respondents serve as data sources. A major advantage of this design is that it allows one to test cause and effect relationships. In socialization studies, for example, parent-child correlations, often used as evidence of the child's modeling of the parent's behavior, also might be explained as reverse modeling—that is, the child's behavior influences the parent's rather than vice versa (McLeod and O'Keefe 1972; Surlin et al. 1978). Cross-lagged correlations, as well as causal modeling with and without lagged variables, can be used with panel data.

One other question that might take a considerable amount of research data to answer deals with how a person's acquisition of consumer behaviors relates to the development of other types of orientations, as well as how the behaviors relate to specific social structures and social systems. It is possible that consumer behavior is best understood in its relationship with other kinds of behaviors as dependent variables and that consumer behavior might represent too narrow a scope for an adequate research program (McLeod and O'Keefe 1972). This would make both socialization processes and consumer behavior dependent on the person's socialization into a more general role. This conceivably would add a sixth element to the consumer socialization model. For example, one fruitful area of future research might be understanding a person's personality development throughout the life-span and studying how such development affects specific aspects of consumer behavior. Similarly, changes in consumer orientations over the life cycle might reflect changes in the person's environment rather than effects of specific socialization processes and their antecedents.

While this book has summarized the findings of several studies, some of the speculations might not be well-founded for at least two reasons. First, when attempts were made to explain empirical findings, little theory was available to guide the development of propositions. Second, many of the data used as a basis for proposition development came from studies using different methods (measurement, sampling, and data analysis). More rigorous methods for secondary means of data integration, such as metanalysis, might have produced better results.

Given these limitations and caveats in consumer socialization research, many directions for future research have been suggested by the data presented here. To begin with the criterion variables, we must understand the types of consumer behavior that are likely to develop at various stages in a person's life cycle, the processes by which they develop, and the reasons for their emergence. We also would benefit a great deal from knowledge regarding modifications of the acquired orientations. Finally, we must learn when or whether earlier acquired orientations disappear or are replaced by other orientations. We also must better understand the processes leading to the acquisition of specific consumption orientations over the life cycle and the role various socialization agents play in this process. Understanding both desirable and undesirable consumer socialization could help us in controlling or modifying specific socialization processes to bring about desirable outcomes.

Perhaps it is time to start considering a more specific variable than age or life cycle that would be associated with, for example, the development of specific consumption orientations. Such a variable that would measure changes in need structures due to sociopsychological changes might be more useful in understanding consumer socialization over the life span than, for example, age, which measures maturation and a host of other factors and cumulative experiences associated with advancing age. Perhaps building measures of cognitive maturation based on consumer decision demands placed on us as a result of our dynamic environment and social interactions might be better predictors of consumer socialization. Progression through such stages of maturation affects our demands for information, which are likely to result in more active interaction with socialization agents and one's environment in an effort to acquire the needed information.

One of the more challenging tasks for researchers would be to identify stages in the life cycle at which various consumption orientations begin to develop, since learning to behave in a particular fashion does not occur simultaneously with the social or biological transition into the next stage. A fruitful approach to understanding the dynamic changes in the individual in the context of the general model of consumer socialization is to begin with studying actual and anticipatory changes in the individual's position within a particular social structure (such as marriage, parenthood, employment, or retirement) and the corresponding needs for consumer information and consumption in general that such changes are likely to have. This might include exploring the types of consumer roles these needs are likely to define or modify and the information required for learning to enact such roles. This might help us understand patterns of interaction with socialization agents and the acquisition of norms and behaviors related to consumption. Very little research has been conducted on the acquisition of consumer roles for later life. We must understand the changes in consumer skills and the development of those orientations that would help the older person function more effeciently and effectively as a consumer in later life.

Finally, questions remain unanswered regarding how the effects of early experiences and the formation of consumer orientations in earlier life affect the learning of other consumption-related norms and behaviors in later life. This is perhaps one of the more demanding research tasks because it requires longitudinal designs to guard against possible cohort and period effects.

Expanding the Scope of Consumer Socialization

The methodology for studying consumer behavior presented here could be applied to different settings. It already has been shown that deviant consumer behavior can be viewed from a socialization perspective. Other situations might be amenable to investigations using the socialization framework. The introduction of new products and services into the marketplace often make new demands on consumers who are unfamiliar with their use. Such new developments often require people to make modifications in their consumer behavior before they can adopt them effectively. This process could be viewed from a socialization perspective because it falls into the category of resocialization.

Similarly, the socialization of new residents into an environment different from the one to which they are accustomed might be viewed from a socialization perspective. New residents must develop new patterns of consumer behavior, especially those related to store patronage. Understanding the process underlying these developments would be useful to marketers, who already seem to attempt to intervene in the process with promotions such as the welcome wagon.

The socialization perspective generally seems to be an appropriate framework for research whenever learning or relearning of a role is involved. It is possible that the framework can be applied to those areas of marketing in which role prescriptions exist. For example, it is possible to view the development (training) of salespeople and marketing practitioners from a socialization standpoint, using perspectives already available in socialization of occupations (see, for example, Goslin 1969). Understanding the processes leading to the acquisition of such roles might help us create not only more effective consumers but also more efficient sellers of goods and services, thus contributing to a more efficient functioning of our economic system.

References

Abedl-Ghany, Mohamed, and Gordon E. Bivens (1976). "Correlates of Consumption of Food Nutrients." *Advances in Consumer Research,* vol. 3, edited by B. Anderson, 229–37. Cincinnati, OH: Association for Consumer Research.

Adler, Richard P., B. Friedlander, G. Lesser, L. Meringoff, T. Robertson, J. Rossiter, and S. Ward (1977). *Research on the Effects of Television Advertising on Children.* Report prepared for Research Applied to National Needs Program, National Science Foundation. Washington: Government Printing Office.

———. (1980). *The Effects of Television Advertising on Children.* Lexington, MA: Lexington Books.

Advertising Age (1984). *Seventeen* advertisement, *Advertising Age* (October 22): 9.

Adweek (1981). "Simmons Study Finds Male Teens Are More Brand Loyal Than Females." *Adweek* 2, no. 41 (September 28): 28.

Ahammer, I. (1973). "Social Learning Theory as a Framework for the Study of Adult Personality Development." In *Life-Span Developmental Psychology: Personality and Socialization,* edited by P. Baltes and W. Schaie, 253–84. New York: Academic Press.

Albrecht, G., and H. Gift (1975). "Adult Socialization: Ambiguity and Adult Life Crises." In *Life-Span Developmental Psychology: Normative Life Crises,* edited by N. Catan and L. Ginsburg, 237–51. New York: Academic Press.

Alderson, Wroe (1957). *Marketing Behavior and Executive Action.* Homewood, IL: Richard D. Irwin.

Aldous, Joan (1974). "Commentaries on Ward, Consumer Socialization." *Journal of Consumer Research* 1 (September): 15–16.

Alexander, Alec (1964). *Greek Industrialists.* Athens: Center for Productivity and Economic Research.

Alexander, R.J. (1947). "Some Aspects of Sex Differences in Relation to Marketing." *Journal of Marketing* 12 (July): 158–72.

Alexis, Marcus (1962). "Some Negro-White Differences in Consumption." *American Journal of Economics and Sociology* 21 (January): 11–28.

Allen, Carole (1981). "Over 55: Growth Market of the 80's." *Nation's Business* 69 (April): 23–32.

Allen, Richard L., and Steven H. Chaffee (1977). "Racial Differences in Family Communication Patterns." *Journalism Quarterly* 55 (Spring): 8–13, 57.

Allen, R.L., and S.H. Chaffee (1979). "Mass Communication and the Political Participation of Black Americans." In *Communication Yearbook,* vol. 3, edited by D. Nimmo, 407–522. New Brunswick, NJ: Transaction Books.

Allen, R.L., and D.E. Clarke (1980). "Ethnicity and Mass Media Behavior: A Study of Blacks and Latinos." *Journal of Broadcasting* 24 no. 1 (Winter): 23–24.

Allison, Neil K. (1978). "A Psychometric Development of a Test for Consumer Alienation from the Market Place." *Journal of Marketing Research* 15 (November): 565–75.

Alvarez, Rodolfo (1971). "The Unique Psycho-Historical Experience of the Mexican American People." *Social Science Quarterly* 52 (June): 15–29.

Amann, A., B. Doberauer, W. Doberauer, J. Hoerl, and G. Majce (1980). "Austria." In *International Handbook on Aging: Contemporary Development and Research,* edited by Erdman Palmore, 3–38. Westport, CT: Greenwood Press.

Anderson, J.E. (1936). "The Young Child in the Home: A Survey of Three Thousand American Families." Report of the Committee on the Infant and Preschool Child, White House Conference on Child Health and Protection. New York: Appleton-Century.

Andreasen, Alan R. (1982). "Disadvantaged Hispanic Consumers: A Research Perspective and Agenda." *Journal of Consumer Affairs* 16 no. 1 (Summer): 46–61.

Angrist, Shirley S., Richard Mickelsen, and Anthony N. Penna (1977). "Sex Differences in Sex-Role Conceptions and Family Orientation of High School Students." *Journal of Youth and Adolescence* 6, no. 2 (June): 179–86.

Ardagh, John (1973). *The New France: A Society in Transition.* London: Penguin Books.

Arndt, Johan (1971). "A Research Note on Intergenerational Overlap of Selected Consumer Variables." *Markeds Kommunikasjon* 3: 7–8.

———. (1976). "Reflections on Research in Consumer Behavior." In *Advances in Consumer Research,* vol. 3, edited by B. Anderson, 213–21. Cincinnati, OH: Association for Consumer Research.

———. (1979). "Family Life Cycle as a Determinant of Size and Composition of Household Expenditure." In *Advances in Consumer Research,* vol. 6, edited by W.L. Wilkie, 128–32. Ann Arbor, MI: Association for Consumer Research.

Arnold, David O. (1970). *The Sociology of Subcultures.* Berkeley, CA: Glendasary Press.

Assael, Henry (1984). *Consumer Behavior and Marketing Action.* 2d ed. Boston: Kent Publishing Company.

Atchley, Robert C. (1972). *The Social Forces in Later Life: An Introduction to Social Gerontology.* Belmont, CA: Wadsworth.

Atkin, Charles (1975a). "Children's Social Learning from Television: Research Evidence on Observational Modeling of Product Consumption." Paper presented at conference of Association for Consumer Research, Cincinnati.

———. (1975b). "Effects of Television Advertising on Children—First Year Experimental Evidence." *Report #1.* Michigan State University (June).

———. (1975c). "Effects of Television Advertising on Children—Second Year Experimental Evidence." *Report #2.* Michigan State University (June).

———. (1975d). "Effects of Television Advertising on Children—Content Analysis of Children's Television Commercials." *Report #5.* Michigan State University (June).

———. (1975e). "Effects of Television Advertising on Children—Survey of Pre-Adolescent's Responses to Television Commercials." *Report #6.* Michigan State University (June).

———. (1975f). "Effects of Television Advertising on Children—Parent-Child Communication in Supermarket Breakfast Selection." *Report #.* Michigan State University (June).

——. (1975g). "Effects of Television Advertising on Children—Survey of Children's and Mother's Responses to Television Commercials." *Report #8*. Michigan State University (June).

——. (1976a). "Children's Social Learning from Television Advertising: Research Evidence on Observational Modeling of Product Consumption." In *Advances in Consumer Research*, vol. 3, edited by B. Anderson, 513–19. Cincinnati, OH: Association for Consumer Research.

——. (1976b). "Mass Media and the Aging." In *Aging and Communication*, edited by H.J. Oyer and E.J. Oyer, 99–118. Baltimore: University Press.

——. (1978a). "Observation of Parent-Child Interaction in Supermarket Decision Making." *Journal of Marketing* 42: 41–45.

——. (1978b). "Effects of Drug Commercials on Young Viewers." *Journal of Communication* 28, no. 4 (Fall): 71–79.

——. (1982). "Television Advertising and Socialization to Consumer Roles." In *Television and Behavior*, edited by K. Pearl et al., 191–200. Rockville, MD: U.S. Department of Health and Human Services.

Atkin, Charles K., and Martin Block (1984). "The Effects of Alcohol Advertising." In *Advances in Consumer Research*, vol. 11, edited by T. Kinnear, 688–93. Provo, UT: Association for Consumer Research.

Atkin, C., M. Block, and L. Reid (1980). "Advertising Effects on Alcohol Brand Images and Preferences." Paper presented at the meeting of the Association for Education in Journalism, Boston.

Atkin, Charles K., and Walter Gantz (1978). "Television News and Political Socialization." *Public Opinion Quarterly* 42, no. 2 (Summer): 183–98.

Atkin, C., and W. Gibson (1978). "Children's Nutrition Learning from Television Advertising." Unpublished manuscript, Michigan State University.

Atkin, Charles, and Bradley S. Greenberg (1974). *Public Television and Political Socialization*. Report prepared for Corporation of Public Broadcasting. East Lansing, MI: Department of Communication, Michigan State University (March).

Atkin, Charles, Bradley Greenberg, Felipe Korzenny, and Steven McDermott (1979). "Selective Exposure to Televised Violence." *Journal of Broadcasting* 23 (Winter): 5–13.

Atkin, C., B. Reeves, and W. Gibson (1979). "Effects of Television Food Advertising on Children." Paper presented at the meeting of the Association for Education in Journalism, Houston.

Ausubel, D.P. (1960). "The Use of Advanced Organizers in the Learning and Retention of Meaningful Verbal Material." *Journal of Educational Psychology* 51 (October): 267–72.

Ausubel, D.P., and F.G. Robinson (1969). *School Learning*. New York: Holt, Rinehart and Winston.

Avery, R.K. (1979). "Adolescents' Use of the Mass Media." *American Behavioral Scientist* 23 (September/October): 53–70.

Axiom Market Research Bureau (1979). *Target Group Index*. New York: Axiom Market Research Bureau.

Baldwin, Alfred L. (1969). "A Cognitive Theory of Socialization." In *Handbook of Socialization*, edited by D.A. Goslin, 325–46. Chicago: Rand McNally.

Baltes, Paul, ed. (1978). *Life Span Development and Behavior*, vol. 1. New York: Academic Press.

Baltes, P., and G. Labouvie (1973). "Adult Development of Intellectual Performance: Description, Explanation and Modification." In *The Psychology of Adult Development and Aging,* edited by C. Eisdorfer and M. Lawton, 157–219. Washington: American Psychological Association.

Baltes, Paul B., H.W. Reese, and Lewis P. Lipsitt (1980). "Life Span Developmental Psychology." *Annual Reviews in Psychology* 31: 65–110.

Baltes, Paul, H.W. Reese, and J.R. Nesselroade (1977). *Life-Span Developmental Psychology: Introduction to Research Methods.* Belmont, CA: Wadsworth.

Baltes, P.B., and K.W. Schaie, eds. (1973). *Life-Span Developmental Psychology: Personality and Socialization.* New York: Academic Press.

Bandura, A. (1965). "Vicarious Processes: A Case of No-Trial Learning." In *Advances in Experimental Social Psychology,* vol. 2, edited by L. Berkowitz, 1–55. New York: Academic Press.

———. (1969). "Social-Learning Theory of Identification Processes." In *Handbook of Socialization Theory and Research,* edited by D. Goslin, 213–62. Chicago: Rand McNally.

———. (1971a). *Modeling Influences on Children.* Testimony to the Federal Trade Commission.

———. (1971b). *Social Learning Theory.* New York: General Learning Press.

———. (1973). *Aggression: A Social Learning Analysis.* Englewood Cliffs, NJ: Prentice-Hall.

———. (1978). "Social Learning Theory of Aggression." *Journal of Communication* 28, no. 3 (Summer): 12–29.

Barak, B., and L. Schiffman (1981). "Cognitive Age: A Non-Chronological Age Variable." In *Advances in Consumer Research,* vol. 8, edited by K. Monroe, 602–06. Ann Arbor, MI: Association for Consumer Research.

Barak, Benny, and Steven Gould (1985). "Alternative Age Measures: A Research Agenda." In *Advances in Consumer Research,* vol. 12, edited by E. Hirschman and M. Holbrook, 53–58. Provo, UT: Association for Consumer Research.

Baranowski, Marc D. (1978). "Adolescents' Attempted Influence on Parental Behaviors." *Adolescence* 13, no. 52: 585–604.

Barnes, Nora Ganim, and Michael P. Peters (1982). "Modes of Retail Distribution: Views of the Elderly." *Akron Business and Economic Review* 13 (Fall): 26–31.

Barry, Thomas E., and Anees Sheikh (1977). "Race as a Dimension in Children's TV Advertising: The Need for More Research." *Journal of Advertising* 6 (Summer): 5–10.

Bartos, Rena (1980). "Over 49: The Invisible Consumer Market." *Harvard Business Review* 58 (January/February): 140–48.

Bauer, R.A. (1964). "The Obstinate Audience: The Influence Process from the Point of View of Social Communication." *American Psychologist* 19 (May): 319–28.

———. (1967). "Games People and Audiences Play." Paper presented at Seminar in Contemporary Society, the University of Texas (March 27).

Bauer, Raymond A., and Scott M. Cunningham (1970). "The Negro Market." *Journal of Advertising Research* 10, no. 1 (February): 3–13.

Bauer, Raymond, Scott Cunningham, and Lawrence Wortzel (1965). "The Marketing Dilemma of Negroes." *Journal of Marketing* 29, no. 3 (July): 1–6.

Baumgarten, Steven A., Tanniru R. Rao, and L. Winston Ring (1976). "A Descriptive Model of Consumer Choice Processes Among Nursing Home Patients." In *Advances in Consumer Research,* vol. 3, edited by B. Anderson, 457–60. Urbana, IL: Association for Consumer Research.

Bayer, A.E. (1975). "Sexist Students in American Colleges: A Descriptive Note." *Journal of Marriage and the Family* 37: 391–97.

Bealer, C., and F.K. Willits (1961). "Rural Youth: A Case Study in the Rebelliousness of Adolescents." *Annals of the American Academy of Political and Social Science* 338: 63–69.

Bearden, William O., J. Barry Mason, and Edward M. Smith (1979). "Perceived Risk and Elderly Perceptions of Generic Drug Prescribing." *The Gerontologist* 19, no. 2: 191–95.

Bearden, William O., Jesse E. Teel, and Richard M. Durand (1978). "Media Usage, Psychographic, and Demographic Dimensions of Retail Shoppers." *Journal of Retailing* 53 (Spring): 65–74.

Becherer, Richard C., and Fred Morgan (1982). "Informal Group/Influence Among Situationally/Dispositionally Oriented Consumers." *Journal of the Academy of Marketing Science* 10 (Summer): 269–81.

Becker, Lee B. (1979). "Measurement of Gratifications." *Communications Research* 6, no. 1 (January): 54–73.

Bee, H.L., and S.K. Mitchell (1980). *The Developing Person: A Life-Span Approach*. New York: Harper & Row.

Belch, George E., and Michael A. Belch (1984). "An Investigation of the Effects of Repetition on Cognitive and Affective Reactions to Humorous and Serious Television Commercials." In *Advances in Consumer Research*, vol. 11, edited by Thomas Kinnear, 4–10. Provo, UT: Association for Consumer Research.

Belch, George, Michael A. Belch, and Gayle Ceresino (1985). "Parental and Teenage Child Influences in Family Decision Making." *Journal of Business Research*, 13, no. 2 (April): 163–76.

Belk, Russell W. (1985). "Materialism: Trait Aspects of Living in the Material World." *Journal of Consumer Research* 12 (December): 265–80.

Belk, Russell W., Kenneth D. Bahn, and Robert N. Mayer (1982). "Developmental Recognition of Consumption Symbolism." *Journal of Consumer Research* 9 (June): 4–17.

Belk, Russell, Robert Mayer, and Amy Driscoll (1984). "Children's Recognition of Consumption Symbolism in Children's Products." *Journal of Consumer Research* 10 (March): 386–97.

Belk, Russell W., Gifford Rice, and Randall Harvey (1985). "Adolescents' Reporting Saving, Giving, and Spending as a Function of Sources of Income." In *Advances in Consumer Research*, vol. 11, edited by Elizabeth Hirschman and Morris Holbrook, 42–46. Provo, UT: Association for Consumer Research.

Bellenger, Danny, Elizabeth Hirschman, and Dan Robertson (1976–1977). "Age and Education as Key Correlates of Store Selection for Female Shoppers." *Journal of Retailing* 52 (Winter): 71–78.

Bellenger, Danny N., and George P. Moschis (1981). "A Socialization Model of Retail Patronage." In *Advances in Consumer Research*, vol. 8, edited by K. Monroe, 373–78. Ann Arbor, MI: Association for Consumer Research.

Bellenger, Danny N., Dan H. Robertson, and Barnett Greenberg (1977). "Shopping Center Patronage Motives." *Journal of Retailing* 52 (Summer): 29–37, 94, 95.

Bellenger, Danny N., and Humberto Valencia (1982). "Understanding the Hispanic Market." *Business Horizons* 25, no. 3 (May/June): 47–50.

Bennett, P.D., and H.H. Kassarjian (1972). *Consumer Behavior*. Englewood Cliffs, NJ: Prentice-Hall.

Benson, P. (1967). "Individual Exposure to Advertising and Changes in Brands Bought." *Journal of Advertising Research* 7, no. 4: 27–31.

Berelson, Bernard, and G.A. Steiner (1964). *Human Behavior: Shorter Edition: Poverty, Minorities and Marketing.* New York: Harcourt Brace Jovanovich.

Berey, L.A., and R.W. Pollay (1968). "Influencing Role of the Child in Family Decision Making." *Journal of Marketing Research* 5, no. 1 (February): 70–72.

Berger, Joan (1985). " 'The New Old': Where The Economic Action Is." *Business Week* (November 25): 138–40.

Bergman, M. (1980). *Aging and the Perception of Speech.* Baltimore: University Press.

Berkman, Harold W., and Christopher C. Gilson (1978). *Consumer Behavior: Concepts and Strategies.* Encino, CA: Dickenson Publishing Co.

Bernard, Jessie (1976). "Change and Stability in Sex-Role Norms." *Journal of Social Issues* 32, no. 3: 207–23.

Bernhardt, K. (1981). "Consumer Problems and Complaint Actions of Older Americans: A National View." *Journal of Retailing* 57 (Fall): 107–25.

Bernhardt, K., and T. Kinnear (1976). "Profiling the Senior Citizen Market." In *Advances in Consumer Research,* vol. 3, edited by B. Anderson, 449–52. Cincinnati, OH: Association for Consumer Research.

Berry, Leonard, and Paul J. Solomon (1971). "Generalizing about Low-Income Food Shoppers: A Word of Caution." *Journal of Retailing* 47 (Summer): 259.

Berry, Lewis A., and Richard W. Pollay (1968). "The Influencing Role of the Child in Family Decision Making." *Journal of Marketing Research* 5 (February): 70–72.

Bikson, T., et al. (1976). "Decision Making Processes Among Elderly Consumers." In *The Elderly Consumer,* edited by F. Waddell, 449–65. Columbia, MD: The Human Ecology Center, Antioch College.

Birren, J.E. (1964). *The Psychology of Aging.* Englewood Cliffs, NJ: Prentice-Hall.

———. (1974). "Translations in Gerontology—From Lab to Life: Psychophysiology and Speed of Response." *American Psychologist* 29: 808–15.

Birren, J.E., and D.S. Woodruff (1973). "Human Development Over the Life Span Through Education." In *Life Span Developmental Psychology: Personality and Socialization,* edited by P.S. Baltes and K.W. Schaie, 306–39. New York: Academic Press.

Blau, Zena S. (1956). "Changes in Status and Age Identification." *American Sociological Review* 21 (April): 198–202.

———. (1973). *Old Age in a Changing Society.* New York: Franklin Watts, Inc.

Block, Carl E., and Bert J. Kellerman (1978). "Variation in Exposure Patterns to Commercial Sources of Information: An Empirical Analysis of the Differences Among the Poor Living in Rural and Urban Environments." *Journal of Advertising* 7 (Fall): 36–39.

Blumler, J.G., and E. Katz, eds. (1974). *The Uses of Mass Communications.* Berverly Hills, CA: Sage.

Boddweyn, Jean J. (1981). "Comparative Marketing: The First Twenty-Five Years." *Journal of International Business Studies* 12 (Spring): 61–70.

Bodec, Ben (1980). "Market With a Future—Retirement." *Marketing & Media Decisions* (December): 74–120.

Bogart, L. (1967). *Strategy in Advertising.* New York: Harcourt, Brace and World.

Boone, Louis E., David L. Kurtz, James C. Johnson, and John A. Bonno (1974). "City Shoppers and Urban Identification Revisited." *Journal of Marketing* 38 (July): 67–69.

Boote, Alfred S. (1982–1983). "Psychographic Segmentation in Europe." *Journal of Advertising Research* 22 (December/January): 19–25.

Botwinick, Jack (1978). *Aging and Behavior: A Comprehensive Integration of Research Findings.* 2d ed. New York: Springer.

Bowen, Howard R. (1977). "The Effects of Going to College." *The Chronicle of Higher Education* 15, no. 9 (October 31): 3–4.

Bowerman, Charles E., and John W. Kinch (1959). "Changes in Family and Peer Orientation of Children Between Fourth and Tenth Graders." *Social Forces* 37 (March): 206–11.

Boyd, Neal R., and Warren J. Huffman (1984). "The Relationship Between Emotional Maturity and Drinking and Driving Involvement Among Young Adults." *Journal of Safety Research* 15 (Spring): 1–6.

Breen, Miles P., and Jon T. Powell (1973). "The Relation Between Attractiveness and Credibility of Television Commercials as Perceived By Children: A Replication." Paper presented to Central States Speech Association, Minneapolis.

Brim, Orville G., Jr. (1960). "Personality Development as Role Learning." In *Personality Development in Children,* edited by I. Iscoe and H.W. Stevenson, 127–59. Austin, TX: University of Texas Press.

———. (1966). "Socialization Through the Life Cycle." In *Socialization after Childhood: Two Essays,* edited by O.G. Brim, Jr., and S. Wheeler, 1–49. New York: John Wiley and Sons.

———. (1968). "Adult Socialization." In *Socialization and Society,* edited by J.A. Clausen, 182–226. Boston: Little Brown.

Brim, Orville G., and Stanton Wheeler (1966). *Socialization After Childhood: Two Easays.* New York: John Wiley and Sons.

Brinberg, David, and Nancy Schwenk (1985). "Husband-Wife Decision Making: An Exploratory Study of Iteration Process." In *Advances in Consumer Research,* vol. 12, edited by E. Hirschman and M. Holbrook, 487–91. Provo, UT: Association for Consumer Research.

Brittain, Clay V. (1963). "Adolescent Choices and Parent-Peer Cross Pressures." *American Sociological Review* 28 (June): 385–91.

Broadcasting (1976). "Arbitron Says Blacks and Women Watch the Most TV." *Broadcasting* 91 (October 18); 42.

Brucks, Merrie, Marvin E. Goldberg, and Gary M. Armstrong (1986). "Children's Cognitive References to Advertising." In *Advances in Consumer Research,* vol. 13, edited by Rich Lutz, 650–54. Provo, UT: Association for Consumer Research.

Bureau of Labor Statistics (1972–1973). *Consumer Expenditure Survey, 1972–73.* Bulletin 1982. Washington: Bureau of Labor.

Burgoon, Judee K., and Michael Burgoon (1980). "Predictors of Newspaper Readership." *Journalism Quarterly* 57, no. 4 (Winter): 589–96.

Burnett, John J. (1981). "Psychographic and Demographic Characteristics of Blood Donors." *Journal of Consumer Research* 8 (June): 62–66.

Burr, Pat, and Richard M. Burr (1977). "Product Recognition and Premium Appeal." *Journal of Communication* 27 (Winter): 115–17.

Burton, John R., and Charles B. Hennon (1980). "Consumer Concerns of Senior Citizen Center Participants." *Journal of Consumer Affairs* 14, no. 2 (Winter): 366–82.

Busby, Linda J. (1975). "Sex-Role Research on the Mass Media." *Journal of Communication* 25, no. 4 (Autumn): 107–31.

Bush, D., B. Hutchinson, R.G. Simmons, and D. Blyth (1977–1978). "Adolescent Perception of Sex-Roles in 1968 and 1975." *Public Opinion Quarterly* 41: 459–74.

Byrne, Gary (1969). "Mass Media and Political Socialization of Children and Pre-Adults." *Journalism Quarterly* 46 (Spring): 149–42.

Cameron, M.O. (1964). *The Booster and the Snitch: Department Store Shoplifting.* New York: Free Press.

Cameron, Tracy L. (1982). "Drinking and Driving Among American Youth: Beliefs and Behaviors." *Drug and Alcohol Dependence* 10 (September): 1–33.

Campbell, Ernest Q. (1969). "Adolescent Socialization." In *Handbook of Socialization Theory and Research,* edited by D.A. Goslin, 821–59. Chicago: Rand McNally.

Campbell, J.D. (1964). "Peer Relations in Childhood." In *Review of Child Development Research,* vol. 1, edited by M.L. Hoffmen, 289–322. New York: Russell Sage Foundation.

———. (1974). "Illness Is a Point of View: The Development of Children's Concepts of Illness." *Child Development* 46 (March): 92–100.

Campisi, P.J. (1947). "A Scale of the Measurement of Acculturation." Doctoral dissertation, University of Chicago.

Cannon, Kenneth C., Ruth Staples, and Irene Carlson (1952). "Personal Appearance as a Factor in Personal Acceptance." *Journal of Home Economics* 44 (November): 710–13.

Capon, Noel, and Deanna Kuhn (1980). "A Developmental Study of Consumer Information-Processing Strategies." *Journal of Consumer Research* 7 (December): 225–33.

Capon, Noel, Deanna Kuhn, and Maria Carmel Gurucharri (1981). "Consumer Information Processing Strategies in Middle and Late Adulthood." *Journal of Applied Developmental Psychology* 2, no. 1: 1–12.

Caron, Andre, and Scott Ward (1975). "Gift Decisions by Kids and Parents." *Journal of Advertising Research* 15 (August): 15–20.

Carter, J.H. (1982). "The Effects of Aging on Selected Visual Functions: Color Vision, Glare Sensitivity, Field of Vision, and Accommodation." In *Aging and Human Visual Function,* edited by R. Sekuler, D. Kline, and K. Dismukes, 121–30. New York: Alan R. Liss.

Carter, Richard F. (1965). "Communication and Affective Relations." *Journalism Quarterly* 42 (Spring): 203–12.

Cassata, M.B., P.A. Anderson, and T.D. Skill (1980). "The Older Adult in Daytime Social Drama." *Journal of Communication* 30 (Winter): 48–49.

Cateora, Phillip R. (1963). *An Analysis of the Teenage Market.* Austin, TX: Bureau of Business Research, University of Texas.

Cattell, Raymond B. (1978). *The Scientific Use of Factor Analysis in Behavioral and Life Sciences.* New York: Plenum Press.

Cervantes, F.J. (1980). "The Forgotten Consumers: The Mexican-Americans." In *Proceedings, 1980 Marketing Educators Conference,* edited by R. Bagozzi, L. Bernhardt, P. Bush, D. Cravens, J. Hair, Jr., and C. Scott, 180–83. Chicago: American Marketing Association.

Chaffee, Steven H. (1973). "Applying The Interpersonal Perception Model to the Real World." *American Behavioral Scientist* 16, (March/April): 465–68.

Chaffee, Steven H., and Jack M. McLeod (1968). "Sensitization in Panel Design: A Coorientational Experiment." *Journalism Quarterly* 45 (Winter): 661–69.

———. (1972). "Adolescent Television Use in the Family Context." In *Television and Social Behavior,* vol. 3: *Television and Adolescent Aggressiveness,* edited by G. Comstock and E. Rubinstein, 149–72. Washington: Government Printing Office.

———. (1973). "Consumer Decisions and Information Use." In *Consumer Behavior: Theoretical Sources,* edited by Scott Ward and Thomas Robertson, 385–415. Englewood Cliffs, NJ: Prentice-Hall.

Chaffee, Steven H., Jack M. McLeod, and Charles K. Atkin (1971). "Parental Influences on Adolescent Media Use." *American Behavioral Scientist* 14 (January/February): 323–40.

Chaffee, Steven, Jack McLeod, and Daniel B. Wackman (1966). "Family Communication and Political Socialization." Paper presented to the Association for Education in Journalism, Iowa City, Iowa.

Chaffee, Steven H., and Albert R. Tims (1976). "Interpersonal Factors in Adolescent Television Use." *Journal of Social Issues* 32, no. 4 (Fall): 98.

Chaffee, Steven H., L. Scott Ward, and Leonard P. Tipton (1970). "Mass Communication and Political Socialization." *Journalism Quarterly* 47 (Winter): 647–59.

Chaffee, S.H., and D. Wilson (1975). "Adult Life Cycle Changes in Mass Media Use." Paper presented to the Association for Education in Journalism, Ottawa, Ontario, Canada.

Chance, Norman (1965). "Acculturation, Self-Identification, and Personality Adjustment." *American Anthropologist* 67 (March): 372–93.

Chap, J.B., and J. Sinnot (1977–1978). "Performance of Institutionalized and Community Active Old Persons on Concrete and Formal Piagetian Tasks." *International Journal of Aging and Human Development* 8, no. 3: 269–78.

Chiles-Miller, Pamela (1975). "Reactions to Marital Roles in Commercials." *Journal of Advertising Research* 15 (August): 45–49.

Chinoy, Ely (1955). *Automobile Workers and the American Dream.* New York: Doubleday.

Christiansen, J.B. (1979). "Television Role Models and Adolescent Occupational Goals." *Human Communication Research* 5, no. 4 (Summer): 335–37.

Christman, R.J. (1979). *Sensory Experience.* 2d ed. New York: Harper & Row.

Churchill, Gilbert A., Jr., and George P. Moschis (1979). "Television and Interpersonal Influences on Adolescent Consumer Learning." *Journal of Consumer Research* 6 (June): 23–35.

Cicarelli, James (1974). "On Income, Race, and Consumer Behavior." *American Journal of Economics and Sociology* 33 (July): 243–48.

Clancy, J. (1975). "Preliminary Observations on Media Use and Food Habits of the Elderly." *Gerontologist* 15 (December): 529–32.

Clancy-Hepburn, K., A.A. Hickey, and G. Neville (1974). "Children's Behavior Responses to TV Food Advertisements." *Journal of Nutrition Education* 6 (September): 93–96.

Clark, Lincoln H., ed. (1955). *Consumer Behavior* vol. 2: *The Life Cycle and Consumer Behavior.* New York: New York University Press.

Clark, M., and B.G. Anderson (1967). *Culture and Aging: An Anthropological Study of Older Americans.* Springfield, IL: Charles C. Thomas.

Clarke, A.C. (1956). "The Use of Leisure and Its Relation to Levels of Occupational Prestige." *American Sociological Review* 21 (June): 301–06.

Clarke, P. (1971). "Children's Response to Entertainment: Effects of Co-orientation on Information Seeking." *American Behavioral Scientist* 14 (January/February): 353–69.

———. (1973). "Teenagers' Coorientation and Information Seeking About Pop Music." *American Behavioral Scientist* 16 (April): 551–66.

Clausen, J.A. (1967). "Introduction." In *Socialization and Society,* edited by J.A. Clausen, 3–17. Boston: Little Brown.

Clausen, John A. (1968a). "A Historical and Comparative View of Socialization Theory and Research." In *Socialization and Society,* 18–73. *See* Clausen 1967.

———. (1968b). "Perspectives on Childhood Socialization," in *Socialization and Society,* edited by John Clausen, 130–81. Boston: Little Brown.

Clayton, A. (1985). "Youth and Traffic Safety." *Alcohol, Drugs and Drinking* 1, no. 1–2 (June): 107–10.

Cobb, Cathy J. (1985). "Television Clutter and Advertising Effectiveness." In *AMA Educator's Proceedings,* edited by Robert F. Lusch et al., 41–47. Chicago: American Marketing Association.

Cobb, Henry V. (1954). "Role Wishes and General Wishes of Children and Adolescents." *Child Development* 25 (September): 161–71.

Colavita, F.B. (1978). *Sensory Change in the Elderly.* Springfield, IL: Charles C. Thomas.

Coleman, J.S. (1961). *The Adolescent Society.* New York: Free Press.

Coleman, Richard P. (1983). "The Continuing Significance of Social Class to Marketing." *Journal of Consumer Research* 10 (December): 265–80.

Coles, Robert (1986). "How TV Shapes Our Values." *TV Guide* (June): 5–7.

Comstock, G. (1978). "The Impact of Television on American Institutions." *Journal of Communication* 28 (Spring): 12–28.

Comstock, G., S. Chaffee, N. Katzman, M. Mccombs, and D. Roberts (1978). *Television and Human Behavior.* New York: Columbia University Press.

Cooley, Charles (1902). *Human Nature and the Social Order* Boston: Scribner.

———. (1912). *Social Organization.* New York: Scribner.

Copp, James H. (1965). "Family Backgrounds of Rural Youth." In *Rural Youth in Crisis: Facts, Myths, and Social Change,* edited by L.G. Burchinal, 35–44. Washington: Government Printing Office.

Corcoran, Mary, Christopher Jencks, and Michael Olneck (1976). "The Effects of Family Background on Earnings." *American Economic Review* 66 (May): 430–35.

Cort, Stanton, and Luis V. Dominguez (1977–1978). "Cross Shopping as Incremental Business in Concentric Growth Strategies." *Journal of Retailing* 53 (Winter): 3–16, 96.

Courtney, Alice E., and Thomas W. Whipple (1979). *Sex Stereotyping in Advertising: An Annotated Bibliography.* Cambridge, MA: Marketing Science Institute.

Cowgill, D. (1979). "The Reevaluation of Age." In *The Age of Aging: A Reader in Social Gerontology,* edited by A. Monk, 63–71. New York: Prometheus Books.

Cowgill, D., and N. Baulch (1962). "The Use of Leisure Time by Older People." *Gerontologist* 2 (March): 47–50.

Cox, Howard (1971). "A Study of the Influence of Consumer Characteristics Upon Buying Behavior in Competing Retail Establishments." In *Proceedings of the American Marketing Association,* vol. 33, edited by F. Allvine, 423–27. Chicago: American Marketing Association.

Crandall, J.J., S. Orleans, A. Preston, and A. Rabson (1958). "Development of Social Compliance in Young Children." *Child Development* 29 (September): 429–43.

Crockett, Jean (1976). "The Choice Between Spending and Saving." In *Selected Aspects of Consumer Behavior,* edited by Robert Ferber, 149–62. Washington: Government Printing Office.

Crosby, Richard W. (1969). "Attitude Measurement in a Bilingual Culture." *Journal of Marketing Research* 6 (November): 421–26.

Culley, J., and R. Bennett (1976). "Selling Women, Selling Blacks." *Journal of Communication* 26, no. 4 (Autumn): 160–74.

Cumming, Elaine, and W. Henry (1961). *Growing Old: The Process of Disengagement.* New York: Basic Books.

Cunningham, W.H., T.W. Anderson, and John H. Murphy (1974). "Are Students Real People?" *Journal of Business* 47 (July): 399–409.

The Dade Latin Market (1980). *The Dade Latin Market.* Miami: Strategy Research Corporation.

Dalrymple, Douglass J., Thomas S. Robertson, and Michael Y. Yoshino (1971). "Consumption Behavior Across Ethnic Categories." *California Management Review* 14 (Fall): 65–70.

Danowski, J. (1975). "Informational Aging: Implications for Alternative Features of Societal Information Systems." Paper presented at the International Communication Association Convention, Chicago.

Darden, W., and Dub Ashton (1974–1975). "Psychographic Profiles of Patronage Preference Groups." *Journal of Retailing* 50 (Winter): 99–112.

Darden, William R., John J. Lennon, and Donna K. Darden (1978). "Communicating with Interurban Shoppers." *Journal of Retailing* 54 (Spring): 51–63.

Darley, William F., and Jeen-Su Lim (1986). "Family Decision Making in Leisure-Time Activities: An Exploratory Investigation of the Impact of Locus of Control, Child Age Influence Factor and Parental Type of Perceived Child Influence." In *Advances in Consumer Research,* vol. 13, edited by Richard J. Lutz, 370–74. Provo, UT: Association for Consumer Research.

Davis, Harry L. (1971). "Measurement of Husband-Wife Influence in Consumer Purchase Decisions." *Journal of Marketing Research* 8 (August): 305–12.

———. (1976). "Decision Making Within the Household." *Journal of Consumer Research* 2 (March): 241–60.

Davis, R.H., and A.E. Edwards (1975). *Television: A Therapeutic Tool for the Aged.* Los Angeles: University of Southern California.

Davis, Richard H., A.E. Edwards, D.J. Bartel, and D. Martin (1976). "Assessing Television Viewing Behavior of Older Adults." *Journal of Broadcasting* 20 (Winter): 69–76.

Davis, Richard, and Robert W. Kubey (1982), "Growing Old on Television and With Television." In *Television and Behavior,* edited by D. Pearl, L. Bouthilet, and J. Lazar, 201–08. Rockville, MD: US Department of Health and Human Services.

DeFleur, M., and L. DeFleur (1967). "The Relative Contribution of Television as a Learning Source of Children's Occupational Knowledge." *American Sociological Review* 32: 777–89.

Denhardt, R.B., and P.W. Jeffress (1971). "Social Learning and Economic Behavior: The Process of Economic Socialization." *The American Journal of Sociology* 30: 113–26.

Dervin, B., and B.S. Greenberg (1972). "The Communication Environment of the Urban Poor." In *Current Perspectives in Mass Communication Research,* edited by F.G. Kline and P.J. Tichenor, 195–235. Beverly Hills, CA: Sage.

Deutsch, M., and H.B. Gerard (1955). "A Study of Normative and Informational Social Influence Upon Individual Judgment." *Journal of Abnormal and Social Psychology* 51: 629–36.

Dewey, J. (1922). *Human Nature and Conduct.* New York: Holt.

Dichter, Ernest (1962). "The World Customer." *Harvard Business Review* (July): 113–22.

Dimmick, John W., Thomas A. McCain, and W. Theodore Bolton (1979). "Media Use and the Life Span: Notes on Theory and Method." *American Behavioral Scientist* 23 (September/October): 7–31.

Dodge, Robert E. (1962). "Purchasing Habits and Market Potentialities of the Older Consumer." *Law and Contemporary Problems* 27 (Winter): 146–47.

Dollard, J. (1935). *Criteria for the Life History—With Analysis of Six Notable Documents.* New Haven, CT: Yale University Press.

——. (1939). "Culture, Society Impulse, and Socialization." *American Journal of Sociology* 45 (July): 50–63.

Dominick, J.R., and B.S. Greenberg (1970). "Mass Media Functions Among Low-Income Adolescents." In *Use of the Mass Media by the Urban Poor,* edited by B.S. Greenberg and B. Dervin, 31–49. New York: Praeger.

Dominick, J., and G. Rauch (1972). "The Image of Women in Network TV Commercials." *Journal of Broadcasting* 16 (Summer): 259–65.

Donohue, Thomas R. (1975a). "Effect of Commercials on Black Children." *Journal of Advertising Research* 15 (December): 41–47.

——. (1975b). "Emotionally Disturbed Adolescents' Perceptions of TV Characters as Models of Antisocial Behavior." Paper presented to the Speech Communication Association, Houston.

Donohue, T.R., W.A. Donohue, and T.P. Meyer (1976). "Black, White, White Gifted and Emotionally Disturbed Children's Perceptions of the Reality in TV Programming." Paper presented at the International Communication Association, Portland, OR.

Donohue, Thomas R., Timothy P. Meyer, and Lucy L. Henke (1978). "Black and White Children: Perceptions of TV Commercials." *Journal of Marketing* 42 (October): 34–40.

Donohue, William A., and Loretta Sheehan (1980). "A Model for Understanding the Impact of Conflict from Product Request Denials." Paper Presented at the Association for Education in Journalism Conference, Boston (August).

Doolittle, J.C. (1979). "News Media Used by Older Adults." *Journalism Quarterly* 56, no. 2 (Summer): 311–17, 345.

Dorvan, Elizabeth, and Joseph Adelson (1966). *The Adolescent Experience.* New York: Urley.

Douglas, Susan P. (1976). "Cross-National Comparisons and Consumer Stereotypes: A Case Study of Working and Non-Working Wives in the U.S. and France." *The Journal of Consumer Research* 3, no. 1 (June): 12–20.

——. (1977). "Do Working Wives Read Different Magazines from Non-Working Wives?" *Journal of Advertising* 6 (Winter): 40–43.

——. (1979). "A Cross National Exploration of Husband-Wife Involvement in Selected Household Activities." In *Advances in Consumer Research,* vol. 6, edited by W.L. Wilkie, 364–71. Ann Arbor, MI: Association for Consumer Research.

Dowd, J. (1980). *Stratification Among the Aged.* Monterey, CA: Brooks/Cole Publishing Company.

Dowd, J., R. Sisson, and D. Kern (1981). "Socialization to Violence Among the Aged." *Journal of Gerontology* 36, no. 3: 350–61.

Doyle, Peter, and Jan Fenwick (1974–1975). "How Store Image Affects Shopping Habits in Grocery Chains." *Journal of Retailing* 50 (Winter): 39–52.

Duesere, S. (1976). "The Effects of Television Advertising on Children's Eating Habits." Unpublished doctoral dissertation, University of Massachusetts, Amherst.

Duncan, Otis D. (1961). "A Socioeconomic Index of All Occupations." In *Occupations and Social Status,* edited by Albert J. Reiss, Jr., 109–38. New York: Free Press.

Dunn, Marie S. (1960). "Marriage Role Expectations of Adolescents." *Marriage and Family Living* 22: 99–104.

Dunn, S. Watson (1962). "French Retailing and the Common Market." *Journal of Marketing* 29 (January): 19–22.

Eisenstadt, S.N. (1962). "Archetypal Patterns of Youth." *Daedalus* (Winter): 28–46.

Elder, Glen N., Jr. (1968). *Adolescent Socialization and Personality Development.* Chicago: Rand McNally.

Elkind, D. (1967). "Egocentrism in Adolescence." *Child Development* 38: 1025–34.

Elliott, W.R., and C.P. Quattlebaum (1979). "Similarities in Patterns of Media Use: A Cluster Analysis of Media Gratification." *Western Journal of Speech Communication* 43: 61–72.

Ellis, Seth, James McCullough, Melanie Wallendorf, and Chion Tion Tan (1985). "Cultural Values and Behavior: Chineseness within Geographic Boundaries." In *Advances in Consumer Research*, vol. 12, edited by E. Hirschman and M. Holbrook, 126–28. Provo, UT: Association for Consumer Research.

Emmerich, Helen Jones (1978). "The Influence of Parents and Peers on Choices Made by Adolescents." *Journal of Youth and Adolescence* 7, no. 2 (June): 175–80.

Engel, James F., and Roger D. Blackwell (1982). *Consumer Behavior.* 4th ed. Hinsdale, IL: The Dryden Press.

Engel, James, Roger D. Blackwell, and David T. Kollat (1978). *Consumer Behavior.* New York: Holt, Rinehart and Winston.

Engel, James F., David T. Kollat, and Roger D. Blackwell (1973). *Consumer Behavior.* 2d ed. New York: Holt, Rinehart and Winston.

Enis, Ben, and G. Paul (1970). "Store Loyalty as a Basis for Market Segmentation." *Journal of Retailing* 46 (Fall): 42–56.

Eswara, H.S. (1968). "An Interpersonal Approach to the Study of Social Influence: Family Communication Patterns and Attitude Change." Unpublished doctoral dissertation, School of Journalism and Mass Communication, University of Wisconsin.

Exter, Thomas G. (1985). "50 Plus Discovers Diversity." *American Demographics* (February): 19, 42.

Faber, R.J., J.D. Brown, and J.M. McLeod (1979). "Coming of Age in the Global Village: Television and Adolescence." In *Children Communicating*, edited by E. Wartella, 215–49. Beverly Hills, CA: Sage.

Fannin, Rebecca (1985). "The Greening of the Maturity Market." *Marketing and Media Decisions* (March): 72–80, 146–52.

Fauman, B.C. (1966). "Determinants of Adolescents' Brand Preferences." Unpubilshed thesis, MIT Sloan School of Management.

Feldman, Laurence P., and Alvin D. Star (1968). "Racial Factors in Shopping Behavior." In *A New Measure of Responsibility for Marketing*, edited by Keith Cox and Ben Enis, 216–26. Chicago: American Marketing Association.

Ferber, M.A., and B.G. Birnbaum (1977). "The 'New Home' Economics: Retrospects and Prospects." *Journal of Consumer Research* 4, no. 1 (June): 19–28,

Ferber, Robert, ed. (1976). *Selected Aspects of Consumer Behavior.* Washington: National Science Foundation.

Ferguson, Clara B. (1975). "Preadolescent Children's Attitude Toward Television Commercials." *Studies in Marketing #21.* Austin, TX: Bureau of Business Research, University of Texas.

Feshbach, Norman, T.S. Jordan, A.S. Dillman, R. Choate, S. Feshbach, and M. Zolotow (1976). "The design of a Graphic to Convey Nutritional Information to Children: Pilot Studies." Council on Children, Media and Merchandising (October).

Festinger, L. (1954). "A Theory of Social Comparison Processes." *Human Relations* 72: 117–40.

Finch, C., and L. Hayflick, eds. (1977). *Handbook of the Biology of Aging.* New York: Van Nostrand.

Flavell, J.H. (1970). "Cognitive Changes in Adulthood." In *Life-Span Developmental Psychology: Research and Theory,* edited by L. Goulet and P. Baltes, 249. New York: Academic Press.

Flessati, Eugene, and Gregory Fouts (1985). "Effects of Time-Compressed Television and Children's Activity Levels on Observational Learning." A paper presented to the International Communication Association, Honolulu (May).

Fouts, G. (1984). "Time Alteration of Cartoon Viewing by Children." *Canadian Journal of Communication* 10, no. 2: 67–80.

Freedman, K., and J. Rothman (1979). *The "Slob" Campaign: An Experimental Approach to Drunk-Driving Mass Media Communications (Sydney, Australia).* New South Wales Department of Motor Transportation, Roseberry, New South Wales.

French, W.A., and M.R. Crask (1977)., "The Credibility of Media Advertising for the Elderly." In *Educators' Conference Proceedings,* edited by B.A. Greenberg and D.N. Bellenger, 74–77. Chicago: American Marketing Association.

Freuth, T., and P.E. McGhee (1975). "Traditional Sex Role Developmental and Amount of Time Spent Watching TV." *Developments Psychology* 11, no. 1 (January): 109.

Frideres, James S. (1973). "Advertising, Buying Patterns and Children." *Journal of Advertising Research* 13 (February): 34–36.

Friedman, M.P., and Ira M. Wasserman (1978). "A Community Survey of Purchase Experiences of Older Consumers." *Journal of Consumer Affairs* 12, no. 2 (Winter): 300–08.

Fritzche, David J. (1981). "An Analysis of Energy Consumption Patterns by Stage of Family Life Cycle." *Journal of Marketing Research* 18 (May): 227–32.

Fry, Joseph N., David C. Shaw, C. Kaehling Von Lanzenauer, and Cecil R. Dipchaud (1973). "Consumer Loyalty to Banks: A Longitudinal Study." *Journal of Business* 46 (October): 517–25.

Fujitake, A. (1978). "Television and Home Life." In *Hoso-Bunka Foundation Symposium on the Cultural Role of Broadcasting: Summary Report,* 53–61. Tokyo: Hoso-Bunka Foundation.

Fulgraff, B. (1978). "Social Gerontology in West Germany: A Review of Recent and Current Research." *Gerontologist* 18 (February): 42–58.

Galst, J., and M. White (1976). "The Unhealthy Persuader: The Reinforcing Value of Television and Children's Purchase Influence Attempts at the Supermarket." *Child Development* 47: 1089–96.

Gans, H.J. (1962). *The Urban Villagers.* New York: Free Press.

Gantz, W., H.M. Gartenberg, and C.K. Rainbow (1980). "Approaching Invisibility: The Portrayal of the Elderly in Magazine Advertisements." *Journal of Communication* 30 (Winter): 56–60.

Gavian, Ruth W., and Louis G. Nanassy (1955). "Economic Competence as Goal of Elementary School Education." *Elementary School Journal* 55 (January): 270–73.

Gelb, Betsy D. (1982). "Discovering the 65+ Consumer." *Business Horizon* 25, no. 3 (May/June): 42–46.

Gelb, Betsy D., Jae W. Hong, and George M. Zinkhan (1985). "Communications Effects of Specific Advertising Elements: An Update." In *Current Issues and Research in Advertising,* vol. 2, edited by James Leigh and Claude R. Martin, Jr., 75–98. Ann Arbor, MI: University of Michigan, Graduate School of Business, Division of Research.

Gelb, Betsy D., and Charles M. Pickett (1983). "Attitude-Toward-the-Ad: Link to Humor and to Advertising Effectiveness." *Journal of Advertising* 12, no. 2: 33–41.

Gene Reilly Group (1973a). *The Assumption by the Child of the Role of the Consumer.* Darien, CT: The Gene Reilly Group, Inc.

———. (1973b). "Meals and Snacking: The Child and What He Eats." The Child, vol. 2. Darien, Conn.: The Gene Reilly Group, Inc.

Gensch, Dennis H. (1970). "Media Factors: A Review Article." *Journal of Marketing Research* 7 (May): 216–25.

Gerbner, G., L. Gross, N. Signorielli, and M. Morgan (1980). "Aging with Television: Images on Television Drama and Conceptions of Social Reality." *Journal of Communication* 30 (Winter): 37–47.

Gerson, Walter M. (1966). "Mass Media Socialization Behavior." *Social Forces* 45 (September): 40–50.

Gerwirtz, Jacob L. (1969). "Mechanisms of Social Learning: Some Roles of Stimulation and Behavior in Early Human Development." In *Handbook of Socialization Theory and Research,* edited by David A. Goslin, 57–212. Chicago: Rand McNally.

Gibbs, Mary (1963). "Decision-Making Procedures by Young Consumers." *Journal of Home Economics* 55 (May): 359–60.

Gilkison, Paul (1965). "What Influences the Buying Behavior of Teenagers?" *Journal of Retailing* 41 (Fall): 33–41.

———. (1973). "Teenagers' Perceptions of Buying Frame of Reference: A Decade of Retrospect." *Journal of Retailing* 49 (Summer): 25–37.

Gillet, P.L., and R.A. Scott (1974). "Shopping Opinions of Mexican-American Consumers: A Comparative Analysis." In *1974 Combined Proceedings,* edited by R.C. Curhan, 135–41. Chicago: American Marketing Association.

Gilly, Mary C., and Valarie A. Zeithaml (1985). "The Elderly Consumer and Adoption of Technologies." *Journal of Consumer Research* 12 (December): 353–57.

Gilson, Edith (1982). "We're All Getting Older." *Madison Avenue* (October): 76–80.

Glass, D.C., J. Neulinger, and O.G. Brim (1974). "Birth Order, Verbal Intelligence, and Educational Aspiration." *Child Development* 45 (September): 807–11.

Glasser, Gerald J., and Gale D. Metzger (1981). "Radio Usage by Blacks: An Update." *Journal of Advertising Research* 21, no. 2 (April): 47–50.

Gold, M. (1970). *Delinquency in an American City.* Belmont, CA: Brooks/Cole Publishing Company.

Goldberg, Marvin E., and Gerald J. Gorn (1976). "Material vs. Social Preferences, Parent-Child Relations, and the Child's Emotional Response: Three Dimensions of Response to Children's TV Advertising." Unpublished paper, McGill University, Faculty of Management, Montreal.

———. (1978). "Some Unintended Consequences of TV Advertising to Children." *Journal of Consumer Research* 5, no. 1 (June): 22–29.

Goldberg, Marvin E., Gerald J. Gorn, and Wendy Gibson (1978). "TV Messages for Snack and Breakfast Foods: Do They Influence Children's Preferences?" *Journal of Consumer Research* 5 (September): 73–81.

Goldberg, Marvin E., Gerald J. Gorn, David S. Litvak, and Jerry A. Rosenblatt (1986). "TV and the Elderly: An Experiment Assessing the Effects of Informational and Emotional Appeals." In *Advances in Consumer Research,* vol. 13, edited by M. Houston and R. Lutz, 215–19. Provo, UT; Association for Consumer Research.

Goldman, A. (1974). "Outreach of Consumers and the Modernization of Urban Food Retailing in Developing Countries." *Journal of Marketing* 38 (October): 8–16.

———. (1977–1978). "The Shopping Style Explanation for Store Loyalty." *Journal of Retailing* 53 (Winter): 33–46, 94.

Goldstein, S. (1968). "The Aged Segment of the Market, 1950 and 1960." *Journal of Marketing* 32 (April: 62–68.

Goldthorpe, John M. et al. (1969). *The Affluent Worker in the Class Structure.* Cambridge, MA: Cambridge University Press.

Gordon, Milton M. (1947). "The Concept of Sub-Culture and Its Application." *Social Forces* 26 (October): 40–42.

Gordon, Wendy (1981). "The Life Style of the Affluent Middle Aged." *Admap* 17 (February): 71–74.

Gorn, Gerald J. (1982). "The Effects of Music in Advertising on Choice Behavior: A Classical Conditioning Approach." *Journal of Marketing* 46 (Winter): 94–101.

Gorn, Gerald J., and Marvin E. Goldberg (1976). "Children's TV Commercials and the Hierarchy of Effects Hypothesis." Unpublished paper, McGill University, Faculty of Management, Montreal.

———. (1977). "The Impact of Television Advertising on Children from Low Income Families." *Journal of Consumer Research* 4 (September): 86–88.

———. (1980). "Notes and Comments: Children's Responses to Repetitive Television Commercials." *Journal of Consumer Research* 6 (March): 421.

———. (1982a). "Behavioral Evidence of the Effects of Televised Food Messages on Children." *Journal of Consumer Research* 9 (September): 200–05.

———. (1982b). "Increasing the Involvement of Teenage Smokers in Anti-Smoking Campaigns." *Journal of Communication* 32, no. 1 (Spring): 75–86.

Gorney, R., D. Love, and G. Steele (1977). "Impact of Dramatized Television Entertainment on Adult Males." *American Journal of Psychiatry* 34 (February): 170–74.

Goslin, D.A., ed. (1969). *Handbook of Socialization Theory and Research.* Chicago: Rand McNally.

Granbois, Donald H., Dennis L. Rosen, and Franklin Acito (1986). "A Developmental Study of Family Financial Management Practices." In *Advances in Consumer Research,* vol. 13, edited by R. Lutz, 170–74. Provo, UT: Association of Consumer Research.

Graney, M., and E. Graney (1974). "Communications Activity Substitutions in Aging." *Journal of Communication* 24, no. 4 (Autumn): 88–96.

Graves, Theodore D. (1967). "Psychological Acculturation in a Tri-ethnic Community." *Southern Journal of Anthropology* 23 (Winter): 337–50.

Gredal, Karen (1966). "Purchasing Behavior in Households." *Readings in Danish Theory of Marketing,* edited by Max Kjaer-Hausen, 84–100. Copenhagen: Einar Harcks Fozlag.

Green, R.T., and I.C.M. Cunningham (1980). "Family Purchasing Roles in Two Countries: United States and Venezuela." *Journal of International Business Studies* 11 (Spring/Summer): 92–97.

Green, R.T., W.H. Cunningham, and I.C.M. Cunningham. (1975). "The Effectiveness of Standardized Global Advertising." *Journal of Advertising* 4, no. 3 (Summer): 25–29.

Green, Robert T., and Eric Langeard (1975). "A Cross-National Comparison of Consumer Habits and Innovator Characteristics." *Journal of Marketing* 39 (July): 34–41.

Green, Robert, Jean-Paul Leonardi, Jean-Louis Chandon, Isabella Cunningham, Bronis Verhage, and Alain Strazzieri (1983). "Societal Development and Family Purchasing Roles: A Cross-National Study." *Journal of Consumer Research* 9 (March): 436–42.

Green, R.T., B.J. Verhage, and I.C.M. Cunningham (1981). "Household Purchasing Decisions: How Do American and Dutch Consumers Differ?" *European Journal of Marketing* 15, no. 1: 68–77.

Greenberg, Bradley S. (1982). "Television and Role Socialization: An Overview." In *Television and Behavior*, edited by D. Pearl et al., 179–80. Rockville, MD: U.S. Department of Health and Human Services.

Greenberg, B.S., and B. Dervin (1970). "The Role of the Mass Media for Urban Poor Adults." In *The Use of Mass Media by the Urban Poor*, edited by B. Greenberg and B. Dervin, 3–29. New York: Praeger.

Greenberg, Bradly S., and J.R. Dominick (1969). "Race and Social Class Differences in Teenagers' Use of Television." *Journal of Broadcasting* 13 (Fall): 331–44.

Greenberg, Bradley S., and H. Kumata (1968). "National Sample Reductions of Mass Media Use." *Journalism Quarterly* 45 (Winter): 641–46.

Greenberg, Bradley S., and B. Reeves (1976). "Children and the Perceived Reality of Television." *Journal of Social Issues* 32, no. 4 (Fall): 86–97.

Guest, Lester P. (1942). "The Genesis of Brand Awareness." *Journal of Applied Psychology* 26 (December): 800–08.

———. (1944). "A Study of Brand Loyalty." *Journal of Applied Psychology* 28 (February): 16–27.

———. (1955). "Brand Loyalty: Twelve Years Later." *Journal of Applied Psychology* 39 (April): 93–97.

———. (1964). "Brand Loyalty Revisited: A Twenty Year Report." *Journal of Applied Psychology* 48 (April): 93–97.

Haefner, James E., and John J. Leckenby (1975). "Consumers' Use and Awareness of Consumer Protection Agencies." *Journal of Consumer Affairs* 9, no. 1 (Winter): 205–11.

Haefner, James E., John Leckenby, and Steven L. Goldman (1975). "The Measurement of Advertising Impact on Children." Paper presented at the American Psychological Association (August).

Hair, Franklin J., Jr., and Ralph E. Anderson (1972). "Culture, Acculturation and Consumer Behavior: An Empirical Study." In *1972 Combined Proceedings, American Marketing Association*, edited by Bonis W. Becker and Helmut Becker, 423–28. Chicago: American Marketing Association.

Haller, Archibald O., and Alejandro Portes (1973). "Status Attainment Processes." *Sociology of Education* 46 (Winter): 51–91.

Haller, Thomas F. (1974). "What Students Think of Advertising." *Journal of Advertising Research* 14 (February): 34–38.

Hamilton, Janice, and Jessie Warden (1966). "Student's Role in a High School Community and His Clothing Behavior." *Journal of Home Economics* 58: 781–91.

Harris, H.E., and J. Bodden (1978). "An Activity Group Experience for Disengaged Elderly Persons." *Journal of Consulting and Clinical Psychology* 24 (April): 325–30.

Hartup, Willard (1970). "Peer Interaction and Social Organization." In *Manual of Child Psychology*, vol. 2, 3d ed., edited by Paul H. Mussen, 361–456. New York: John Wiley and Sons.

Havighurst, Robert (1968). "A Social-Psychological Perspective on Aging." *Gerontologist* 8 (Spring): 67–71.

Hawes, D.K., S. Gromo, and J. Arndt (1978). "Shopping Time and Leisure Time: Some Preliminary Cross-Cultural Comparisons of Time Budget Expenditures." In *Advances in Consumer Research*, vol. 5, edited by K. Hunt, 151–59. Ann Arbor, MI: Association for Consumer Research.

Hawkins, Calvin H. (1977). "A Study of the Use of Consumer Education Concepts by High School Graduates." *Journal of Consumer Affairs* 11, no. 1 (Summer): 122–27.

Hawkins, Del I., and Kenneth A. Coney (1974). "Peer Group Influences on Children's Product Preferences." *Journal of the Academy of Marketing Science* 2, no. 2 (Spring): 322–30.

Hawkins, Robert P., and Suzanne Pingree (1982). "Television's Influence on Social Reality." In *Television and Behavior*, vol. 3, edited by David Pearl, Lorraine Bouthilet, and Joyce Lazar, 224–47. Rockville, MD: U.S. Department of Health and Human Services.

Heatherton, Todd, and Gregory Fouts (1985). "Television and the Older Viewer: Effects of Changes in the Visual and Auditory Systems." Paper presented to the International Communications Association, Honolulu (May).

Heinzerling, Barbara (1984). "ACCI Consumer Education Workshop." In *Proceedings of the American Council on Consumer Interests.* edited by K.P. Goebel, 222–25. Columbia, Mo: American Council on Consumer Interests.

Henderson, Caroline M., Robert Kopp, and Scott Ward (1980). "Influences on Children's Product Requests and Mothers' Answers: A Multivariate Analysis of Diary Data, "Report #80-106. Marketing Science Institute Research Program—A Working Paper" (September).

Hendricks, J., and C. Hendricks (1977). *Aging in Mass Society: Myths and Realities.* Cambridge, MA: Winthrop.

Henry, W.A. (1976). "Cultural Values Do Correlate with Consumer Behavior." *Journal of Marketing Research* 13 (May): 121–27.

Hepner, H. (1949). *Effective Advertising.* 2d ed. New York: McGraw-Hill.

Herberg, Will (1955). *Protestant, Catholic, Jew: An Essay in American Religious Sociology.* Garden City, NJ: Doubleday & Company.

Herbst, P.G. (1952). "The Measurement of Family Relationships." *Human Relations* 5 (February): 3–35.

Heskel, Dennis, and Richard J. Semenik (1983). "An Anthropological Perspective for Consumer Research Issues." In *1983 AMA Educators' Proceedings*, no. 49, edited by Patrick E. Murphy et al., 118–22. Chicago: American Marketing Association.

Hess, B. (1972). "Friendship." In *Aging and Society*, vol. 3, edited by M. Riley, M. Johnson, and A. Foner. New York: Russell Sage Foundation.

Hess, Robert D. (1970). "Social Class and Ethnic Influence Upon Socialization." In *Manual of Child Psychology*, 3rd ed., edited by Paul Mussen, 457–559. New York: John Wiley and Sons.

Hess, R.D., and J.V. Torney (1967). *The Development of Political Attitudes in Children.* Chicago: Aldine Publishing Company.

Hill, Reuben L. (1965). "Decision Making and the Family Life Cycle." In *Social Structure and the Family: Generational Relations*, edited by E. Shanas and G. Streib, 113–39. Englewood Cliffs, NJ: Prentice-Hall.

Hill, Reuben, and J. Alders (1969). "Socialization for Marriage and Parenthood." In *Handbook of Socialization Theory and Research*, edited by D. Goslin, 951–83. Chicago: Rand McNally.

Hill, Reuben, Alvin Katz, and Richard Simpson (1957). "An Inventory of Marriage and Family Research." *Marriage and Family Living* 19 (February): 89–92.

Hiltz, S.T. (1971). "Why Black Families Own Less Life Insurance," *Journal of Risk and Insurance*, 38, no. 2 (June): 225–33.

Himmelweit, H., A. Oppenheim, and P. Vince (1958). *Television and the Child.* London: Oxford.

Hirschman, Elizabeth C. (1979). "Differences in Consumer Purchase Behavior by Credit and Payment System." *Journal of Consumer Research* 6 (June): 58–66.

———. (1981). "American Jewish Ethnicity: Its Relationship to Some Selected Aspects of Consumer Behavior." *Journal of Marketing* 45 (Summer): 102–10.

———. (1985a). "Primitive Aspects of Consumption in Modern American Society." *Journal of Consumer Research* 12 (September): 142–54.

———. (1985b). "Ethnicity as a Predictor of Media Content Preferences." In *Proceedings of the AMA Educators' Winter Conference,* edited by Michael Houston and Richard Lutz, 209–14. Chicago: American Marketing Association.

———. (1986). "Marketing as an Agent of Change in Subsistence Cultures: Some Dysfunctional Consumption Consequences." In *Advances in Consumer Research,* vol. 13, edited by Rich Lutz, 99–104. Provo, UT: Association for Consumer Research.

Hisrich, Robert D., Ronald J. Dornoff, and Jerome B. Kernan (1972). "Perceived Risk in Store Selection." *Journal of Marketing Research* 9 (November): 435–39.

Hisrich, Robert D., and Michael P. Peters (1974). "Selecting the Superior Segmentation Correlate." *Journal of Marketing* 38 (July): 60–63.

Hoffman, L.W. (1972). "Early Childhood Experiences and Women's Achievement Motives." *Journal of Social Issues* 28, no. 2: 129–55.

Hornik, Jacob (1980). "Comparative Evaluation of International vs. National Advertising Strategies." *Columbia Journal of World Business* 15 (Spring): 36–45.

Hornik, Robert, Mark Gonzalez, and June Gould (1980). "Susceptibility to Media Effects." Paper presented at International Communication Association Conference, Acapulco.

House, A.S., C. Williams, H. Hecker, and K. Kryter (1965). "Articulation-Testing Methods: Consonantal Differentiation with a Closed-Response Set." *Journal of Acoustical Society of America* 37: 158–66.

Howard, John A., James Hulbert, and D.R. Lehmann (1973). "An Exploratory Analysis of the Effect of Television Advertising on Children." In *AMA Educators' Proceedings,* edited by B. Greenberg and D. Bellenger, 465–70. Chicago: American Marketing Asociation.

———. (1977). "An Exploratory Analysis of the Effect of Televison Advertising on Children.' A working paper described in Adler et al. 1977, 184.

Howard, J., and J. Sheth (1969). *The Theory of Buyer Behavior.* New York: John Wiley and Sons.

Hoy, Mariea Garebbs, and Raymond P. Fisk (1985). "Older Consumers and Services: Implications for Marketers." In *AMA Educators Proceedings,* edited by Robert F. Lusch et al., 50–55. Chicago: American Marketing Association.

Hoyer, Wayne D., and Rohit Deshpande (1982). "Cross-Cultural Influences on Buyer Behavior: The Impact of Hispanic Ethnicity." In *AMA Educators Conference Proceedings,* edited by B. Walker, W. Bearden, W. Darden, P. Murphy, J. Nevin, J. Olson, and B. Weitz, 89–92. Chicago: American Marketing Association.

Hulbary, W.E. (1975). "Race, Deprivation and Adolescent Self-Images." *Social Science Quarterly* 56, no. 1 (June): 105–14.

Hulbert, James (1974). "Applying Buyer Behavior Analysis to Social Problems: The Case of Drug Use." In *Proceedings of the American Marketing Association,* edited by Ronald C. Curhan, 289–92. Chicago: American Marketing Association.

Hur, K.K., and S.J. Baran (1979). "One-Parent Children's Identification with Television Characters and Parents." *Communication Quarterly* 27, no. 3 (Summer): 31–36.

Hurlock, Elizabeth B. (1955). *Adolescent Development.* New York: McGraw-Hill.

——. (1968). *Developmental Psychology.* 3d ed. New York: McGraw-Hill.

Hurt, Mary Lee (1961). *Teenagers and Their Money.* Washington: National Education Association.

Inkeles, Alex (1968). "Society, Social Structure and Child Socialization." In *Socialization and Society,* edited by John A. Clausen, 73–219. Boston: Little Brown.

——. (1969). "Social Structure and Socialization." In *Handbook of Socialization Theory and Research,* edited by D.A. Goslin, 615–32. Chicago: Rand McNally.

Isler, Leslie, Edward Pappa, and Scott Ward (1977). "Children's Purchase Requests Methods Report." *Research Briefs.* Cambridge, MA: Marketing Science Institute.

James, Alice, Herbert H. Lehman, and William L. James (1985). "Gift Giving in Rural Ireland: An Analysis of Necoprioty." In *AMA Educator's Proceedings,* edited by Robert F. Lusch, G. Ford, G. Frazier, R. Howell, C. Ingene, M. Reilly, and R. Stampfl, 26–47. Chicago, IL: American Marketing Association.

James, Don L. (1971). *Youth, Media, and Advertising.* Austin, TX: Bureau of Business Research, University of Texas.

Jaworski, Bernard, and William J. Sauer (1985). "Cohort Variation." In *Advances in Consumer Research,* vol. 12, edited by E. Hirschman and M. Holbroook, 32–36. Provo, UT: Association for Consumer Research.

Jennings, Kent M., and Richard G. Niemi (1968). "Patterns of Political Learning." *Howard Educational Review* 38 (Summer): 443–67.

Johnston, John (1971). *Econometric Methods.* 2d ed. New York: McGraw-Hill.

Joseph, Benoy W. (1982). "The Credibility of Physically Attractive Communications: A Review." *Journal of Advertising* 1, no. 3: 15–24.

Kagan, Jerome (1977). "The Child in the Family." *Daedalus* (Spring): 33–56.

Kagan, Jerome, and Howard Moss (1962). *Birth to Maturity.* New York: John Wiley and Sons.

Kahl, Joseph A. (1953). "Educational and Occupational Aspirations of 'Common Man' Boys." *Harvard Educational Review* 23, no. 3, (Summer): 186.

Kahle, Lynn R.C. (1986). "The Nine Nations of North America and the Value Basis of Geographic Segmentation." *Journal of Marketing* 50 (April): 37–47.

Kahle, Lynn R., and Pamela Homer (1985). "Androgyny and Midday Mastication: Do Real Men Eat Quiche?" In *Advances in Consumer Research,* vol. 12, edited by E. Hirschman and M. Holbrook, 242–46. Provo, UT: Association for Consumer Research.

Kandel, Denise, and Gerald S. Lesser (1972). *Youth in Two Worlds.* San Francisco: Jossey-Bass.

Kassarjian, H. (1971). "Personality and Consumer Behavior: A Review." *Journal of Marketing Research* 81 (November): 409–18.

Katona, George, and Eva Mueller (1955). " A Study of Purchase Decisions." In *Consumer Behavior: The Dynamics of Consumer Reaction,* edited by Lincoln Clark, 30–87. New York: New York Univesity Press.

Katz, E., and P.L. Lazarsfeld (1955). *Personal Influence.* Glencoe, IL: The Free Press.

Katz, Elihu, Jay G. Blumler, and Michael Gurevitch (1974). "Utilization of Mass Communication by the Individual." In *The Uses of Mass Communications,* edited by J.G. Blumler and E. Katz, 19–34. Beverly Hills, CA: Sage.

Katz, F.M. (1964). "The Meaning of Success: Some Differences in Value Systems of Social Classes." *Journal of Social Psychology* 62 (February): 141–48.

Keiser, Stephen K., and P.G. Kuehl (1972). "Social Class and Income Influences on External Search Processes of Adolescents." In *Proceedings, Third Annual Conference of the Association for Consumer Research*, edited by M. Venkatesan, 602–31. Iowa City: Association for Consumer Research.

Kelly, Robert F. (1967). "The Role of Information in the Patronage Decision: A Diffusion Phenomenon." In *Marketing for Tomorrow . . . Today*, edited by M.S. Mayer and R.E. Vosbuzgh, 119–29. Chicago: American Marketing Association.

Kelman, H.C. (1961). "Processes of Opinion Change." *Public Opinion Quarterly* 25 (Spring): 57–78.

Kenkel, W.F. (1961). "Family Interaction in Decision Making on Spending." In *Household Decision-Making*, edited by Nelson N. Foote, 140–64. New York: New York University Press.

Kimmel, D.C. (1974). *Adulthood and Aging.* New York: John Wiley and Sons.

King, Robert L., and Earl Robert DeManche (1969). "Comparative Acceptance of Selected Private-Branded Food Products by Low-Income Negro and White Families." In *Marketing Involvement in Society*, edited by R.R. McDonald, 63–69. Chicago: American Marketing Association.

Kizilbash, A.H., and E.T. Garman (1975–1976). "Grocery Retailing in Spanish Neighborhoods." *Journal of Retailing* 51 (Winter): 15–21.

Klapper, Joseph T. (1960). *The Effects of Mass Communication.* New York: Free Press.

Klemke, Lloyd W. (1982). "Exploring Juvenile Shoplifting." *Sociology and Social Research* 67, no. 1: 59–75.

Kline, F.G. (1971). "Media Time Budgeting as a Function of Demographics and Life Style." *Journalism Quarterly* 48 (Summer): 211–21.

Kline, F.G., P.V. Miller, and A.J. Morrison (1974). "Adolescents and Family Planning Information: An Exploration of Audience Needs and Media Effects." In *The Uses of Mass Communications*, edited by J. Blumler and E. Katz, 113–136. Beverly Hills, CA: Sage.

Klippel, E., and J. Sweeney (1974). "Use of Information Sources by the Aged Consumer." *Gerontologist* 14 (April): 163–66.

Kogan, Nathan (1973). *Creativity and Cognitive Style: A Life-Span Perspective.* edited by Paul B. Baltes and K.W. Schaie. New York: New School for Social Research.

Kohlberg, Lawrence (1969). "Stage and Sequence: The Cognitive Developmental Approach to Socialization." In *Handbook of Socialization Theory and Research*, edited by D.A. Goslin, 347–480. Chicago: Rand McNally.

———. (1973). "Continuities in Childhood and Adult Moral Development Revisited." In *Life-Span Developmental Psychology: Personality and Socialization*, edited by V.L. Bengston and D.K. Black, 179–204. New York: Academic Press.

———. (1976). "Moral Stages and Moralization: The Cognitive-Developmental Approach." In *Moral Development and Behavior: Theory, Research and Social Issues*, edited by T. Lickona, 31–53. New York: Holt, Rinehart and Winston.

Kohn, M.L. (1963). "Social Class and Parent-Child Relationships." *American Journal of Sociology* 68, no. 4 (January): 471–80.

Korgaonkar, Pradeep, and George P. Moschis (1986). "The Effects of Perceived Risk and Social Class on Consumer Preferences for Distribution Outlets." Working paper, Florida Atlantic University College of Business, Boca Raton.

Krugman, Herbert E. (1965). "The Impact of Advertising: Learning Without Involvement." *Public Opinion Quarterly* 29 (Fall): 349–56.

Kubey, R.W. (1980). "Television and Aging: Past, Present and Future." *Gerontologist* 20 (January): 16–35.

Kuhn, Manford H. (1954). "Factors in Personality: Socio-Cultural Determinants as Seen Through the Amish." In *Aspects of Culture and Personality,* edited by F.L.K. Hsu, 43–65. New York: Abeard-Schumann, Inc.

Kuypers, J., and V. Bengston (1973). "Social Behavior and Competence: A Mode of Normal Aging." *Human Development* 16, no. 3: 181–201.

LaForge, M., W. French, and M. Crask (1981). "Segmenting the Elderly Market." Paper presented to the American Institute for Decision Sciences Conference, Boston (December).

Laing, R.D., H. Phillipson, and A.R. Lee (1966). *Interpersonal Perception: A Theory and Method of Research.* New York: Springer.

Lambert, Zarrel V. (1979). "An Investigation of Older Consumers' Unmet Needs and Wants at the Retail Level." *Journal of Retailing* 55 (Winter): 35–57.

———. (1980). "Elderly Consumers' Knowledge Related to Medigap Protection Needs." *Journal of Consumer Affairs* 14 no. 2 (Winter): 434–51.

Lambiri, Ioanna (1967). *Social Change in a Greek Country Town.* Monograph no. 13. Athens: Center for Productivity and Economic Research.

Langrehr, Frederick W. (1979). "Consumer Education: Does It Change Students' Competencies and Attitudes?" *Journal of Consumer Affairs* 13, no. 1 (Summer): 41–53.

Langrehr, Frederick W., and Barry Mason (1977). "The Development and Implementation of the Concept of Consumer Education." *Journal of Consumer Affairs* 11 (Winter): 63–79.

Langton, Kenneth (1969). *Political Socialization.* New York: Oxford University Press.

Langton, Kenneth P., and Kent Jennings (1973). *Socialization to Politics: A Reader.* edited by Jack Dennis. New York: John Wiley and Sons.

Larson, C., and H. Wales (1970). "Slogan Awareness in the Chicago Market." *Journal of Advertising Research* 10, no. 6 (December): 38–43.

Larson, Lyle E. (1972). "The Relative Influence of Parent-Adolescent Affect in Predicting the Salience Hierarchy Among Youth." *Pacific Sociological Review* 15, no. 1 (January): 83–102.

Laughlin, Meagan, and Roger Jon Desmond (1981). "Social Interaction in Advertising Directed to Children." *Journal of Broadcasting* 25, (Summer): 303–07.

Laurent, Clint R. (1985). "A Comparison of Consumer Attitudes Within Hong Kong Society." In *Historical Perspective in Consumer Research,* edited by Chin Tiong Tan and N. Sheth, 331–35. Singapore: National University of Singapore.

Lavidge, R.J., and G.A. Steiner (1965). "A Model for Predictive Measurement of Advertising Effectiveness." *Journal of Marketing* 25, no. 4 (October): 45–55.

Lawton, J.T. (1977). "The Use of Advance Organizers in the Learning and Retention of Logical Operations and Social Studies Concepts." *American Educational Research Journal* 14 (winter): 25–43.

Lazar, William, and Robert Wyckham (1969). "Perpetual Segmentation of Department Store Market." *Journal of Retailing* 45 (Summer): 3–14.

Lemmon, Bruce W., Vern Bengston, and James Peterson (1972). "An Exploration of the Activity Theory of Aging: Activity Types of Life Satisfaction Among In-Movers to a Retirement Community." *Journal of Gerontology* 27 (October): 511–23.

Lepisto, Lawrence R. (1985). "A Life-Span Perspective of Consumer Behavior." In *Advances in Consumer Research*, vol. 12, edited by E. Hirschman and M. Holbrook, 47–52. Provo, UT: Association for Consumer Research.

Levine, Adeline (1976). "Educational and Occupational Choice: A Synthesis of Literature from Sociology and Psychology." In *Selected Aspects of Consumer Behavior*, edited by R. Ferber, 131–48. Washington: Government Printing Office.

Levy, Sidney J. (1966). "Social Class and Consumer Behavior." In *On Knowing the consumer*, edited by J.W. Newman, 55–57. New York: John Wiley and Sons.

Lewin, K. (1951). *Field Theory and Social Science: Selected Theoretical Papers*, edited by D. Cartwright. New York: Harper & Row.

Liebert, R.M., J.M. Neale, and E.S. Davidson (1973). *The Early Window: Effects of Television on Children and Youth.* New York: Pergamon.

Lipman, A. (1961). "Role Perceptions and Morale of Couples in Retirement." *Journal of Gerontology* 16 (July): 267–71.

Loether, H.J. (1975). *Problems of Aging: Sociological and Social Psychological Perspectives.* 2d ed. Encino, CA: Dickenson Publishing Co.

London, L. (1976). "The Senior Citizen: An Underdeveloped Market Segment." In *Proceedings*, edited by H. Nash and D. Tobin, 124–26. Southern Marketing Association and Mississippi State University.

Long, Huey B. (1980). "In Search of a Theory of Adult Cognitive Development." *Journal of Research and Development in Education* 13 (Spring): 1–10.

Long, H., K. McCrary, and S. Ackerman (1980). "Adult Cognitive Development: A New Look at Piagetian Theory." *Journal of Research and Development in Education* 13 (Spring): 11–20.

Longman, D.S., and H.O. Pruden (1972). "Alienation from the Marketplace: A Study in Black, Brown, and White." In *Combined Proceedings 1971 Spring and Fall Conferences*, edited by F.C. Allvine, 616–19. Chicago: American Marketing Association.

Lorimore, E.S., and S.W. Dunn (1968–1969). "Use of the Mass Media in France and Egypt." *Public Opinion Quarterly* 32 (Winter): 680–87.

Loudon, D.L., and A.J. Della-Bitta (1979). *Consumer Behavior: Concepts and Applications.* New York: McGraw-Hill.

Louis Harris and Associates, Inc. (1975). *The Myth and Reality of Aging in America.* Washington: National Council on Aging.

Lull, James (1980a). "The Social Uses of Television." *Human Communication Research* 6 (Spring): 197–209.

———. (1980b). "Family Communication Patterns and the Social Uses of Television." Paper presented at Conference of International Communication Association, Acapulco.

Lumpkin, James R., and Barnett A. Greenberg (1982). "Apparel Shopping Patterns of the Elderly Consumer." *Journal of Retailing* 58, no. 4 (Winter): 68–89.

Lumpkin, James R., Barnett A. Greenberg, and Jac L. Goldstucker (1985). "Marketplace Needs of the Elderly: Determinant Attributes and Store Choice." *Journal of Retailing* 61, no. 2 (Summer): 75–105.

Lyle, J., and H.R. Hoffman (1972). "Children's Use of Television and Other Media." In *Television and Social Behavior*, vol. 4: Television in Day-to-Day Life: Patterns of Use, edited by E. Rubinstein, G. Comstock, and J. Murray, 129–257. Washington: Government Printing Office.

Lynn, D.B. (1959). " A Note on Sex Differences in the Development of Masculine and Feminine Identification." *Psychological Review* 66 (March): 126–35.

McCall, Luzanne H. (1977). "Meet the Workwife." *Journal of Marketing* 41 (July): 55–65.

McCandless, Boyd R. (1969). "Childhood Socialization." In *Handbook of Socialization Theory and Research*, edited by D. Goslin, 791–819. Chicago: Rand McNally.

McClelland, David C. (1961). *The Achieving Society*. New York: Free Press.

Maccoby, E.E. (1954). "Why Do Children Watch Television?" *Public Opinion Quarterly* 18, no. 3 (Fall): 239–44.

———. (1968). "The Development of Moral Values and Behavior in Childhood." In *Socialization and Society*, edited by J.A. Clousen, 227–69. Boston: Little Brown.

McCombs, M.E., and D.L. Shaw (1972). "The Agenda-Setting Function of Mass Media." *Public Opinion Quarterly* 36 (Summer): 176–87.

McCombs, M.E., and D. Weaver (1973). "Voter's Need for Orientation and Use of Mass Media." Paper presented to the International Communication Association, Montreal.

McCullough, James, Ching Tiong Tan, and John Wong (1986). "Effect of Stereotyping in Cross Cultural Research: Are the Chinese Really Chinese?" In *Advances in Consumer Research*, vol. 13, edited by Rich Lutz, 576–78. Provo, UT: Association for Consumer Research.

McGhee, James D. (1984). "A Profile of the Black, Single, Female-Headed Household." In *The State of Black America*, edited by J.D. Williams. New York: National Urban League.

McGuire, William J. (1969). "The Nature of Attitudes and Attitude Change." In *The Handbook of Social Psychology*, vol. 3, 2d ed., edited by G. Lindsey and E. Aronson, 136–314. Reading, MA: Addison-Wesley.

———. (1974). "Psychological Motives and Communication Gratification." In *The Uses of Mass Communications*, edited by J.G. Blumler and E. Katz, 167–96. Beverly Hills, CA: Sage.

McLeod, Jack M. (1974). "Commentaries on Ward, 'Consumer Socialization.' " *Journal of Consumer Research* 1 (September): 15–16.

McLeod, Jack M., and Lee B. Becker (1974). "Testing the Validity of Media Gratification Through Political Effects Analysis." In *The Uses of Mass Communications*, edited by J.G. Blumler and E. Katz, 137–66. Beverly Hills, CA: Sage.

McLeod, Jack M., Carl R. Bybee, and Jean A. Duvall (1982). "Evaluating Media Performance by Gratifications Sought and Received." *Journalism Quarterly* 60, no. 1 (Spring): 3–12.

McLeod, Jack M., and Steven H. Chaffee (1972). "The Construction of Social Reality." In *The Social Influence Process*, edited by J.T. Tedeschi, 50–99. Chicago: Aldine-Atherton.

———. (1973). "Interpersonal Approaches to Communication Research." *American Behavioral Scientist* 16 (April): 469–99.

McLeod, Jack M., Mary Ann Fitzpatrick, Carroll J. Glynn, and Susan F. Fallis (1982). "Television and Social Relations: Family Influences and Consequences for Interpersonal Behavior." In *Television and Behavior*, edited by D. Pearl et al., 272–86. Rockville, MD: U.S. Department of Health and Human Services.

McLeod, Jack M., and Garrett O'Keefe, Jr. (1972). "The Socialization Perspective and Communication Behavior." In *Current Perspectives in Mass Communication Research*, edited by G. Kline and P. Tichenor, 121–68. Beverly Hills, CA: Sage.

McLeod, Jack, Scott Ward, and Karen Tancil (1965–1966). "Alienation and Uses of the Mass Media." *Public Opinion Quarterly* (Winter): 583–94.

McMahon, James (1976). "Buying Behavior of the Older American Consumer." *Hearing Rehabilitation Quarterly* (Winter): 12–14.

McMillan, Pat, and George P. Moschis (1985). *The Silver Wave: A Look at the 55+ Consumer Market.* Atlanta: BellSouth Corp.

McNeal, James U. (1964). *Children as Consumers.* Marketing Study Series no. 9. Austin, TX: Bureau of Business Research, University of Texas.

———. (1969). "An Exploratory Study of the Consumer Behavior of Children." In *Dimensions of Consumer Behavior,* 2d ed., edited by J.U. McNeal, 255–85. New York: Appleton-Century-Crofts.

McQuail, D., and M. Gurevitch (1974). "Explaining Audience Behavior: Three Approaches Considered." In *The Uses of Mass Communications,* edited by J.G. Blumler and E. Katz. Beverly Hills, CA: Sage.

Madden, Thomas J., and Marc G. Weinberger (1984). "Humor in Advertising: A Practitioner View." *Journal of Advertising Research* 24, no. 4 (August/September): 23–29.

Maddox, G.L., Jr. (1964). "Disengagement Theories: A Critical Evaluation." *Gerontologist* 4 (March): 80–82, 103.

Madison Avenue (1980). "Seventeen Makes a Sales Call." *Madison Avenue* 22, no. 10 (November): 85, 88–91, 94–95.

Maki, M.J., A. Tallqvist, and J. Prigogine (1975). Prepared for Organization for Economic Cooperation and Development. *Young Driver Accidents: A Report.* Paris: OECD, Road Research Group.

Marmor, M. (1977). "The Eye and Vision in the Elderly." *Geriatrics* 32: 63–67.

Marquez, F.T. (1979). "Cross-Cultural Research: A Decision Factor in Standardized Versus Non-Standardized Global Advertising." *Gazette* 25, no. 3: 150–62.

Marshall, Helen, and Lucille Magruder (1960). "Relations Between Parent, Money, Education Practices and Children's Knowledge and Use of Money." *Child Development* 31 (June): 253–84.

Martin, B. (1975b). "Parent-Child Relations." In *Review of Child Development Research,* vol. 4, edited by F.D. Horonitz, 463–540. Chicago: University of Chicago Press.

Martin, Claude R., Jr. (1975a). "A Trans-Generational Comparison: The Elderly Fashion Consumer." In *Advances in Consumer Research,* vol. 3, edited by B. Anderson, 453–56. Cincinnati, OH: Association for Consumer Research.

Mason, J.B., and W.O. Bearden (1978). "Profiling the Shopping Behavior of Elderly Consumers." *Gerontologist* 18 (October): 454–61.

Mason, J.B., and B.E. Smith (1974). "An Exploratory Note on the Shopping Behavior of the Low Income Senior Citizen." *Journal of Consumer Affairs* 8 (Winter): 204–10.

Mason, Karen O., John L. Czajka, and Sara Arber (1976). "Change in U.S. Women's Sex-Role Attitudes 1964–1974." *American Sociological Review* 41 (August): 573–96.

Matosian, Jackline (1982). "Effectiveness of Different Coupon Delivery Methods in Building Mass Transit Ridership." *Journal of Advertising Research* 22 (June/July): 54–56.

Mauldin, C. (1976). "Communication and the Aging Consumer." In *Aging and Communication,* edited by H.J. Oyer and E.J. Oyer, 119–28. Baltimore: University Press.

Mauro, J.B. (1979). "Newspaper Readership Among Public School Children Grades 7–12." *American Newspaper Publishers Association News Research Report no. 23,* 7. Washington: ANPA News Research Center (October 31).

Mayer, Robert N., and Russell Belk (1982). "Acquisition of Consumption Stereotypes by Children." *Journal of Consumer Affairs* 16, no. 2 (Winter): 307–21.

Mayes, Sandra L., and K.B. Valentine (1979). "Sex Role Stereotyping in Staurday Morning Cartoon Shows." *Journal of Broadcasting* 23 (Winter): 41–50.

Mead, G.H. (1934). *Mind, Self, and Society.* Chicago: University of Chicago Press.

Mead, M. (1970). *Culture and Commitment: A Study of the Generation Gap.* Garden City, NY: Doubleday.

Meadow, H.L., S. Cosmas, and A. Plotkin (1981). "The Elderly Consumers: Past, Present, and Future." In *Advances in Consumer Research,* vol. 8, edited by K. Monroe, 742–47. Ann Arbor, MI: Association for Consumer Research.

Media Decisions (1977). "Don't Overlook the $200 Billion 55-Plus Market." *Media Decisions* (October): 59–61, 116–122.

Mehrotra, Sunil, and Sandra Torges (1977). "Determinants of Children's Influence on Mothers' Buying Behavior." In *Advances in Consumer Research,* vol. 4, edited by W. Perreault, 56–60. Atlanta, GA: Association for Consumer Research.

Mehta, Subhash C., and Kam Ah Keng (1985). "Correlates of Materialism: A Study of Singapore Chinese." In *Historical Perspective in Consumer Research,* edited by Chin Tiong Tan and N. Sheth, 326–30. Singapore: National University of Singapore.

Mendelsohn, H. (1968). *Radio in Contemporary American Life.* Denver, Co: Communications Arts Center, University of Denver.

Merton, Robert K. (1957). *Social Theory and Social Structure.* Glencoe, IL: The Free Press.

Messina, Irene, and Marshall E. Reddick (1980). *Mexican-American Buyer Behavior.* Los Angeles: Bureau of Business and Economic Research.

Meyer, Timothy P., Thomas J. Donohue, and Lucy L. Henke (1978). "How Black Children See TV Commercials." *Journal of Advertising Research* 18 (October): 51–58.

Milavsky, J. Ronald, Berton Pekowsky, and Horst Stipp (1975–1976). "TV Drug Advertising and Proprietary and Illicit Drug Use Among Teenage Boys." *Public Opinion Quarterly* 39 (Winter): 457–81.

Miller, D.L. (1955). "The Life Cycle and the Impact of Advertising." In *The Life Cycle and Consumer Behavior,* edited by L.W. Clark, 61–65. New York: New York University Press.

Miller, D.R., and G.E. Swanson (1958). *The Changing American Parent.* New York: John Wiley and Sons.

Miller, John P. (1978). "Piaget, Kohlberg and Erickson: Developmental Implications for Secondary Education." *Adolescence* 13, no. 50 (Summer): 237–50.

Miller, N.E., and J. Dollard (1941). *Social Learning and Imitation.* New Haven, CT: Yale University Press.

Miller, Patricia (1979). "Female Delinquency: Fact and Fiction." In *Female Adolescent Development,* edited by Max Sugar, 126. New York: Brunner/Mazel Publishers.

Milliman, Ronald M. (1982). "Using Background Music to Affect the Behavior of Supermarket Shoppers." *Journal of Marketing* 46 (Summer): 86–91.

Millson, C.A. (1966). "Conformity to Peers Versus Adults in Early Adolescence." Doctoral dissertation, Cornell University.

Moore, Bernice M., and Wayne H. Holtzman (1965). "Youth Present a Case for Education for Homemaking and Family Life." In *Tomorrow's Parents: A Study of Youth and Their Families,* edited by Bernice M. Moore and Wayne H. Holtzman, 231–54. Austin, TX: University of Texas Press.

Moore, Roy L., and George P. Moschis (1978a). "Teenagers' Reaction to Advertising." *Journal of Advertising* 7 (Fall): 24–30.

——. (1978b). "Family Communication Patterns and Consumer Socialization." Paper presented to the Mass Communication and Society Division, Association for Education in Journalism Annual Convention, Seattle (August).

——. (1979a). "Social Interaction and Social Structural Determinants in Adolescent Consumer Socialization." Paper presented at the Annual Conference of the Association for Consumer Research, San Francisco, CA (October).

——. (1979b). "Role Perceptions in Adolescent Consumer Learning." *Home Economics Research Journal* 8 (September): 66–74.

——. (1980). "Family and Media Influences in Consumer Socialization." Paper presented at International Communication Association 30th International Conference on Communication, Acapulco, (May).

——. (1981a). "The Impact of Newspaper Reading on Adolescent Consumers." *Newspaper Research Journal* 2, no. 4 (July): 1–8.

——. (1981b). "The Effects of Family Communication and Mass Media Use on Adolescent Consumer Learning." *Journal of Communication* 31, no. 4 (Fall): 42–51.

——. (1983). "Role of Mass Media and the Family in Development of Consumption Norms." *Journalism Quarterly* 80, no. 1 (Spring): 67–73.

Moore, Roy L., Goerge P. Moschis, and Lowndes F. Stephens (1975). "An Exploratory Study of Consumer Role Perceptions in Adolescent Consumer Socialization." Paper presented at the International Communication Association Conference, Chicago (April).

Moore, Roy L., and Lowndes F. Stephens (1975). "Some Communication and Demographic Determinants of Adolescent Consumer Learning." *Journal of Consumer Research* 2 (September): 80–92.

Moore, Roy L., Lowndes F. Stephens, and George P. Moschis (1976). "Mass Media and Interpersonal Influence in Adolescent Consumer Socialization." Paper presented to Mass Communication Division, International Communication Association, Portland, OR (April).

Moroz, Paul (1979). "Discovering the Over-55 Set." *Business Week* (November): 194–95.

Morrison, A.J. (1979). "Mass Media Use by Adults." *American Behavioral Scientist* 23, no. 1 (September/October): 71–93.

Moschis, George P. (1976a). "Acquisition of the Consumer Role by Adolescents." Unpublished doctoral dissertation, Graduate School of Business, University of Wisconsin, Madison.

——. (1976b). "Social Comparison and Informal Group Influence." *Journal of Marketing Research* 13 (August): 237–44.

——. (1976c). "Shopping Orientations and Consumer Uses of Information." *Journal of Retailing* 52 (Summer): 61–70, 93.

——. (1978a). *Acquisition of the Consumer Role by Adolescents.* Research Monograph no. 82. Atlanta: Bureau of Business Research, Georgia State University.

——. (1978b). "Teenagers' Responses to Retailing Stimuli." *Journal of Retailing* 54 (Winter): 80–93.

——. (1979). "Formal Consumer Education: An Empirical Assessment." In *Advances in Consumer Research*, vol. 6, edited by W. Wilkie, 456–59. Ann Arbor, MI: Association for Consumer Research.

——. (1980). "Consumer Information Use: Individual Versus Social Predictors." *Communication Research* 7 (April): 139–60.

Moschis, George P. (1981a). "Patterns of Consumer Learning." *Journal of the Academy of Marketing Science* 9 (Spring): 110–24.

——. (1981b). "Socialization Perspectives and Consumer Behavior." In *Review of Marketing 1981,* edited by B.M. Enis and K.J. Roering, 43–56. Chicago: American Marketing Association.

——. (1984). "A Longitudinal Study of Consumer Socialization." *Proceedings of the Winter Educators' Conference.* Chicago: American Marketing Association.

——. (1985). "The Role of Family Communication in Consumer Socialization of Children and Adolescents." *Journal of Consumer Research* 11, no. 4 (March): 898–13.

Moschis, George P., and Daniel C. Bello (1987). "Decision Making Patterns Among International Vacationers." *Psychology and Marketing* 4, no. 1 (forthcoming).

Moschis, George P., and Gilbert A. Churchill, Jr. (1977). "Mass Media and Interpersonal Influences on Adolescent Consumer Learning." In *Educators' Proceedings,* edited by B. Greenberg and D. Bellenger, 68–71. Chicago: American Marketing Association.

——. (1978). "Consumer Socialization: A Theoretical and Empirical Analysis." *Journal of Marketing Research* 15 (November): 599–609.

——. (1979). "An Analysis of the Young Consumer." *Journal of Marketing* 43 (Summer): 40–48.

Moschis, George P., Jac L. Goldstucker, and Thomas J. Stanley (1985). "At Home Shopping: Will Consumers Let Their Computers do the Walking?" *Business Horizons* 28, no. 2 (March/April): 22–28.

Moschis, George P., Joseph T. Lawton, and Ronald W. Stampfl (1980). "Preschool Children's Consumer Learning." *Home Economics Research Journal* 9 (September): 64–71.

Moschis, George P., and Linda G. Mitchell (1986). "Television Advertising and Interpersonal Influences on Teenager's Participation in Family Consumer Decisions." In *Advances in Consumer Research,* 13, edited by Richard J. Lutz, 181–86. Provo, UT: Association for Consumer Research.

Moschis, George P., and Roy L. Moore (1978). "An Analysis of the Acquisition of Some Consumer Competencies Among Adolescents." *Journal of Consumer Affairs* 12 (Winter): 276–91.

——. (1979a). "Mass Media and Personal Influences on Adolescent Consumer Learning." In *Developments in Marketing Science,* vol. 2, edited by H. Gitlow and F. Wheatley. Coral Gables, University of Miami.

——. (1979b). "Decision Making Among the Young: A Socialization Perspective." *Journal of Consumer Research* 6 (September): 101–12.

——. (1979c). "Family Communication Patterns and Consumer Socialization." *1979 Educators' Conference Proceedings,* edited by N. Beckwith et al., 226–30. Chicago: American Marketing Association.

——. (1979d). "Family Communication and Consumer Socialization." In *Advances in Consumer Research,* vol. 6, edited by W.L. Wilkie, 757–59. Ann Arbor, MI: Association for Consumer Research.

——. (1980). "Purchasing Behavior of Adolescent Consumers." In *Marketing in the 80's: Change and Challenges,* edited by R.P. Baaozzi et al., 89–92. Chicago: American Marketing Association.

——. (1981a). "A Study of Acquisition of Desires for Products and Brands." In *1981 AMA Educators' Conference Proceedings,* edited by K.L. Bernhardt et al., 201–04. Chicago: American Marketing Association.

———. (1981b). "Racial and Socioeconomic Influence on Adolescent Consumer Behavior." In *1981 AMA Educators' Conference Proceedings,* 261–65. *See* Moschis and Moore 1981a.

———. (1981c). "A Model of Brand Preference Formation." Unpublished paper, Georgia State University.

———. (1982). "A Longitudinal Study of Television Advertising Effects." *Journal of Consumer Research* 9 (December): 279–87.

———. (1983). " A Longtidunal Study of the Development of Purchasing Patterns." *Proceedings of the Educators' Conference,* edited by P. Murphy et al., 114–17. Chicago: American Marketing Association.

———. (1984). "Anticipatory Consumer Socialization." *Journal of the Academy of Marketing Science* 12, no. 4 (Fall): 109–23.

———. (1985). "Racial and Socioeconomic Influences on the Development of Consumer Behavior." In *Advances in Consumer Research,* vol. 12, edited by E. Hirschman and M. Holbrook, 525–31. Provo, UT: Association for Consumer Research.

Moschis, George P., Roy L. Moore, and Ruth B. Smith (1984). "The Impact of Family Communication on Adolescent Consumer Socialization." In *Advances in Consumer Research,* edited by Thomas C. Kinnear, 314–19. Provo, UT: Association for Consumer Research.

Moschis, George P., Roy L. Moore, and Thomas J. Stanley (1984). "An Exploratory Study of Brand Loyalty Development." In *Advances in Consumer Research,* vol. 11, edited by Thomas C. Kinnear, 412–17. Ann Arbor, MI: Association for Consumer Reearch.

Moschis, George P., Roy L. Moore, and Lowndes F. Stephens (1977). "Purchasing Patterns of Adolescent Consumers." *Journal of Retailing* 53 (Spring): 17–26, 92.

Moschis, George P., Andjali E. Prahasto, and Linda G. Mitchell (1986). "Family Communication Influences on the Development of Consumer Behavior: Some Additional Findings." In *Advances in Consumer Research,* vol. 13, edited by Richard J. Lutz, 365–69. Provo, UT: Association for Consumer Research.

Moschis, George P., Dena S. Cox, and James Kellaris (1987). "An Exploratory Study of Adolescent Shoplifting Behavior." In *Advances in Consumer Research,* vol. 14, edited by Paul Anderson. Provo, UT: Association for Consumer Research (forthcoming).

Moschis, George P., and Ruth B. Smith (1985). "Consumer Socialization: Origins, Trends and Directions for Future Research." In *Proceedings of the International Conference of the Association for Consumer Research,* edited by C.T. Tan and J.N. Sheth, 275–81. Singapore: National University of Singapore.

Murphy, Patrick E., and William A. Staples (1979). "A Modernized Family Life Cycle." *Journal of Consumer Research* 6 (June): 12–22.

Murray, John P. (1980). *Television & Youth: 25 years of Research and Controversy.* Boys Town, NE: The Boys Town Center for Study of Youth Development.

Murray, John P., and Susan Kippax (1978). "Children's Social Behavior in Three Towns with Differing Television Experience." *Journal of Communication* 28 (Winter): 19–29.

Myers, James H., and John F. Mount (1973). "More on Social Class vs. Income as Correlates of Buying Behavior." *Journal of Marketing* 37 (April): 71–73.

Neeley, J.J., R.V. Hickel, and H.M. Leichtman (1973). "The Effect of Race of Model and Response Consequences to the Model on Imitation in Children." *The Journal of Social Psychology* 89: 225–31.

Nettler, G.A. (1967). "A Measure of Alienation." *American Sociological Review* 22 (December): 870.

Neugarten, B. (1968). *Middle Age and Aging: A Reader in Social Psychology.* Chicago: University of Chicago Press.

——. (1972). "Personality and the Aging Process." *Gerontologist* 1 (Spring): 9–15.

Neugarten, Bernice (1964). *Personality in Middle and Late Life.* New York: Athron Press.

Neugarten, B., R. Havighurst, and S. Tobin (1968). "Personality and Patterns of Aging." In *Middle Age and Aging,* edited by B. Neugarten, 173–77. Chicago: University of Chicago Press.

Neugarten, Bernice, Joan Moore, and John Lowe (1968). "Age Norms, Age Constraints, and Adult Socialization." In *Middle Age and Aging,* 22–28. *See* Neugarten, Havighurst, and Tobin 1968.

Newcomb, T.M. (1953). "An Approach to the Study of Communicative Acts." *Psychological Review* 60 (November): 393–404.

Newspaper Advertising Bureau (1977). *How the Public Gets Its News.* New York: Newspaper Advertising Bureau.

Newspaper Research Bureau (1981). *Senior Citizens and Newspapers.* New York: Newspaper Research Project.

Nicosia, F.M. (1966). *Consumer Decision Processes.* Englewood Cliffs, NJ: Prentice-Hall.

Nicosia, Francesco M., and Robert M. Mayer (1976). "Toward a Sociology of Consumption." *Journal of Consumer Research* 3 (September): 65–75.

Nielsen, A.C. (1975). *The Television Audience: 1975.* Chicago: A.C. Nielsen Company.

Nielsen Report (1982). *Nielsen Report on Television.* Chicago: A.C. Nielsen Company (November).

Nunnally, Jum C. (1967). *Psychometric Theory.* New York: McGraw-Hill.

——. (1978). *Psychometric Theory.* 2nd ed. New York: McGraw-Hill.

O'Guinn, Thomas C., and Ronald J. Faber (1985). "New Perspectives on Acculturation: The Relationship of General and Role Specific Acculturation with Hispanics' Consumer Attitudes." In *Advances in Consumer Research,* vol. 12, edited by E. Hirschman and M. Holbrook, 113–17. Ann Arbor, MI: Association for Consumer Research.

O'Guinn, Thomas C., Ron Faber, and Giovano Inperia (1986). "Subcultural Influences on Family Decision Making: A Comparison of Mexican-American and Anglo Families." *Psychology and Marketing* 4, no. 4 (December, forthcoming).

O'Guinn, Thomas C., Wei-Na Lee, and Ronald Faber (1986). "Acculturation: The Impact of Divergent Paths on Buyer Behavior." In *Advances in Consumer Research,* vol. 13, edited by Rich Lutz, 579–83. Ann Arbor, MI: Association for Consumer Research.

O'Keefe, Garrett J., Jr. (1973). Coorientation Variables in Family Studies." *American Behavioral Scientist* 16 (April): 513–36.

Olbrich, Erhard, and Hans Thomas (1978). "Empirical Findings to a Cognitive Theory of Aging." *International Journal of Behavioral Development* 1: 67–82.

Olmedo, Esteban L., Joe L. Martinez, Jr., and Sergio R. Martinez (1981). "A Measure of Acculturation for Chicano Adolescents." *Psychological Reports* 42 (February): 159–70.

Olmedo, Esteban L., and Amado M. Padilla (1978)j. "Empirical and Construct Validation of a Measure of Acculturation for Mexican-Americans." *Journal of Psychology* 105: 179–87.

Olshavsky, Richard W., and Donald H. Granbois (1979). "Consumer Decision-Making—Fact or Fiction?" *Journal of Consumer Research* 6 (September): 93–101.

Olson, A.V., and C.L. Rosen (1967). "A Comparison of Reading Interests of Two Populations of Ninth Grade Students." *Adolescence* 1: 321–26.

Oppenheim, Irene (1969). *The Family as Consumers*. New York: Macmillan.

Ordy, J., K. Brizzee, and H. Johnson (1982). "Cellular Alterations in Visual Pathways and the Limbic System: Implications for Vision and Short-Term Memory." In *Aging and Human Visual Function*, edited by R. Sekuler, D. Kline, and K. Dismukes, 79–114. New York: Alan R. Liss.

Osmond, M.W., and P.Y. Martin (1975). "Sex and Sexism: A Comparison of Male and Female Sex-Role Attitudes." *Journal of Marriage and Family* 37 (November): 744–58.

Owsley, C., R. Sekuler, and C. Boldt (1981). "Aging and Low-Contrast Vision: Face Perception." *Investigative Ophthalmology & Visual Science* 21: 362–65.

Papalia, D.E. (1972). "The Status of Several Conservation Abilities Across the Life Span." *Human Development* 15, no. 2: 229–45.

Park, C. Whan, and V. Parker Lessig (1977). "Students and Housewives: Differences in Susceptibility to Reference Group Influence." *Journal of Consumer Research* 4 (September): 102–10.

Park, R.E., and E.W. Burgess (1921). *Introduction to the Science of Sociology*. Chicago: University of Chicago Press.

Parke, R.D. (1972). *Recent Trends in Social Learning Theory*. New York: Academic Press.

Parsons, Jacquelynne E., Diane N. Ruble, Karen L. Hodges, and Ava W. Smith (1976). "Cognitive-Developmental Factors in Emerging Sex Differences in Achievement-Related Expectancies." *Journal of Social Issues* 32, no. 3: 47.

Parsons, T. (1949). "Age and Sex in the Social Structure of the United States." In *Essays in Sociological Theory, Pure and Applied*, edited by T. Parsons, 218–32. Glencoe, IL: The Free Press.

Parsons, T., R.F. Bales, and E.A. Shils (1953). *Working Papers in the Theory of Action*. Glencoe, IL: The Free Press.

Pasdirtz, G.W. (1969). "An Approach to the Study of Interaction Processes." Paper presented to the Association for Education in Journalism, Berkeley, CA.

Payment Systems (1982). *Payment Systems Perspectives '82*. Atlanta: Payment Systems, Inc.

Penn, Roger J. (1977). "Measuring Intergenerational Value Differences." *Social Science Quarterly* 58, no. 2 (September): 293–301.

Peters, John F. (1985). "Adolescents as Socialization Agents to Parents." *Adolescence* 19 (Winter): 921–34.

Peters, W.H., and N. Ford (1972). "A Profile of Urban In-House Shoppers: The Other Half." *Journal of Marketing* 36 (January): 62–64.

Peterson, Robert A., and Alain J.P. Jolibert (1976). "A Cross-National Investigation of Price and Brand as Determinants of Perceived Product Quality." *Journal of Applied Psychology* 61 (August): 533–36.

Phelan, Gladys K., and Jay D. Schvaneveldt (1969). "Spending and Saving Patterns of Adolescent Siblings." *Journal of Home Economics* 61 (February): 104–09.

Philibert, Michael A. (1965). "The Emergence of Social Gerontology." *Journal of Social Issues* 21 (October): 4–12.

Phillips, L., and B. Sternthal (1977). "Age Differences in Information Processing: A Perspective on the Aged Consumer." *Journal of Marketing Research* 14 (November): 444–57.

Piaget, Jean (1926). *The Language and Thought of the Child*. London: Kegan Paul, French, Trubner.

———. (1932). *The Moral Judgment of the Child*. London: Kegan Paul, French, Trubner.

———. (1952). *The Origins of the Intelligence in Children*. New York: International Universities Press.

Piaget, Jean. (1970). *The Science of Education and the Psychology of the Child.* New York: Viking Press.

——. (1972). "Intellectual Evolution from Adolescence to Adulthood." *Human Development* 15, no. 1: 1–12.

Pitts, D.G. (1982). "The Effects of Aging on Selected Visual Functions: Dark Adaptation, Visual Acuity, Stereopsis, and Brightness Contrast." In *Aging and Human Visual Function,* edited by R. Sekuler, D. Kline, and K. Dismukes, 131–59. New York: Alan R. Liss.

Pollack, Andrew (1982). "The Home Computer Arrives." *New York Times* (June 17): 33, 38.

Poulos, R. (1975). "Unintentional Negative Effects of Food Commercials on Children: A Case Study." Unpublished manuscript, Media Action Research Center, New York.

Powell, Judith D., and George P. Moschis (1986). "A Study of Juvenile Shoplifting Behavior." Working paper, Georgia State University.

Powell, Marvin (1963). *The Psychology of Adolescence.* New York: Bobbs-Merrill.

Prasad, V. (1975). "Socioeconomic Product Risk and Patronage Preferences of Retail Shoppers." *Journal of Marketing* 39 (July): 42–47.

Pressey, S.L., and R.G. Kuhlen (1957). *Psychological Development Through the Life Span.* New York: Harper & Row.

Prisuta, Robert H. (1979). "The Adolescent and Television News: A Viewer Profile." *Journalism Quarterly* 56, no. 2 (Summer): 277–86.

Prisuta, Robert H., and Richard E. Kriner (1985). "Communications Technology and Older Persons: Attitudes, Uses, and Needs." A paper submitted to the International Communication Association, Special Interest Group on Human Communication Technology, Honolulu (May 22–25).

Pruden, H.O., and D.O. Longman (1972). "Race, Alienation, and Consumerism." *Journal of Marketing* 36 (July): 58–63.

Psathas, George (1957). "Ethnicity, Social Class and Adolescent Independence from Parental Control." *American Sociological Review* 22 (August): 415–23.

Quick Frozen Foods (1979). "Teen-age Girls a Critical Market for FF, Purchase 35 Per Cent of Family Foods." *Quick Frozen Foods* 42 (November): 18–21.

Ray, Michael, and Scott Ward (1975). "The Relevlance of Consumer Information Processing Studies to Communication Research." *Communication Research* 2 (July): 195–202.

——. (1976). "Experimentation for Pretesting Public Health Programs: The Case of the Anti-Drug Abuse Campaigns." In *Advances in Consumer Research,* vol. 3, edited by B. Anderson, 278–86. Cincinnati, OH: Association for Consumer Research.

Real, M.R., N. Anderson, and M. Harrington (1980). "Television Access for Older Adults." *Journal of Communication* 30 (Winter): 74–76.

Reece, Bonnie B. (1986). "Children and Shopping: Some Public Questions." *Journal of Marketing and Public Policy* 5: 185–94.

Reichard, S., F. Livson, and P. Peterson (1962). *Aging and Personality.* New York: John Wiley and Sons.

Reid, Irvin D., David F. Preusser (1983). "The Impact of Alternative Consumer Education Strategies on Safety Knowledge Behavior." *Journal of the Academy of Marketing Science* 11: 382–403.

Reid, Leonard N., Jesse E. Teel, and Bruce G. Vanderbergh (1980). "Perceived Risk and Interest in Rick Reducing Information of the Elderly." In *Proceedings,* Southern Marketing Association, edited by J. Summey and R. Taylor, 123–26. Carbondale, IL: Southern Illinois University.

Reily, Michael D. (1982). "Working Wives and Convenience Consumption." *Journal of Consumer Research* 8 (March): 407–18.

Reinecke, John A. (1975). "Supermarkets, Shopping Centers and the Senior Shopper." *Marquette Business Review* (Fall): 105–07.

Remmers, H.H., and D.H. Radler (1957). *The American Teenager.* New York: Bobbs-Merrill.

Resnik, A., and B.L. Stern (1977). "Children's Television Advertising and Branch Choice: A Laboratory Experiment." *Journal of Advertising* 6: 11–17.

Reynolds, Fred D., William R. Darden, and Warren S. Martin (1974). "Developing an Image of the Store-Loyal Customer." *Journal of Retailing* 50 (Winter): 73–84.

Reynolds, Fred D., and Joseph O. Rentz (1981). "Cohort Analysis: An Aid to Strategic Planning." *Journal of Marketing* 45 (Summer): 62–70.

Reynolds, F.D., and W.D. Wells (1977). *Consumer Behavior.* New York: McGraw-Hill.

Rich, Stuart, and S. Jain (1968). "Social Class and Life Cycle as Predictors of Shopping Behavior." *Journal of Marketing Research* 5 (February): 41–49.

Richarde, Stephen R. (1980). "Notes and Communication." *Journal of Marketing* 44 (Summer): 107–08.

Riegel, K.F. (1975). "Adult Life Crises: A Dialectic Interpretation of Development." In *Life-Span Developmental Psychology: Normative Life Crises,* edited by N. Data and L.H. Ginsburg, 98–128. New York: Academic Press.

Riesman, David, Nathan Glazer, and Paul Denny (1956). *The Lonely Crowd.* New Haven, CT: Yale University Press.

Riesman, David, and Howard Roseborough (1955). "Careers and Consumer Behavior." In *Consumer Behavior* vol. 2: *The Life Cycle and Consumer Behavior,* edited by Lincoln Clark, 1–18. New York: New York University Press.

Riley, Matilda W., Anne Foner, Beth Hess, and Marcia L. Toby (1969). "Socialization For the Middle and Later Years." In *Handbook of Socialization Theory and Research,* edited by D. Goslin, 951–82. Chicago: Rand McNally.

Ritchie, L. David (1985). "Family Communication Patterns—or Parent Communication Pattern." A paper presented to the Mass Communication Division of the International Communication Association, Honolulu (May).

Robertson, Thomas S. (1976). "Low-Commitment Consumer Behavior." *Journal of Advertising Research* 16 (April): 19–24.

———. (1979). "Parental Mediation of Television Advertising Effects." *Journal of Communication* 29 (Winter): 12–25.

Robertson, T.S., D.J. Dalrymple, and M. Yoshino (1968). "Cultural Compatibility in Product Adoption." In *Marketing Involvement in Society and the Economy,* edited by P.R. McDonald, 70–75. Chicago: American Marketing Association.

Robertson, Thomas S., and Shel Feldman (1976). "Children as Consumers: The Need for Multitheoretical Perspectives." In *Advances in Consumer Research,* vol. 3, edited by B. Anderson, 508–12. Cincinnati, OH: Association for Consumer Research.

Robertson, Thomas S., and John R. Rossiter (1975). "Children's Consumer Disappointment." Working Paper, Center for Research on Media and Children, University of Pennsylvania (April).

———. (1976a). "Short-Run Advertising Effects on Children: A Field Study." *Journal of Marketing Research* 13 (February): 68–70.

———. (1976b). "Children's Consumer Socialization." Working Paper, Center for Research on Media and Children, University of Pennsylvania.

Robertson, T.S., J.R. Rossiter, and T.C. Gleason (1979). "Children's Receptivity to Proprietary Medicine Advertising." *Journal of Consumer Research* 6, no. 3 (December): 247–55.

Robertson, Thomas S., John R. Rossiter, and Scott Ward (1985). "Consumer Satisfaction Among Children." In *Advances in Consumer Research*, vol. 12, edited by E. Hirschman and M. Holbrook, 279–84. Provo, UT: Association for Consumer Research.

Robertson, Thomas S., and Scott Ward (1973). "Consumer Behavior Research: Promise and Prospects." In *Consumer Behavior: Theoretical Sources*, edited by Scott Ward and Thomas S. Robertson, 3–42. Englewood Cliffs, NJ: Prentice-Hall.

Robertson, Thomas S., Joan Zielinski, and Scott Ward (1984). *Consumer Behavior*. Glenview, IL: Scott, Foresman and Co.

Robin, G.D. (1963). "Patterns of Department Store Shoplifting." *Crime and Delinquency* 9, no. 29 (April): 163–72.

Robinson, Patricia A., C.P. Rao, and S.C. Mehta (1985). "Historical Perspectives of Black Consumer Research in the United States: A Critical Review." In *Historical Perspectives in Consumer Research*, edited by C.T. Tan and J. Sheth, 46–50. Singapore: National University of Singapore.

Rodman, Hyman (1972). "Marital Power and the Theory of Resources in Cross-Cultural Context." *Journal of Comparative Family Studies* 29 (Spring): 337–44.

Roedder-John, Deborah, and Catherine A. Cole (1986). "Age Differences in Information Processing: Understanding Deficits in Young and Elderly Consumers." *Journal of Consumer Research* (forthcoming).

Roedder-John, Deborah, and John C. Whitney, Jr. (1986). "The Development of Consumer Knowledge in Children: Cognitive Structure Approach." *Journal of Consumer Research* 12 (March): 406–17.

Ronen, Simcha, and Allen I. Kraut (1977). "Similarities Among Countries Based on Employee Work Values and Attitudes." *Columbia Journal of World Business* (Summer): 94.

Rook, Dennis W. (1985). "The Ritual Dimension of Consumer Behavior." *Journal of Consumer Research* 12 (December): 251–64.

Rose, Arnold M. (1956). "Reference Groups of Rural High School Youth." *Child Development* 27 (September): 351–63.

———. (1965). "Group Consciousness Among the Aging." In *Older People and Their Social World*, edited by A.M. Rose and W.A. Peterson, 19–36. Philadelphia: Davis.

Rosen, B.C. (1964). "Family Structure and Value Transmission." *Merrill-Palmer Quarterly* 10, no. 1 (January): 59–76.

Roslow, Peter, and Sydney Roslow (1980). "How U.S. Latins Use Radio." *Journal of Advertising Research* 20, no. 3 (June): 19–24.

Rosow, I. (1970). "Old People: Their Friends and Neighbors." *American Behavioral Scientist* 14 (September/October): 59–69.

———. (1974). *Socialization to Old Age*. Berkeley, CA: University of California Press.

Rossiter, John R. (1977). "Reliability of a Short Test Measuring Children's Attitudes Toward TV Commercials." *Journal of Consumer Resarch* 13 (March): 179–84.

———. (1979). "Does TV Advertising Affect Children?" *Journal of Advertising Research* 19 (February): 49–53.

Rossiter, John, and John Robertson (1975). "Children's Television Viewing: An Examination of Parent-Child Consensus." *Sociometry* 38 (September): 308–26.

Rossiter, John R., and Thomas S. Robertson (1974). "Children's TV Commercials: Testing for Defenses." *Journal of Communication* 24, no. 4 (Autumn): 137–44.

———. (1979). "Children's Independence from Parental Mediation in Learning about OTC Drugs." In *1979 Educators Conference Proceedings*, edited by N. Beckwith, M. Houston,

R. Millelstaedt, K. Monroe, and S. Ward, 653–57. Chicago: American Marketing Association.

Rubin, Alan M. (1979). "Television Use by Children and Adolescents." *Human Communication Research* 5, no. 2 (Winter): 109–20.

———. (1982). "Directions in Television and Aging Research." *Journal of Broadcasting* 26, no. 2: 537–51.

Rubin, A., and R. Rubin (1981). "Contextual Age and Television Use." *Human Communication Research* 8, no. 3 (Spring): 228–44.

———. (1982). "Older Person's TV Viewing Patterns and Motivations." *Communication Research* 9, no. 2 (April): 287–313.

Rudd, Nancy M., and Marilyn M. Dunsing (1972). "A Three-Pronged Look at Family Saving." *The Journal of Consumer Affairs* 6, no. 1 (Summer): 35–44.

Runyon, Kenneth E. (1977). *Consumer Behavior and the Practice of Marketing.* Columbus, OH: Charles E. Merrill.

Ryles, Tim (1980). "Consumer Education in the 80's: New Conditions and New Strategies." Paper presented to 1980 Conference of the Committee in Support of National Consumer Education Week, Washington (October 6).

Samli, A.C. (1967). "The Elusive Senior Citizen Market." *Dimensions.* 1 (November): 7–16.

Samli, A., and F. Palunbiskas (1972). "Some Lesser Known Aspects of the Senior Citizen Market—A California Study." *Akron Business Review* 3: 47–55.

Samli, A. Coskun, and H. Nicholas Windeshausen (1965). Teenagers as a Market." *University of Washington Business Review* 24 (February): 53–58.

Samuelson, M.R., R.F. Carter, and W.L. Ruggels (1963). "Education, Available Time and Use of the Mass Media." *Journalism Quarterly* 40 (Autumn): 491–96.

Saunders, Josephine R., A. Coskun Samli, and Enid F. Tozier (1973). "Congruence and Conflict in Buying Decisions of Mothers and Daughters." *Journal of Retailing* 49, no. 3 (Fall): 3–18.

Scammon, Debra L., and Carole L. Christopher (1981). "Nutrition Education with Children via Television: A Review." *Journal of Advertising* 10, no. 2: 26–36.

Scanzoni, John H. (1975). *Sex Roles, Life Styles and Childbearing.* New York: Free Press.

———. (1976). "Sex Role Change and Influences on Birth Intentions." *Journal of Marriage and Family* 38 (February): 43–60.

———. (1977). "Changing Sex Roles and Emerging Directions in Family Decision Making." *Journal of Consumer Research* 4 (December): 185–88.

Schachter, S. (1959). *The Psychology of Affiliation.* Stanford, CA: Stanford University Press.

Schaninger, Charles M., Jacques C. Bourgeois, and W. Christian Buss (1985). "French-English Canadian Subcultural Consumption Differences." *Journal of Marketing* 43 (Spring): 82–92.

Scheff, T.J. (1967). "Toward a Sociological Model of Consensus." *American Sociological Review* 32 (Februray): 32–46.

Schewe, Charles D. (1984). "Buying and Consuming Behavior of the Elderly: Findings from Behavioral Research." In *Advances in Consumer Research,* vol. 11, edited by T. Kinnear, 558–62. Provo, UT: Association for Consumer Research.

———. (1985). "Gray America Goes to Market." *Business* 35, no. 2 (April/June): 3–9.

Schiffman, L.G. (1971). "Sources of Information for the Elderly." *Journal of Advertising Research* 11 (October): 33–37.

Schiffman, L.G. (1972a). "Perceived Risk in New Product Trial by Elderly Consumers." *Journal of Marketing Research* 9 (May): 106–08.

———. (1972b). "Social Interaction Patterns of the Elderly Consumer." In *AMA Combined Conference Proceedings,* edited by B.W. Becker and H. Becker, 445–51. Chicago: American marketing Association.

Schiffman, Leon G., Joseph F. Dash, and William R. Dillon (1977). "The Contribution of Store-Image Characteristics to Store-Type Choice." *Journal of Retailing* 53 (Summer): 3–14.

Schiffman, L.G., W.R. Dillon, and F.E. Ngumah (1982). "The Influence of Subcultural and Personality Factors on Consumer Acculturation. *Journal of International Business Studies* 12 (Fall): 137–43.

Schiffman, Leon G., and Leslie Lazar Kanuk (1983). *Consumer Behavior.* 2d ed. Englewood Cliffs, N.J.: Prentice-Hall

Schmuck, R. (1963). "Sex of Siblings, Birth Order, and Female Disposition to Conform in Two-Child Families." *Child Development* 34, no. 4 (December): 913–18.

Schow, R.L., J.M. Christensen, J.M. Hutchinson, and M.A. Nerbonne (1978). *Communication Disorders of the Aged: A Guide for Health Professionals.* Baltimore: University Press.

Schramm, W. (1969). "Aging and Mass Communication." In *Aging and Society,* vol. 2: *Aging and the Professions,* edited by M. Riley and M. Johnson, 352–75. New York: Russell Sage Foundation.

Schramm, W., J. Lyle, and E.B. Parker (1961). *Television in the Lives of Our Children.* Stanford, CA: Stanford University Press.

Schreiber, E.S., and D.A. Boyd (1980). "How the Elderly Perceive Television Commercials." *Journal of Communication* 30, no. 1 (Winter): 61–70.

Sebald, Hans (1968). *Adolescence: A Sociological Analysis.* New York: Appleton-Century-Crofts.

Segal, D.R., and M. Felson (1973). "Social Stratification and Family Economic Behavior." In *Family Economic Behavior,* edited by E.B. Sheldon, 143–64. Philadelphia: J.B. Lizzinratt.

Segal, Madhav N., and Sosa Lionel (1983). "Marketing to the Hispanic Community." *California Management Review* 26, no. 1 (Fall): 120–34.

Sekuler, R., D. Kline, and K. Dismukes (1982). *Aging and Human Visual Function.* New York: Alan R. Liss.

Sethi, S. Prakash (1971). "Comparative Cluster Analysis for World Markets." *Journal of Marketing Research* 8, no. 3 (August): 348–54.

Shaak, Bruce, Lori Annes, and John R. Rossiter (1975). "Effects of the Social Success Theme on Children's Product Preference." Paper presented at the 1975 Conference on Culture and Communications, Temple University, Philadelphia (March).

Sharaga, S. (1974). "The Effect of Television Advertising on Children's Nutrition Attitudes, Nutrition Knowledge, and Eating Habits." Unpublished doctoral dissertation, Cornell University.

Shaw, M.E., and P.R. Costanzo (1970). *Theories of Social Psychology.* New York: McGraw-Hill.

Sheikh, Anees A., and L. Martin Moleski (1977). "Conflict in the Family Over Commercials." *Journal of Communication* 27, no. 1 (Winter): 152–57.

Sherman, Elaine, and Leon G. Schiffman (1984). "Applying Age-Gender Theory from Social Gerontology to Understand the Consumer Well-Being of the Elderly." In *Advances in*

Consumer Research, vol. 11, edited by T. Kinnear, 569–73. Provo, UT: Association for Consumer Research.

Sheth, Jagdish N., and Gary L. Frazier (1982). "A Model of Strategy Mix Choice for Planned Social Change." *Journal of Marketing* 46 (Winter): 15–26.

Shimp, T., and I. Preston (1981). "Deceptive and Nondeceptive Consequences of Evaluative Advertising." *Journal of Marketing* 45 (Winter): 22–32.

Silvenus, Scott (1979). "Packaging for the Elderly." *Modern Packaging* 52 (October): 38–39.

Slovic, P., and S. Lichtenstein (1971). "Comparison of Bayesian and Regression Approaches to the Study of Information Processing in Judgment." *Organizational Behavior and Human Performance* 6: 649–744.

Smart, R., and D. Fejer (1974). "The Effects of High and Low Fear Messages about Drugs." *Journal of Drug Education* 4: 225–35.

Smith, Ruth Belk (1982). "Consumer Socialization of the Elderly." Ph.D. disseration, Georgia State University.

Smith, Ruth, and George P. Moschis (1984a). "Consumer Socialization of the Elderly: An Explanatory Study." In *Advances in Consumer Research*, vol. 2, edited by Thomas C. Kinnear, 548–52. Ann Arbor, MI: Association for Consumer Research.

———. (1984b). "Effects of Advertising on the Elderly Consumer: An Investigation of Social Breakdown Theory." In *Proceedings of The Annual Educators' Conference*, edited by R. Belk, R. Peterson, G. Albaum, M. Holbrook, R. Kerin, N. Malhotra, and P. Wright, 1–5. Chicago: American Marketing Association.

———. (1985a). "A Socialization Perspective on Selected Consumer Characteristics of the Elderly." *Journal of Consumer Affairs* 19, no. 1 (Spring/Summer): 74–95.

———. (1985b). "Effects of Mass Media Advertising and Interpersonal Communication on the Elderly Consumer." Paper presented at the International Communication Association Conference, Honolulu (May).

———. (1987). "A Socialization Approach to the Study of the Elderly Consumer." In *Advances in Consumer Research*, vol. 14, edited by Paul Anderson. Provo, UT: Association for Consumer Research (forthcoming.)

Smith, Ruth B., George P. Moschis, and Roy L. Moore (1981). "The Impact of Mass Communication On Consumer Decision Making Among the Elderly." Paper presented to the Mass Communication and Society Division, Association for Education in Journalism Annual Convention, Michigan State University.

———. (1982). "Social Effects of Advertising on the Elderly Consumer." Paper presented to the Theory and Methodology Division, Association for Education in Journalism Annual Convention, Athens, OH (July).

———. (1985). "Some Advertising Influences on the Elderly Consumer: Implications for Theoretical Considerations." In *Current Issues and Research in Advertising*, vol. 1, edited by J. Leigh and C. Martin, 187–201. Ann Arbor, MI: University of Michigan.

———. (1986). "Social Effects of Advertising and Personal Communications on the Elderly Consumer." In *Research in Marketing*, edited by M.J. Sheth. Greenwich, CT: Jai Press.

Sofranko, A.J., and M.F. Nolan (1972). "Early Life Experiences and Adult Sports Participation." *Journal of Leisure Research* 4, no. 1 (Winter): 6–18.

Sohn, Ardyth Broadrick (1978). "A Longitudinal Analysis of Local Nonpolitical Agenda-Setting Effects." *Journalism Quarterly* 55, no. 2 (Summer): 325–33.

Soldow, Gary F. (1983). "The Processing of Information in the Young Consumer: The Impact of Cognitive Developmental Stage In Television, Radio and Print Advertising." *Journal of Advertising* 12 (September): 4–14.

Solomon, Daniel (1963). "Influences on the Decisions of Adolescents." *Human Relations* 16 (February): 45–60.

Solow, Robert M. (1968). "The Truth Further Refined: A Comment on Marris." *Public Interest* 11 (Spring): 47–52.

Stack, Carol (1974). *All Our Kin: Strategies for Survival in a Black Community*. New York: Harper & Row.

Stampfl, Ronald W. (1978). "The Consumer Life Cycle." *Journal of Consumer Affairs* 12 (Winter): 209–19.

Stampfl, Ronald W., George P. Moschis, and Joseph T. Lawton (1978). "Consumer Education and the Preschool Child." *Journal of Consumer Affairs* 12 (Summer): 12–29.

Stang, D.J. (1974). "Methodological Factors in Mere Exposure Research." *Psychological Bulletin* 81 (December): 1014–25.

Stanley, Thomas J., Murphy A. Sewall, and George P. Moschis (1982). *Consumer Profiles by Payment Types*. Atlanta: Payment Systems, Inc.

Steilen, Charles F. (1972). "New Dimensions in Market Segmentation." *Atlanta Economic Review* 22 (May): 4–6.

Steiner, Gary A. (1963). "The People Look at Television." *Journal of Business* 39 (April): 272–304.

Stephens, Nancy (1981). "Media Use and Media Attitude Changes with Age and with Time." *Journal of Advertising* 10, no. 1, (Winter): 38–47.

———. (1982). "The Effectiveness of Time-Compressed Television Advertisements with Older Adults." *Journal of Advertising* 11, no. 3 (Fall): 48–55.

Stephens, Nancy, and Robert A. Warrens (1983–1984). "Advertising Frequency Requirements for Older Adults." *Journal of Advertising Research* 23, no. 6 (December/January): 23–30.

Stephenson, William (1967). *The Play Theory of Mass Communication*. Chicago: University of Chicago Press.

Sternglanz, S.H., and L.A. Serbin (1974). "Sex Role Stereotyping in Children's Television Programs. *Developmental Psychology* 10: 710–15.

Stinnett, N., S. Talley, and J. Walters (1973). "Parent–Child Relationships of Black and White High School Students." *The Journal of Social Psychology* 91, pp. 349–50.

Stone, Gregory P. (1955). "Comments on: Careers and Consumer Behavior." In *Consumer Behavior vol. 2: The Life Cycle and Consumer Behavior*, edited by Lincoln H. Clark, 21–27. New York: New York University Press.

Stone, Vernon A., and Steven H. Caffee (1970). "Family Communication Patterns and Source-Message Orientation." *Journalism Quarterly* 47 (Summer): 239–46.

Strategy Research. (1980). "A Comprehensive Study of U.S. Hispanics—A Market Profile." Miami, FL: Strategy Research Corp.

Straus, M.A. (1962a). "Deferred Gratifications, Social Class and the Achievement Syndrome." *American Sociological Review* 27 (June): 326–35.

———. (1962b). "Work Roles and Financial Responsibility in the Socialization of Farm, Fringe and Town Boys." *Rural Sociology* 27 (September): 257–74.

Streib, Gordon (1968). "Are the Aged a Minority Group?" In *Middle Age and Aging*, edited by B. Neugarten, 35–46. Chicago: University of Chicago Press.

Strickland, Donald E. (1982). "Alcohol Advertising: Orientation and Influence." *Journal of Advertising* (United Kingdom) 1, no. 4 (October/December): 307–19.

Sturdivant, Frederick D. (1968). "Better Deal for Ghetto Shoppers." *Harvard Business Review* 46 (March/April): 130–39.

———. (1969). "Business and the Mexican-American Community." *California Management Review* 11 (Spring): 73–80.

———. (1973). "Subculture Theory: Poverty, Minorities and Marketing." In *Consumer Behavior: Theoretical Sources,* edited by Scott Ward and Thomas Robertson, 459–520. Englewood Cliffs, NJ: Prentice Hall.

Surlin, Stuart H., Alan Wurtzel, and Linda Whitener (1978). "Parental Control of Children's Television Viewing Behavior: Support for the Reverse Modeling Principle." Paper presented to Mass Communication Division, International Communication Association, Chicago (April).

Sutherland, Max, and John Galloway (1981). "Role of Advertising: Persuasion or Agenda Setting." *Journal of Advertising Research* 21, no. 5 (October): 25–29.

Talmon, Yonina (1963). "Comparative Analysis of Adult Socialization." Paper presented at the Social Science Research Council Conference on Socialization Through the Life Cycle, New York.

Tan, Alexis S. (1980). "Causal Influence in Mass Communication and Political Socialization Research." Paper presented at annual Conference of International Communication Association, Acapulco.

Tan, A.S., and D. Gunter (1979). "Media Use and Achievement of Mexican-American High School Students." *Journalism Quarterly* 56, no. 4 (Winter): 827–31.

Tan, Chin Tiong, and James McCullough (1985). "Relating Ethnic Attitudes and Consumption Values in an Asian Context." In *Advances in Consumer Research,* vol. 12, edited by E. Hirschman and M. Holbrook, 122–25. Provo, UT: Association for Consumer Research.

Tannenbaum, Percy H., and Jack M. McLeod (1967). "On the Measurement of Socialization." *Public Opinion Quarterly* 21 (Spring): 27–37.

Tannis, Macbeth Williams (1981). "How and What Do Children Learn from Television?" *Communication Research* 7, no. 2 (Winter): 180–92.

Tate, Russell S. (1961). "The Supermarket Battle for Store Loyalty." *Journal of Marketing* 25 (October): 8–13.

Teel, S.J., J.E. Teel, and W.O. Bearden (1979). "Lessons Learned from the Cigarette Advertising Ban." *Journal of Marketing* 43 (January): 45–50.

Terpstra, Vern (1972). *International Marketing.* New York: Holt, Rinehart, and Winston.

Thibodeau, Janice (1980). "Adult Performance on Piagetian Cognitive Tasks: Implications for Adult Education." *Journal of Research and Development in Education* 13, no. 3: 25–32.

Thomas, W.I., and F. Znaniecki (1918–1920). *The Polish Peasant in Europe and America.* 4 vols. Boston: Richard C. Badger.

Thorelli, Hans B., and Gerald D. Sentell (1982). *Consumer Emancipation and Economic Development: The Case of Thailand.* Greenwich, CT, Jai Press Inc.

Thorton, Russell, and Peter M. Nardi (1975). "The Dynamics of Role Acquisition." *American Journal of Sociology* 80 (January): 870–84.

Tichenor, P.J., G.A. Donohue, and C.N. Blien (1970). "Mass Media Flow and Differential Growth in Knowledge." *Public Opinion Quarterly* 34 (Summer): 159–70.

Time, Inc. (1985). *The Expert's Guide to the Baby Boomers.* New York: Time, Inc.

Tims, Albert R., and Jonathan L. Masland (1985). "Measurement of Family Communication Patterns." *Communication Research* 12, no. 1 (January): 35–57.

Towle, J.G., and C.R. Martin (1976). "The Elderly Consumer: One Segment or Many?" In *Advances in Consumer Research,* vol. 3, edited by B. Anderson, 463–68. Cincinnati, OH: Association for Consumer Research.

Turner, Josephine, and Jeanette Brandt (1978). "Development and Validation of a Simulated Market to Test Children for Selected Consumer Skills." *Journal of Consumer Affairs* (Winter): 266–76.

Urban, Christine D. (1977). "A Cross-National Comparison of Consumer Media Use Patterns." *Columbia Journal of World Business* 12 (Winter): 53–64.

———. (1980). "Correlates of Magazine Readership." *Journal of Advertising Research* 20, no. 4: 73–84.

U.S. Bureau of the Census (1979). *Demographic Aspects of Aging and the Older Population in the United States.* Special Studies Series P-23, no. 59. Washington: Government Printing Office.

U.S. Department of Health and Human Services (1979). Washington: Public Health Service.

Utsey, Marjorie Fox, and Victor J. Cook (1984). "Demographics and Propensity to Consume." In *Advances in Consumer Research,* vol. 11, edited by T.C. Kinnear, 718–23. Provo, UT: Association for Consumer Research.

Valdez, Armando (1979). "Socialization Influences of Television Commercials on Preschool-Age Children." Ph.D. dissertation, Stanford University.

Valencia, Humberto (1982). "Shopping Orientations Among Hispanics and Anglos in the United States." Ph.D. dissertation, Georgia State University.

———. (1985). "Developing an Index to Measure Hispanicness." In *Advances in Consumer Research,* vol. 12, edited by E. Hirschman and M. Holbrook, 118–21. Provo, UT: Association for Consumer Research.

Valentine, Deborah, Martha Williams, and Robert K. Young (1978). *Age Related Factors in Driving Safety, Draft Report.* University of Texas at Austin, Council for Advanced Transportation Studies.

Van Zelst, Raymond H. (1952). "Empathy Test Scores of Union Leaders." *Journal of Applied Psychology,* vol. 36 (October): 293–95.

Velilla, Martin (1967). *2,000,000 People to Captivate: New York Greater Hispanic Market.* New York: The Thunder Book Company.

Vener, A.M. (1957). "Adolescent Orientation to Clothing: A Social Psychological Interpretation." Doctoral dissertation, Michigan State University.

Vener, A.M., and C.V. Hoffer (1959). *Adolescent Orientation to Clothing.* Technical Bulletin 270. East Lansing, MI: Michigan State University Agricultural Experiment Station.

Veroff, Joseph (1978). "Social Motivation." *American Behavioral Scientist* 21, no. 5 (May/June): 709–29.

Wackman, Daniel B., Greg Reale, and Scott Ward (1972). "Racial Differences in Responses to Advertising Among Adolescents." In *Television and Social Behavior,* vol. 4: *Television in Day to Day Use: Patterns of Use,* edited by Eli A. Rubinstein, George H. Comstock, and John Murray, 543–53. Washington: Government Printing Office.

Wade, S.E., and W. Schramm (1969). "The Mass Media as Sources of Public Affairs, Science, and Health Knowledge." *Public Opinion Quarterly* 33 (Summer): 197–209.

Wagner, Janet, and Sherman Hanna (1983). "The Effectiveness of Family Life Cycle Variables in Consumer Expenditure Research." *Journal of Consumer Research* 10, no. 3 (December): 281–91.

Wallendorf, Melanie, and Michael D. Reilly (1983). "Ethnic Migration, Assimilation, and Consumption." *Journal of Consumer Research* 10 (December): 292–301.

Ward, Scott (1974a). "Consumer Socialization." *Journal of Consumer Research* 1 (September): 1–16.

———. (1974b). "Consumer Socialization." Working paper, Marketing Science Institute, Cambridge, MA.

———. (1978). "Contributions of Socialization Theory to Consumer Behavior Research." *American Behavioral Scientist* 21, no. 4 (March/April): 501–14.

Ward, Scott, Donna M. Klees, and Thomas S. Robertson (1987). "Consumer Socialization in Different Settings: An International Perspective." In *Advances in Consumer Research*, vol. 14, edited by Paul Anderson. Provo, UT: Association for Consumer Research (forthcoming).

Ward, Scott, and Greg Reale (1972). "Student Attitudes Toward Business and Marketing Institutions and Practices." Working paper, Marketing Science Institute, Cambridge, MA (May).

Ward, Scott, and Thomas Robertson (1970). "Family Influence on Adolescent Consumer Behavior." Paper presented to the American Psychological Association, Consumer Psychology Division, Miami, FL (September).

———. (1972) "Adolescent Attitudes Toward Television Advertising." In *Television and Social Behavior*, vol. 4: *Television in Day to Day Use: Patterns of Use*, edited by Eli A. Rubinstein, George H. Comstock, and John Murray, 526–42. Washington: Government Printing Office.

Ward, Scott, Thomas S. Robertson, Donna M. Klees, and Hubert Gatignon (1986). "Children Purchase Requests and Parental Yielding: A Cross-National Study." In *Advances in Consumer Research*, vol. 13, edited by R. Lutz, 629–32. Provo, UT: Association for Consumer Research.

Ward, Scott, and Daniel Wackman (1971). "Family and Media Influences on Adolescent Consumer Learning." *American Behavioral Scientist* 14 (January/February): 415–27.

———. (1972). "Children's Purchase Influence Attempts and Parental Yielding." *Journal of Marketing Research* 9 (November): 316–19.

———. (1973). "Effects of Television Advertising on Consumer Socialization." Working paper, Marketing Science Institute, Cambridge, MA.

Ward, S., D.B. Wackman, and E. Wartella (1977). *How Children Learn to Buy: The Development of Consumer Information Processing Skills*, Beverly Hills, CA: Sage Publications.

Warner, James A., and Donald M. Derlinger (1969). *The Gentle People: A Portrait of The Amish*. New York: Grossman Publishers.

Warner, Lloyd W. (1972). "Classes Are Real." In *Issues and Social Inequality*, edited by G.W. Thubar and S. Feldman. Boston: Little Brown.

Wartella, E., A. Alexander, and D. Lemish (1979). "The Mass Media Environment of Children." *American Behavioral Scientist* 23 (September/October): 33–52.

Warwick, Walsh, and Miller, Inc., ed. (1981). *A Study of Consumer Attitudes Toward TV Programming and Advertising*. New York: Warwick, Walsh, and Miller, Inc.

Watanabe, M. (1981). "A Profile Goes to New Heights." *Advertising Age* (April 6): A-1.

Webb, Peter H. (1979). "Consumer Initial Processing in a Difficult Media Environment." *Journal of Consumer Research* 6 (December): 225–36.

Weeks, William A. (1986). "Applying Disengagement Theory from Social Gerontology to Predict and Explain Segments within the Senior Market." In *Advances in Consumer Research*, vol. 13, edited by Rich Lutz, 673. Provo, UT: Association for Consumer Research.

Welch, R.L., A. Huston-Stein, J.E. Wright, and R. Phehal (1979). "Subtle Sex-Role Cues in Children's Commercials." *Journal of Communication* 29 (Summer): 202–9.

Wells, William D. (1965). "Communicating with Children." *Journal of Advertising Research* 5 (June): 2–14.

Wells, William D. (1975). "Psychographics: A Critical Review." *Journal of Marketing Research* 12 (May): 191–213.

Wells, William, and George Gubar (1966). "Life Cycle Concept in Marketing Research." *Journal of Marketing Research* 3 (November): 355–63.

Wells, William D., and Leonard A. LoSciuto (1966). "Direct Observation of Purchasing Behavior." *Journal of Marketing Research* 3 (August): 227–33.

Wenner, L. (1976). "Functional Analysis of TV Viewing for Older Adults." *Journal of Broadcasting* 20: 79–88.

Wheeler, S. (1969). "Socialization in Correctional Institutions." In *Handbook of Socialization Theory and Research,* edited by D. Goslin, 1005–27. Chicago: Rand McNally.

Whipple, T.W., and L.A. Neidell (1971–1972). "Black and White Perceptions of Competing Stores." *Journal of Retailing* 47, no. 4 (Winter): 5–20.

White, Kathryn, and Jane D. Brown (1981). "The Effects of Androgynous Televised Portrayals on Children's Sex Role Preferences." Paper presented to the Theory and Methodology Division, Association for Education in Journalism.

Wilkie, William L., and Edgar A. Pessemier (1973). "Issues in Marketing's Use of Multi-Attribute Attitude Models. *Journal of Marketing Research.* 10 (November): 428–41.

Williams, Jerome D. (1985). "African & European Roots of Multiculturalism in the Consumer Behavior of American Blacks." In *Historical Perspective in Consumer Research,* edited by C.T. Tan and J. Sheth, 52–55. Singapore: National University of Singapore.

Williams, J.W. (1970). "A Gradient of the Economic Concepts of Elementary School Children and Factors Associated with Cognition." *Journal of Consumer Affairs* 4 (Summer): 113–23.

Williams, T.M. (1981). "What Do Children Learn from Television?" *Human Communication Research* 7, no. 2 (Winter): 180–92.

Winick, Charles (1961). "Anthropology's Contributions to Marketing." *Journal of Marketing* 25 (July): 53–60.

Wohlwill, J.F. (1970). "Methodology and Research Strategy in the Study of Developmental Change." In *Life-Span Developmental Psychology: Research and Theory,* edited by L.K. Goulet and P.B. Baltes, 50–190. New York: Academic Press.

Won, George, and George Yamamoto (1968). "Social Structure and Deviant Behavior: A Study of Shoplifting." *Sociology and Social Research* 53, (October): 44–55.

Woodside, Arch G. (1973). "Patronage Motives and Marketing Strategies." *Journal of Retailing* 49 (Spring): 35–44.

Yankelovich, Skelly, and White (1981). *Spanish USA, A Study of the Hispanic Market in the United States.* New York: Yankelovich, Skelly & White, Inc.

Yarrow, M.R. (1963). "Appraising Environment." In *Processes of Aging* vol. 1: *Social Psychological Perspectives,* edited by R.H. Williams, C. Tibbitts, and W. Donahue, 201–22. New York: Aldine.

Yau, Oliver H.M. (1985). "Consumer Research in Hong Kong: An Overview." In *Historical Perspectives in Consumer Research: National and International Perspectives,* edited by C.T. Tang and J. Sheth, 196–200. Singapore: National University of Singapore.

Young, Donald R. (1969). "The Socialization of American Minority Peoples." In *Handbook of Socialization Theory and Research,* edited by D.A. Goslin, 1103–40. Chicago: Rand McNally.

Young, T.H. (1975). "An Image Analysis of the Stimulus Concepts 'Senior Citizen' and 'You When You Are a Senior Citizen.' " Paper presented to the International Communication Association, Portland, OR.

———. (1979). "Use of the Media by Older Adults." *American Behavioral Scientist* 23 (September/October): 119–36.

Youth Research Institute (1967). *The Dynamics of the Youth Explosion.* Los Angeles: Los Angeles Chamber of Commerce.

Zajonc, R.B. (1968). "Attitudinal Effects of Mere Exposure." *Journal of Personality and Social Psychology Monograph* (Supplement) 9 (June): 1–27.

Zaltman, Gerry, R.K. Srivastava, and R. Deshpande (1978). "Perceptions of Unfair Marketing Practices: Consumerism Implications." In *Advances in Consumer Research,* vol. 5, edited by K. Hunt, 24–53. Ann Arbor, MI: Association for Consumer Research.

Zbytniewski, Jo Ann (1979). "The Older Shopper: Over 65 and Overlooked?" *Progressive Grocer* (November): 109–11.

Zedek, S., J. Frisch, and R. Zawadski (1974). "Information Processing and Decision Making as Influenced by Product Proliferation." *Technological Change, Product Proliferation and Consumer Decision Processes,* vol. 3, edited by F. Nicosia and K. Lancaster. Washington: National Science Foundation, DA 39496 and DA 39497.

Zigler, E., and I.L. Child (1969). "Socialization." In *The Handbook of Social Psychology: The Individual in a Social Context* (2nd ed.), vol. 3, edited by G. Lindzey and E. Aronson, 450–89. Reading, MA: Addison-Wesley.

Subject Index

Author Index

About the Author

George P. Moschis is research professor of marketing and director of the Center for Mature Consumer Studies at Georgia State University, Atlanta, Georgia. He has served as a marketing consultant for several major corporations, specializing in consumer behavior and communication behavior of special segments, and in home information systems and communication technologies.